CASS SERIES ON THE SOVIET (RUSSIAN) STUDY OF WAR
Series Editor: David M. Glantz

KURSK 1943
A Statistical Analysis

CASS SERIES ON SOVIET (RUSSIAN) MILITARY EXPERIENCE
Series Editor: David M. Glantz
ISSN: 1462-0944

This series focuses on Soviet military experiences in specific campaigns or operations

1. David M. Glantz, *From the Don to the Dnepr, Soviet Offensive Operations, December 1942 to August 1943* (ISBN 0 7146 3401 8 cloth, 0 7146 4064 6 paper)
2. David M. Glantz, *The Initial Period of War on the Eastern Front: 22 June–August 1941* (ISBN 0 7146 3375 5 cloth, 0 7146 4298 3 paper)
3. Carl Van Dyke, *The Soviet Invasion of Finland, 1939–40* (ISBN 0 7146 4653 5 cloth, 0 7146 4314 9 paper)
4. Leonid Grenkevich, *The Soviet Partisan Movement 1941–1944*, edited and with a Foreword by David M. Glantz (ISBN 0 7146 4874 4 cloth, 0 7146 4428 5 paper)
5. Tony Le Tissier, *Race for the Reichstag: The 1945 Battle for Berlin* (ISBN 0 7146 4929 5 cloth, 0 7146 4489 7 paper)

CASS SERIES ON THE SOVIET (RUSSIAN) STUDY OF WAR
Series Editor: David M. Glantz
ISSN: 1462-0960

This series examines what Soviet military theorists and commanders learned from the study of their own military operations.

1. Harold S. Orenstein, translator and editor, *Soviet Documents on the Use of War Experience*, Volume I, *The Initial Period of War 1941*, with an Introduction by David M. Glantz. (ISBN 0 7146 3392 5 cloth)
2. Harold S. Orenstein, translator and editor, *Soviet Documents on the Use of War Experience*, Volume II, *The Winter Campaign 1941–1942*, with an Introduction by David M. Glantz. (ISBN 0 7146 3393 3 cloth)
3. Joseph G. Welsh, translator, *Red Armor Combat Orders: Combat Regulations for Tank and Mechanized Forces 1944*, edited and with an Introduction by Richard N. Armstrong. (ISBN 0 7146 3401 8 cloth)
4. Harold S. Orenstein, translator and editor, *Soviet Documents on the Use of War Experience*, Volume III, *Military Operations 1941 and 1942*, with an Introduction by David M. Glantz. (ISBN 0 7146 3402 6 cloth)
5. William A. Burhans, translator, *The Nature of the Operations of Modern Armies* by V.K. Triandafillov, edited by Jacob W. Kipp, with an Introduction by James J. Schneider. (ISBN 0 7146 4501 X cloth, 0 7146 4118 9 paper)
6. Harold S. Orenstein, translator, *The Evolution of Soviet Operational Art, 1927–1991: The Documentary Basis*, Volume I, *Operational Art, 1927–1964*, with an Introduction by David M. Glantz. (ISBN 0 7146 4547 8 cloth, 0 7146 4228 2 paper)
7. Harold S. Orenstein, translator, *The Evolution of Soviet Operational Art, 1927–1991: The Documentary Basis*, Volume II, *Operational Art, 1965–1991*, with an Introduction by David M. Glantz. (ISBN 0 7146 4548 6 cloth, 0 7146 4229 0 paper)
8. Richard N. Armstrong and Joseph G. Welsh, *Winter Warfare: Red Army Orders and Experiences*. (ISBN 0 7146 4699 7 cloth, 0 7146 4237 1 paper)
9. Lester W. Grau, *The Bear Went Over the Mountain: Soviet Combat Tactics in Afghanistan*. (ISBN 0 7146 4174 4 cloth, 0 7146 4413 7 paper)
10. David M. Glantz and Harold S. Orenstein, *The Battle for Kursk 1943: The Soviet General Staff Study* (ISBN 0 7146 4933 3 cloth, 0 7146 4493 5 paper)
11. Niklas Zetterling and Anders Frankson, *Kursk 1943: A Statistical Analysis* (ISBN 0 7146 5052 8 cloth, 0 7146 8103 2 paper)
12. David M. Glantz and Harold S. Orenstein, *Belorussia 1944: The Soviet General Staff Study* (ISBN 0 7146 5102 8)

KURSK 1943
A Statistical Analysis

NIKLAS ZETTERLING
and
ANDERS FRANKSON

FRANK CASS
LONDON • PORTLAND, OR

First published in 2000 in Great Britain by
FRANK CASS PUBLISHERS
Newbury House, 900 Eastern Avenue
London, IG2 7HH

and in the United States of America by
FRANK CASS PUBLISHERS
c/o ISBS, 5804 N.E. Hassalo Street
Portland, Oregon, 97213-3644

Website: www.frankcass.com

British Library Cataloguing in Publication Data

Zetterling, Niklas
Kursk 1943: a statistical analysis. – (Cass series on
Soviet (Russian) study of war)
1. Kursk, Battle of, 1943 2. Kursk, Battle of, 1943 – Sources –
Evaluation
I. Title II. Frankson, Anders
940.5'421'735

ISBN 0-7146-5052-8 (cloth)
ISSN 1462-0960

Library of Congress Cataloging-in-Publication Data

Zetterling, Niklas.
Kursk 1943: a statistical analysis / Niklas Zetterling and Anders Frankson.
p. cm. – (Cass series on the Soviet (Russian) study of war, ISSN 1462-0960)
Includes bibliographical references and index.
ISBN 0-7146-5052-8 (cloth)
1. Kursk, Battle of, 1943. I. Frankson, Anders. II. Title. III. Series.
D764.3.K8 Z48 2000
940.54'21735–dc21   00-021357

Typeset by Vitaset, Paddock Wood, Kent
Printed in Great Britain by
MPG Books Ltd, Bodmin, Cornwall

Contents

List of Tables and Figures   vii

List of Maps   x

Foreword by David M. Glantz   xi

Preface   xiii

List of Abbreviations   xvii

1   Background   1

2   The Assembly of Forces   15

3   Structure of Involved Forces   25

4   Tanks Employed at Zitadelle   58

5   The Air War   74

6   Chronology of the Offensive   84

7   Prokhorovka   101

8   The Cost of the Battle   111

9   An Analysis of the Battle   132

10   The Consequences of the Battle   145

Appendices

   1. Soviet Order of Battle   153

   2. German Order of Battle   166

   3. Soviet Tank Units Facing Army Group South   174

   4. The Panther Tank in Zitadelle   177

5. *Deliveries of New Tanks to the Eastern Front, June–August 1943*   181

6. *Daily Tank Strength in Army Group South*   185

7. *The Condition of 8th Army, 30 August 1943*   191

8. *Examples of Causes of German Tank Losses*   193

9. *Number of German Tanks and Assault Guns on the Eastern Front, April–December 1943*   195

10. *Further Information on German Casualties*   197

11. *Tank Data*   209

12. *Tank and AT Gun Data*   211

13. *Armour-Penetration Capabilities*   213

14. *Information on German Tank Losses*   216

15. *Ration Strength of the 4th Panzer Army*   224

16. *Divisional Structure for German Forces on 4 July 1943*   226

Bibliography   238

Index   263

Tables and Figures

TABLES

		page
1.1	Comparative strength, 1 July 1942	2
1.2	Comparative strength, 1 July 1943	5
1.3	Soviet strength in the Kursk area, 10 April 1943	11
2.1	German strength in the Kursk area, 1 July 1943	18
2.2	German combat units in the Kursk area, 1 July 1943	19
2.3	Soviet strength in the Kursk area, 1 July 1943	20
2.4	Soviet combat units in the Kursk area, 1 July 1943	21
3.1	656th Tank Destroyer Regiment, 4 July 1943	27
3.2	Tanks and SP artillery of divisions in XXXXVII Panzer Corps in early July 1943	27
3.3	Distribution of tanks and SP artillery available in Model's Mobile Reserve in early July 1943	28
3.4	Distribution of tanks, assault guns and SP artillery within mobile divisions of XXXXVIII Pz Corps in early July 1943	29
3.5	Distribution of tanks, assault guns and SP artillery within the mobile divisions of II SS-Pz Corps in early July 1943	30
3.6	Distribution of tanks, assault guns and SP artillery within the panzer divisions of III Pz Corps in early July 1943	31
3.7	Distribution of tanks and assault guns in von Manstein's Mobile Reserve in early July 1943	31
3.8	Attacking forces on 4 July 1943	32
3.9	Central Front anti-tank reserve	34
3.10	23rd Guards Rifle Corps' arsenal of guns, 4 July 1943	35
3.11	Voronezh Front anti-tank reserve	36
3.12	Tank strength in 1st Tank Army	37
3.13	Ration strength compared with combat strength in German divisions, 4 July 1943	38

3.14   Combat strength in battalions of 6th ID, 31st ID and 20th
       PzD   39
3.15   German infantry division T/O&E strength   41
3.16   German artillery in infantry divisions   41
3.17   German anti-tank guns in infantry divisions   42
3.18   Number of anti-tank guns in some infantry divisions,
       1 July 1943   42
3.19   Anti-tank battalions in 6th and 167th Infantry Divisions   43
3.20   German infantry divisions, 4 July 1943   44
3.21   Units in a panzer division and a GD or SS panzergrenadier
       division compared   45
3.22   Initial AFV strength for the panzer divisions, 4 July 1943   46
3.23   T/O&E of SPWs in I (armoured battalion)/12th
       Panzergrenadier Regiment (4th Panzer Division)   46
3.24   Soviet tank army, 1943   47
3.25   The five tank armies present in July 1943   48
3.26   Number of tanks and self-propelled guns in Soviet tank
       armies in August 1943   49
3.27   Organization of a Soviet tank corps, July 1943   49
3.28   Organization of tank corps deployed on the Voronezh and
       Central Fronts, 4 July 1943   50
3.29   Organization of tank corps reinforcing Voronezh Front
       during Zitadelle   50
3.30   T/O&E of a Soviet tank brigade, July 1943   51
3.31   Soviet independent tank corps in the defensive phase, July
       1943   51
3.32   Organization of Soviet mechanized corps, July 1943   52
4.1   Deployment of Tiger tanks engaged in operation Zitadelle,
       July 1943   59
4.2   Independent StuG battalions, 4 July 1943   65
4.3   Divisional StuG battalions, 4 July 1943   66
5.1   Numbers of aircraft in Soviet air army units on 4 July 1943   76
5.2   German air losses between 5 and 15 July 1943   77
5.3   Soviet air losses, 5–8 July 1943   78
7.1   Operational tanks and assault guns with Army Detachment
       Kempf, 11–15 July 1943   102
7.2   II SS-Pz Corps' operational tanks and assault guns,
       11–16 July 1943   103
7.3   II SS-Pz Corps' manpower losses, 11–16 July 1943   105
7.4   Soviet tanks and SP guns in 5th Guards Tank Army,
       12 July 1943   106

7.5   Distribution of 5th Guards Tank Army attacking units   107
8.1   Casualties suffered by the German 9th Army   113
8.2   Casualties suffered by Army Detachment Kempf, 4–20 July
       1943   114
8.3   Casualties suffered by 4th Panzer Army, 4–20 July 1943   115
8.4   German casualties, June–September 1943   116
8.5   German casualties on the eastern front for each army,
       1 July–31 August 1943   117
8.6   Casualties suffered by the Red Army during operation
       Zitadelle   119
8.7   Casualties suffered by the Red Army during major
       operations in summer 1943   119
8.8   Destroyed tanks in Army Group Centre, 5–14 July 1943   121
8.9   Tank losses among units in Army Group Centre during
       July 1943   121
8.10   Destroyed tanks in Army Group South, 5–17 July 1943   122
8.11   German aircraft losses and sorties during Zitadelle   123
8.12   Losses in 2nd Tank Army during the defensive phase, July
       1943   126
8.13   Equipment losses of the Red Army during major
       operations in summer 1943   127
10.1   German tanks and assault guns sent to the eastern front
       during 1943   147
10.2   German tank and assault gun losses on the eastern front,
       July–December 1943   148

FIGURES

10.1   German tanks on the eastern front, April–December 1943   146
10.2   Accumulated German casualties on the eastern front,
       22 June 1941–31 May 1944   150

Maps

		page
1.	The eastern front, 1942–43	3
2.	Central Front defensive dispositions	7
3.	9th Army attacks, 5–6 July	86
4.	9th Army attacks, 11–12 July	89
5.	XLVIII Panzer Corps attacks, 5–10 July	93
6.	German territorial gains in the Prokhorovka area, 12–15 July	104

Series Editor's Foreword

Midway through the Soviet–German War of 1941–45, in July 1943, the German Wehrmacht and the Soviet Red Army fought one of the most titanic battles in military history in the region around the Russian city of Kursk. Along with Stalingrad, the name Kursk was etched into historical record and people's minds to symbolize the nature of a war whose scale, ferocity, costs and consequences were both unprecedented and unfathomable. The Battle of Kursk's fame has rested on two distinct pillars. First, historians have portrayed it, and the accompanying massive tank encounter at Prokhorovka, as the greatest tank battle in history. Second, they have described the battle as the principal turning point in the war, when the Red Army defeated German Blitzkrieg and set the Soviet Union on the path toward victory over Nazi Germany.

Its fame notwithstanding, the Battle of Kursk has also generated a mythology of its own, one which evolved largely because of the paucity of reliable source materials necessary to document all aspects of its conduct. In short, Kursk also came to symbolize how little Westerners and even Russian citizens themselves knew about a battle and a war that so materially shaped the fate of the Soviet nation and its peoples, if not of Europe and the world as a whole. Most accounts of the battle were based either on recollections of Germans who fought there or on research undertaken by Soviet historians. As often as not, the latter were writing as much to demonstrate how Soviet socialism had triumphed over Western capitalism or to educate their military establishment, as to relate an accurate picture of the battle. To be sure, these histories contained more than just a grain of truth. For example, they described when and where the battle was fought, why, and to what effect with fair accuracy. Even here, however, German and Soviet historians differed over what constituted the battle's definition in terms of scope and duration. Owing to the relative paucity of archival materials on the Soviet side, however, they had greater difficulty addressing how the battle was fought or at what cost. Nor were the historians on either side able to state precisely what made the battle and its Prokhorovka engagement the largest tank battle in history, instead relying on the time-honored statement that 1,200–1,500 tanks met in combat on the field of Prokhorovka.

Nonetheless, recent histories have begun to address and dispel these myths. The doors to the Soviet archives are slowly opening, and the Russian government has been releasing archival materials and semi-archival studies, and Western authors have been preparing new studies that exploit German archival materials to a greater extent than before.[1] Others have written more complete and definitive histories based on these sources about how both sides conducted the battle.[2] Yet, as is the case with the war as a whole, the process of illuminating the Battle of Kursk is an incremental one that is likely to continue for some time.

One of the most vexing aspects of the Battle of Kursk has been the absence of reliable data concerning the strength of and losses suffered by both sides in the struggle. This is all the more perplexing, since, although available, requisite materials on the German side have yet to be exploited fully. The publication of this book corrects that long-standing deficiency. Within the context of a sound chronological narrative of the battle, Zetterling and Frankson offer an imposing statistical analysis of the Battle of Kursk. By exploiting all available German archival sources, they offer a definitive view of the strength, losses, and loss rates of German forces, particularly panzer, during the Battle of Kursk. They juxtapose this against a fair representation of like figures on the Red Army side. In doing so, the authors put to rest many of the myths concerning the battle and offer a work that superbly complements the best of new literature now appearing about the battle. One can only hope that the Russians will respond to this volume's candor by releasing appropriate data on the Red Army; but until they do, this book will justifiably remain the last word on the subject.

DAVID M. GLANTZ
Carlisle, PA, March 2000

NOTES

1. See, for example, David M. Glantz and Harold S. Orenstein, trans. and ed., *The Battle for Kursk 1943: The Soviet General Staff Study* (London: Frank Cass, 1999), and George M. Nipe Jr, *Decision in the Ukraine Summer 1943, II SS and III Panzerkorps* (Winnipeg, Canada: J. J. Fedorowicz, 1996).
2. See, for example, David M. Glantz and Jonathan M. House, *The Battle of Kursk* (Lawrence, KS and London: University Press of Kansas and Ian Allen, 1999 and 2000).

Preface

Several years have passed since we began working on this book and it is difficult to recollect why the work was initiated. Probably it began with the bewilderment we felt. This was caused by the different definitions of the battle we found in the literature. After a while two main definitions crystallized and it became clear that they originated from the different perspectives of the battle held by the Germans and the Soviets during the war. According to official Soviet history, the Battle of Kursk began on 5 July 1943 and ended on 23 August 1943. The battle is divided into three parts, the defensive phase, the offensive against Orel and the offensive against Belgorod–Kharkov. For the Germans these formed three different battles, Operation Zitadelle, the summer fighting around Orel and the fourth battle of Kharkov. The main reason for this is probably that Army Group South had to shift forces from Operation Zitadelle to fight along the Mius river far to the south and then react to another Soviet offensive directed against Belgorod–Kharkov. Our aim with this book is to make a thorough analysis of Operation Zitadelle or, to use the Soviet definition of the battle, only the defensive phase of the Battle of Kursk.

This was the first problem we encountered, but further difficulties appeared. The second was that despite claims that the battle did produce losses from which the German army never recovered, no previous author seems to have made any serious effort to establish the level of German losses. This is surprising, considering that the answer can be found in the German Military Archives in Freiburg (or in the copy-documents on microfilm in the National Archives in Washington, DC). Instead many figures of dubious background have been reiterated.

Third, the balance of forces has been sketchily described at best. This is also surprising, since material for this can be readily found, both with regard to the overall situation and to the engagements within the frame of the battle.

Fourth, in many cases the use of sources has been at fault. It is our conviction, for example, that information on losses must not be taken from sources on the opposing side. This is valid for the battle studied here, as well as for most other military operations. Consequently, both Soviet and German sources must be used in parallel. In this book we have tried to do this. In references for sources concerning the Soviet side the reader may occasionally find titles in German. Unless otherwise noted, these are Soviet books translated into German, usually in the former East Germany.

Fifth, more can be done to put the battle in its proper perspective, to give it the role it actually played during the war. How decisive was the battle? What were the short and long term effects? Was it the 'Swan song of German armour'?

Sixth, many errors in details persist, errors that could have been eradicated with little effort long ago had it not been for a tendency among writers to rewrite what a previous author had already written, without carefully checking the facts against other sources.

These points provided our ambitions for the present work. It is for the reader to judge whether they have been achieved.

We would also like to add a comment on the sources. Since at least the 1970s there has been a strong faction that has argued that the history of the eastern front has largely been dominated by the German view. Superficially this may seem plausible, but closer scrutiny reveals several flaws with this line of argument. Mainly there is not one 'German view', rather there are several. The sources available from the German side are many: archival documents, memoirs, various publications by more or less skilled historians, etc. These do not present a unified 'view'.

Second, it is not true to say that the history of the eastern front has been conditioned by German sources. Judging from the literature published in English on the battle at Kursk, it seems that a majority of the information originates from post-war Soviet publications. Often these are better described as propagandist rather than sincere and skilled attempts at uncovering the truth. Hence, almost all information given in English-language publications on German strength and losses is wrong, and is often considerably off the mark.

This book is based mainly on research in the German military archives. For this operation it is obvious that this source has been used far too little, and it seems that this is also true for many of the other battles on the eastern front. It is understandable that Soviet archival documents have been virtually unused by Western historians before the present decade. However, it is difficult to understand why the German archives, which have long been available, have been so little used.

We are indebted to John and Ljubica Erickson for helping us with material when we started this project. This has been very useful to us. We also want to thank Charles C. Sharp for providing us with material we needed. Mr Chris Lawrence at the Dupuy Institute has taken time to discuss some questions we had concerning the reliability of various items of information. Dr Alfred Price kindly allowed us to quote from one of his books. We are grateful for the assistance and help we have received from the staff at Bundesarchiv-Militärarchiv (Freiburg), Lietuvos Nacionaline Martyno Mazvydo Biblioteka (Vilnius) and Försvarshögskolans bibliotek (Stockholm).

Finally, we are most indebted to Försvarshögskolan (National Swedish Defence College) and thank them for the support provided for this project.

Abbreviations

AA	anti-aircraft
A/C	armoured car
AG	assault gun
AP	armour piercing
Arko	Artillery Commander
Art	artillery
AT	anti-tank
Aufkl	*Aufklärung*, reconnaissance
BA-MA	Bundesarchiv-Militärarchiv, Freiburg
Bde	brigade
Bef	*Befehls*, command (adjectival prefix)
Bn	battalion
Bty	battery
Coy	company
Eng	engineer
Fkl	*Funk-lenk*, remote-controlled
Flak	*Fliegerabwehrkanone*, anti-aircraft gun
Flamm	*Flammpanzer*, flame-thrower equipped tank
GD	*Großdeutschland*, Greater Germany (name on a division)
Gds	guards
Geb	*Gebirgs*, mountain (adjective – type of soldiery)
GHQ	General Headquarters
How	howitzer
ID	infantry division
IG	infantry gun
Jäg	*Jäger*, light infantry
K	*Korps*, corps
KTB	*Kriegstagebuch*, war diary
lg.	*lang*, long
Lt, le	light

MC   motorcycle
Mtn   mountain
Mtr   mortar
Nbw   *Nebelwerfer*, smokeprojector (German codename for rocket
        artillery)
Pak   *Panzerabwehrkanone*, anti-tank gun
PD   Panzer division
Pz   Panzer
r.   Russian
RD   rifle division
Rdfr   *Radfahrer*, cyclist
Recce   reconnaissance
RVGK   *Reserv Verkhovnogo Glavnogo Komandovaniya*, High
        Command's Reserve
s.   *schwere*, heavy
SP   self-propelled
SPW   *Schützenpanzerwagen*, armoured personnel carrier
StuG   *Sturmgeschütz*, assault gun
SU   self-propelled guns in the Red Army
T/O&E   Table of Organization and Equipment

1

Background

When the Wehrmacht launched operation Barbarossa on 22 June 1941, it met an adversary which in many respects was of similar size, at least in terms of manpower and artillery systems.[1] The large Soviet numerical superiority in tanks and aircraft was to a great extent negated by the Red Army's poor leadership, communication systems and doctrine. During the summer and autumn, the Wehrmacht managed to inflict losses on the Red Army almost as quickly as the Soviet Union could feed new units into the battle, but when the 'mud' period began in the autumn, the German forces could not impose as high an attrition rate on the enemy as they had previously. Worse was to come. As the Red Army went over to the offensive in December 1941, it was no longer the Germans deciding the loss rate to be suffered by the Soviet forces. The spring of 1942 provided further time for force build-up, and it was not the Germans who benefited most from it. As can be seen in Table 1.1, the Red Army had about a 2:1 numerical superiority on the main front at the end of June 1942. According to Soviet literature, the balance was much more even, but that results from an exaggeration of German strength.

Despite this, the Germans succeeded in taking the initiative and delivering a heavy blow to the Soviet forces in eastern Ukraine. The German forces between Kursk and Rostov inflicted 586,834 casualties on the enemy between 28 June and 24 July,[2] thus paving the way for the advances towards Stalingrad and the Caucasus. To lose about 600,000 men in a month on what amounted to less than a third of the front line between Leningrad and the Black Sea was hard even for the Red Army. However, the German offensive gradually ran out of steam, thus reducing the attrition rate. With the German offensive contained, the Red Army could itself grasp the initiative and inflict a telling defeat on the Axis powers. It was not only the forces in and around Stalingrad that were struck by the Soviet attack, for during the following winter the offensive was successively expanded to involve forces from Orel southwards. The situation

TABLE 1.1: COMPARATIVE STRENGTH, 1 JULY 1942

	Manpower	Tanks and Assault Guns	Guns and Mortars	Aircraft
Soviet strength[3]				
Main front	5,217,000	5,850	55,700	2,350
Stavka reserve[4]	750,000	900	9,500	2,150
Total	5,967,000	6,750	65,200	4,500
Finnish front	298,000	150	4,571	240
Other fronts*	1,800,000	1,900	15,000	2,000
Axis strength				
German forces				
On eastern front	2,635,000[5]	2,535[6]	23,000†	2,750[7]
On Finnish front	150,000[8]	~25[9]	700†	264[10]
Ostgebiete**	212,000[11]	–	–	–
Other areas***	951,000[12]	3,100[13]††	?	2,192[14]
German satellites****	648,000[15]	?	?	?
Finnish forces[16]	210,000	<100	?	~250

Notes:
*   Other fronts include the Far East and the Soviet southern border. Figures are estimates only.
**   Includes the rear occupied areas in eastern Europe.
*** Includes forces in Norway, Netherlands, Belgium, France, Italy, Africa, Balkans and Germany.
**** Includes Hungarian, Italian, Rumanian and Slovakian troops on the eastern front. Figures apply to 10 September 1942, additional satellite units had arrived since 1 July. The strength on that date must consequently have been lower.
†   Estimates based on T/O&E strength and number of units.
††   Includes tanks accepted by the army but not yet supplied to units, tanks with training units as well as tanks with combat units, also included are 2,192 tanks considered unsuitable for front-line employment.

Guns and Mortars include AT guns, AA guns, mortars and indirectly firing artillery pieces.

became especially critical for the Axis forces, when the Hungarian 2nd Army and the Italian 8th Army were defeated and a large gap extended from Voronezh to the lower Don.

· Soviet ambitions were, however, thwarted by the brilliant counter-stroke orchestrated by von Manstein, who succeeded in defeating the Red Army spearheads in the Ukraine and in stabilizing the front along much the same line as when the Germans launched their summer offensive of 1942. The outstanding difference lay in the two huge salients, which characterized the new front line. These were located around the towns of

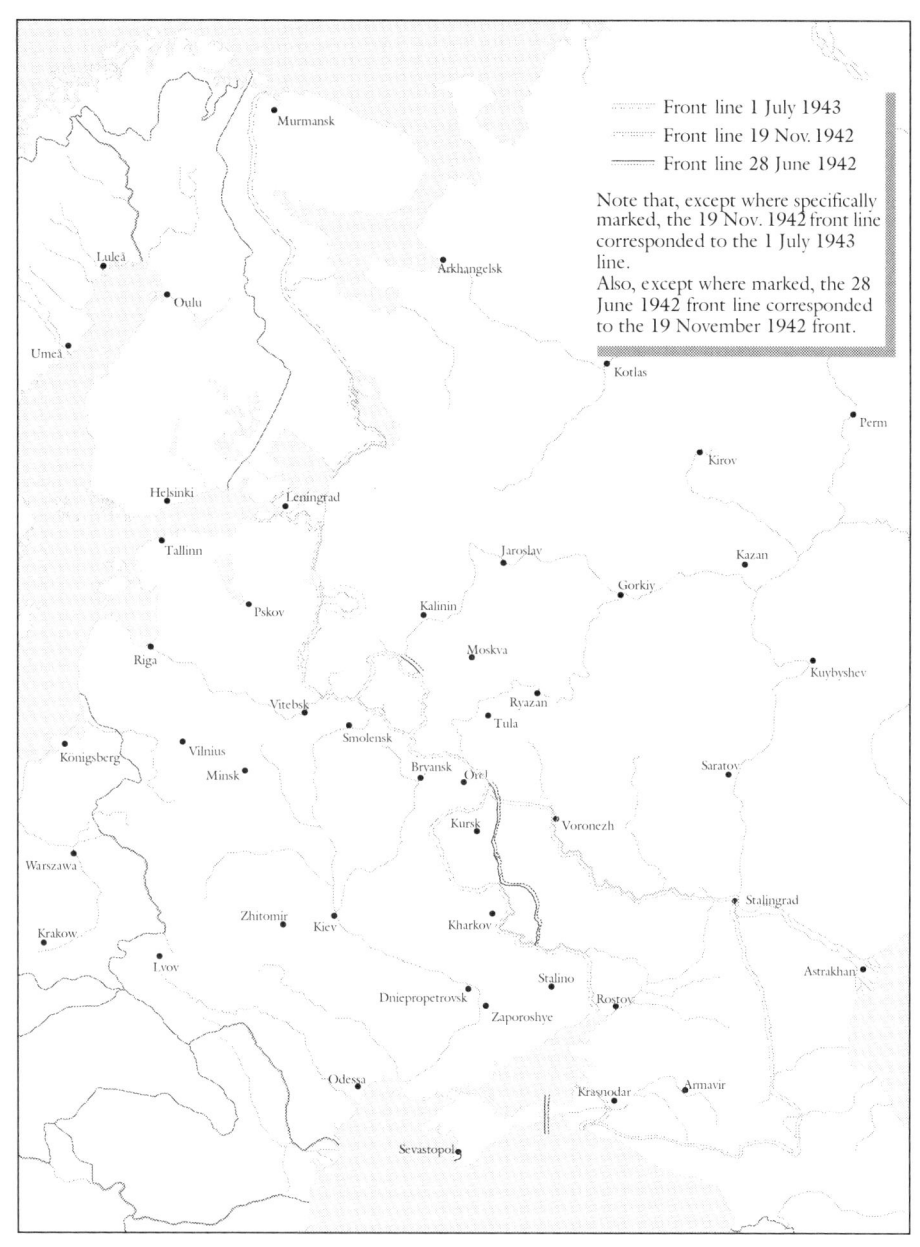

Front line 1 July 1943
Front line 19 Nov. 1942
Front line 28 June 1942

Note that, except where specifically marked, the 19 Nov. 1942 front line corresponded to the 1 July 1943 line.
Also, except where marked, the 28 June 1942 front line corresponded to the 19 November 1942 front.

Map 1. The eastern front, 1942–43

Orel and Kursk, two towns which, until Word War II at least, were relatively unknown. Since the German-held Orel salient formed the northern shoulder of the Soviet-held Kursk salient, operations against either of the salients were likely to involve forces in the other. Both areas offered the prospects of cutting off considerable enemy forces if a successful attack could be launched. Thus it is no surprise that this area did attract the eyes of the men in Berlin and Moscow when they gathered around their maps.

The strategic situation in the spring of 1943 was in many respects different from the circumstances that had shaped the events during the summer campaign season of the previous year. The disaster at Stalingrad cast its shadow over the German high command, even though the German Army was actually stronger in 1943 than it had been in 1942. In terms of manpower, the German Army in the east had increased by nearly 20 per cent. The number of tanks and assault guns had risen from 2,535[17] to 3,524[18] in the same period. The quality of the tanks had also improved, as had the German AT guns. This was the encouraging side of the coin, but two more ominous facts also had to be considered. The first was the severe decline in the contribution made by Germany's allies since the summer of 1942. The Italian forces were gone altogether, while Rumania and Hungary fielded much smaller forces in the spring of 1943 compared with the contribution they had made during the summer of 1942. The second, and most serious change, lay in the increasing strength of the Red Army, although the German generals were perhaps only partly aware of this. The change lay not so much in manpower, but in the increase in tanks, artillery and aircraft (see Tables 1.1 and 1.2 for a direct comparison). Tanks not only increased in numbers, but the more powerful vehicles were receiving a greater share of production resources. In 1942, medium and heavy tanks made up 61 per cent of all those produced, while their quota was 86 per cent in 1943.[19] Artillery almost doubled in numbers, while the Soviets developed firing techniques suitable for their means of communication and fire direction. Thus, the summer of 1943 promised to be a much more challenging season for the Wehrmacht than the previous year had been.

Essentially, there were three choices for the German forces in Russia: (1) try a static defence; (2) use a mobile defence; or (3) try their fortunes with offensive action. Of these, the first was inevitably used over a large portion of the front. Most of the infantry units had only limited mobility and it had become more and more evident that the cost of attacks made by infantry without adequate tank support was not commensurate with the results, at least not in the longer term. A mobile defence was possible if the proportion of infantry units to mobile units was not too great.

TABLE 1.2: COMPARATIVE STRENGTH, 1 JULY 1943

	Manpower	Tanks and Assault Guns	Guns and Mortars	Aircraft
Soviet strength[20]				
Main front	5,745,800	9,888	91,791	6,532
Stavka reserve	1,111,000	2,688	16,782	662
Total	6,856,800	12,576	108,573	7,194
Finnish front	320,100	311	4,571	299
Other fronts*	1,955,000	3,200	18,800	4,500
Axis strength				
German forces				
On eastern front	3,138,000[21]	3,524[22]	25,000**	3,180***[23]
On Finnish front	80,000[24]	~25[25]	600**	235***[26]
In other areas††	1,237,000[27]	2,807†[28]	?	3,321***[29]
Satellite forces****	~225,000[30]			
Finnish forces[31]	230,000	<100		~250

Notes:
* Other fronts include the Far East and the Soviet southern border. Figures apply to 1 April 1943, not 1 July 1943.
** This is an estimate, based on T/O&E strength of the units on the eastern front.
*** Figure applies to 31 May 1943. Includes all types of aircraft, including transport and liaison planes.
**** Includes Hungarian, Rumanian and Slovakian troops on the eastern front.
† Includes tank and assault gun units being set up, also includes vehicles no longer regarded as suitable for combat, but still retained by the Army.
†† Of the manpower in other areas, 296,000 were in the Balkans, 195,000 were in Italy and 746,000 were in western Europe.[32]

Guns and Mortars include AT guns, AA guns, mortars and indirectly firing artillery pieces.

In the Army Group North area the number of infantry divisions was 38, while only one panzergrenadier division and not a single panzer division was subordinated to the army group.[33] In addition it had three Jäger divisions and one mountain division, which at least had somewhat better mobility than the infantry divisions. This was clearly not sufficient to mount a truly mobile defence at army-group level; neither did the terrain favour mobile operations. The final nail in the mobile defence coffin for Army Group North was Leningrad. It was unthinkable that Hitler would loosen the German grip on this city, even though it had been dented in January 1943, when the Red Army had opened a narrow land corridor to the besieged city.

In the Army Group Centre area, the prospects for a mobile defence were better, since the terrain, while not ideal, was more suitable. No specific geographical features tied the ground forces to certain positions, and the proportion of mobile units was higher, 11 mobile divisions compared with 64 infantry divisions.[34] It is doubtful however, if it would have been possible to stage such a defence over more than limited sectors of the front, owing to the relatively limited number of mobile units.

In the Army Group South area the conditions for a successful mobile defence were more propitious than for any other army group. The number of mobile divisions was 13, while the infantry divisions amounted to 29 (including one mountain division).[35] While even this presented rather a low ratio, it was considerably higher than the average for the German armed forces as a whole. The Wehrmacht simply could not expect anything better. While this ratio certainly was not ideal, it at least made mobile defence a viable option, especially since the Red Army had an even lower proportion of mobile units in their forces. The geography was also favourable to this type of defence. No large area in Europe provided better terrain for a mobile defence than the Ukraine. But more ominous for this defence alternative was the fact that Kharkov, the fourth-largest city in the Soviet Union, was located only 35 kilometres from the front line along the Donets River. To compound matters for the German field commanders, the important industrial region around Stalino was equally perilously close to the front. For Hitler these were objectives that had to be denied to Stalin. This ruled out mobile defence in the Ukraine, at least until Soviet pressure had forced the Germans out of Kharkov and the Donets industrial region. However, by then it could be too late.

Whether a mobile defence would or would not have been successful is, of course, open to debate. Ever since the campaigns in 1941 had faltered, the fighting on the eastern front had increasingly turned into a grinding war of attrition. Historians tend to focus on the overwhelming Soviet manpower resources and their considerably greater production of weapons. To this has been added the fact that Germany had to devote resources to the Mediterranean and to the defence of western Europe, even though the eastern front clearly was the main concern. The implication of this was that the larger Soviet resources made a German victory in a war of attrition impossible.

In a war of attrition, however, it is not only the ability to feed new troops, tanks, guns and planes into the fighting that matters: the ability to inflict losses on the enemy is equally important. In this respect, the German Army had a substantial superiority. As it turned out, during 1943 Germany lost 1,803,755 men on the eastern front (killed, wounded and missing), of which 1,442,654 were combat losses.[36] This can be compared

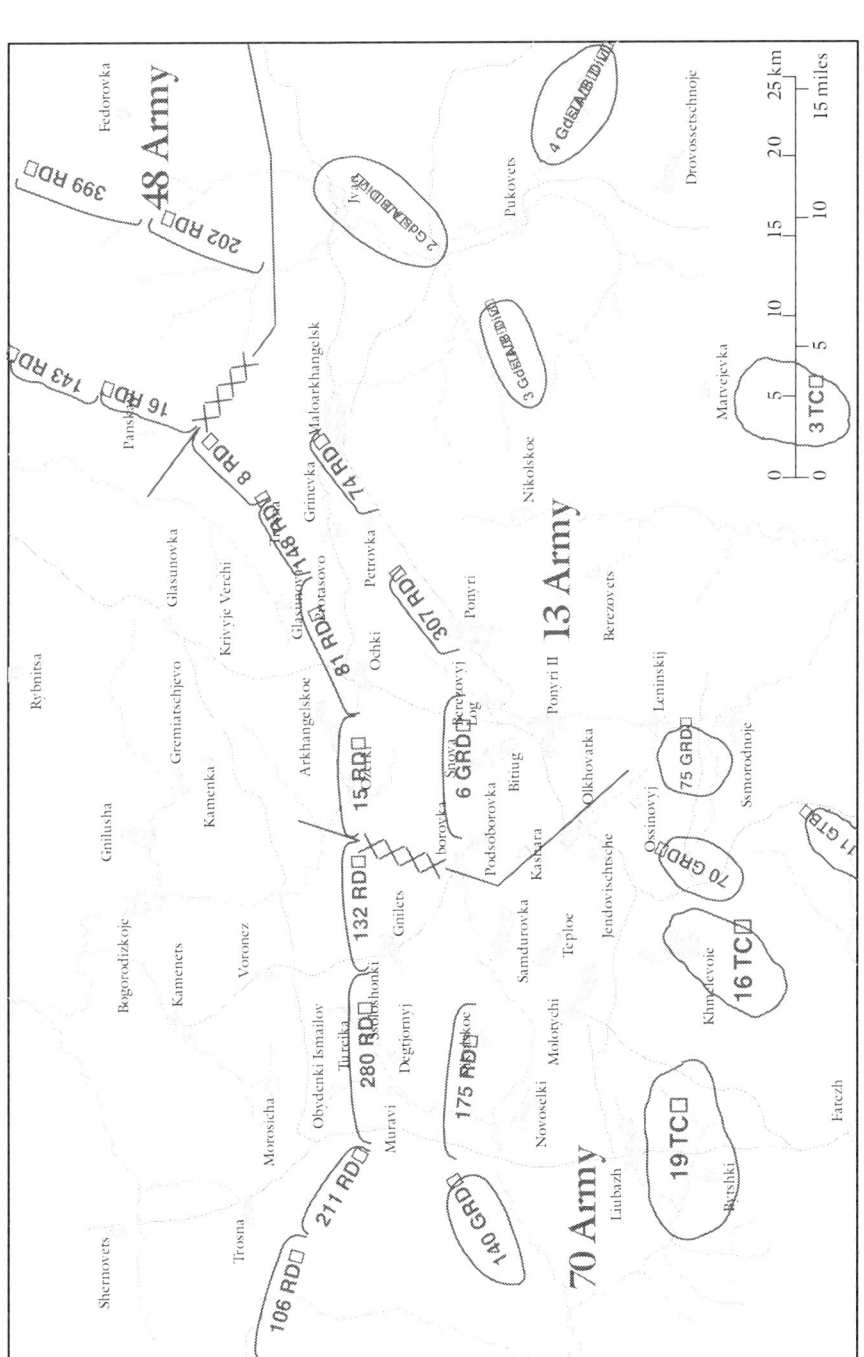

Map 2. Central Front defensive dispositions

with Soviet casualties amounting to 7,857,503,[37] or more than four times higher, during 1943. In a war of attrition it is not possible to win if the loss ratio is too unfavourable, when the losses sustained exceed the rate of replacement. In this case the relative difference in losses was greater than the relative difference in population size.[38] According to this calculation it was the Red Army which could be expected to run out of men first, not the German Army. Two facts, though, altered the situation in favour of the Soviet Union. The first was the impossibility for Germany to send all its newly conscripted soldiers to Russia, since it also had to take into consideration strengthening the defence in the west. Second, the German population was older than the Soviet one, making a smaller proportion suitable for military service.

Similarly, German tank and assault gun losses (on all fronts) during 1943 amounted to 8,067,[39] while Soviet losses were approximately 23,500,[40] which can be compared with the German production of 10,747[41] and the Soviet production of 24,006 tanks and assault guns.[42] Again, the ratio between Soviet and German losses is greater than the ratio between Soviet and German production. In this respect, it must be remembered, the Red Army was aided by the fact that it received lend-lease tanks.

The implication of these figures is that the Soviet margin for victory in the war of attrition as events actually took place was slight and it cannot be regarded as having been inevitable. A German mobile defence could have been used to exact an even more favourable kill rate on the enemy, but whether this would have been sufficient to change the outcome of the war in the east is a subject of its own and outside of the scope of this book.

Since a mobile defence was not on the agenda, recourse had to be made to the other two possibilities. In this situation it was not surprising that the two salients around Orel and Kursk attracted the minds of the men in the German high command. If the Kursk salient could be pinched off, two positive results might be reaped. The Red Army would suffer serious losses and the Orel salient would become much less exposed. The opinions of the senior German commanders were divided concerning the feasibility, or even the advisability of such an offensive. Among the opponents was the recently appointed inspector-general of armoured troops, Heinz Guderian. He considered the whole idea pointless, since it was certain to result in heavy tank losses among the panzer divisions which were resting and refitting with new equipment during the spring. On the contrary, he thought it would be more appropriate to concentrate on strengthening the defences in the west.[43]

The idea of an offensive aimed at nipping off the Kursk salient seems to have appeared as early as March 1943. Indeed, it was a logical continuation of von Manstein's counteroffensive. He had assembled his striking force, largely built around the SS-Panzer corps, in the vicinity of Pavlograd and, as a first step, defeated the Soviet forces that had crossed the Donets river around Izyum. Having accomplished this, von Manstein directed his troops in a northerly direction. Kharkov was retaken and, in conjunction with the Großdeutschland division attacking from the west, the SS-Panzer corps continued, retaking Belgorod on 18 March.[44] It is doubtful whether the Germans had expected to get any further. The thaw was in full swing and gradually turning the country into a morass. This is also evident from Hitler's *Operationsbefehl Nr. 5*, which was issued on 13 March, five days before the fall of Belgorod.[45] In this directive, Army Group South was ordered to build up a strong panzer army north of Kharkov, in order to attack northwards in conjunction with forces from Army Group Centre. This latter army group was then to build its striking forces from the units released when the Rzhev salient had been evacuated, a move which was accomplished on 25 March. These forces were to be inserted in the Orel salient. The assembly of the attacking forces were to be completed in mid-April, which indicates that the Germans did not expect to take Kursk in March.

Events were not going to develop at that pace though. In his *Operationsbefehl Nr. 6* Hitler explained his decision to proceed with the attack, which had by now received the name 'Zitadelle', as soon as the weather permitted.[46] According to the directive, the attack *had* to be quickly and resoundingly successful and it *had* to give the German forces the initiative for the rest of the spring and the summer. From this directive, issued on 12 April, it was reasonable to expect the attack to start no later than the middle of May.

According to von Manstein, he envisioned the operation as a kind of pre-emptive attack. The idea, as he saw it, was to defeat the Soviet forces before they had completely refitted and replenished their units. Thereby he hoped to be able to destroy units completely, not even leaving cadres around which units might be reformed. If this were not achieved, he did not regard the attack to be a sensible operation.[47]

The attack was delayed, however. The principal reason for this was probably the desire to mount the attack with the greatest possible number of modern tanks. During spring 1943 the brand-new Panther tank had entered production. This tank outclassed all previous tanks in terms of fire power and frontal armour protection, as shown in the Tables in the Appendices. Also taking into account the fact that the Panther was the fastest German tank, with the best power-to-weight ratio and the fact that optics and communication equipment were excellent, the desire to use this tank in the planned offensive is understandable. The main uncertainty with the new tank concerned teething troubles. General Guderian did not consider the Panther combat-worthy at its present stage. He expressed this view on 4 May at a conference in Munich where the chief of the General Staff of the Army Kurt Zeitzler, the chief of the General Staff of Luftwaffe Hans Jeschonnek, the commander of the 9th Army Walter Model, the commander of Army Group Centre Günther von Kluge, the commander of Army Group South Erich von Manstein and the minister of armaments Albert Speer had gathered with Hitler. Another discouraging fact was presented by Model. Recently taken aerial photographs showed that Soviet defensive positions of considerable strength and depth were being prepared. Model, concluding that the prospects of achieving surprise were gone, was negative to the Zitadelle plan. Guderian was more firmly than ever against the attack and was supported by Speer. Zeitzler and von Kluge were in favour of attack, while von Manstein thought that an attack in April might have stood a good chance of success but did not believe that the prospects for the attack were good at this late stage. The conference was dissolved without any decision being made.[48]

This was not the last time that the decision about whether the offensive should be launched or not was postponed; and with every postponement the possibilities for the Red Army to prepare their defences improved. Also, the photographs Model had received from the Luftwaffe reconnaissance units were telling the truth. The Stavka had realized, at least a month earlier, that the Kursk salient was likely to be the subject of a German attack. On 8 April, Zhukov had sent a report to Stalin in which he concluded that a German attack, with the aim of cutting off the Kursk salient, was going to be launched from the area around Belgorod in the south and from the Orel–Kromy area in the north. Concerning the possible alternatives for meeting this threat, Zhukov preferred the construction of strong defences in the threatened sectors, rather than launching a pre-emptive attack.[49] This proved to be the alternative the Red Army was going to settle for. However, they still had concerns about the ability of the troops to withstand a German summer offensive, therefore Steppe Military District (hereafter Steppe Front[50]) was formed and deployed behind the bulge. This was not the only reason, since it could also reinforce the front forces when the Red Army launched its counter-offensives. Table 1.3 gives the strength of the Red Army forces in the Kursk area on 10 April 1943.

As can be seen in Table 1.3, the Voronezh Front still lacked guns and mortars compared with the other two fronts. Probably, all losses from von Manstein's counterstroke had not yet been replaced. The Central Front

10

TABLE 1.3: SOVIET STRENGTH IN THE KURSK AREA, 10 APRIL 1943[51]

	Manpower	Tanks and Assault Guns	Guns and Mortars	Aircraft
Central Front	538,480	950	7,860	660
Voronezh Front	419,430	270	3,835	470
Reserve Front[52]	269,142	120	7,406	177
Total	1,227,052	1,340	19,101	1,307

had 42 divisions at this time,[53] while Voronezh had 32[54] and the Reserve had 33.[55] The three fronts could field 107 divisions. When the battle started these three fronts had 123 divisions. This is not in itself a considerable difference but a closer look at the amount of equipment amassed to meet the German summer offensive reveals important changes.

NOTES

1. The Red Army had 2,680,000 men and 37,500 guns and mortars in the western military districts, Leningrad, Baltic, Western, Kiev and Odessa (*Istoriya Vtoroi Mirovoi Voiny*, Vol. 4, pp. 25ff.). The Wehrmacht had 3,050,000 men (OKH Gen St d h/Gen Qu Abt. H. Vers./Qu. 1 Nr 1/0740/41 g.kdos., BA–MA RH 2/1326) available (OKH Gen. St. d. h./Gen. Qu. Abt. H.Vers./Qu. 1 Nr 1/0740/41 g.Kdos. den 20. Juni 1941, BA–MA RH 2/1326), but of these about half a million were OKH reserves, which were committed a couple of weeks after 22 June 1941. The army had detailed 4,760 light artillery pieces and 2,252 heavy pieces plus 172 other guns (General der Artillerie beim Ob. d. H. (Ia) Nr 132/41 g.K.Chef.S. den 20. Juni 1941, BA–MA RH 2/1326). This does not include mortars and light guns (mainly AT-guns) as do the Soviet figures. On the basis of T/O&E strength it can be estimated that the Germans had about 12,000 of these weapons.
2. G.F. Krivosheyev, *Grif Sekretnosti Sniat* (Voenizdat, Moscow, 1993), pp. 177ff. We have previously offered considerable criticism of this book (see N. Zetterling and A. Frankson, 'Analyzing World War II Eastern Front Battles', article in *Journal of Slavic Military Studies*, March 1998), hence it may seem strange that we use this source here. However, our criticisms focus on errors that may result in Soviet casualty figures during German offensive operations being too low. If this is the case during this operation too, it reinforces our argument.
3. *Geschichte des Zweiten Weltkrieges*, Vol. 5, pp. 176–7 (Table 15), p. 133 (strength of reserves), p. 118 (strength on other fronts).
4. This is an estimate based on the number of units in STAVKA Reserve. The estimate should be considered as conservative. Information on the STAVKA reserve has been taken from *Geschichte des Zweiten Weltkrieges*, Vol. 5, p. 395, table 18.
5. Überschlägige Kräfteberechnung für das Jahr 1943 und ihre Auswirkung auf die Kampfkraft der Ostfront. OKH Org.Abt. den 8.8.1942. BA–MA RH 2/429. The figures refer to Iststärke.
6. The number of tanks is taken from Panzerlage Ost Januari 1942 – März 1943 (BA–MA RH 10/68). To this is added an estimated 475 assault guns (based on the fact that

11

15⅓ assault gun battalions were present with the army groups on the eastern front 15 June 1942 (Zahlenmäßige Übersicht über die Verteilung der AOK, Gen.Kdos., Divn. und Heerestruppen, Stand 15.6. 1942, BA-MA RH 2/340K) and a strength of 31 assault guns per battalion (T/O&E strength).

7. Williamson Murray, *Luftwaffe* (Grafton, London, 1988), p. 173.

8. Überschlägige Kräfteberechnung für das Jahr 1943 und ihre Auswirkung auf die Kampfkraft der Ostfront. OKH Org.Abt. den 8.8.1942. BA-MA RH 2/429. The figure refers to actual strength.

9. Estimate, based on the fact that the only German tank unit in the area was the 211th Tank Battalion, equipped with captured tanks.

10. This is the strength of Luftflotte 5 according to Earl F. Ziemke, *The German Northern Theater of Operations 1940–1945* (Dept. of the Army Pamphlet, no. 20-271, Washington, 1959), p. 239.

11. Überschlägige Kräfteberechnung für das Jahr 1943 und ihre Auswirkung auf die Kampfkraft der Ostfront. OKH Org.Abt. den 8.8.1942. BA-MA RH 2/429. The figure refers to actual strength.

12. Überschlägige Kräfteberechnung für das Jahr 1943 und ihre Auswirkung auf die Kampfkraft der Ostfront. OKH Org.Abt. den 8.8.1942. BA-MA RH 2/429. The figure refers to actual strength.

13. Calculated by subtracting the number of tanks on the eastern front from the total German tank and assault gun stock given by Müller-Hillebrand, *Das Heer*, Vol. III, Anhang B (Mittler & Sohn, Frankfurt am Main, 1969).

14. Calculated by subtracting the number of aircraft on the eastern front from the total number of aircraft in the Luftwaffe, given by W. Murray, *Luftwaffe* (Grafton, London, 1988), p. 197.

15. Gen.St.d.Heeres/Org.Abt. den 20.9.1942. BA-MA RH 2/429. The figure refers to Verpflegungsstärke (ration strength).

16. K.J. Mikola, Finlands Försvarsmakt 50 år (Aktuellt och Historiskt, Stockholm, 1968).

17. The number of tanks is taken from Panzerlage Ost Januari 1942–März 1943 (BA-MA RH 10/68). To this is added an estimated 475 assault guns (based on the fact that 15⅓ assault gun battalions were present with the army groups on the eastern front, 15 June 1942 (Zahlenmäßige Übersicht über die Verteilung der AOK, Gen.Kdos., Divn. und Heerestruppen, Stand 15.6.1942, BA-MA RH 2/340K) and a strength of 31 assault guns per battalion (T/O&E strength).

18. Panzerlage Ost (Nach Gen Qu) 1943, BA-MA RH 10/61 and StuG-Lage Ost (Nach Gen Qu) 1943, BA-MA RH 10/62 and PAK-Lage Ost, BA-MA RH 10/63. The figure includes 984 assault guns and 90 Ferdinands.

19. The percentages are taken from the table on page 225 in *Soviet Tanks and Combat Vehicles of WWII* by S.J. Zaloga and J. Grandsen.

20. *Istoriya Vtoroi mirovoi voiny 1939–1945*, Vol. 7 (Voenizdat, Moscow, 1976), p. 120 (Table 15), p. 104 (strength of reserves), p. 96 (on other fronts). Further forces existed in the interior military districts; the strengths given in Table 1.2 show forces available on 1 July 1943.

21. OKH/Gen.St.d.H./Org.Abt. Nr. I/18941/44 g.Kdos, v. 7.9.44 (National Archives, Microfilm Publication T78, Roll 414, Frame 6383114). The figures do not include forces in Finland. Waffen-SS and ground combat units from the Luftwaffe are included.

22. Panzerlage Ost (Nach Gen Qu) 1943, BA-MA RH 10/61 and StuG-Lage Ost (Nach Gen Qu) 1943, BA-MA RH 10/62 and PAK-Lage Ost, BA-MA RH 10/63. The figure includes 984 assault guns and 90 Ferdinands.

23. Olaf Groehler, *Geschichte des Luftkriegs 1910 bis 1970* (Militärverlag der Deutschen

Demokratischen Republik, Berlin, 1975), p. 376.
24. W. Victor Madej, *The Russo-German War, July 1943–May 1945* (Valor Publishing Company, Allentown, PA, 1986), p. 187. The author does not state his sources for the table from which the figure has been taken, but we have been able to check some of the figures from original documents in file BA-MA RH 2/1341. The documents and Madej's figures are in good agreement.
25. This is an estimate, the only tank unit in the area was the 211th Tank Battalion, which had two tank companies equipped with captured tanks – see Georg Tessin, *Verbände und Truppen der Deutschen Wehrmacht und Waffen-SS* (Mittler & Sohn, Frankfurt am Main (Vols 1–5), Biblio Verlag, Osnabrück (Vols 6–14), 1966–1975).
26. Groehler, *Geschichte des Luftkriegs*, p. 376.
27. OKH/GenStdH/Org.Abt. Nr I/18941/44, v. 7.9.44 (National Archives T78, R414, Frames 6383112-4.
28. Figure obtained by using the total number of tanks and assault guns given in Müller-Hillebrand, *Das Heer*, Vol. III, Anhang B and subtracting the tanks on the eastern front.
29. Groehler, *Geschichte des Luftkriegs*, p. 376.
30. Estimate based on the number of divisions (15 according to KTB OKW 1943, pp. 731–4) and an assumed divisional slice of 15,000 (slightly lower than the slice in 1942, when the units were more up to strength).
31. K.J. Mikola, *Finlands Försvarsmakt 50 år*, pp. 127–30.
32. OKH/GenStdH/Org.Abt. Nr I/18941/44, v. 7.9.44 (National Archives T78, R414, Frames 6383112-4).
33. KTB OKW, Vol. III, p. 736. The figures refer to 7 July 1943.
34. Ibid.
35. Ibid.
36. BA-MA RH 2/1343. According to figures presented by KTB OKW 1943, p. 1482, men killed constituted about 13.5 per cent of overall losses.
37. Krivosheyev, *Grif Sekretnosti Sniat*, p. 146.
38. The data on Soviet population on the eve of operation Barbarossa is uncertain, but it seems that the population of the USSR amounted to approximately 200,000,000 at the beginning of 1941, which can be compared to a German population of approximately 80,000,000 (see e.g. B.V. Sokolov, *The Cost of War: Human Losses for the USSR and Germany 1939–1945, Journal of Slavic Military Studies*, Vol. 9, no. 1, March 1996, pp. 164ff.). This means that the Soviet population was only about 2.5 times greater than the German population.
39. Müller-Hillebrand, *Das Heer*, Vol. III, Anhang B.
40. Krivosheyev, *Grif Sekretnosti Sniat*, p. 357.
41. Müller-Hillebrand, *Das Heer*, Vol. III, Anhang B
42. Zaloga/Grandsen, *Soviet Tanks and Combat Vehicles*, p. 225.
43. Guderian, *Panzer Leader*, p. 307.
44. Von Manstein, *Verlorene Siege*, pp. 459–72.
45. See E. Klink, *Das Gesetz des Handelns* (Deutsche Verlagsanstalt, Stuttgart, 1966), p. 277.
46. Ibid., p. 292.
47. Manstein, *Verlorene Siege*, p. 485.
48. Guderian, *Panzer Leader*, p. 307.
49. G.K. Zhukov, *The Memoirs of Marshal Zhukov*, pp. 433–4 (Natraj, New Delhi, 1985).
50. The Steppe Military District became the Steppe Front on 9 July 1943. *Rysskii Arkhiv: Velikaya Otechestvennaya 4(4), Kurskaya Bitva, Dokumenti i Materiali 27 Marta – 23 Avgusta 1943 goda* (Terra, Moscow, 1997), p. 48.

51. *Rysskii Arkhiv: Velikaya Otechestvennaya 4(4), Kurskaya Bitva, Dokumenti i Materiali 27 Marta – 23 Avgusta 1943 goda*, p. 394.
52. Reserve Front is the nucleus for the forces which became Steppe Front later on.
53. 38 Rifle Divisions and 4 Mobile Corps (Tank/Mech). These corps equal divisions in size.
54. 31 Rifle Divisions and 1 Mobile Corps (Tank/Mech). This corps equals a division in size.
55. 31 Rifle Divisions and 2 Mobile Corps (Tank/Mech). These corps equal divisions in size.

2

The Assembly of Forces

When fighting petered out in mud at the end of March 1943, both sides could begin to rebuild their battered forces. This was not an easy process, but it became easier due to the unexpectedly long lull before operation Zitadelle began. Although not known at the time, the respite before major combat operations were initiated again was unusually long for the eastern front. This also provided an opportunity to train newly arrived replacements jointly with the veterans among the units.

For the Germans the emphasis on the panzer units was of course great. The overall number of tanks on the eastern front reached a new peak and they were of more powerful types than ever. Of all the tanks on the eastern front about 70 per cent were deployed for operation Zitadelle.[1] This was a concentration of armour seldom surpassed, but it was more than matched by the Red Army. The Panzer III and Panzer IV were still the dominant types, though the majority of them were now fitted with longer and more powerful guns. The newer models, the Tigers and Panthers, only made up some 14 per cent of the tanks on the eastern front.[2]

The German forces north of the Kursk salient were somewhat weaker than those south of the salient. Some Soviet accounts maintain that they did expect the more powerful blow from the north. No explanation for this estimate has been found. Probably the Red Army had relatively correct information about the German order of battle and it seems rather strange that such a mistake should occur since 9th Army in the north had fewer mechanized divisions. However, there is one possible explanation for this. Ninth Army was stronger in one respect. It had heavier artillery due to its larger number of non-divisional artillery units. For Red Army breakthrough operations this was a good indicator of where the main emphasis lay. It is possible that the Red Army evaluated the enemy by assuming that he behaved similarly. This was not the case however. In Soviet breakthrough operations one part of the force performed the initial assault, while other units, usually tank and mechanized corps, waited to exploit the gap once created. The Wehrmacht, however, did not use that method, unless factors such as terrain necessitated it. The preferred method was to let Panzer units create and exploit holes, that is to say a unit first broke through and then immediately exploited, with no unit passing through it.

The German choice is probably a reflection of two phenomena. First, the superior German effectiveness in inflicting casualties made it far more likely for the German unit to suffer acceptable losses during the initial period than was the case for a Soviet unit, which could be severely mauled in the process. Second, the German method was dependent upon initiative at all levels, since a breakthrough is inevitably a confused process, making it difficult to control from above. It is not easy for a unit, engaged in confusing and intensive combat, suddenly to thrust deeply, without initiative at all levels. If however a higher commander has a fresh unit available when the moment appears, he can exercise greater control. The disadvantage of such a method is of course traffic control when the newly committed units pass through the units making the initial assault. Also it can be more difficult for a higher commander to grasp the opportunity when a gap occurs than for men on the spot. Overall the German method produced quicker breakthroughs and exploitations, but this could as well be a result of the skill with which the method is implemented than a result of inherent characteristics of the method. In retrospect, it seems that both sides chose the method which best fitted their available forces.

Thus, according to Soviet operational methods, the German dispositions could indicate a main effort in the north, while, according to German operational thinking, the dispositions indicated that the southern attack was the more powerful. This is, of course, only speculation, since no substantial information has been found in the available Soviet sources, but as an explanation it is not wholly implausible.

The Orel salient was held by the German 2nd Panzer Army and the 9th Army. The 2nd Panzer Army, its impressive name notwithstanding, did not possess a single panzer division,[3] and only one panzer grenadier division.[4] Also 2nd Panzer Army had 13 infantry divisions.[5] This army took no part in Zitadelle, and did not face the Soviet Central Front. Rather, the Soviet units opposing it were part of the Bryansk Front.

The German 9th Army was much better furnished with powerful units. It had six panzer divisions, one panzer grenadier division and 14 infantry divisions.[6] Also it was unusually well provided (for a German Army) with non-divisional artillery support. The 9th Army covered the front sector between Bogodukhova and Sevsk. The opposing forces on the Soviet side were part of the Central Front.

16

The western side of the Kursk salient was defended by the 2nd Army. This was rather weak, with only seven infantry divisions plus remnants of two other infantry divisions.[7] The army was short of 14,000 men and had no real offensive capability. Consequently, it was allotted the static task of guarding the western face of the salient. It did not even undertake attacks to hold Soviet units in place.

The German unit able to deliver the most concentrated punch was probably the 4th Panzer Army, led by the very experienced panzer commander Hermann Hoth. This army consisted of three corps. The LII on the left flank possessed three infantry divisions and was given a rather passive role in the battle. The XXXXVIII Panzer Corps with two panzer divisions and the elite panzer grenadier division Großdeutschland had considerable striking power and was of course one of the spearhead corps of Army Group South. To the right Hoth deployed the II SS-Panzer Corps consisting of the three SS-panzer grenadier divisions Leibstandarte, Das Reich and Totenkopf. Naturally this corps was also one of the main attacking units. The 4th Panzer Army also deployed the 167th Infantry Division on the boundary between XXXXVIII Panzer Corps and II SS-Panzer Corps. Including all types the 4th Panzer Army had almost 1,100 tanks and assault guns (if vehicles in workshops are included). This was a number probably never exceeded by any German Army during the war.

Army Group South intended the 4th Panzer Army to be the main striking force, but Army Detachment Kempf on the right flank was also to advance to cover the right flank of 4th Panzer Army. For this purpose Kempf used the Corps Raus – later called XI Corps – and III Panzer Corps. The latter was commanded by Hermann Breith, who had assumed command on 3 January 1943. Except for two short periods, Breith remained in command of the corps for the remainder of the war. It was quite unusual to remain in command of a panzer corps for such a long period. Corps Raus consisted of two infantry divisions, while III Panzer Corps had at its disposal three panzer divisions and one infantry division. An additional infantry division was sent to Raus shortly after the initiation of the operation.

The strength of the German forces committed around the Kursk salient is given in Table 2.1. The figures here differ from the traditional ones exemplified by the *History of the Great Patriotic War of the Soviet Union*: 900,000 men, 2,700 tanks and 10,000 guns.[8] These figures have been reiterated many times but the figures we present above are based on primary German sources, while the traditional figures were estimates made by the Soviets.

It should also be remembered that the manpower strength given in

TABLE 2.1: GERMAN STRENGTH IN THE KURSK AREA, 1 JULY 1943

	Manpower	Tanks and Assault Guns	Guns and Mortars*	Aircraft
9th Army	335,000[9]	920[10]	3,630	–
2nd Army	110,000[11]	31[12]	940	–
4th Pz Army	223,907[13]	1,089[14]	1,774	–
Army Det. Kempf**	108,000[15]	419[16]	1,073	–
VIII Air Corps***	–	–	–	1,100[17]
1st Air Division****	–	–	–	730[18]
Total	777,000	2,451	7,417	1,830

*   These numbers are estimates, based on T/O&E strength and the number of units given in Table 2.2. The same definition of guns and mortars as used by Soviet writing have been applied.
**   Not including XXXXII Corps, which took no part in the battle.
***   The part of Luftflotte 4 which was committed to the battle.
****   The part of Luftflotte 6 which was committed to the battle.

Notes: All figures on German manpower strength refer to ration strength.
        Figures on tank strength include command tanks, recovery tanks, artillery observation tanks and flame-thrower tanks. Older types of tanks and tanks in workshops are included.
        Figures for Army Detachment Kempf do not include the XXXXII Corps, since this corps faced the Soviet Southwestern Front, which took no part in the battle.

Table 2.1 refers to ration strength. Thus non-combat personnel are included too, as are non-military men who received their subsistence from the army. Also included are men in hospitals and prisoners of war. Hence, ration strength figures give an inflated picture of the strength, a phenomenon which seems to have been both common and well known according to German documents.[19] Consequently, the manpower strengths given in Table 2.1 should be regarded as upper limits.

As has been touched upon, the 9th Army was considerably better off in terms of GHQ units than the attacking armies of Army Group South. This did to some extent compensate for the lower number of tanks. Table 2.2 presents the number of combat units, both divisions and GHQ units, in the armies around the Kursk salient.

These then were the forces poised for the attack on the Kursk salient, but although they were impressively large, the defending forces were even larger. The Central Front, commanded by K.K. Rokossovsky, was slightly stronger than F.N. Vatutin's Voronezh Front on the southern side of the salient. However, the Red Army did not only deploy massive forces in the German attack sectors. Its large resources made it possible for it to form

TABLE 2.2: GERMAN COMBAT UNITS IN THE KURSK AREA, 1 JULY 1943

	9th Army[20]	2nd Army[21]	4th Panzer Army[22]	Army Det. Kempf*[23]
Infantry divisions	14	7	4	3
Panzer divisions	6	–	2	3
Panzer grenadier divisions	1	–	4†	–
Infantry regiments	1	–	–	–
Tank battalions	1	–	2	1
Assault tank battalions**	1	–	–	–
Heavy tank destroyer battalions***	2	–	–	–
Tank destroyer battalions***	–	2	–	–
Assault gun battalions	7	1	1	2
Assault gun batteries	–	–	–	1
Fkl tank companies****	3	–	–	–
7.5cm gun battalions	1	–	–	–
10.5cm howitzer battalions	8	1	2	2
10cm gun battalions	3	–	1	2
10cm gun batteries	–	2	–	–
Mixed artillery battalions*****	2	1	–	–
15cm howitzer battalions	5	–	1	1
15cm gun batteries	3	1	1	–
17cm gun batteries	1	–	–	–
21cm howitzer battalions	3	–	1	1
21cm howitzer batteries	2	–	–	–
Nebelwerfer regiments	3	–	3	3
Mortar battalions	2	–	–	–
Jäger battalions	5	–	–	–

Notes:
*   Only those units of Army Detachment Kempf which faced the Soviet Voronezh Front are included. Units facing the Southwest Front are not included.
**   Assault tank battalions were equipped with the Sturm Pz IV.
***   Tank destroyer battalions were either equipped with lightly armoured, open topped vehicles carrying the 7.5cm PAK 40 (in 2nd Army), or equipped with Ferdinands (in 9th Army). In the latter case they are called heavy.
****   Fkl (*Funk-lenk*) tank companies had remote controlled mini-tanks which carried explosive charges.
*****Mixed artillery battalions had 10cm guns and 15cm howitzers, with a total of 12 pieces in the battalion according to T/O&E.
†   Note that these panzer grenadier divisions were better equipped and had a larger organization than regular army panzer grenadier divisions.

impressive reserves, something which the Germans lacked. This was not necessarily a reflection of differences in operational thinking. When the Germans had resources about equal to the opponents they too had reserves. In the campaign in the west in 1940, the OKH held about two dozen divisions in reserve, and similarly the OKH held considerable forces in reserve when the Germans launched operation Barbarossa. But in 1943, the Red Army had such a numerical superiority at the front that it was not possible for the Germans to form theatre reserves. The Russians, on the other hand, had large forces in reserve, and of particular interest for operation Zitadelle is of course Konev's Steppe Front.[24] This was deployed in the area immediately west of the Don, north and south of Voronezh. It was intended to be used for offensive operations when the German attack had run out of steam, but it could of course be called upon if a critical situation should occur on the Voronezh or Central Fronts. The Steppe Front constituted about half the Stavka reserves.

TABLE 2.3: SOVIET STRENGTH IN THE KURSK AREA, 1 JULY 1943

	Manpower	Tanks and SP Guns	Guns and Mortars	Aircraft[25]
Central Front[26]	711,575	1,785	12,453	1,050
Voronezh Front[27]	625,591	1,704	9,751	881
Steppe Front[28]	573,195	1,639	9,211	563
17th Air Army[29]	–	–	–	735
Long Range Bomber Command				320
Total	1,910,361	5,128	31,415	3,549

Note: 17th Air Army belonged to Southwest Front, but it did take part in the battle in July.

The combined manpower strength of the Central and Voronezh Fronts was 1,337,166 men, or close to double the strength of the German forces. Additionally, the Steppe Front could be counted upon. The exact Soviet strength is given in Table 2.3. The number of tanks given in Table 2.3 marginally exceeds the T/O&E strength of the armoured units on the respective fronts. Probably, the fronts had a few extra tanks to cover losses, but the discrepancy is not very significant. These men, tanks and guns were distributed in the combat units shown in Table 2.4.

It has quite often been asserted that Soviet units were smaller than their German equivalents. The consequence of this, allegedly, is that a cursory counting of divisions would not present a true picture of the strength ratio. Perhaps German divisions were stronger according to T/O&E figures, but that is only part of the story. In a theatre where both sides regularly fought with units reduced to mere skeletons, the T/O&E strength may mean little (as shown in Chapter 3). But of great importance also is the number of GHQ units available. In that respect, the Red Army was considerably better off, as indicated by Tables 2.3 and 2.4.

20

TABLE 2.4: SOVIET COMBAT UNITS IN THE KURSK AREA, 1 JULY 1943

	Central Front[30]	Voronezh Front[31]	Total
Rifle divisions	41	35	76
Rifle brigades	4	–	4
Tank corps	4	4	8
Mechanized corps	–	1	1
Tank brigades	3	6	9
Tank regiments	15	8	23
Artillery divisions	3	–	3
Artillery brigades	–	4	4
Artillery regiments	3	9	12
Self-propelled artillery regiments	3	3	6
Destroyer brigades	3	–	3
Anti-tank brigades	3	7	10
Anti-tank regiments	8	27	35
Mortar brigades	1	1	2
Mortar regiments	10	11	21
Armoured train battalions	4	3	7
Guards Rocket Artillery division	1	–	1
Guards Rocket Artillery regiments	10	11	21
Guards Rocket Artillery battalions	1	–	1

Notes: Only separate units have been included; units which formed part of larger combat units are not included. Tank and mechanized corps were not included in the original source, the tank, mechanized and motorized infantry brigades of these corps have been subtracted from the numbers given in the original tables.

Another approach is to look at divisional slices, that is to say, adding together the overall manpower strength and dividing it by the number of divisions. The Voronezh and Central Fronts had a combined strength of 85 divisions (equating tank and mechanized corps with divisions). This means that the fronts had an average divisional slice of 15,731 men. The Germans, on the other hand, had 777,000 men and 44 divisions, resulting in a slice of 17,659 men. However, the German strength is ration strength and the Soviet strength most likely is not.[32] The effect of this is that the divisional slice differs little between the opponents. However, similar calculations can be made for tanks and guns and mortars too. The Germans had 7,417 guns and mortars, which equates to 169 per division. This can be compared with 261 pieces per division for the Voronezh and Central Fronts. If we look at tanks, we see that the Germans had 2,451 tanks and assault guns spread over 15 panzer and panzer grenadier divisions or 164 per division. The two Soviet fronts had 3,489 tanks and assault guns dispensed among nine tank and mechanized

21

corps or 388 per corps. This latter figure clearly shows that it is very important to consider non-divisional units too when comparing strength. Two things can be concluded from this. The first is that comparing numbers of divisions does not necessarily give an inflated picture of Soviet strength; actually it can be to the contrary. Second, it dispels the myth, if anyone should still believe it so, of the Red Army being a horde of infantrymen. The figures above, in fact, indicate a ratio of guns and mortars to manpower twice as high in the Red Army as in the German forces. Again, it should be remembered that the German manpower strength is ration strength, while the Red Army strength probably does not include all the categories of men included in the German strength. This would most likely redress the balance to a certain extent.

But for the Red Army the preparations were not limited to the assembling of men and weapons. Equally important were the preparations of the field defences with minefields, barbed wire, trenches, tank ditches, bunkers, command posts, battery positions, the improvement of roads and the expansion of airfields. Civilian labour was used extensively. Already in April no less than 105,000 civilians were digging trenches and tank ditches, constructing bunkers, improving roads and expanding airfields.[33] This number increased during the spring, and reached 300,000 by June.[34] In their minefields the two fronts laid down 503,663 anti-tank mines and 439,348 anti-personnel mines.[35] These extensive field works were noticed by the German reconnaissance but if the Germans had waited even longer to attack for the purpose of bringing forward more troops it would have given the Red Army even more time to prepare.

Furthermore, the partisan activity increased to disturb the German assembly of forces, especially in the rear area of Army Group Centre.[36] The German command launched several operations[37] to clear the rear area for the army group. These operations involved forces which were going to take part in operation Zitadelle (6th Infantry, 7th Infantry, 10th Panzer Grenadier, 4th Panzer, 18th Panzer Divisions).[38] To fight against the partisans the Germans also deployed many units formed of eastern volunteers.[39] The Germans reported 1,092 partisan attacks against the railways during June (they also reported 409 disabled engines and 54 disabled bridges during this month).[40] Thus, their rear area was not entirely secure.

NOTES

1. Sources for this calculation are B. Müller-Hillebrand, *Das Heer*, Vol. III (Mittler & Sohn, Frankfurt am Main, 1969), pp. 220–1, BA-MA RH 21-4/450, BA-MA RH 10/61, BA-MA RH 10/62 and BA-MA RH 10/63.
2. Pz-Lage Ost (Nach Gen Qu) 1943, BA-MA RH 10/61.
3. There were two German panzer divisions, 5th and 8th, positioned behind 2nd Panzer Army and 4th Army. These were army group reserves and had had lower priority when it came to deliveries of tanks. No less than 60 Panzer IV were despatched to 5th Panzer Division in mid-June, while 42 were sent to 8th Panzer Division 5–9 July (Lieferungen der Panzerfahrzeuge, Band ab Mai 1943, BA-MA RH 10/349).
4. KTB OKW, Vol. III, p. 753.
5. KTB OKW, Vol. III, p. 753.
6. KTB OKW, Vol. III, p. 753. In the total, the divisions of Gruppe Esebeck (which was located in the 9th Army Area, but nominally under Army Group control) has been included, since these were committed during the battle.
7. KTB OKW, Vol. III, p. 753.
8. See for example *Geschichte des Großen Vaterländischen Krieges der Sowjetunion*, Vol. III (Deutscher Militärverlag, East Berlin, 1965), p. 290.
9. AOK 9/O.Qu., Beilage zum KTB, Tätigkeitsbericht der Abteilung IVa, vom 27.6. bis 4.7. 1943 (NARA T312, R317, F7885270).
10. See Chapter 3 below.
11. This is an estimate, based on average divisional slice for 9th Army, but with a reduction allowing for the fact that the army was short of 14,400 men (according to E. Klink, *Das Gesetz des Handelns* (Deutsche Verlags-Ansalt, Stuttgart, 1966), p. 176).
12. KTB AOK 2, Ia, Fernschreiben 5.7.43, *Betr:* Kampfstärken, National Archives, Microfilm publication T312, Roll 1665, Frame 001099f.
13. Pz.AOK 4, Anlage 7 zum KTB, Meldungen (Beute, Verpflegungsstärken) von 1.7.1943 bis 31.12.1943, BA-MA RH 21-4/422.
14. See Chapter 3 below.
15. This is an estimate, based on the average divisional slice in 9th Army and 4th Panzer Army. There are indications that the divisional slice was smaller in Kempf's units compared to 4th Panzer Army. The 19th Pz.Div. for example had a ration strength of 13,221 men on 1 July (Anlagenband 5 zum KTB Nr 2 19. Pz.Div., BA-MA RH 27-19/14).
16. See Chapter 3 below.
17. Hermann Plocher, *The German Air Force versus Russia 1943* (US Air Force historical studies no. 155, Arno Press, New York, 1967), p. 83.
18. Ibid.
19. We have discussed this extensively in an article in the *Journal of Slavic Military Studies*. See Niklas Zetterling and Anders Frankson, 'Analysing WWII East Front Battles' (*JSMS*, March 1998).
20. Kriegsgliederung Gruppe Weiss 30.6.1943, BA-MA RH 20-9/135 (Gruppe Weiss was used as code name for 9th Army forces).
21. Klink, *Das Gesetz des Handelns – Die Operation Zitadelle 1943* (Deutsche Verlagsanstalt, Stuttgart, 1966), p. 332.
22. Kriegsgliederung Pz.AOK 4 6.7.1943, BA-MA RH 21-4/133.
23. Klink, *Das Gesetz des Handelns*, p. 334.
24. On 1 July 1943 Konev's force's designation was Steppe Military District, later it was renamed Steppe Front. We have chosen to use the latter throughout the text.

25. G.A. Koltunov and B.G. Solovev, *Kurskaya Bitva* (Voenizdat, Moscow, 1973), pp. 76–7.
26. *Dokumenty i Materiali: Kurskaya Bitva v Tsifrakh in Voenno-Istroricheskii Zhurnal*, no. 6, 1968. Various sources give marginally different figures, but this source was preferred since it does present information on the number of weapons with a finer subdivision of types of weapons and categories. It does also more clearly specify what is included in, for example, 'guns'. The number of aircraft is however taken from G.A. Koltunov and B.G. Solovev, *Kurskaya Bitva* (Voenizdat, Moscow, 1973), pp. 76–7 since the main source does not provide *all* information.
27. Ibid.
28. Ibid.
29. O. Groehler, *Geschichte des Luftkriegs 1910–1970* (Militärverlag der Deutschen Demokratischen Republik, Berlin, 1975), p. 364.
30. *Boevoy Sostav Sovetskoy Armii, chast III* (East View Publications).
31. Ibid.
32. Probably Soviet strength figures correspond to what Germans call 'Iststärke', i.e. actual strength. This is inevitably lower than ration strength.
33. *Geschichte des Großen Vaterländischen Krieges*, Vol. 3, p. 303.
34. Ibid.
35. *Dokumenty i Materiali: Kurskaya Bitva v Tsifrakh in Voenno-Istroricheskii Zhurnal*, no. 6, 1968, p. 66.
36. For a Soviet account of the Partisan activity in the rear area of Army Group Centre see *Voenno-Istoricheskii Zhurnal*, no. 2, 1980, N. Azyasskii: *O Vklade Partisan v razgrom gruppi armii 'Tsentr'*, pp. 29–35.
37. Operation Nachbarhilfe, Freischütz and Zigeunerbaron.
38. W. Haupt, *Die Schlachten der Heeresgruppe Mitte 1941–1944* (Podzun-Pallas, Freiberg, 1983), pp. 204–5.
39. Example of an army with a lot of rear area responsibility is 2nd Panzer Army. The Eastern Volunteers under command of 2nd Panzer Army had a ration strength of 25,998 on 6 June 1943. BA-MA RH 21-2/509 Meldung 6.1943 Pz.AOK 2. This does not include any *Hilfswillige* employed with German divisions.
40. Fritz Hahn, *Waffen und Geheimwaffen des deutschen Heeres 1933–45*, Band 2 (Bernard & Graefe Verlag, Koblenz, 1987), pp. 236–7.

3

Structure of Involved Forces

This chapter attempts to provide an in-depth analysis of the involved forces. To understand better how they fought it is necessary to look deeper into how the two combatants organized their forces and resources. Also it will be shown that even if units have the same designation, they do not necessarily have the same size or resources (manpower and weapons).

THE ATTACKING FORCES

During the offensive not all troops were involved to the same extent. Here focus will be on the forces that took part in the main fighting during this short but intensive offensive.

Forces in the north

9th Army
Two Corps-Commands XXXXI Panzer and XXXXVII Panzer were going to make the main attack while two corps protected the flanks. The XXIII Corps was to advance to cover the left flank while XXXXVI Panzer Corps was to advance on the right flank of the main attacking forces. The Army had one more, XX Corps, which protected the right flank of the Army. XX Corps was not involved in the offensive.[1] The army had three mobile divisions in reserve, 4th Panzer, 12th Panzer and 10th Panzer Grenadier, ready to exploit any success.

XXIII Corps
This Corps had three divisions, 216th Infantry, 383rd Infantry and 78th Assault. The last division was a modified infantry division which demanded much larger resources than a normal infantry division and only one of these was formed on the eastern front. This division (78th Assault)

did most of the corps offensive action. To support these divisions the Corps had 87th Grenadier Regiment (two battalions), two independent Jäger Battalions (8th and 13th), two Assault Gun Battalions (185th and 189th), the equivalent of ten GHQ artillery battalions and 51st Rocket Artillery Regiment. The total artillery strength was 214 field artillery pieces (divisional and GHQ) and 57 Nebelwerfers.[2]

All the 62 Assault Guns available to the corps were in the two assault gun battalions (185th had 27 Stug III lg and 4 StuH while 189th had 31 Stug III lg). The corps had no other tanks or assault guns. Even though the Corps had few armoured vehicles it had a strong anti-tank capacity thanks to 78th Assault Division which had 71 7.5cm Pak 40 (towed) and 25 Marders. The Corps also had two armoured engineer companies (811th and 813th) equipped with Goliats.[3] Each of these companies had 12 SPW (Radio-Control Vehicles) and 96 Goliats.[4]

XXXXI Panzer Corps

The XXXXI Panzer Corps had three divisions, 18th Panzer, 86th Infantry and 292nd Infantry. The panzer division was a panzer division only in name. It had a large deficit of motor vehicles for its panzer grenadiers and few tanks. The divisional panzer battalion had 38 Panzer IV and 31 Panzer III available for the offensive.[5] Neither of the two infantry divisions was at full strength; both had only six infantry battalions. In their support they had two assault-gun battalions, 177th and 244th (each with 22 Stug III lg and 9 StuH) and 656th Tank Destroyer Regiment, which had a rather unique composition: 653rd and 654th Heavy Tank Destroyer Battalion, 216th Assault Panzer Battalion, 313th and 314th Panzer Companies (Funk-lenk).[6] This regiment had 171 tanks and assault guns (see Table 3.1 below).

Additional fire support was provided by 6⅓ GHQ artillery battalions, one heavy mortar battalion and a Nebelwerfer-regiment. To control and co-ordinate indirect fire an independent artillery regiment staff belonged to the Corps. The German Army did not have independent artillery regiments, rather it had independent Artillery-Regiment Staffs which were used to control and co-ordinate independent artillery battalions when needed. The XXXXI Panzer Corps had 304 tanks and assault guns available, of which over 90 per cent were operational on the morning of 5 July. The number of field artillery pieces available was 180 (divisional and GHQ). To this should be added 36 15cm Nebelwerfers and 18 21cm Nebelwerfers.

TABLE 3.1: 656TH TANK DESTROYER REGIMENT, 4 JULY 1943[7]

Equipment	Operational	Repairable within 14 days	Repairable over 14 days
Elefants	83	4	2
Brummbärs	42	1	2
Pz III Bef	5		
Pz III L24	3		
Pz III L60	7		
Pz III L42	10	2	
Pz II	2		
Stug III lg	10		
Sdkfz 301	72		

XXXXVII Panzer Corps

The second corps that was part of the main attack was XXXXVII Panzer Corps with three panzer divisions and one infantry division, 2nd Panzer, 9th Panzer and 20th Panzer plus 6th Infantry. One of the panzer divisions (20th) was nothing more than a weak panzer grenadier division. On the other hand, the 2nd Panzer Division was one of the best equipped on the eastern front. The infantry division only had six infantry battalions as was common among the infantry divisions in 9th Army (see Table 3.2).

TABLE 3.2: TANKS AND SP ARTILLERY OF DIVISIONS IN
XXXXVII PANZER CORPS IN EARLY JULY 1943

	Pz II	Pz III	Pz IV	Wespe	Hummel
2nd Panzer Div[8]	1	32	66	12	6
9th Panzer Div[9]	–	28	61	–	6
20th Panzer Div[10]	–	15	35	–	–
Total	1	75	162	12	12

To support these divisions the Corps had the 505th Heavy Tank Battalion. When the offensive began, the battalion had only two of its three companies available, thus it only had 31 Tiger I tanks. The third company, with 14 Tigers, arrived on 8 July. Further the corps had two assault gun battalions (904th with 31 Stug III lg and 245th with 22 Stug III lg and 9 StuH). Also the Corps had the 312th Panzer Company (Funk-lenk) attached for the offensive. For indirect fire the Corps had 3⅓ GHQ artillery battalions and a heavy Nebelwerfer regiment. Altogether the

27

XXXXVII Panzer Corps had 331 tanks and assault guns available of which over 90 per cent were operational on the morning of 5 July. The number of field artillery pieces available was 178 (divisional and GHQ). These were augmented by 18 15cm Nebelwerfers and 36 30cm Nebelwerfers.

XXXXVI Panzer Corps

Even though this was a Panzer Corps it did not have a single mobile division on 5 July, only four infantry divisions (7th, 31st, 102nd and 258th). These four divisions were supported by 909th Assault Gun Battalion, 3⅔ Artillery Battalions and three Jäger Battalions (9th, 10th and 11th). The corps had 180 field artillery pieces (divisional and GHQ).[11] One division, the 102nd, took little part in battle since its main mission was to protect the right flank of the corps.

The 909th Assault Gun Battalion had 27 Stug III lg and 4 Stug III kurz. The Corps had one Panzer Company (6th) from 12th Panzer Division attached. The company had eight Panzer IV lg and one Panzer III kurz (these are included in 12th Pz Div total below).

Model's Mobile Reserve

Despite having changed its name from 10th Motorized Infantry Division to 10th Panzer Grenadier Division, the unit had received no new types of equipment. Thus the division was without tanks and assault guns. The 4th Panzer Division on the other hand was well equipped with panzers and SPWs but, since its SPW battalion had only recently received all its vehicles, it was still in training. It performed this training at the same time as it acted as divisional reserve behind the lines during the battle. The two panzer divisions had at their disposal the number of tanks as shown in Table 3.3. In total, Model's reserve had 14 infantry battalions, 168 tanks and 101 field artillery pieces on hand to exploit any success.

TABLE 3.3: DISTRIBUTION OF TANKS AND SP ARTILLERY AVAILABLE IN MODEL'S MOBILE RESERVE IN EARLY JULY 1943

	Pz III	Pz IV	Wespe	Hummel
4th Panzer Div [12]	17	76	12	6
12th Panzer Div [13]	38	37	–	–
Total	55	113	12	6

Forces in the south

In the south, two armies took part in the main offensive action, making the role of Army Group South more active in the co-ordination of the offensive when compared with the situation on the northern side of the Kursk salient. Also three corps were used as main attack forces, while their flanks were protected by two corps. From left to right, LII, XXXXVIII Panzer, II SS-Panzer, III Panzer and Corps Raus were deployed. The last two belonged to Army Detachment Kempf and the first three belonged to 4th Panzer Army. In reserve Army Group South had XXIV Panzer Corps.

LII Corps

This Corps was not initially involved in the offensive. To improve co-ordination the Corps initially had 332nd Infantry Division attached to XXXXVIII Panzer Corps. The Corps merely covered the left flank while 332nd Infantry Division bore the brunt of the fighting. This division suffered 74 per cent of all casualties in LII Corps during the offensive.[14]

XXXXVIII Panzer Corps

Among the units in XXXXVIII Panzer Corps was the strongest division in the German Army, Panzer Grenadier Division 'Großdeutschland'. This corps also had two panzer divisions, the 3rd and 11th. Two-thirds of 167th Infantry Division started within XXXXVIII Panzer Corps sector. To support these 3⅔ divisions the corps had two Panther battalions (51st and 52nd), 911th Assault Gun battalion (22 Stug III lg and 9 StuH)[15] and three GHQ artillery battalions. To assist the co-ordination of the indirect-fire support an independent artillery regiment staff was attached to the corps. The corps also had temporarily attached from LII Corps the 332nd Infantry Division and a Heavy Nebelwerfer regiment for support during the initial phase. In all, the Corps had 595 tanks and assault guns available

TABLE 3.4: DISTRIBUTION OF TANKS, ASSAULT GUNS AND SP ARTILLERY WITHIN MOBILE DIVISIONS OF XXXXVIII PZ CORPS IN EARLY JULY 1943

	Pz II	Pz III	Flamm Pz	Pz IV	Pz VI	Stug	Wespe	Hummel
3rd Panzer Div[16]	7	59	–	23	–	2	–	–
11th Panzer Div[17]	8	62	13	26	–	–	–	6
Pz.Gr.Div. GD[18]	4	28	14	68	15	35	12	6
Total	19	149	27	117	15	37	12	12

29

for battle of which over 90 per cent were operational on the morning of 5 July. Fire support was provided by the 244 field artillery pieces (divisional and GHQ) and 23 15cm and 36 30cm Nebelwerfers available to the corps.

II SS-Panzer Corps

II SS-Panzer Corps had three SS-Panzer Grenadier divisions plus a third of 167th Infantry Division within II SS-Panzer Corps sector. This gave 21 infantry battalions. For indirect fire support the Corps had several GHQ units, two artillery battalions, two Nebelwerfer regiments and one Nebelwerfer battalion attached.

TABLE 3.5: DISTRIBUTION OF TANKS, ASSAULT GUNS AND SP ARTILLERY WITHIN THE MOBILE DIVISIONS OF II SS-PZ CORPS IN EARLY JULY 1943

	Pz II	Pz III	Pz IV	Pz VI	Stug	T-34	Wespe	Hummel
1st SS-PzGr[19]	7	13	83	13	35	–	12	6
2nd SS-PzGr[20]	1	70	33	14	34	26	12	6
3rd SS-PzGr[21]	–	63	52	15	35	–	12	6
Total	8	146	168	42	104	26	36	18

This gave the Corps a strength of 494 tanks and assault guns, of which over 90 per cent were operational on the morning of 5 July. Also, 179 field artillery pieces (divisional and GHQ) and 138 Nebelwerfers were available.

III Panzer Corps

Three Panzer Divisions and one Infantry Division constituted the strike force of III Panzer Corps. The divisions were 6th Panzer, 7th Panzer, 19th Panzer and 168th Infantry. The 503rd Heavy Tank Battalion (45 Tiger I) and 228th Assault Gun Battalion (31 Stug III lg) were attached to the Corps. One Artillery Regiment Staff was attached together with three artillery battalions, one Nebelwerfer regiment and two Flak regiments for fire-support. Total strength of the corps included 375 tanks and assault guns available, of which over 90 per cent were operational on the morning of 5 July. Altogether 200 field artillery pieces (divisional and GHQ) and 54 Nebelwerfers were available (see Table 3.6).

Corps Raus

Only two infantry divisions (106th and 320th) made up Corps Raus. It had three GHQ Artillery Battalions and four Nebelwerfer Battalions to provide artillery fire support. The total number of guns was 117 field

TABLE 3.6: DISTRIBUTION OF TANKS, ASSAULT GUNS AND SP ARTILLERY WITHIN THE
PANZER DIVISIONS OF III PZ CORPS IN EARLY JULY 1943

	Pz I	Pz II	Pz III	Flamm	Pz IV	Wespe	Hummel
6th Panzer Div[22]	–	13	52	13	28	–	–
7th Panzer Div[23]	–	12	62	–	38	6	6
19th Panzer Div[24]	3	2	38	0	38	–	–
Total	3	27	152	13	104	6	6

artillery pieces (divisional and GHQ) and 72 Nebelwerfers.[25] To increase
artillery fire support the Corps used its heavy flak guns in GHQ units for
indirect fire support initially. This added 72 8.8cm Flak (six battalions,
each with 12 guns) to the fire support available. The Corps had 44 assault
guns (905th Stug Bn had 23 Stug III lg and 9 StuH while 393rd Stug Bty
had 12 Stug III lg). Later, on 9 July, the Corps received one more infantry
division, the 198th, from Army Group South reserves.

Manstein's Reserve, XXIV Panzer Corps
This corps had only two divisions on 4 July but a third division was
attached on 7 July. The first two were the 17th Panzer Division and SS-
Panzer Grenadier Division 'Wiking'. The division that was added was the
23rd Panzer Division. Together, these could add 181 tanks and assault
guns and 13 infantry battalions to the attacking forces. Their field artillery
amounted to 123 pieces (see Table 3.7).

TABLE 3.7: DISTRIBUTION OF TANKS AND ASSAULT GUNS AVAILABLE IN
VON MANSTEIN'S MOBILE RESERVE IN EARLY JULY 1943

	Pz II	Pz III	Pz IV	Stug	T-34	Sturm IG[26]
17th Panzer Div[27]	4	29	32	–	2	–
SS-Wiking[28]	4	24	17	6	–	–
23rd Panzer Div[29]	–	23	33	–	–	7
Total	8	76	82	6	2	7

Summary of the attacking forces
Initially 14 divisions were available in the north and a further three were
in reserve. Of these 14, 12 actually took part in the offensive. Army Group
South initially committed 14 divisions to the attacks. There existed an
important difference between the reserves for Army Group South and

those belonging to Model in the north. It was Hitler who approved the use of XXIV Panzer Corps, which meant that von Manstein had had to get a release order from Berlin before he could use it. Model and von Kluge, on the other hand, had had greater control over their reserves.

Table 3.8 compares the strength of the forces on the northern and southern shoulders of the Kursk salient. In the table motorized infantry battalions, armoured infantry battalions and jäger battalions are included in the category of 'infantry battalions' (but not reconnaissance battalions).

TABLE 3.8: ATTACKING FORCES ON 4 JULY 1943

		Infantry Battalions	Tanks and Assault Guns	Field Artillery	Rocket Artillery
9th Army	XXIII Corps*	23	62	214	57
	XXXXI Pz Corps	16	304	180	54
	XXXXVII Pz Corps	18	331	178	54
	XXXXVI Pz Corps*	27	40	180	–
	AG Centre Total	84	747	752	165
4th Pz Army	LII Corps*	12	–	91	–
	XXXXVIII Pz Corps	29	595	244	39
	II SS-Pz Corps	21	494	179	138
Kempf	III Pz Corps	21	375	200	54
	Corps Raus	18	44	117	72
	AG South Total	101	1,508	831	303

Note: *These Corps did not involve all their forces in the offensive (see below).

Table 3.8 makes it clear that the forces in the south had a far more powerful armoured striking force. The southern force was also stronger in infantry and artillery. The comparison for infantry is not entirely correct though, since parts of the forces did not take an active part in the offensive. It would be more appropriate to say that 72 and 89 infantry battalions were involved respectively.

THE DEFENDING FORCES

Central Front

In the north one army, 13th Army, was deployed to cover most of the sector where the Germans were expected to attack. Its forces were deployed in three echelons, but it could be reinforced with tank and anti-tank units from Central Front reserves.

13th Army

The 13th Army was commanded by General N.P. Pukhov. According to Kozlov,[30] he had under his command 150,000 soldiers, even though this figure probably does not include the same manpower categories as do the manpower figures for German armies.[31] The area in which the army was deployed covered 32km of the front line and had a depth of 30km. The army had three main defence lines. The first line had a depth of 5–6 km and there were four rifle divisions deployed in it. From right to left 8th, 148th, 81st and 15th Rifle Division. In the second line there were three rifle divisions supported by five tank regiments. The divisions were the 74th, 307th and 6th Guards. Finally in the army's last defence line there were five divisions and one tank brigade (129th). These belonged to 18th Guards Rifle Corps (2nd Guards, 3rd Guards and 4th Guards Airborne Rifle Division) and 17th Guards Rifle Corps (70th Guards and 75th Guards Rifle Division). The 6th Guards Rifle Division, which was deployed in the second line, also belonged to this corps. Under Pukhov's command too was 4th Breakthrough Artillery Corps with two breakthrough artillery divisions and one rocket artillery division.[32] This huge artillery corps controlled over 700 guns and mortars with a calibre of 76mm or greater and 432 M-30 launchers for the rocket-artillery.[33]

The Army had much RVGK artillery attached from the start, actually 44 per cent of Central Front's resources. Altogether, the army had in its arsenal 2,939 guns and mortars. More specifically it amounted to 694 field guns, 757 anti-tank guns[34] and 1,488 mortars (82–120mm). In addition, there were 105 BM-8/-13 and 432 M-30 rocket artillery[35] for fire support. The army had 223 tanks and 47 assault guns for armoured support.[36]

Since preparations against a full-scale panzer attack had been fully completed, the army had built up its anti-tank defences to a very great extent. No less than 51,000 anti-tank mines and 29,000 anti-personnel mines had been placed in the army's area. The first line of defence had 44 anti-tank strongpoints (with 204 guns), the second line had 34 of these (with 160 guns) and the third defence-line had 60 positions (with 342 guns).[37] Also the army had five anti-tank mine task forces, each with 4 trucks with anti-tank mines and one company of sappers ready to move and create a blocking minefield in the path of the attackers.

Central Front's reserves

Since the 13th Army had a depth of three echelons the Central Front mainly had tank units and anti-tank units in reserve ready to reinforce once the Germans had showed their cards. The number of anti-tank guns in Central Front anti-tank reserve units is given in Table 3.9. The front

TABLE 3.9: CENTRAL FRONT ANTI-TANK RESERVE[38]

	76mm	45mm	
1st Anti-Tank Brigade	40	20	
13th Anti-Tank Brigade	40	20	
130th Anti-Tank Regiment	24	–	
563rd Anti-Tank Regiment	–	20	
4th Destroyer Brigade	16	12	
Total	120	72	=192 AT-guns

had a tank army in reserve. It was the 2nd Tank Army with two tank corps (3rd and 16th) and one tank brigade (11th Guards). In addition, the front had two independent tank corps (9th and 19th) and one self-propelled artillery regiment (SU) in reserve. These units had 843 tanks and assault guns all together, which formed 47 per cent of the total armoured strength in the Central Front.

Without shifting any forces from neighbouring armies (48th and 70th), the Central Front could deploy 1,113 tanks and assault guns and 949 anti-tank guns to stop 9th Army. The two neighbouring armies had 303 tanks and assault guns that could be redeployed in support of 13th Army.[39] The 1st Guards Artillery Division, which was part of 70th Army, could also be deployed to provide fire support for the defending forces. Its T/O&E strength was 192 field guns, which the division probably had.[40]

Voronezh Front

For this front it was not perfectly clear where the enemy would attack. Hence, the forces deployed to meet the attack were organized into two armies, 6th Guards and 7th Guards. The two armies were divided into two defensive echelons, while the third line of defence was composed of front reserves. These were the 1st Tank Army, 69th Army, 35th Guards Rifle Corps, 2nd Guards Tank Corps and 5th Guards Tank Corps.

6th Guards Army

This army was commanded by I.M. Chistyakov. It covered 60km of the front line and was organized in two echelons. The two guards rifle corps (22nd and 23rd) within the army deployed two rifle divisions up front and one rifle division in second echelon. Accordingly the first line of defence had four divisions, from left to right 375th, 52nd Guards, 67th Guards and 71st Guards Rifle Division. The army had a further three guards rifle divisions in the second line, one being directly subordinated to the Army.

Each rifle division within the Army had about 70km of trenches. To strengthen the defences 69,688 anti-tank mines and 64,430 anti-personnel mines were placed with the first line of defence. A further 20,200 anti-tank mines and 9,097 anti-personnel mines were used in the second line of defence. Due to the importance of protection against German tanks 28 anti-tank strong points had been constructed.

In its arsenal the 6th Guards Army had 1,682 guns and mortars of which 316 were field guns, 573 anti-tank guns[41] and 793 mortars (82–120mm). The rocket artillery contributed with 88 katyushas for the army. The army had 135 tanks and 20 assault guns to support the rifle units in combat.[42]

To provide an impression of how the types of weapons were distributed in a corps, an example from the 23rd Guards Rifle Corps can be illuminating. The 23rd Guards Rifle Corps, with 51st Guards, 52nd Guards and 375th Rifle Division had in its deployment area the weapons (including contributions from GHQ-units) shown in Table 3.10.

TABLE 3.10: 23RD GUARDS RIFLE CORPS' ARSENAL OF GUNS, 4 JULY 1943[43]

Weapons	51st GRD	52nd GRD	375rd RD	Total
45mm anti-tank guns	42	60	63	165
76mm regimental field guns	32	12	12	56
76mm divisional field guns	10	44	79	133
122mm howitzers	–	30	30	60
152mm howitzers	–	18	–	18
50mm mortars	45	48	46	139
82mm mortars	74	65	68	207
120mm mortars	18	24	54	96
BM-13	–	16	41	57

In addition the corps had the 96th Tank Brigade (61 tanks) and 230th Tank Regiment (39 tanks) as support. The 89th Guards Rifle Division, which was subordinated directly to 6th Guards Army, was deployed in the second echelon on the army's extreme left flank. Tactically it was deployed in such a way that it could either support the army's own left flank (the 23rd Guards Rifle Corps) or support 7th Guards Army's right flank.

7th Guards Army
This army was commanded by M.S. Shumilov. It covered 55km of the front line and was organized in two echelons. The two guards rifle corps (24th and 25th) within the army deployed two rifle divisions up front and one rifle division in second echelon. The independent 213th Rifle Division was deployed in second echelon on the army's centre enabling it

35

to support either corps if necessary. The four guards rifle divisions up front were, from left to right, 36th Guards, 72nd Guards, 78th Guards, 81st Guards.

For protection against German tanks 27 anti-tank strong points had been constructed within the area of the army. Equally important were minefields. In the deployment area of 81st Guards Rifle Division, which confronted the German bridgehead at Belgorod, for example, there were 2,133 anti-tank mines and 2,626 anti-personnel mines per kilometre of front line.[44]

The 7th Guards Army had 1,573 guns and mortars in its inventory, of which 290 were field guns, 506 anti-tank guns[45] and 777 mortars (82–120mm). It also had 47 Katyusha rocket launchers for indirect fire support. The army had 224 tanks and 22 assault guns in two tank brigades, three tank regiments and two SU-Regiments as a mobile armoured force.[46] The three tank regiments were deployed in direct support of the three Rifle Divisions initially, 262nd Tank Regiment with 81st Guards Rifle Division, 167th Tank Regiment with 73rd Guards Rifle Division and finally 148th Tank with 15th Guards Rifle Division.

Voronezh Front's reserves

A total of eight rifle divisions were in the front's reserves. Of these, five were with 69th Army, while three guards rifle divisions were with 35th Guards Rifle Corps. These forces provided the third line of defence. To strengthen the anti-tank capacity of the defending armies, the front had two AT brigades and two AT regiments ready to reinforce the front line with anti-tank guns (see Table 3.11).

TABLE 3.11: VORONEZH FRONT ANTI-TANK RESERVE[47]

	76mm	45mm	
14th Anti-Tank Brigade	60	–	
31st Anti-Tank Brigade	24	20	
1076th Anti-Tank Regiment	20	–	
1689th Anti-Tank Regiment	19	–	
Total	123	20	=143

Not only had the front rifle and anti-tank units with which to support the two main armies when the German offensive started, it also had large armoured forces in reserve ready to move forward to meet the attacker. The front had 1,011 tanks in reserve in its five armoured corps (2nd Guards, 5th Guards, 6th and 31st Tank Corps plus 3rd Mechanized Corps). The latter three of these corps belonged to 1st Tank Army commanded by M.E. Katukov. This tank army was deployed behind the right flank of 6th Guards Army.

TABLE 3.12: TANK STRENGTH IN 1ST TANK ARMY[48]

	T-34	T-70	
3rd Mechanized Corps	195	35	
6th Tank Corps	155	32	
31st Tank Corps	175	42	
Total tank strength	525	109	= 634

For indirect fire support, the front reserves had 69 field guns (76mm or larger) and 553 mortars (82–120mm) in 69th Army, 108 field guns (76mm or larger) and 332 mortars (82–120mm) in 35th Guards Rifle Corps and 80 field guns (76mm or larger) and 271 mortars (82–120mm) in 1st Tank Army. A further 72 field guns (76mm or larger) and 327 mortars (82–120mm) were in independent units.[49]

GERMAN DIVISIONAL ORGANIZATION

Three types of divisions – infantry, panzer and panzer grenadier – were present among the forces assembled for operation Zitadelle. Including 2nd Army, but excluding XXXXII Corps,[50] the total number of divisions was 44. This amounted to almost 24 per cent of all the divisions on the eastern front.[51]

German divisions displayed considerable variation in organization, equipment and strength even when they were of the same type. This can make comparisons more difficult. For example, Army Group South committed eight infantry divisions[52] while Army Group Centre committed ten Infantry Divisions,[53] which would indicate that the infantry in Army Group South was weaker. However, if we count infantry battalions among the infantry divisions we find that Army Group South committed 66 infantry battalions while Centre had 63 battalions. The number of battalions in a division could indeed vary considerably (see Table 3.20).

To complicate matters further, the German Army had several ways of reporting the manpower strength of a unit. The most common were *Verpflegungsstärke*, *Iststärke* and *Gefechtstärke*. *Verpflegungsstärke* corresponds to the English term 'ration strength'. This could include any men that the unit had to provide with food and other necessities. Consequently it could include civilians and even POWs. *Iststärke*, on the other hand, included men belonging to the unit and also men attached to the unit. However, included in the *Iststärke* were also wounded and sick, who were expected to return to duty within eight weeks. Also men detached and men on leave were included in the *Iststärke*. Finally, *Gefechtstärke* is usually translated as combat strength. However, this can be somewhat misleading, since the Germans used another term, *Kampfstärke*, sometimes also translated as combat strength. The difference between *Gefechtstärke* and *Kampfstärke* is that the former term included men belonging to the combat arms (infantry, armour, anti-tank, cavalry, artillery, engineer and field replacement units) excluding their baggage sections and workshops, while the latter included those soldiers that were employed as riflemen or in direct support of riflemen. Neither of these two terms included men that were sick, wounded, detached or on leave.[54]

Here the word 'combat strength' will be used as a translation of *Gefechtstärke*. There exists one further term, *Tagesstärke*, that is worth discussing. It depicts the men available for service with the unit at the date indicated by the report. Thus it is the *Iststärke* minus sick, wounded and men detached or on leave.[55] The *Tagesstärke* would for many purposes be the best indicator of the strength of a unit, but unfortunately it is very rare in German documents. The most common are *Verpflegungsstärke*, *Iststärke* and *Gefechtstärke*. An example of the difference between ration strength (*Verpflegungsstärke*) and combat strength (*Gefechtstärke*) is given in Table 3.13

TABLE 3.13: RATION STRENGTH COMPARED WITH COMBAT STRENGTH IN GERMAN DIVISIONS, 4 JULY 1943

	Ration strength[56]	Combat strength[57]
2nd SS–Pz Gr	20,659	7,350
3rd Panzer	14,141	5,170
167th Infantry	17,837	6,776

Naturally, most losses a division suffered were usually confined to the combat units, in particular the infantry. Thus most of the losses will be confined to the part of a division that is included in the combat strength. If it is stated that a division had 1,000 infantrymen left for example, it could still have a ration strength of over 10,000. Three examples of how divisions could be depleted are given in Table 3.14.

From Table 3.14 we can see that 75 per cent of the casualties suffered by 31st ID were confined to the infantry and engineers. The same percentage applies to 20th PzD where it is the panzer grenadiers who suffered the greatest losses. In 6th ID the infantry battalions accounted

TABLE 3.14: COMBAT STRENGTH IN BATTALIONS OF 6TH ID, 31ST ID AND 20TH PZD[58]

6th Infantry Division		
	2 July	*10 July*
I/18th Inf Bn	422	197
II/18th Inf Bn	435	228
I/37th Inf Bn	405	236
III/37th Inf Bn	399	260
I/58th Inf Bn	379	171
III/58th Inf Bn	386	206
Reconnaissance Bn	331	269
Pioneer Bn	364	284
Total strength	3,121	1,851
Difference (losses)		1,270
Total Div cas.[59]		1,479

31st Infantry Division		
	3 July	*10 July*
I/12th Inf Bn	422	269
III/12th Inf Bn	427	312
I/17th Inf Bn	472	378
III/17th Inf Bn	474	229
I/82nd Inf Bn	457	256
II/82nd Inf Bn	459	278
Pioneer Bn	357	261
Total strength	3,068	1,983
Difference (losses)		1,085
Total Div cas.[59]		1,443

20th Panzer Division		
	3 July	*10 July*
I/59th PzGr Bn	477	297
II/59th PzGr Bn	484	353
I/112th PzGr Bn	479	247
II/112th PzGr Bn	530	229
Armd. Recce Bn	542	372
Pz. Pioneer Bn	325	253
Total strength	2,837	1,751
Difference (losses		1,086
Total Div cas.[59]		1,445

for an even greater part of the casualties, 86 per cent. It should be remembered that these figures apply to divisions attacking. In defence, at least if the enemy manages to break through or overrun parts of the divisions, the distribution of casualties may be different.

An important part of the German system for replacing casualties was the field replacement battalion that formed part of most divisions. This could be filled up before an operation, providing the division with an ability to replace some of its losses, thus increasing its staying power. The main reason for the existence of the replacement battalions was, however, to provide the final training of the replacements and to provide acquaintance with the new unit and its personnel.

A particular characteristic of operation Zitadelle was that most of the units on both sides had been rested and refitted. Consequently the units had few wounded soldiers subject to medical care. During operations where units had been in sustained combat for a longer period, the units could have expected convalescents to return and thereby provide some reinforcement.[60] This was however not the case at Zitadelle. An effect of this is that initial strength minus final strength, as given in Table 3.14, effectively constitutes losses. Another phenomenon typical of operations with worn units is that men from non-combat units will be inserted into the infantry battalions to provide some replacements for losses. Again this was not prevalent during Zitadelle.

Table 3.14 only depicts the strength within the battalions, not in the infantry or panzer grenadier regiments as a whole. The combined combat strength of the battalions is less than the combat strength of the regiment they belong to. Also there are other combat units in a division than those given in Table 3.14. This is especially true for the panzer divisions, which is evident when comparing the data on 20th Panzer Division in Table 3.14 for example with the data on 3rd Panzer Division in Table 3.13.

Infantry division

At the beginning of operation Barbarossa an infantry division had three infantry regiments with three infantry battalions each. As losses mounted, the Germans experienced difficulties keeping the units at their prescribed strength. The raising of new divisions further compounded this. Consequently, several divisions had to make alterations to their structure. One common change was to reduce the number of infantry battalions in the infantry regiments from three to two. However, some divisions retained the three-battalion regiments, but kept only two regiments, rather than three. In October 1943 a new T/O&E was issued for the infantry divisions,

TABLE 3.15: GERMAN INFANTRY DIVISION T/O&E STRENGTH[61]

	June 1941	October 1943
Manpower	16,860	13,656
Machine-guns	535	541
5cm mortars	84	–
8.1cm mortars	54	72
12cm mortars	–	21
AT rifles	90	–
3.7cm AT guns	75	6
5cm AT guns	–	24
7.5cm AT guns	–	18
7.5cm light inf. guns	20	18
15cm heavy inf. guns	6	6
10.5cm howitzers	36	24
15cm howitzers	12	12

and this confirmed the two-battalion regiments that had already become common. The other important change that occurred in October was the removal of one light artillery battalion from each artillery regiment, thus the regiment went from 48 howitzers to 36 howitzers. This was logical, given the reduction of infantry battalions. Previously the division had had one 10.5cm howitzer battery for each infantry battalion. The new organization retained that ratio. At Kursk a reduction in the number of artillery pieces had already occurred in several divisions, since many had artillery battalions with 9 howitzers rather than the original number of 12. Two types of artillery piece dominated the German divisional artillery, the 10.5cm howitzer and the 15cm howitzer.

TABLE 3.16: GERMAN ARTILLERY IN INFANTRY DIVISIONS[62]

	Weight in action kg	Range m	Rate of fire rds/min.	Shell weight kg
10.5cm l FH 18	1,985	10,670	6–8	14.8
15cm s FH 18	5,512	13,250	4–5	43.5

Also the anti-tank capabilities of the divisions were altered. According to the old organization the division was meant to have 75 anti-tank guns and 90 anti-tank rifles but according to the new organization it had 48 AT guns and no AT rifles. Later Panzerschrecks and Panzerfausts were added.[63] In the infantry division the guns were found either in the anti-tank battalion (T/O&E of 36 guns) or in anti-tank companies (T/O&E of 12) that existed in each infantry regiment. According to the old T/O&E

all AT guns were 3.7cm Pak 35/36 and, when more powerful weapons became available, the divisions gradually received the newer types. When the units changed from an older gun to a more powerful one, the exchange ratio was not 1:1, rather 4:3 (for every four old the divisions received three new). According to the new T/O&E (October 1943) the infantry divisions were intended to have six 3.7cm Pak 35/36, 24 5cm Pak 38 and 18 7.5cm Pak 40.[64]

TABLE 3.17: GERMAN ANTI-TANK GUNS IN INFANTRY DIVISIONS[65]

	Weight in action kg	Rate of fire rds/min.	Shell weight kg(AP)	Muzzle velocity m/sec
3.7cm Pak 35/36	435	16	0.68	745
5cm Pak 38	986	14	2.10	835
7.5cm Pak 40	1,425	10-12	6.80	792

Very few divisions at Kursk conformed to the T/O&E. This is demonstrated in Table 3.18. Indeed no less than four of the ten divisions in the table had five different types of anti-tank guns, all of them requiring different ammunition. Almost invariably the guns were towed, but the 31st Infantry Division was an exception. It had the advantage of having 13 self-propelled anti-tank guns. The eight 7.5cm Pak 40 and four 7.62cm Pak 36 (r) were probably standard production Marders. The 7.5cm Pak 41 on the other hand was probably a conversion made by the division itself. The value of self-propelled anti-tank guns was more pronounced with the heavier guns needed to defeat the thicker armour carried by the tanks in 1943. Later the Germans made considerable efforts to equip each infantry division with one company (14 vehicles) of assault guns (StuG III G or Hetzer) to improve both the offensive and the defensive capabilities of the infantry division.

TABLE 3.18: NUMBER OF ANTI-TANK GUNS IN SOME INFANTRY DIVISIONS, 1 JULY 1943[66]

	Infantry Division									
	6th	7th	31st	39th	106th	167th	198th	216th	255th	258th
3.7cm Pak 35/36	27	42	18	–	–	–	–	18	18	28
5cm Pak 38	12	15	18	12	30	21	27	8	8	14
7.5cm Pak 40	7	5	8(sf)	21	24	24	27	4	21	3
7.5cm Pak 97/38	9	–	–	9	9	9	–	10	3	–
T–34/76	–	–	2	–	–	–	–	–	–	–
7.62cm Pak 36 (r)	1	–	4(sf)	–	–	–	–	7	6	5
7.5cm Pak 41	–	3	1(sf)	–	–	–	–	–	–	–
8.5cm Pak (r)	–	5	–	–	–	–	–	–	–	–
Total no. of guns	56	70	51	42	63	54	54	47	56	50

Since the number and types of anti-tank guns varied, the anti-tank battalions of various divisions did not have the same capacity to combat enemy tanks. An example of how differently the anti-tank battalions could be organized is given in Table 3.19. The 6th Infantry Division was part of 9th Army, while 167th was committed on the right flank of XXXXVIII Panzer Corps in the south.

TABLE 3.19: ANTI-TANK BATTALIONS IN 6TH AND 167TH INFANTRY DIVISIONS[67]

	6th AT-Bn (6th ID)	238th AT-Bn (167th ID)
1st Coy	6 3.7cm Pak 35/36, 4 7.5cm Pak 40	12 7.5cm Pak 40
2nd Coy	6 Pak 35/36, 2 Pak 40, 1 7.5cm Pak 97/38	12 7.5cm Pak 40
3rd Coy	7 Pak 35/36, 1 Pak 40, 2 7.5cm Pak 97/38	11 2cm anti-aircraft guns

The anti-tank battalion in 167th ID had the new organization that had become established in October 1943. In the new T/O&E, the third company of the battalion was an anti-aircraft company rather than an anti-tank company. These 2cm Flak guns were not only used against aircraft, they could be very effective against enemy unarmoured troops.

As can be understood from what has been presented thus far, the German infantry divisions were involved in a prolonged transformation. This process did not proceed at the same pace with every unit. Consequently the divisions could differ considerably. This is shown in Table 3.20, which gives the number of battalions of the main types and also the number of howitzers the divisions possessed. It should be noted that some divisions had no reconnaissance battalion. In most such cases, the divisional anti-tank battalion was a mixture of reconnaissance and anti-tank components and was termed a *Schnelle Abteilung*, a fast unit.

As can be seen in Table 3.20 few divisions had nine infantry battalions and a full artillery regiment (48 howitzers). The four that had such a strong organization were all found in Army Group South.

Even if two divisions had the same number of infantry battalions the combat strength for each division might be quite different depending on how strong the battalions were. For example the average combat strength for an infantry battalion of 31st Infantry Division was 452 soldiers while for a battalion in 102nd Infantry Division it was 367 soldiers.[68]

Panzer division and panzer grenadier division

During this battle many of the panzer divisions had a weak panzer regiment. Normally, a panzer regiment ought to have had 160 tanks arranged in two battalions but no division reached that level. The division with the

43

TABLE 3.20: GERMAN INFANTRY DIVISIONS, 4 JULY 1943[69]

	Army	Corps	Inf.Bn	Recce Bn	AT Bn	lFH	sFH
6th ID	9th	XXXXVII Pz	6	1	1	27	8
7th ID	9th	XXXXVI Pz	6	1	1	27	9
26th ID	2nd	VII	6	1	1	18	17
31st ID	9th	XXXXVI Pz	6	1	1	27	8
39th ID	Kempf	XXXXII	6	–	1	25	8
68th ID	2nd	VII	8	1	1	27	9
72nd ID	9th	XX	6	1	1	27	4
75th ID	2nd	VII	7	1	1	27	8
82nd ID	2nd	XIII	6	–	1	25	6
86th ID	9th	XXXXI Pz	6	1	1	27	9
88th ID	2nd	VII	7	–	1	16	–
102nd ID	9th	XXXXVI Pz	6	–	1	25	7
106th ID	Kempf	Raus	9	1	1	36	12
161st ID	Kempf	XXXXII	8	–	1	36	12
167th ID	4th Pz	XXXXVIII Pz	9	1	1	36	12
198th ID	AG South	–	9	–	1	36	12
216th ID	9th	XXIII	6	1 coy	1	26	8
255th ID	4th Pz	LII	6	1	1	27	12
258th ID	9th	XXXXVI Pz	7	1	1	25	5
282nd ID	Kempf	XXXXII	9	–	1 coy	24	12
320th ID	Kempf	Raus	9	–	1	24	12
327th ID	2nd	XIII	8	1	1	30	11
332nd ID	4th Pz	LII	9	1	1	36	12
340th ID	2nd	XIII	7	–	1	2	6
383rd ID	9th	XXIII	8	1 coy	1	22	8

Notes: lFH= 10.5cm howitzer or similar, sFH= 15cm howitzer or similar.
383rd ID also had 22 15cm Nebelwerfers.

greatest number of tanks was SS-Das Reich which had 144 tanks (including 26 T-34),[70] but this division was not yet designated as a panzer division.[71] Das Reich was called a panzer grenadier division but was rather a mixture of panzer division and motorized division. It was much more powerful than a normal panzer grenadier division. This also applies to Großdeutschland, Leibstandarte and Totenkopf, but not to 10th Panzer Grenadier Division, which had no tanks at all.

Table 3.21 compares the basic T/O&E for a panzer division and a GD or SS panzer grenadier division.

Usually the battalions had the same T/O&E, one exception being the anti-aircraft battalion which was somewhat stronger in the four panzer grenadier divisions. Both Großdeutschland and Leibstandarte Adolf Hitler had larger motorized infantry battalions than the rest (five companies compared to four companies). Not all divisions had yet received a

TABLE 3.21: UNITS IN A PANZER DIVISION AND A GD OR SS PANZERGRENADIER DIVISION COMPARED[72]

	Panzer Division	*GD or SS PzGr Division*
Panzer Battalions	2	2
Heavy Tank Coy[73]	–	1
Motorized Infantry Bn	3	5
Armoured Infantry Bn	1	1
Light Artillery Bn	1	2
Heavy Artillery Bn	1	1
SP Artillery Bn	1	1
Reconnaissance Bn	1	1
Anti-Tank Bn	1	1
Assault Gun Bn	–	1
Anti-Aircraft Bn (Flak)	1	1(+)

self-propelled artillery battalion. Those units without had retained their towed guns, these panzer divisions having two light artillery battalions instead.

At Zitadelle a panzer division had on average fewer tanks than the panzer divisions participating in the Ardennes in December 1944, but the number of panzer divisions was greater at Zitadelle.[74] Table 3.22 gives the number of tanks on hand, that is to say, the number of operational tanks plus the tanks in workshops. However, at the beginning of Zitadelle, the vast majority of the tanks were operational. Any vehicles on their way from Germany to the divisions have not been included.

Many divisions lacked one of their panzer battalions, which were in Germany or France to be re-equipped with Panthers. Two Panther battalions had hitherto arrived from Germany but they were present at the battlefield as independent battalions. They originally belonged to 9th Panzer Division and 11th Panzer Division. Later they returned to their parent units, to the 9th in September 1944 and to the 11th in October 1943.[75] The German Army often sent the Panther battalions where the need was urgent, rather than to its parent division. In Normandy for example both Panzer-Lehr and 116th Panzer Division operated Panther battalions belonging to other divisions. This practice was not the case with the Waffen-SS because these divisions were usually themselves sent to the hot spot.

Not all divisions had an armoured infantry battalion, since the production of SdKfz 251 and SdKfz 250 was not sufficient to cope with demand. These versatile vehicles were used as armoured troop carriers (Schützenpanzerwagen, or SPW) for infantry, engineer and reconnaissance and for various other specialized tasks. Total production before 1943 was only 3,956 vehicles.[76] However, in 1943 German war production

45

TABLE 3.22: INITIAL AFV STRENGTH FOR THE PANZER DIVISIONS, 4 JULY 1943[77]

	Lt Pz	Pz III	Flamm Pz	Pz IV	Pz VI	T-34	Stug	Total	Marder	Wespe	Hum.	Armoured Inf. Bn
2nd Panzer	1	32	–	66	–	–	–	99	30	12	6	Yes
3rd Panzer	7	59	–	23	–	–	2	91	14	–	–	No (2 coys)
4th Panzer	–	17	–	76	–	–	–	93	25	12	6	Yes
6th Panzer	13	52	13	28	–	–	–	106	14	–	–	Yes
7th Panzer	12	62	–	38	–	–	–	112	6	6	6	Yes
9th Panzer	–	28	–	61	–	–	–	89	16	–	6	Yes
11th Panzer	8	62	13	26	–	–	–	109	11	–	6	No (2 coys)
12th Panzer	–	38	–	37	–	–	–	75	16	–	–	No (1 coy)
18th Panzer	–	31	–	38	–	–	–	69	8	–	–	No
19th Panzer	5	38	–	38	–	–	–	81	12	–	–	No (1 coy)
20th Panzer	–	15	–	35	–	–	–	50	30	–	–	No (1 coy)
PzGr GD	4	28	14	68	15	–	35	164	20	12	6	Yes
1st SS PzGr	7	13	–	83	13	–	35	151	21	12	6	Yes
2nd SS PzGr	1	70	–	33	14	26	34	178	12	12	6	Yes
3rd SS PzGr	–	63	–	52	15	–	35	165	11	12	6	Yes
Total	58	608	40	702	57	26	141	1,632	230	78	54	

reached much higher levels than previously. This is amply demonstrated by the fact that SPW production in that year amounted to 7,153,[78] or almost twice the entire production of the period from 1939 to 1942. Of course, losses had occurred among previously produced vehicles. On the eastern front, from 22 June 1941 to 31 December 1942 1,731 armoured cars and SPWs were lost as total write offs.[79] All of this meant that not all panzer divisions had received enough vehicles to render any one battalion fully armoured.

TABLE 3.23: T/O&E OF SPWs IN I (ARMOURED BATTALION)/
12TH PANZERGRENADIER REGIMENT (4TH PZ DIV)[80]

Sdkfz	251/1	251/2	251/3	251/4	251/7	251/8	251/9	251/10	251/11	251/16	Total
T/O&E	39	6	11	8	6	1	12	10	3	6	102
Actual 5 July	32	6	11	9	6	1	12	10	3	6	96

But the armoured infantry battalion was not the only unit to have these types of vehicles in a division. According to a document in the archives at least 222 SPWs of type 251 were needed in a division (T/O&E 1944) when it had one armoured infantry battalion calling for 86 Sdfkz 251 SPWs.[81] Similar demands existed also in 1943 for such vehicles in the panzer grenadiers regimental staffs, in one engineer company in the engineer battalion, in the recon battalion and in the panzer regiment in a panzer division.

Evidently, the Germans experienced great difficulties in reaching the T/O&E strength of their units, despite the long lull on the eastern front. Also the German divisions exhibited significant variations in actual structure and strength. This could be expected after a prolonged period of fighting, but again, the three months of rest between the end of major operations in March and Zitadelle were not sufficient to redress the deficiencies. Clearly, German industrial and manpower resources were insufficient to cope with demand. The Germans tried to solve these problems in two ways. The first was further to improve the efficiency of the industry and to discontinue the production of less vital products to free facilities for the production of more important items. The other method the Germans employed was to reduce the authorized strength of their units.

The Germans were not alone with these problems however. To some extent the Red Army experienced difficulties of the same kind.

ORGANIZATION OF SOVIET TANK AND MECHANIZED UNITS DURING ZITADELLE

By summer 1943 the Soviets had five tank armies, only three of these being deployed to meet the German offensive. They were the 1st Tank, 2nd Tank and 5th Guards Tank Armies. The other two, 3rd Guards Tank and 4th Tank Armies, were later used in the Soviet offensive to liberate Orel. The organization of the tank armies was based around tank corps and according to Soviet T/O&E for tank armies the organization was as shown in Table 3.24.

TABLE 3.24: SOVIET TANK ARMY, 1943[82]

2 Tank Corps, each of 168 tanks
1 Mechanized Corps of 175 Tanks[83]
1 Motorcycle Regiment
1 Air-Defence Artillery Division
2 Anti-Tank Artillery Regiments
1 Self-propelled Artillery (SU) Regiment
1 Howitzer Artillery Regiment
1 Guards Mortar Regiment
2 Mortar Regiments
1 Engineer Battalion
1 Independent Tank Brigade or Regiment of 53 tanks or 39 tanks
Total number of tanks: 564 or 550.

47

But, as shown in the order of battle in Appendix 1, not all armies had this structure. This was probably caused by lack of time to form and organize all the supporting units, of which a tank army was supposed to be composed. It should be noted that a Soviet tank army, compared with a German panzer army, was more of a 'pure' armoured army. The main reason for this seems to have been a matter of command and control.

The Red Army had tried an organization similar to the German pattern but it had failed since the Soviet tank army commanders had great problems in co-ordinating their forces of different types (tank, infantry, cavalry and artillery). The reasons for this were lack of effective communications between units and also lack of well-trained men and officers at all levels. Hence, the tank armies were intended to be the tools available to fronts for exploiting breakthroughs rather than creating them (while their German counterpart did both). This led the Red Army to make its tank armies as mobile as possible. No major changes occurred in the T/O&E for the tank armies for the rest of the war except that the corps received more tanks and some more support units, mainly SU regiments and heavy tank regiments.

TABLE 3.25: THE FIVE TANK ARMIES PRESENT IN JULY 1943

	Entered combat	Front	Tanks and SUs	Tank Corps	Mech Corps
1st Tank Army	6 July	Voronezh	634[84]	6, 31	3
2nd Tank Army	6 July	Central	456[85]	3, 16	–
3rd Guards Tank Army	19 July	Bryansk	799[86]	12, 15	2
4th Tank Army	26 July	Western	735[87]	11, 30	6 Gds
5th Guards Tank Army	12 July	Voronezh	850[88]	2, 18, 29, 2 Gds	5 Gds

One tank army (5th Guards Tank) had a large number of corps. The reason for this is that 2nd Tank Corps and 2nd Guards Tank Corps were attached to 5th Guards Tank Army when it arrived on the battlefield. These corps had already been committed to combat. Later all five tank armies took part in the offensive phase of the Battle of Kursk, even those used earlier in the defensive phase. Three armies – 2nd Tank, 3rd Guards Tank and 4th Tank Army – were used against Army Group Centre at Orel. The 1st Tank Army and 5th Guards Tank Army took part in the offensive towards Kharkov and Belgorod that started on 3 August. Since all five tank armies were involved in heavy fighting during July and August many of them had to be withdrawn to be replenished with tanks, weapons and personnel. Also many armoured corps that had fought independently during the summer had to be replenished.[89]

48

TABLE 3.26: NUMBER OF TANKS AND SELF-PROPELLED GUNS IN SOVIET
TANK ARMIES IN AUGUST 1943

	Tanks and SUs[90]	Date	Replacement tanks received
1st Tank Army	569[91]	2 Aug	200
2nd Tank Army	ca 280[92]	29 July	?
3rd Guards Tank Army	417[93]	4 Aug	200
4th Tank Army	483[94]	4 Aug	0
5th Guards Tank Army	543[95]	2 Aug	?

During the defensive phase not only three tank armies with their corps entered combat; the Red Army also ordered six independent tank corps into the battle. Thus 12 tank corps were committed to battle during Zitadelle but not all of them had the same organization. A tank corps had not only tank brigades but also some supporting units and, since the Red Army was still rebuilding and organizing its armoured forces, not all corps had reached their goal (T/O&E).

TABLE 3.27: ORGANIZATION OF A SOVIET TANK CORPS, JULY 1943[96]

Corps HQ	
3 × Tank Brigades	53 or 65 Tanks
Motorized Rifle Brigade	
Air-Defence Artillery Regiment	16 37mm AA-guns
Guards Rocket Artillery Battalion	8 BM-13 Rocket Launchers
Motorcycle Battalion	
Engineer Battalion	
Mortar Regiment	36 120mm mortars
SU-Regiment (mixed)	8 SU-122 and 9 SU-76[97]
Anti-Tank Regiment	20 AT guns (could be 45mm, 57mm or 76mm)
(Separate) Anti-Tank Battalion	12 85mm AT guns

The (separate) anti-tank battalion with 12 85mm AT guns was an emergency measure to deal with the German Tiger tank. Since no other Soviet tank gun could penetrate the armour of the Tiger, except under very favourable circumstances, the corps needed some weapon that was able to deal with the Tiger. The 57mm anti-tank gun was rare in the Red Army. In January 1943 they had 100 and the production for 1943 was 1,900 guns.[98] Most common as anti-tank guns were the 45mm and 76mm weapons.

As can be seen in Tables 3.28 and 3.29 very few tank corps had the organization presented in Table 3.27 when the German offensive started, while some corps had extra units not included in the T/O&E. For example, 18th Tank Corps and 2nd Guards Tank Corps had a heavy tank regiment and 29th Tank Corps had an Armoured Car Battalion.

TABLE 3.28: ORGANIZATION OF TANKS CORPS DEPLOYED ON THE VORONEZH
AND CENTRAL FRONTS, 4 JULY 1943

	Tank Corps							
	3rd	6th	9th	16th	19th	31st	2nd Gds	5th Gds
Tank Brigade	3	3	3	3	3	3	3	3
Mot Rifle Brigade	1	1	1	1	1	–	1	1
AT Regiment	1	1	–	1	–	–	1	1
AT Battalion	1	–	1	1	–	–	1	–
SU Regiment	–	1	2	1	–	–	–	–
Hvy Tank Reg	–	–	–	–	–	–	1	1
MC Battalion	1	1	–	1	–	–	–	–
AA Regiment	1	–	–	–	–	–	1	1
Mtr Regiment	1	1	–	1	–	–	1	1

TABLE 3.29: ORGANIZATION OF TANK CORPS REINFORCING VORONEZH FRONT
DURING ZITADELLE

	Tank Corps			
	2nd	10th	18th	29th
Tank Brigade	3	3	3	3
Mot Rifle Brigade	1	1	1	1
AT Regiment	1	1	1	1
AT Battalion	–	–	1	1
SU Regiment	–	1	–	1
Hvy Tank Reg	–	–	1	–
MC Battalion	1	1	–	1
A/C Battalion	–	–	–	1
AA Regiment	1	1	1	–
Mtr Regiment	1	1	1	1
Gds Rocket Artillery Bn	1	–	–	–

All tank corps had three tank brigades but since the Red Army was changing the composition of the tank brigade this affected the number of tanks in a tank corps. Hence, the number of tanks depended on which T/O&E applied to their particular tank brigades. The old T/O&E organization is presented below in Table 3.30.

It is to be noted that the brigade had a mixture of light tanks (T-70) and medium tanks (T-34). This did not work well in combat since the T-34 actually had superior mobility. The T-70s were often lagging behind during advances, while obviously the T-34 was also better protected and had greater firepower. But the Red Army had to resort to this mixture since the production of medium tanks was not sufficient to cope with demand. By 1943 the production of medium tanks was much greater than

TABLE 3.30: T/O&E OF A SOVIET TANK BRIGADE, JULY 1943[99]

Unit	Men	T-34	T-70	LtAC	Other Equipment
Brigade HQ	181	1		3	
1st Tank Battalion	151	21			
2nd Tank Battalion	146	10	21		
Motorized Rifle Battalion	498				8 82mm Mtr
AA MG Battery	48				9 12.7mm AA MG
AT Battery	101				4 76.2mm guns
Total	1,173	53 Tanks			

the output of light tanks and the Red Army tried to replace the light tanks with the T-34, but this had not yet been fully accomplished. Also, at this time a new tank brigade organization was introduced. This called for three battalions, each equipped with 21 T-34s, while the brigade HQ had two T-34s. This gave a strength of 65 T-34s and no light tanks. But at Kursk both brigade organizations seem to have been used. Also some brigades with 65 tanks still retained some light tanks, since they had not received sufficient T-34s yet.

Of the six tank corps in the tank armies five seem to have had the old organization of tank brigades with 53 tanks. These were the 3rd, 6th, 16th, 18th and 29th Tank Corps. The one with the new organization of tank brigades was 31st Tank Corps. The six independent tank corps are listed in Table 3.31.

TABLE 3.31: SOVIET INDEPENDENT TANK CORPS IN THE DEFENSIVE PHASE, JULY 1943

	Entered Combat	Front	Organization
2nd Tank Corps	9 July	Voronezh	New
9th Tank Corps	8 July	Central	Old
10th Tank Corps	9 July	Voronezh	New
19th Tank Corps	6 July	Central	Old
2nd Guard Tank Corps	8 July	Voronezh	Old
5th Guard Tank Corps	6 July	Voronezh	Old

The Red Army had a second type of corps, the mechanized corps. They were rather scarce and only two were committed to combat during the defensive phase. These were the 3rd Mechanized Corps in 1st Tank Army and 5th Guards Mechanized Corps in 5th Guards Tank Army. The main differences between a tank corps and a mechanized corps was that a mechanized corps had more infantry and more guns and mortars. This also meant that the mechanized corps was a larger unit demanding more manpower.

TABLE 3.32: ORGANIZATION OF A SOVIET MECHANIZED CORPS, JULY 1943[100]

Corps HQ	
Three Mechanized Brigades	
One or two Tank Brigades[101]	
Motorcycle Battalion	
Armoured Car Battalion	
Guards Rocket Artillery Battalion	8 BM-13
Mortar Regiment	36 120mm mortars
Air-Defence Artillery Regiment	16 37mm AA guns
Anti-Tank Regiment	20 AT guns
SU Regiment (mixed)	8 SU-122 and 9 SU-76[102]
Engineer Battalion	
(Separate) Anti-Tank Battalion	12 85mm AT guns

As was the case with the tank corps, not all support units were available for the two corps, but 5th Guards Mechanized Corps had almost all. The main difference between a mechanized brigade and a motorized rifle brigade in a tank corps was that the mechanized had 39 tanks, a tank regiment within the brigade. In July 1943 there existed 22 Tank Corps and 13 Mechanized Corps in the Red Army.[103] Of these 14 were committed to the defensive phase of the battle of Kursk.

NOTES

1. XX Corps had 320 casualties from between 5 and 10 July while its neighbour, XXXXVI Panzer Corps, that was involved in the offensive had 4,576. BA-MA RH 20-9/939 AOK 9. Abt IIa Verluste.
2. BA-MA RH 24-23/126, Abt Ia Meldung von 3.7.1943.
3. The Goliat was a small remote controlled tracked vehicle with an explosive charge, but these did not work as they were supposed to. Technical problems or enemy fire seriously hampered the Goliats from achieving any success. H. Schäufler, *So lebten und starben sie, Das Buch von Panzer Regiment 35* (Kameradschaft ehem. Pz Reg 35, Bamberg, not dated) p. 134.
4. This is based on a report on how 814th Armoured Engineer Company was organized. We assume that these had similar organization. BA-MA RH 10/306. 814th Armoured Engineer Company.
5. BA-MA RH 10/155, Divisional Report 18th Panzer 1.7.1943.
6. Funk-lenk works quite similarly to Goliat but is a larger variant. The charge-carrier vehicle is Sdkfz 301 (B-IV) a *schwere Ladungsträger*. Each company had 36 of these. These vehicles were either remote-controlled from Panzer IIIs or Sturmgeschütz IIIs or controlled directly by a driver in the vehicle itself. The charge carried had a weight of 500 kg, and was released from the vehicle. The vehicle can reverse before

52

the charge explodes. Data for B-IV, weight of vehicle 3.45 ton, 3.65 metres long, 1.8 metres wide, 1.185 metres high, range 120 km (fuel tank), engine 49 hp. Fritz Hahn, *Waffen und Geheimwaffen des deutschen Heeres 1933–1945*, Band 2: *Panzer- und Sonderfahrzeuge, Wunderwaffen, Vebrauch und Verluste* (Bernard & Graefe Verlag, Koblenz, 1987), pp. 98–9.

7. BA-MA RH 10/246, 656th PzJg.Rgt, 4.7.1943.
8. BA-MA RH 10/141, Divisional Report 2nd Panzer, 1.7.1943.
9. BA-MA RH 10/148, Divisional Report 9th Panzer, 1.7.1943.
10. BA-MA RH 10/157, Divisional Report 20th Panzer, 1.7.1943.
11. BA-MA RH 24-6/98, Fernschreiben von XXXXVI PzK an Gruppe Weiss, 3.7.1943.
12. BA-MA RH 10/143, Divisional Report 4th Panzer Division, 4.7.1943. BA-MA RH 26-46/91, Divisional Report 4th Panzer Division, 3.7.1943.
13. BA-MA RH 10/150, Divisional Report 12th Panzer, 1.7.1943.
14. BA-MA RH 24-52/159, Anlageheft vom 21.7 bis 26.7.1943 zum KTB Nr 6 LII A.K.Ia.
15. During the offensive this battalion fought attached to 11th Panzer Division.
16. BA-MA RH 10/142, Divisional Report 3rd Panzer, 30.6.1943.
17. BA-MA RH 10/149, Divisional Report 11th Panzer, 1.7.1943.
18. BA-MA RH21-4/450, Pz.AOK 4 O.Qu Anlage 11 zum KTB Tätigkeitsberichte v.d.Abteilungen.
19. BA-MA RH 10/312, Divisional Report 1st SS-PzGr, 1.7.1943.
20. BA-MA RH 10/313, Divisional Report 2nd SS-PzGr, 1.7.1943.
21. BA-MA RH 10/314, Divisional Report 3rd SS-PzGr, 1.7.1943.
22. BA-MA RH 10/145, Divisional Report 6th Panzer, 1.7.1943.
23. BA-MA RH 10/146, Divisional Report 7th Panzer, 1.7.1943.
24. BA-MA RH 10/156, Divisional Report 19th Panzer, 1.7.1943.
25. BA-MA RH 24-11/76, Gliederung der Artillerie und Flak beim Gen.kdo Raus, 2.7.1943.
26. The Germans only built 24 of these Sturminfanteriegeschütz 33B. The chassis was based on Panzer III with a 15cm heavy infantry gun mounted in a fully armoured box-like superstructure and it was well armoured (similar to Brummbär).
27. BA-MA RH 21-1/98, Pz.AOK 1 Ia Meldung, 3.7.1943.
28. BA-MA RH 10/316, Divisional Report SS-Wiking, 1.7.1943.
29. BA-MA RH 10/159, Divisional Report 23rd Panzer, 1.7.1943.
30. M.A. Kozlov (ed.), *V Plameni Srazhenii* (Voenizdat, Moscow, 1973) p. 92.
31. With 150,000 men and 12 divisions, the army would have a divisional slice of 12,500 men. This can be compared with the fact that the divisional slice for the entire Central Front was 15,812 (see Tables 2.3 and 2.4). Furthermore, the 13th Army had a greater share of GHQ combat troops than the other armies. Also it can be assumed that the units of 13th Army had received priority for replacements, since they were expected to take the brunt of the German offensive.
   A German Army was to a much greater extent self-sufficient than a Soviet army. The Soviet army had to rely on the front for much of its needs, such as medical and repair facilities, supply and maintenance. Also the Soviet fronts kept control of GHQ combat units to a greater extent. The German Army groups did not have much manpower directly subordinated. This means that Soviet armies cannot be compared directly to German armies.
32. *Voenno-Istoricheskii Zhurnal*, no. 8, 1973, G. Biryokov and A. Tokmakov, *Artilleriya v oborone 13-i armii*, p. 42.
33. K.S. Moskalenko (ed.), *Bitva na Kurskoi Duge* (Nauka, Moscow, 1975), p. 97.

34. Includes regimental artillery, 76mm howitzer.
35. These M-30 frames took time to deploy, each frame fired four rockets and the maximum range was 2.8 km. The short range and the long deployment time limited their use when the enemy was advancing. From 5 July to 12 July the 5th Guards Rocket Artillery Division fired 50 battalion and battery volleys, the total number of rockets used was 6,200. It may be noted that if all M-30 frames were fired at the same time the division would fire 1,728 rockets. V.V. Gurkin and A.E. Ivaschenko, *5-ya Gvardeiskaya Kalinkovichskaya* (Voenizdat, Moscow, 1979), p. 49.
36. G.A. Koltunov and B.G. Soloviev, *Kurskaya Bitva* (Voenizdat, Moscow, 1970), pp. 65, 68, 75.
37. M.A. Kozlov (ed.), *V Plameni Srazhenii* (Voenizdat, Moscow, 1973), p. 91.
38. *Voenno-Istoricheskii Zhurnal*, no. 11, 1974, G. Biryokov and S. Totrov, *Nekotorie Voprosi primeneniya artillerii vo frontovich operatsiyach*, p. 16.
39. 48th Army had 134 Tanks and 44 Assault Guns while 70th Army had 125 Tanks. G.A. Koltunov and B.G. Solovev, *Kurskaya Bitva*, p. 75.
40. C.C. Sharp, *The Soviet Order of Battle World War II*, Vol. VI, *Red Thunder* (George F. Nafziger, West Chester, PA, 1995), pp. 38, 74, 75.
41. Includes regimental artillery, 76mm howitzer.
42. G.A. Koltunov and B.G. Soloviev, *Kurskaya Bitva*, pp. 68, 75.
43. *Voenno-Istoricheskii Zhurnal*, no. 7, 1974, A. Sidorenko, *Oborona 23-go Gvardeiskogo Strelkovogo Korpuca*, p. 39.
44. *Voenno-Istoricheskii Zhurnal*, no. 9, 1972, A. Vinskii, *Primenenie inzhenernich zagrazhdenii v oborone po opitu Velikoy Otechestvennoi Voiny*, p. 73.
45. Includes regimental artillery, 76mm howitzer.
46. G.A. Koltunov and B.G. Soloviev, *Kurskaya Bitva*, pp. 68, 75.
47. *Voenno-Istoricheskii Zhurnal*, no. 11, 1974, G. Biryokov and S. Totrov, *Nekotorie Voprosi primeneniya artillerii vo frontovich operatsiyach*, p. 16.
48. The International TNDM Newsletter, Vol. 1, no. 6, June 1997, p. 27.
49. G.A. Koltunov and B.G. Soloviev, *Kurskaya Bitva*, p. 69.
50. The 42nd Corps was facing the Soviet South-West Front which was not included in the Soviet forces participating in the Kursk battle.
51. According to B. Müller-Hildebrand, *Das Heer*, Vol. III (Mittler & Sohn, Frankfurt am Main, 1969), p. 123. The percentage is calculated by counting divisions on the eastern front not including forces in Finland or Norway.
52. 57th, 106th, 167th, 168th, 198th, 255th, 320th and 332nd Infantry Division.
53. 6th, 7th, 31st, 86th, 102nd, 216th, 258th, 292nd and 383rd Infantry Division plus 78th Assault Division.
54. Oberkommando des Heeres, GenStdH/Org.Abt. Nr. I/2000/44 geh. H.Qu., den 25.4.44, Festlegung der Stärkebegriffe (BA-MA RH 2/60).
55. Ibid.
56. BA-MA RH 21-4/422. Anlage 7 zu KTB PzAOK 4, Meldungen (Beute, Verpflegungsstärken), von 1.7.1943 bis 31.12.1943.
57. K. Sperker, *Generaloberst Erhard Raus, ein Truppenführer im Ostfeldzug*, Appendix: Dokumente (Biblio, Osnabrück, 1988).
58. BA-MA RH 27-20/164. 20.PzD KTB Anlageband Teil 7. RH 24-46/98. Fernschreiben von XXXXVI PzK an Gruppe Weiss. RH 26-6/52. Anlageband V zum Kriegstagenbuch Nr. 7 6.ID.
59. BA-MA RH 20-9/339. AOK 9 Abt IIa Verluste.
60. In the German Army soldiers with light wounds or sickness could stay in the care of their own regiment. They were included on ration strength but not on combat strength. When they became fit again they were sent back to the trenches. O. Schaub,

Aus der Geschichte Panzer-Grenadier-Regiment 12 (SR.12) (Selbstverlag, Bergisch Gladbach, 1957), p. 284.

61. A. Buchner, *Das Handbuch der Deutschen Infanterie 1939–1945* (Podzun-Pallas, Friedberg, 1989), p. 96.

62. The maximum range for a 15cm sFH 18 was 13,250 metres with charge 8 but use of this charge and charge 7 (giving a range of 11,400) required authorization by a higher formation commander. These charges induced considerable strain on the gun. With charge 6 the sFH 18 had a range of 9,725 metres. I. Hogg, *German Artillery of World War Two* (Book Club Edition, London, 1975), pp. 64–5.

63. An Infantry Division got a T/O&E of 130 Panzerschreck and 2,000 Panzerfausts in March 1944. BA-MA RH 10/348, Oberkommando des Heeres H.Qu.OKH den 2 März 1944.

64. A. Buchner, *Das Handbuch der Deutschen Infanterie 1939–1945*, pp. 9 and 97.

65. A. Buchner, *Das Handbuch der Deutschen Infanterie 1939–1945*, pp. 52–5. In *German Artillery of World War Two*, pp. 189 and 194, by I. Hogg, the shell weight for 5cm Pak 38 is 2.25kg with a muzzle velocity of 823 m/sec and the muzzle velocity for 3.7cm Pak 35/36 is 762 m/sec.

66. BA-MA RH 24-46/98, Fernschreiben von XXXXVI PzK an Gruppe Weiss 3.7.1943. I.VII PzK 54633/7, Fernschreiben an Pz.AOK 1 Ia 4.7.1943. RH 20-8/91, Meldung XXXXII AK. RH 24-23/126, Meldung Abt Ia 3.7.1943. RH 26-6/52. Anlageband V zum Kriegstagenbuch, Nr. 7, 6th ID.

67. BA-MA RH 26-6/52. Anlageband V zum Kriegstagenbuch, Nr. 7, 6th ID. RH 26-167/29 Anlagenband Kriegstagebuch des Div Kdos der 167th ID.

68. BA-MA RH 24-46/98, Fernschreiben von XXXXVI PzK an gruppe Weiss, 3.7.1943

69. BA-MA RH 20-2/494, AOK 2.a Ia 6.7.1943: Gefechtsstärke der Gr.Btl stand 5.7.1943. RH 20-8/91, Meldung XXXXII Korps. RH 24-46/98, Fernschreiben von XXXXVI PzK an gruppe Weiss 3.7.1943. RH 20-2/494, Anlage 1 zu AOK 2. Ia Kampfstärkemeldung 4.7.1943. RH 24-23/125, Meldung XXII.AK. RH 24-11/76, Meldung Korps Raus. RH 24/46/91 Gen.Kdo XXXXVI PzK KTB Nr. 7. RH 26-6/52. Anlageband V zum Kriegstagenbuch, Nr. 7, 6th ID.

70. BA-MA RH 21-4/450, Pz.AOK 4 O.Qu Anlage 11 zum KTB Tätigkeitsberichte v.d.Abteilungen.

71. Seven SS-Panzergrenadier Divisions were later in October 1943 designated SS-Panzer Divisions, 1st, 2nd, 3rd, 5th, 9th, 10th and 12th SS-PzGr Div. The divisions did not have the same organizations so not all divisions had the SS-Panzer Division standard. The only division which reached the T/O&E standard by this date was 1st SS Panzer Division.

72. SS-Panzergrenadier Division 'Wiking' was not as strong as the three in II SS-Panzer Corps. See Appendix dealing with German divisional organization.

73. For Großdeutschland the heavy tank company was expanded to a third battalion (heavy) in the panzer regiment in August 1943. For the three SS-divisions it was planned that these companies were going to be the base for the future heavy GHQ tank battalion in SS-Panzer Corps, but as the Waffen-SS had not yet acquired enough Tigers, the companies stayed with the divisions.

74. Here the total for tanks and assault guns was 1,632 in 15 divisions which gives an average of 109. In the Ardennes it was 917 tanks and assault guns in 8 divisions which gives an average of 115 tanks. If we include Jagdpanzer IV as assault guns then the divisions in the Ardennes had an average of 127.

75. R. Stoves, *Die Gepanzerten und Motorisierten Deutschen Grossverbände, 1935–1945* (Podzun-Pallas, Friedberg/H, 1986), pp. 71 and 85.

76. P. Chamberlain and H.L. Doyle, *Encyclopedia of German Tanks of World War II* (Arms & Armour, London, 1978), p. 262.

77. BA-MA RH 21-4/450, Pz.AOK 4 O.Qu Anlage 11 zum KTB Tätigkeitsberichte v.d.Abteilungen. Also RH 10-141 to 143, 145-146, 148-149, 155-157, 209, 312-314 Divisional reports to the General of Panzertroops. Thomas Jentz in *Panzertruppen: The Complete Guide to the Creation & Combat Employment of Germany's Tank Force 1943–45* (Schiffer Military History, Atglen, 1996) presents on pages 78–82 numbers for 1 July 1943 that are sometimes different from those in Table 3.16. One reason for this is the arrival of replacement tanks at the last minute, for example both 9th Panzer Div and 1st SS Panzergrenadier Division received tanks just before the battle. One other reason could be that our main source has been the divisional reports and the practice of writing these was quite new. Thus perhaps not everything was included, such as Befehlspanzers in battalion staffs and regimental staffs.

78. Chamberlain and Doyle, *Encyclopedia of German Tanks of World War II*, p. 262.

79. BA-MA RH 10/114, Der General Inspekteur der Panzertruppen 15.1.45: Deutsche Panzerverluste im Osten in der Zeit vom 22.6.41 bis 31.12.44.

80. O. Schaub, *Aus der Geschichte Panzer-Grenadier-Regiment 12 (SR.12)*, Appendix 25: *Veränderungen im stand an SPW 5.7.1943–29.10.1944.*

81. BA-MA RH 10/101, Der General Inspekteur der Panzertruppen: Freie Gliederung 1944. O. Schaub, *Aus der Geschichte Panzer-Grenadier-Regiment 12 (SR.12).*

82. D.M. Glantz, *From the Don to the Dnepr: Soviet Offensive Operations December 1942–August 1943* (Frank Cass, London, 1991), pp. 220–1. O.A. Losik (ed.), *Stroitelstvo i boevoe primenenie Sovetskikh tankovych Voisk v gody Velikoi Otechestvennoi Voiny* (Voenizdat, Moscow, 1979), p. 71.

83. When the first six mechanized corps were formed they did not have the same numbers of tanks in their organization. Two Corps (1st and 2nd) had 175, two (3rd and 5th) had 224 and two (4th and 6th) had 204, O.A. Losik (ed.), p. 57. Yet on page 70 Losik gives 175 as tank strength for a mechanized corps.

84. Based on Soviet Archival Records in The International TNDM Newsletter, Vol. 1, June 1997, no. 6, p. 27. The tank strength is 631 tanks in two books – M.E. Katukov, *NA Ostrie Glavnogo Udara* (Voenizdat, Moscow, 1974), p. 199, and A.Kh. Babadzhanyan *et al.*, *Lyuki Otkryli v Berline* (Voenizdat, Moscow, 1973), p. 58. Koltunov and Soloviev give the 1st Tank Army a strength of 542. G.A. Koltunov and B.G. Soloviev, *Kurskaya Bitva* (Voenizdat, Moscow, 1970), p. 75.

85. G.A. Koltunov and B.G. Soloviev, *Kurskaya Bitva* (Voenizdat, Moscow, 1970), p. 75.

86. A.I. Radzievskii, *Tankovii Udar* (Voenizdat, Moscow, 1977), p. 262. In another book it is said to have 698 operational tanks and 32 SUs which gives 730 operational on 18 July 1943. A.M. Zvartsev (ed.), *3-ya Gvardeiskaya Tankovaya* (Voenizdat, Moscow, 1982), p. 69.

87. A.I. Radzievskii, *Tankovii Udar*, p. 262.

88. P.Ya. Egorov *et al.*, *Dorogami Podeg (Boevoi put 5-i Gvardeiskoy Armii)* (Voenizdat, Moscow, 1969), p. 28.

89. V.A. Pronko, *Die Sowjetische Strategie im Jahre 1943*, in J. Förster (ed.), *Stalingrad* (R. Piper, München, 1993), p. 322.

90. Including operational tanks and tanks in the workshops.

91. A.Kh. Babadzhanyan *et al.*, *Lyuki Otkryli v Berline*, p. 71.

92. R.N. Armstrong, *Red Army Tank Commanders: The Armored Guards* (Schiffer, Atglen, 1994), p. 123.

93. Ibid., p. 187.

94. A.I. Radzievskii, *Tankovii Udar*, p. 262, 265.

95. P.Ya. Egorov, *et al.*, *Dorogami Podeg (Boevoi put 5-i Gvardeiskoy Armii)*, p. 56.

96. C.C. Sharp, *Soviet Order of Battle World War II*, Vol. II, *School of Battle* (George F. Nafziger, West Chester, OH, 1995), pp. 48–52, 94.

97. By April 1943 the Soviets had started to form two types of SU-regiment, medium and light, instead of mixing the types. A light SU-Regiment had 20 SU-76 and 1 T-34 while a medium regiment had 16 SU-122 and 1 T-34. C.C. Sharp, *Soviet Order of Battle World War II*, Vol. II, *School of Battle*, p. 50.

98. G.F. Krivosheev, *Grif Sekretnosti Snyat* (Voennoe Izdatelstvo, Moscow, 1993), p. 353.

99. C.C. Sharp, *Soviet Order of Battle World War II*, Vol. II, *School of Battle*, p. 94.

100. C.C. Sharp, *Soviet Order of Battle World War II*, Vol. III, *Red Storm*, p. 23.

101. If no tank brigade was available the mechanized corps might have two tank regiments instead.

102. By April 1943 the Soviets had started to form two types of SU-regiment, medium and light, instead of mixing the types. A light SU-Regiment had 20 SU-76 and 1 T-34 while a medium regiment had 16 SU-122 and 1 T-34. C.C. Sharp, *Soviet Order of Battle World War II*, Vol. II, *School of Battle*, p. 50.

103. C.C. Sharp, *Soviet Order of Battle World War II*, Vol. III, *Red Storm*, pp. 28–30.

4

Tanks Employed at Zitadelle

GERMAN ARMOUR

In a battle that would eventually be called the greatest tank battle of all time, the quality of the opposing AFVs is naturally of paramount interest. Additionally, the battle at Kursk was one in which a number of new German tank models were introduced in an attempt to regain the techno-logical superiority which had been lost since the first encounters with the Soviet T-34 and KV tank models. Hitler placed great faith in the ability of the new German tanks to produce a decisive effect on the battlefield. The desire to see as many Tigers, Panthers, Ferdinands and Brummbärs as possible in operation Zitadelle was the main reason for Hitler to delay the offensive. However, despite the delays, the number of new tanks and assault guns did not become significant.

One of the 'new' German tanks had actually seen combat previously, though it was employed in far greater numbers at Kursk. This was the Tiger, a 57 ton behemoth, which had already proved itself superior to enemy tanks in Tunisia and on the eastern front. The Tiger's silhouette resembled a powerful and inflated version of the Panzer IV tank, the most common German tank. This can be an explanation for the many reports among enemy tank units that identified enemy tanks as Tigers. Judging from Soviet, British or American reports or descriptions of engagements, the Tiger should have been a rather common vehicle. However, pro-duction of Tiger I amounted to only 1,354 throughout the war,[1] which can be compared with an overall German wartime production of 24,870 tanks and 17,295 assault guns.[2] The Tiger II, which superseded the Tiger I in the summer 1944 was produced in even more limited numbers, only 489 vehicles.[3]

The total number of Tigers taking part in the offensive was 146.[4] They were organized in two independent heavy tank battalions and four heavy tank companies attached to four Panzer regiments according to the following table:[5]

TABLE 4.1: DEPLOYMENT OF TIGER TANKS ENGAGED IN OPERATION ZITADELLE,
JULY 1943

Army	Unit	Tiger Tanks
9th Army	505th sPz.Abteilung	45 Tigers
4th Pz Army	13th Coy/SS-Pz Regiment 1	13 Tigers
	8th Coy/SS-Pz Regiment 2	14 Tigers
	9th Coy/SS-Pz Regiment 3	15 Tigers
	13th Coy/GD Pz Regiment	14 Tigers
Army-Det. Kempf	503rd sPz.Abteilung	45 Tigers

It should be noted that 503rd heavy-tank battalion did not fight as a battalion initially, the three Panzer divisions in III Panzer Corps each having had one Tiger company attached from 503rd heavy tank battalion. Also 505th heavy tank battalion had to begin the battle with two companies only. The third company arrived on 8 July and entered combat.[6]

As is indicated by its external similarity to the Panzer IV, the Tiger's design had more in common with German prewar design philosophy than any inspiration from the new design philosophy introduced with the revolutionary T-34. Consequently, the Tiger did not employ sloped armour. A departure from previous German design was the fact that the armour plates were fixed to each other by interlocking joints. This made any supportive chassis superfluous, the armour itself produced such stability and integrity as to make the vehicle capable of absorbing severe punishment. The armour plates were thick, but not radically thicker than, for example, the front of the Panzer IV. However, the Tiger did have sufficient thickness to keep out shots from the Soviet 76mm gun, except at very close range, and even at short distances only the sides and rear were vulnerable.[7] Overall it can be said that the Tiger did not carry any extreme armour, especially considering its weight, but the armour was just enough to cause current enemy tanks serious trouble. Improvements in enemy tank armament though, were more or less certain to make the Tiger much more vulnerable, which became clear with the introduction of the T-34/85, half a year after the Kursk battle.

The Tiger's armament consisted of the well-proven 88mm gun, model 1936. This gun was accurate and effective, though not much better than the 75mm gun mounted by the Panzer IV. However, just as was the case with the armour, it was sufficient to deal with current opposition at most realistic distances. Its shell could penetrate the T-34's frontal armour at distances up to about 1,700m. The gun made it the best-armed AFV in the world, save for the Panther and the Ferdinand.

The main disadvantage with the Tiger was its automotive performance. The engine produced 700 HP, which was more than any other tank engine, but it was not sufficient to make the heavy vehicle agile. Also the weight caused problems with bridges, which were often unable to take such a heavy load.[8] The designers had anticipated this and therefore equipped the tank with the ability to travel submerged, up to a depth of 4 metres. However, the weight of the Tiger was causing problems during Zitadelle. Weight also caused problems with recovery, since to be towed the vehicle needed three prime movers. The Tiger was a legend almost before it entered combat, and the vehicle was certainly awesome in many respects, compared to the opposition in 1942, but the construction was not very intelligent, and the Tiger I did not remain in production for more than 26 months.[9]

A much more modern concept was the Panther tank. Its construction had been initiated as a response to the Soviet T-34, encountered in 1941. The experiences of the tank crews facing this enemy tank clearly showed the urgent need for a new medium tank, not only able to match the T-34, but preferably also capable of giving a good account of itself against future enemy tanks. Thus, what was needed was a tank which improved considerably in terms of firepower and protection, without sacrificing automotive performance. In these aspects the designers of the Panther were not going to disappoint the users.

The Panther employed well-sloped armour, on the lines of the T-34. However, the thickness of the armour was considerably greater. The front armour of the Panther was immune save for a rare lucky shot at some vulnerable spot. It seems to be a widespread belief that the Tiger was better protected than the Panther. This is not true, since the Panther had a much better frontal protection than the Tiger I. Side and rear protection was better on the Tiger, however. The frontal armour on the Panther was good enough to render future enemy guns marginally effective at best.

One point must be added however. Initially the Panther had face-hardened armour. This worked well against the enemy guns of 1943. The introduction of enemy guns of larger calibre and rounds with piercing caps caused the Germans to change to homogeneous armour instead. This made the Panther's frontal protection effective, save for very short distances, against the 122mm gun of the Soviet IS-2 tank, though the older vehicles with face-hardened armour could be penetrated more easily. The 85mm gun of the T-34/85 was also unable to penetrate the front of the Panther.[10]

As long as the Soviet tank forces were mainly equipped with T-34/76, the armour configuration of the Panther was not as good that of the Tiger. Since the Soviet 76mm gun had rather poor armour-piercing capabilities, the better frontal protection of the Panther gave it no real advantage over the Tiger. On the other hand, the side armour of the Panther could relatively easily be penetrated by the Soviet 76mm gun, while that gun had considerable difficulties in coping with the side armour of the Tiger. With the introduction of the T-34/85, the situation was altered. Now the Red Army had a tank whose armament had no difficulties with the side armour of even the German heavy tanks. However, the frontal armour of the Panther was still immune, while the frontal armour of the Tiger could be penetrated except at ranges above 1,200 metres. In this situation the Panther clearly was the preferred tank.

Firepower was provided by the 75mm L70 KwK 42 gun, a weapon producing very high muzzle velocity and making the gun very accurate at longer distances. Since the velocity with which a shell strikes its target is the most important factor for armour penetration, the gun excelled in this respect. In fact its armour-piercing capability was superior to all tank guns during the war, with the exception of the long 88mm gun. The shorter 88mm gun on the Tiger I was inferior, despite the popular belief that the Tiger's gun was more powerful. However, the larger 88mm shell could possibly cause greater damage inside a vehicle if it managed to penetrate the armour.

Power to propel the vehicle was provided by the Maybach HL 230 engine with an output of 700 HP. Essentially this was the same engine as that mounted in the Tiger, but the lower weight of the Panther gave the engine an easier task. Automotive performance was not quite on a par with the T-34, but the disadvantage was only marginal. On the other hand, the Panther was more mobile than either the Panzer IV or the Panzer III.

As opposed to the Tiger, the Panther was produced in large numbers. During the last two years of the war the Panther was produced in greater numbers than any German tank; in all, 5,976 were produced from 1943 onwards.[11] It has often been said that the Panther was complicated and expensive to produce; it has even been hinted that it was a mistake for the Germans to choose such a vehicle as the main equipment for the Panzer units. This appears not to be true, however: the cost to produce a Panzer IV was 103,462 Reichsmark, while the cost for the Panther was 117,100.[12] Comparison can also be made with the Tiger I, which cost 250,800 Reichsmark[13] to produce.

Speculation concerning the high cost of producing the Panther also fail to take into account the survivability of the vehicles. What is of importance is not high production numbers, but rather the ability to keep the combat units well provided with tanks. Principally, this can be done in two ways, either by producing and delivering many tanks or by producing vehicles that survive combat. In reality, the combination of the two is what matters. It can be shown that the survivability of the Panther was greater than that of any other medium tank.[14] In fact, it was great enough to more than offset the differences in production cost, thus making the Panther the most cost-effective tank to produce. Such a comparison does not take into account that its greater firepower (and also the fact that its better protection made it easier to apply that firepower) also made the Panther a more effective tank during the time it operated, something which still further improved its cost-effectiveness. One final precautionary note should be mentioned however. If a vehicle exhibits low availability due to frequent mechanical breakdown, the cost-effectiveness of course suffers. This may very well have been the case with the Panther in the beginning, when it did suffer from teething troubles.

Another long-lived myth concerning the Panther was the choice made between the two prototypes produced by MAN and Daimler-Benz. The latter, almost a direct copy of the T-34, was not selected for production, and various reasons have been put forward. It has been implied that the Daimler-Benz prototype was superior, but constructor's pride would not allow it to enter mass production. Another reason that has been voiced is that the engine in the Daimler-Benz prototype was made of aluminium, thus causing production problems. This does not seem plausible since the engine which was eventually selected for the Panther was also made of aluminium. The major reason for selecting the MAN prototype was probably its ability to mount a more powerful armament than was possible in the smaller turret of the Daimler-Benz prototype.[15] The latter was designed to take the 75mm L48 gun, used in the Panzer IV, thus not providing the advantage in armour-piercing capability which the Panther would eventually enjoy during its wartime service.

If any tank deserves the distinction of being described as the best tank during the war, it has to be the Panther. It not only outclassed the opposition in terms of firepower and frontal protection during 1943. It was good enough to keep an advantage over future allied tanks, including the T-34/85, the IS-2 and also the US Pershing tank. Its combat debut in Zitadelle was decided upon despite warnings from Guderian that the tank still suffered from teething troubles.[16]

The main disadvantage with the Panther was its weight. Before Tiger and Panther an upper limit of 30 tonnes was enough for railway transport, bridges and recovery vehicles. But now the Germans had to deal first with the 57 ton weight of the Tiger and then the 44.5 ton Panther. Thus, new wagons had to be ordered for railway transport to cope with this. Also, the engineer units needed new bridge building equipment to be able to construct heavier bridges. Finally, the repair and maintenance units needed heavier recovery vehicles. Therefore, a new recovery vehicle was introduced at operation Zitadelle, the Bergepanther.[17]

For Zitadelle the Panthers were deployed under the command of XXXXVIII Panzer Corps within 4th Panzer Army as part of Army Group South. They were organized in *Abteilungen* (51st and 52nd Panzer Battalions), each with 96 Panthers and two Bergepanther recovery vehicles. They came under 39th Panzer Regiment, which had eight Panthers of its own, and was itself part of 10th Panzer Brigade, comprising staff only. The 200 Panthers fought mainly together with the Großdeutschland Division. It should be noted that the II SS-Panzer Corps did not have any Panthers during the battle, contrary to what many authors claim. Das Reich had Panthers but they belonged to a battalion that was still in Germany. That Panther battalion arrived only after the offensive and made its combat debut on 22 August 1943 outside Kharkov. If it is preferred to define the battle of Kursk to include the fighting up to the Soviet conquest of Kharkov, Das Reich had Panthers during the last two days of the battle.

At the time of operation Zitadelle however, these new tanks made up less than 15 per cent of the German tanks and assault guns.[18] The Panzer III and Panzer IV still constituted the majority of German tanks. By this time the Panzer III was clearly obsolete and production ceased in June 1943.[19] The number of gun-armed Panzer IIIs that took part in Zitadelle was 668, including 40 Pz IIIs armed with flame throwers.[20]

In terms of armour protection and firepower the T-34 had asserted its ascendancy over the Panzer III since 1941. Subsequent up-gunning and up-armouring of the Panzer III had narrowed the gap, but the T-34 still maintained a substantial superiority. Also, the Panzer III had reached the limits of its development potential, making the decision to halt production logical. The automotive performance of the tank was adequate, though not on a par with the Panther nor, more seriously, the T-34. Nevertheless, the German Panzer divisions were going to rely quite heavily on the Panzer III, which was present in several versions. At least four different main weapons were used on the Panzer IIIs employed in the battle. The shorter 50mm L42 gun was still mounted on a few vehicles, but its low muzzle velocity made it useless even against the sides of the T-34. Far more common was the 50mm L60 gun. Its higher muzzle velocity enabled it to penetrate the sides and rear of the T-34 up to distances of about 1,000m, provided the target was hit at a perfect angle. Another weapon used was the short 75mm L24, a gun with very low muzzle velocity. It was unsuited against enemy tanks, but it could fire a more effective HE shell than the 50mm weapons. Finally, a limited number of Panzer III mounted a flame-thrower in the turret. This weapon was of course not usable except at short ranges, but its effect against unprotected infantry could be devastating. It could also be effective against enemy tanks if they came close enough (less than 100m).

The other main German tank was the Panzer IV, which had been in production since 1936.[21] Thus it was about as old as the Panzer III, but it did have one significant advantage over that tank. Its larger turret ring permitted mounting of the 75mm L48 gun, known as the KwK 40. This gun was superior to all enemy tank guns during 1943. It was not much inferior to the 88mm gun mounted in Tiger I, though the 75mm gun of the Panther had an armour piercing capability about 45 per cent better. However, the Panzer IV was spared the dubious pleasure of facing those two tanks. What mattered was that the gun was able to defeat the KV-1 and the T-34, except at longer ranges. The gun was also more accurate than those carried by enemy tanks.

On the debit side was the protection. Initially, the Panzer IV had a frontal protection of 15mm, an almost ludicrous thickness.[22] However, the vast majority of the tanks employed in Zitadelle had the frontal armour increased to a thickness of 80mm. While this was a respectable thickness, the old construction did not employ sloped armour, rendering the protection less efficient. The T-34 had superior frontal armour production, but the Panzer IV had an even greater superiority in gun power, giving it a slight range advantage in a straight gun–armour comparison.

In terms of automotive performance the Panzer IV was only marginally better than the Tiger I and not in the same class as the T-34. In an overall comparison of characteristics the Panzer IV did stand up well against the T-34 however. The superior armament outweighed the better protection carried by the T-34. And while the T-34 was more mobile, the Panzer IV offered a more spacious and better-designed interior, enhancing crew efficiency. Also optics and communications equipment were better in the Panzer IV. Altogether 702 Pz IVs were present with the attacking units assembled for Zitadelle.[23]

Tanks were not the only kind of AFVs employed by the German army. Assault guns also figured in quite significant numbers. These turretless vehicles were originally intended for direct fire support to the infantry, but many of them were more often used as mobile anti-tank guns.[24] They were somewhat cheaper to produce than tanks. A Sturmgeschütz III cost about 82,500 Reichsmark, while a Panzer IV cost 103,462 Reichsmark.[25] The difference between these two vehicles lay in the absence of the revolving turret on the Sturmgeschütz III, but their main guns had similar performance, while the protection was almost identical and also the power to weight ratio was similar.

The Sturmgeschütz III (hereafter called StuG III) was by far the most numerous assault gun, 466 took part in operation Zitadelle.[26] It had first been used in very limited numbers in the campaign in France 1940, when it carried the short-barrelled 75mm gun. It was available in greater numbers in 1941, but production did not become significant until the longer-barrelled 75mm gun was mounted in the vehicle, thus producing an AFV which had the necessary firepower to deal with the T-34 and KV tanks. As has been said, in terms of armament, protection and mobility the StuG III was equal to the Panzer IV, but its lack of revolving turret meant that it was not given more independent offensive tasks, unless of course there were no tanks available.

Also there existed a version armed with a 10.5cm howitzer, the StuH 42. This was far less common and was mainly intended for HE fire. On 30 June 1943, there were 916 StuG with 7.5cm weapon against only 68 with 10.5cm armament on the eastern front.[27] These two vehicles were usually employed in independent assault gun battalions. On 4 July 1943, independent StuG battalions were employed in the Kursk area as shown in Table 4.2.

TABLE 4.2: INDEPENDENT StuG BATTALIONS, 4 JULY 1943

StuG Battalion	Army Area Deployed in	Corps Subordinated to	Number of StuG	Number of StuH
177th	9th	XLI Pz.Korps	22	9
185th	9th	XXIII Korps	27	5
189th	9th	XXIII Korps	31	0
202nd	2nd		31*	0
228th	Kempf	III Pz.Korps	31	0
244th	9th	XLI Pz.Korps	22	9
245th	9th	XLVII Pz.Korps	22	9
904th	9th	XLVII Pz.Korps	31	0
905th	Kempf	Raus	23	9
909th	9th	XLVI Pz.Korps	31**	0
911th	4th Pz.	XLVIII Pz.Korps	22	9
393rd Battery	Kempf	Raus	12	0

*   Of these seven were armed with the short 7.5cm L24 gun.
** Of these four were armed with the short 7.5cm L24 gun.

Source: StuG-Lage, BA-MA RH 10/62.

A few divisions also had assault guns included in their organization, as shown in Table 4.3.

TABLE 4.3: DIVISIONAL StuG BATTALIONS, 4 JULY 1943

StuG Battalion	Army Area Deployed in	Corps Subordinated to	Number of StuG	Number of StuH
Großdeutschland	4th Pz.	XLVIII Pz.Korps	35	0
1st SS	4th Pz.	II. SS-Pz.Korps	35	0
2nd SS	4th Pz.	II. SS-Pz.Korps	34	0
3rd SS	4th Pz.	II. SS-Pz.Korps	35	0

Source: Pz.AOK 4, O.Qu Anlagen zum KTB, Tätigkeitsberichte von der Abteilungen. BA-MA RH 21-4/450.

A much more powerful, though also much less mobile, assault gun was the Ferdinand. It was known by many names, sometimes called Elefant or Porsche-Tiger. When the Tiger project was initiated, Porsche and Henschel were given the task of developing a suitable vehicle. Henschel's version was selected for mass production. Porsche then decided to build another type of vehicle, using components already produced for the refused Tiger version. This ended up as a 65 ton assault gun,[28] armed with the 88mm L71 PAK 43. This gun was so powerful that its shell could penetrate all enemy armour at distances over 3,000m.[29] The frontal armour was 200mm thick, making it totally impervious to any enemy gun. The sides carried thinner armour, 80mm, giving a protection similar to the Tiger I. With a top speed of only 30km/h and a horsepower to weight ratio of 9.2hp/ton,[30] the Ferdinand could hardly be considered a vehicle of rapid movement and exploitation. However, its intended role in operation Zitadelle was rather to be a battering ram, where its heavy armour would allow it to get through the thick Soviet defences. One disadvantage with the vehicle was the lack of machine-guns. This was a deficiency in close combat and it was not rectified until after operation Zitadelle, presumably as a result of experiences in that battle.

Only 90 of these large assault guns were produced and 89 were present on 4 July 1943. Of these 44 each were issued to 653rd Tank Destroyer Battalion and 654th Tank Destroyer Battalion. They fought the battle under command of 9th Army,[31] as part of 656th Tank Destroyer Regiment, which comprised staff only, apart from one Ferdinand of its own.

It should be emphasized that no Ferdinands fought in the Army Group South sector during operation Zitadelle. It is a common mistake in Soviet publications (including western literature based mainly on Soviet sources) to state that Ferdinands were present in 4th Panzer Army.[32]

A vehicle of very different character was the Sturmpanzer IV, or Brummbär (Grizzly Bear). It was constructed as a result of experiences in the Stalingrad fighting. Its main armament was a short-barrelled 15cm howitzer in a fully armoured box-like superstructure. The low muzzle velocity, 280 m/s,[33] rendered it unable to fight enemy tanks, but it could fire a very destructive 38kg HE shell against other targets.[34] Like the Ferdinand the first version of Sturmpanzer IV had no machine-gun in the superstructure. SturmPz IV was built on the Panzer IV chassis, but the armour was thicker and the vehicle heavier. The vehicle was rather specialized though, and was never produced in great number.[35] Only one unit had these Brummbärs in operation Zitadelle and this was 216th Sturmpanzer Abteilung, which belonged to 656th Panzerjäger Regiment in 9th Army. The battalion had 45 Brummbärs when the battle began.[36] It received 10 Brummbär as replacements for losses between 11 and 18 July.[37]

SOVIET ARMOUR

Soviet tanks did not display as great a variation as German AFVs. This has frequently been regarded as a major reason for their greater production numbers. While this certainly did contribute, the main reasons for the greater Soviet production is rather to be found in greater tank production facilities[38] (lend-lease also provided a very important contribution to machine tools necessary for Soviet tank production)[39] and in German slowness in mobilizing all national resources for war production. At this period of the war the main Soviet production was tanks, while production of assault guns was still very small. Therefore the number of assault guns (SUs) in the Red Army was few. Central Front had six SU regiments, which together had 91 SUs of various types and the Voronezh Front had four regiments, with a total of 57 SUs.[40] This compares with the fact that the fronts had 3,341 tanks.[41]

At this stage of the war Soviet AFV production utilized three different chassis.[42] The lightest was the T-70 chassis, which was used both for the T-70 tank and the SU-76 self-propelled gun. The value of a tank carrying a 45mm gun of ordinary qualities coupled with rather poor protection, without any advantage in mobility over medium tanks, was now considered dubious. Also it had a crew of two only. Consequently the T-70 was later phased out of production in October 1943.[43]

The SU-76 resembled the German Marder II, self-propelled anti-tank gun, but its intended role on the battlefield was more similar to the

Sturmgeschütz III. The Soviet 76mm gun did not have armour-piercing capabilities to match the German 7.5cm StuK 40 (similar in performance to the 7.5cm KwK 40 in the Panzer IV). It seems to have been produced due to the desire to utilize existing production lines, rather than due to demands from the crews.[44] It had only been in series production for six months at the time of operation Zitadelle.[45] Thus the vehicle was not widely present. It was not until 1944 the SU-76 was produced in great numbers.[46]

The most important Soviet tank, both numerically and qualitatively, was of course the T-34. Since its combat debut it had seen only minor modifications, a testimony to the soundness of the design. In 1943 it was still more mobile than any other medium tank, and indeed even more mobile than most light tanks. Its revolutionary sloped armour was still above average, indeed it was almost as well protected frontally as the German Tiger I. However, in terms of firepower the T-34 was no longer the dominant tank. Its 76mm gun had a relatively low muzzle velocity compared with the new generation of German tank guns, resulting in poor armour penetration capabilities and inferior accuracy when firing at longer ranges. The gun was not able to penetrate the Tiger I's frontal armour at any range, and even that of the Panzer IV presented difficulties. Added to the lack of gunpower was the poor internal layout of the turret, which only allowed two men to work in the turret, overloading them with the tasks of aiming, loading, observing and commanding.

The need for up-gunning (improving armaments) had been realized for some time, but the examination of a captured Tiger spurred efforts to provide the T-34 with more firepower. Two new models were currently being developed, both carrying the 85mm ZiS-S-53 gun. These were the SU-85 and the T-34/85, the former being a turretless tank destroyer. They did restore superiority over the Panzer IV in terms of armament and armour, and close parity with the Tiger I. The superiority in mobility was still considerable. Neither of these new Soviet vehicles could challenge the Panther in terms of gun power and frontal protection, but still they did present a considerable improvement. Unfortunately for the Red Army, neither of these two vehicles were ready in time for the clash north and south of Kursk, despite some authors stating that one or other of them took part in the battle.[47]

Nevertheless, the T-34 armed with the 76mm gun was a useful and combat-proven vehicle. It must also be remembered that a significant number of the German tanks on the eastern front were of types clearly inferior to the T-34. The process of upgrading the *Panzertruppen* with Tigers, Panthers and late model Panzer IVs would take some time. In the meantime many German tank crews would have to operate their ageing vehicles to the best of their ability.

Another assault gun existed on the T-34 chassis, the SU-122. This resembled the German StuH III, in terms of combat characteristics.[48] It was armed with a short-barrelled 122mm howitzer and was not suitable for employment against enemy tanks. The SU-122's main task was direct-fire support against enemy strongpoints and fortifications, a task for which its armament was very suitable. Later, when heavier ISU (based on the IS-chassis) became available, the production of SU-122 was discontinued.

A vehicle causing more worries than the T-34 was the KV heavy tank. It carried the same gun as the T-34, had only marginally thicker frontal armour (though considerably thicker side and rear armour) and was considerably slower and heavier and also more expensive to produce. The Red Army tried to remedy this with KV-1S which had thinner armour than the KV-1 model 42. Thus the vehicle became lighter but the superiority that the thick armour had provided against German tanks and anti-tanks disappeared in the face of the increasing number of German 75mm guns on the eastern front.[49] The arguments in favour of continued production of the KV were marginal. Production of the KV-1S ceased in 1943, but limited numbers took part in the Kursk battle. Central Front had 100 heavy tanks on 1 July 1943 while Voronezh Front had 105 heavy tanks.[50] The regimental headquarters of a Guards (heavy) Breakthrough Tank Regiment[51] in the summer of 1943 had one HQ tank, a reconnaissance section with three armoured cars, a signal section and a maintenance section. It controlled four Heavy Tank Companies, each with an HQ tank and two platoons of two tanks, giving a total strength of 21 heavy tanks, 3 armoured cars and 214 men.

The KV chassis was also utilized for the SU-152 assault gun. It was designed for close fire support, thus it carried the 152mm ML-30S weapon as main armament. This provided heavy fire power against enemy strong points, though the ammunition carried within the vehicle was limited to only 20 rounds.[52] The gun was also useful against enemy tanks, at least at shorter distances. The relatively low muzzle velocity resulted in limited accuracy at longer ranges. Protection was not as good as on the KV, but the vehicle was still about as heavy, resulting in a similar level of automotive performance. During operation Zitadelle it seems that SU-152 was only deployed on the Central Front.[53]

The opposing tank forces in the summer 1943 were both in a period of transition. Germany, being forced to revamp her tank fleet due to the evident Soviet technological superiority in 1941, now began to harvest the results of the design work as several new types entered service. Kursk was to serve as the ultimate test of the new designs. For the Red Army, new design work had been spurred by the indications of German efforts to introduce more powerful vehicles. Unfortunately for the Red Army the results of the Soviet work did not appear in time for the great clash in July 1943.

NOTES

1. P. Chamberlain and H.L. Doyle, *Encyclopedia of German Tanks of WW II* (Arms & Armour Press, London, 1978), p. 136.
2. Ibid., pp. 261–2. Open topped vehicles are not included in the figures.
3. Ibid., p. 142.
4. The total production of Tiger Is up to 30 June 1943 was 347 Tigers of which 54 had already been lost (write-offs). The German Army had 240 Tigers in their arsenal on 1 July thus almost 61 per cent of Tigers in service was taking part in operation Zitadelle. B. Müller-Hillebrand, *Das Heer 1933–1945*, Vol. III, *Anhang B* (Mittler & Sohn, Frankfurt am Main, 1954–69), and E. Kleine and V. Kühn, *Tiger, Die Geschichte einer legendärischen Waffe 1942–1945* (Motorbuch, Stuttgart, 1981), pp. 79, 84–6.
5. Kleine and Kühn, *Tiger, Die Geschichte einer legendärischen Waffe 1942–1945*, pp. 79, 84–6. BA-MA RH 21-4/450, PzA.O.K 4 O.Qu Anlage 11 zum KTB Tätigkeits-berichte v.d. Abteilungen, Unit reports for 30 June 1943.
6. Kleine and Kühn, pp. 84–6.
7. The Red Army had conducted extensive test firing on a captured Tiger 24–30 April 1943. The test showed that the present armour-piercing round of the 76mm F-34 tank gun had difficulties penetrating the side armour of the Tiger even at distances of 200m. Thus better ammunition was demanded. Istoricheskii Archiv no. 5 1993: *Obespechit Prevoskhodstvo Tankov, Donkladnye zapinksi I.V. Stalin 1942–1944*, p. 108.
8. 3rd company of 503rd Heavy Tank Battalion was attached to 25th Panzer Regiment (7th Panzer Division). During the first day of operation Zitadelle part of 25th Pz.Regt. crossed the Donets over a bridge that could not take vehicles over 30 ton, forcing the Tigers to wait until a new bridge had been constructed. A Rubbel (ed.), *Erinnerungen an die Tigerabteilung 503 1942–45* (Selbstverlag, Bassum, 1990), p. 517.
9. B. Müller-Hillebrand, *Das Heer 1933–1945*, Vol. III, *Anhang B*.
10. This was also confirmed in a report by the former commander of 5th Guards Tank Army, P.A. Rotmistrov in a report to Stalin dated 30 August 1944 (Rotmistrov was appointed deputy commander of Red Army Armoured and Mechanized Forces on 8 August 1944). According to Rotmistrov 'on the whole the T-34 is powerless against the T-V [Tank-V = Panther], especially the 85mm gun'. Istoricheskii Arkhiv no. 5, 1993, *Obespechit Prevoskhodstvo Sovetskikh Tankov, Dokladnye zapinski I.V. Stalin 1942–44*, p. 111.
11. Chamberlain and Doyle, *Encyclopedia of German Tanks*, p. 261.
12. Karl R. Pawlas, *Datenblätter für Heeres-Waffen, Fahrzeuge und Gerät*, Publizistisches Archiv für Militär- und Waffenwesen, Nürnberg, 1976, pp. 143, 148. The prices do not include the cost of the armament and radio. Another way to see the cost is the price per ton, Panzer IV 4,138 RM per ton (103,462 RM/25 ton) while Panther was 2,613 RM per ton (117,100 RM/44.8 ton) and Tiger cost 4,400 RM per ton (250,800 RM/57 ton).

70

13. Ibid., p. 150.
14. Average monthly loss rate for Panthers amounted to 12.7 per cent during the period 1 Jan 1944 to 31 Jan 1945. During the same time the rate for the Pz IV was 14.7 per cent. The calculations are based on the tables of monthly losses and stock in Müller-Hillebrand, *Das Heer*, Vol. III, *Anhang B*. The average has been calculated by weighting the monthly rates with the monthly losses, to make the months with more intensive combat more important in the calculation. Figures of the same quality are not available for tanks of other nations but the US Army suffered losses of medium tanks in Normandy of 26.6 per cent in June, 24.4 per cent in July and 25.3 per cent in August. Both the percentages and absolute numbers were greater than that of any month for the Panther (July 1944 was the peak with 347 lost tanks, resulting in a percentage of 16.4). Figures are taken from Ruppental, *US Army in WWII: Logistical support of the Armies*, Vol I. pp. 522–3. However it must be said that comparisons between armies are somewhat artificial, since tank losses depend heavily on crew training, tactics, leadership, strength of opposition, etc. The main point here is that the Pz IV was a less cost-effective vehicle than the Panther. It should also be remembered that during periods of retreat (quite common for the Germans during the time from which the numbers above are taken) many tanks were lost due to lack of fuel or spare parts, thrown tracks, bogging down, etc. During offensive operations such incidents only cause the vehicle to be out of action for some time, not a total loss. Also, when possible, the Panther battalion in the Panzer divisions was given spearhead roles with the Panzer IVs as flank protection. The loss rates calculated above should thus be seen as representing situations relatively favourable for the Panzer IV compared to the Panther.
15. The turret ring of the Daimler-Benz chassis was 50mm smaller. T. Jentz, *Germany's Panther Tank* (Shiffer, Atglen, 1995), p. 18.
16. H. Guderian, *Panzer Leader* (Futura, London, 1982), p. 310.
17. For further information about Bergepanther see H. Doyle and T. Jentz, *Panther Variants 1942–45* (Osprey, London, 1997), pp. 12–16.
18. 346 Tigers and Panthers of a total strength of 2,459 tanks and assault guns (see Table 2.1 in Chapter 2).
19. Müller-Hillebrand, *Das Heer*, Vol. III, *Anhang B*.
20. BA-MA RH 21-4/450, Pz.A.O.K.4 O.Qu Anlage 11 zum KTB Tätigkeitsberichte v.d.Abteilungen. Also RH 10-141 to 143, 145-146, 148-149, 155-157, 209, 312-314 Divisional reports to the General of Panzertroops.
21. F.M. von Senger und Etterlin, *Die Kampfpanzer von 1916–1966* (J.F. Lehmanns Verlag, 1966, München), p. 68.
22. Chamberlain and Doyle, *Encyclopedia of German Tanks*, p. 89.
23. See Chapter 3.
24. Especially after the introduction of Sturmgeschütz III with a long 75mm gun.
25. Pawlas, *Datenblätter für Heeres-Waffen*, pp. 143, 153. The prices do not include the cost of the armament and radio.
26. BA-MA RH 10/62 and BA-MA RH 21-4/450, PzA.O.K 4 O.Qu Anlage 11 zum KTB Tätigkeitsberichte v.d. Abteilungen, unit reports for 30 June 1943.
27. Panzer-Lage Ost (Nach Gen.Qu.), BA-MA RH 10/61 and StuG-Lage Ost (Nach Gen.Qu.), BA-MA RH 10/62.
28. Another new heavyweight which caused problems for recovery of damaged vehicles. According to a Red Army report of the 21 Ferdinands found on the battlefield in the areas surrounding Ponyri ten vehicles had been left because of AT-mine damage. M. Svirin, *Tyazheloe Shturmovoe Orudie Ferdinand* (Armada, Moscow, 1999), p. 46.
29. See charts in Appendix 13.

30. Chamberlain and Doyle, *Encyclopedia of German Tanks*, p. 140.

31. BA-MA RH 10/246. 656. PzJg Reg, Meldung vom 1 July 1943.

32. Zitadelle is far from the only operation where Soviet literature gives an exaggerated number of Ferdinands. Grylev talks about 6 Ferdinand battalions with a T/O&E strength of 45 vehicles per battalion in January 1944 (A. N. Grylev, *Dnepr, Karpaty, Krym* (Nauka, Moscow, 1970), pp. 15–16). Moskalenko states that 253 new Ferdinand assault guns were with Army Group South in July 1943. Either he has confused Ferdinands with assault guns (which mainly were of the type StuG III G) or else he is completely misinformed (K.S. Moskalenko, *Ha Yugo Zapadnom Napravlenii 1943–45* (Nauka, Moscow, 1973)), p. 16. It should be remembered that only 90 Ferdinands were ever produced. A plausible explanation as to why Soviet sources report too many Ferdinands, proposed by M. Svirin in *Tyazheloe Shturmovoe Orudie Ferdinand*, is that during the years 1943–49 in archival material almost all German self-propelled guns are referred to as Ferdinands.

33. Chamberlain and Doyle, *Encyclopedia of German Tanks*, p. 245.

34. Pawlas, *Datenblätter für Heeres-Waffen*, p. 79.

35. 298 were produced during the war (Chamberlain and Doyle, *Encyclopedia of German Tanks*, p. 101).

36. BA-MA RH 10/246. 656. PzJg Reg, Meldung vom 1 July 1943.

37. BA-MA RH 20-9/446. A.O.Kraft O.U den 18.7.1943. An gep.kfz sind eingetroffen a/ [*sic*].

38. During the period 1930–39, the Soviet union produced 25,903 tanks, with a peak in 1936 (4,803 tanks), according to S.J. Zaloga and J. Grandsen, *Soviet Tanks and Combat Vehicles of WWII* (Arms & Armour Press, London, 1984), p. 108. This actually exceeded German wartime production (excluding assault guns).

39. B.V. Sokolov, *The Role of Lend-Lease in Soviet Military Efforts, 1941–1945*, pp. 580–1, article in *Journal of Slavic Military Studies*, Vol. 7, no. 3 (Frank Cass, London, September 1994).

40. Central had 25 SU-152, 32 SU-122, 18 SU-76 and 16 SU-76 (on Pz III chassis) while Voronezh had 24 SU-122 and 33 SU-76. M. Kolomiets and M. Svirin, *Kurskaya Duga* (EksPrint NV, Moscow, 1998), p. 7 and *Boevoy Sostav Sovetskoy Armii, chast III* (Voenizdat, Moscow, 1972).

41. *Voenno-Istoricheskii Zhurnal*, no. 4, 1968, *Dokumenty i Materiali: Kurskaya Bitva v Tsifrakh*, p. 61.

42. S.J. Zaloga and J. Grandsen, *Soviet Tanks and Combat Vehicles of WWII*, p. 225.

43. Ibid., p. 140.

44. Ibid., pp. 156–9.

45. Ibid.

46. Production in 1942 was 26 vehicles, in 1943 it was 1,928, while during 1944 they produced 7,155 SU-76. Zaloga and Grandsen, ibid., p. 225.

47. Stated in R. Cross, *Citadel* (Michael O'Mara, London), p. 189, for example. However, Zaloga and Grandsen, p. 165, make it clear that the SU-85 was not rolling from the production lines until August 1943. See also Zaloga and Grandsen on the even later introduction of the T-34/85.

48. The total production of StuH III was 1,217 vehicles while the total production of SU-122 was 1,100. The production of SU-122 was ended in summer 1944.

49. Panzer IV F2, Panzer IV G, Marder II, Marder III, Sturmgeschütz IIIF8, Sturmgeschütz IIIG and 7.5cm Pak 40 which had been introduced in 1942.

50. *Dokumenty i Materialy; Kurskaya Bitva v Tsifrakh* (Vizh, no. 6, 1968), p. 61.

51. Charles C. Sharp, *Soviet Order of Battle World War II*, Vol. III, *'Red Storm' Soviet Mechanized Corps and Guards Armored Units 1942 to 1945* (George F. Nafziger,

West Chester, OH, 1995), p. 90.

52. Zaloga and Grandsen, *Soviet Tanks and Combat Vehicles*, p. 179.

53. According to *Dokumenty i Materialy: Kurskaya Bitva v Tsifrakh* (Vizh, no. 6, 1968, pp. 61, 63) only the Central Front had heavy SUs on 1 July 1943. Neither the Voronezh nor the Steppe Front had any.

5

The Air War

THE GERMAN AIR EFFORT

When discussing ground operations it is comparatively easy to define the geographical limits of a battlefield and establish which ground units operated within the area. Also, ground units tend to move relatively slowly in or out of that area, making it comparatively easy to keep track of these movements. Air units, on the other hand, owing to their range, are much more difficult to tie to a particular battle. From a single base, an air unit can conceivably participate in many battles or operations taking place simultaneously.

The land battle started in July but the summer campaign in the sky had already started in May. An important object was of course to attain air superiority. Also, great efforts were made to slow down the opponent's movements of units and supplies to the Kursk area. However, since the offensive was delayed, these efforts had little effect on the respective ground forces, but it did tie down air power resources.

During the preparations for Zitadelle both sides committed air assets to the Kuban bridgehead in the south. According to Soviet history the air campaign over Kuban started on 17 April and ended on 7 June. The Red Air Force reported that it flew 35,000 sorties during this campaign and made a claim of 800 kills in air combat.[1] It should be noted that claims are quite often very exaggerated. They are however included here, since they at least give some measure of the magnitude of air battles fought. The Soviet claims given here can be compared with the fact that the Germans, on the entire eastern front during the three months from April to June, lost 256 fighters, 245 bombers and 115 dive-bombers.[2]

The air campaign for the summer battles of 1943 around Kursk started on 6 May when Soviet aircraft from several air armies raided German airfields. The Soviets expected that the German offensive against Kursk would start between 10 and 12 May and they hoped to cripple the

74

Luftwaffe before the offensive. For three days Soviet units attacked German airfields and claimed that the Germans had lost 506 aircraft while the Red Air force had lost only 122.[3]

The Red Air Force also attacked railway lines, roads and troop-concentration areas with the purpose of delaying the German build-up. The 2nd and 16th Air Armies made 1,909 sorties against German communication lines. Against the German assembly areas around the Kursk bulge, the Red Air Force carried out 7,987 sorties.[4]

Since Hitler was delaying the start of the offensive, the Luftwaffe took advantage of this delay to start a strategic air campaign against Soviet industry. Hans Jeschonnek, the Luftwaffe's chief of staff, was a strong supporter of air support to the army, thus the demands for air support for the army had priority over strategic air war.[5] Now, however, an opportunity existed for a limited strategic campaign. Luftwaffe bombers attacked Gorki (tank-production plant), Saratov (ball-bearing plant and oil refinery) and Yaroslavl (rubber industry). The Germans staged almost 1,200 sorties against these three cities.[6] The German losses of bomber aircraft were low. For example, *Kampfgeschwader* 55 flew 300 sorties during this campaign and lost only two aircraft.[7]

THE SOVIET AIR EFFORT

The Red Air force reacted to this strategic air campaign by staging attacks on German bomber airfields. Air units from three air armies (1st, 2nd, 15th) and the bomber force (long-range aviation) attacked German airfields during the three days from 8 to 10 June. They claimed to have destroyed 249 German aircraft (168 on the ground and 81 in the air) during these missions.[8]

The Red Army assigned air armies to front-commands, enabling ground forces to take full advantage of the air support. Usually, one front had one air army assigned. The following air armies were in the area around Kursk: 1st Air Army (West Front), 2nd Air Army (Voronezh Front), 5th Air Army (Steppe Front), 15th Air Army (Bryansk Front), 16th Air Army (Central Front) and 17th Air Army (South-Western Front). Of these six air armies, according to Soviet sources, three took part in the defensive fighting initially. These were the 2nd, 16th and 17th Air Army. The 5th Air Army entered combat in mid-July. When the Red Army started the counter-offensive against Orel two more entered the fighting, the 1st and 15th.

An air army had as its basic unit the air division, which normally controlled three air regiments (resulting in 124 aircraft, unless it was a bomber division, in which case it had 98 aircraft). Thus, an air regiment usually had 40 aircraft (except bomber regiments, which had 32 aircraft). When the war started air divisions existed that were mixed but later this was not very common. The division had one category of regiments – fighter, bomber or attack. However, the types could be mixed at the air-corps level. One air corps controlled two or three divisions. Of the 14 air corps in the defensive phase six were mixed.[9]

TABLE 5.1: NUMBERS OF AIRCRAFT IN SOVIET AIR ARMY UNITS ON 4 JULY 1943[10]

	Fighters	Sturmoviks	Day-bombers	Night-bombers	Recce Aircraft	Total
2nd Air Army	389	276	172	34	10	881
16th Air Army	455	241	260	74	22	1,052
17th Air Army	218	383	70	64	–	735
Total	1,062	900	502	172	32	2,668

To these aircraft should be added 320 bombers belonging the Red Air Force Bomber Command[11] and 208 fighters belonging to the Air Defence Forces (PVO)[12] around Kursk. Further, to these forces it has to be taken into account that 1st and 15th Air Army soon joined in and that also 5th Army entered the combat during July. This would add an additional 2,787 aircraft.[13] Thus, the Red Air Force had around Kursk almost 6,000 aircraft, a mighty force to be encountered by the Luftwaffe.

THE COST OF THE BATTLE

German air losses

The Germans on the eastern front had divided their air units into four large air commands called *Luftflotten*. They were numbered 1st, 4th, 5th and 6th. The size of them varied a lot. For example on 31 May 1943 the smallest (5th) had only 235 aircraft and the largest (4th) had 1,728 aircraft.[14] In Zitadelle and the battles that followed it two air commands took part (6th Luftflotte with Army Group Centre and 4th Luftflotte with Army Group South) but not all of their units because the battlefield of Zitadelle was only a small part of their area of responsibility. The units from 6th Luftflotte that participated were controlled by 1st Air Division and those from 4th Luftflotte were controlled by VIIIth Air Corps.

The basic unit for the Luftwaffe was the *Geschwader* which had three Groups (*Gruppen*). Usually a *Geschwader* had 94 aircraft (4+30+30+30) but as for ground forces, the strength of the units was adapted to the demands of war, for example a fighter *Geschwader* might have four Groups each with 67 aircraft. By enlarging the Group (thereby becoming a mini-*Geschwader*) it could stay longer in combat, important in defence of the *Reich*.[15]

TABLE 5.2: GERMAN AIR LOSSES BETWEEN 5 AND 15 JULY 1943[16]

	1st Air Division		VIIIth Air Corps	
	Number of Sorties	Aircraft Lost	Number of Sorties	Aircraft Lost
5 July	2,088	7	2,387	19
6 July	1,023	7	1,686	7
7 July	1,687	3	1,829	10
8 July	1,173	2	1,686	5
9 July	877	5	1,621	11
10 July	1,136	7	682	3
11 July	933	2	1,039	14
12 July	1,111*	13	654	11
13 July	1,113	18	656	5
14 July	979	20	1,452	9
15 July	703	10	706	5
Total	12,823	94	14,398	99

Note: *Most sorties were made in support of 2nd Panzer Army.

The two German air commands together had almost 2,000 aircraft as their initial strength. Roughly one-third were bombers, one-third were fighters and one-third were ground-attack planes.[17] Some of the ground attack aircraft were very capable of air-to-air combat, since they were Fw 190F.[18] As seen from Table 5.2 the Germans did not lose many aircraft but the number that remained operational became much lower. For example, *Jagdgeschwader* 51 had 88 Fw 190 A operational at the start of the battle and five days later it was down to 37.[19] During this time the unit had lost seven pilots. With an initial strength of 2,000 aircraft and with over 27,000 sorties in support of the offensive most pilots (crews) had to do several missions over the battlefield each day. Even the bombers had to do that. *Kampfgeschwader* 55 flew 899 sorties in support of the offensive during eight flying days between 6 and 17 July and the day they had the highest number of sorties was 7 July with 178 sorties.[20] They had initially no more than 70 aircraft (He 111H).

Soviet air losses

The Germans[21] claimed to have shot down 923 aircraft between 5 and 8 July and the Soviets admit to having lost 566 aircraft. The claim does not represent confirmed victories, rather what the units claimed to have achieved. Table 5.3 shows all air armies that conducted missions to support the defensive fighting.

TABLE 5.3: SOVIET AIR LOSSES 5–8 JULY 1943[22]

	Number of Sorties	Aircraft Lost
5 July	3,385	176
6 July	2,800	171
7 July	2,770	122
8 July	2,280	97
Total	11,235	566

Over the defensive period as a whole the Red Air Force admitted that it lost almost 1,000 aircraft.[23] The Soviet air units had heavy losses. For example, between 5 and 10 July 2nd Air Army lost 153 fighters, representing 40 per cent losses.[24] 16th Air Army was down to 706 aircraft by 10 July.[25] The Soviet air units claim that during the period from 5 to 8 July they shot down 878 enemy aircraft and destroyed 70 aircraft on the ground.[26] Compared with the real German losses it appears that these claims were grossly exaggerated. Between 5 July and 23 August 1943 the Soviet claim was 3,500 air victories in the battle of Kursk.[27] In the defensive period[28] of the battle 1,400 of them are said to have occurred. They also write that the Germans had 2,980 combat aircraft[29] on the whole eastern front in summer 1943, so it easy to see that something is not correct. Also, if one includes the Soviet claims of aircraft destroyed on the ground and those shot down by Soviet air defence artillery, a total of almost 5,000 will be reached.

One thing though the Soviet forces managed to estimate with almost pinpoint accuracy. They recorded 4,298 enemy sorties on 5 July when the Germans made 4,475 sorties and on the next day they registered 2,100 sorties while the Germans performed 2,709.[30] The total number of sorties the Soviet Army Air force made from 5 to 23 August was 118,000, of which 28,000 were made during the defensive period.[31] Of the sorties during the defensive phase 75 per cent were made by front aviation, 18 per cent by Bomber Command and finally 6 per cent by the air–defence units (PVO) in the area.[32] Based on numbers given above and other sources, 2nd Air

Army flew 11,000 missions[33] during the defensive phase, 16th Air Army 5,870[34] and 17th Air Army 4,230 missions.[35] The two air armies in the south flew 15,230 missions and the single Army in the north only 5,870, the reason for this being that the defensive phase of the battle lasted longer in the south. All missions made by 16th Army after 11 July are recorded as having taken place during the offensive phase.

AIRCRAFT

Considering the quality of aircraft, the Red Air Forces had managed to narrow the gap between them and the Luftwaffe. Most of the German aircraft were of the same basic types as in 1942. The two most important exceptions were the Focke-Wulf 190 and the Henschel 129. The FW 190 was the best piston-engine fighter produced by the Germans during the war. The Hs 129 was not at all so successful as the Fw 190. It was intended to be Germany's counterpart to the Soviet Sturmovik but only 876[36] were accepted by the Luftwaffe. This can be compared with Soviet production of the Sturmovik, which amounted to 36,136.[37] Hence, the Luftwaffe had to use Fw 190 F, Hs 129 and Ju 87 for ground attack.[38] The fighters used were mainly the Messerschmidt Bf 109 G and the Fw 190 A, while the He 111 and the Ju 88 formed the backbone of the bomber force.

The Soviets on the other hand had greatly improved their equipment. The Sturmovik (Il-2) equipped all ground-attack regiments and almost all were the new two-seater version Il-2m3, which had a rear gunner. The Red Air Force had steadily improved their use of ground-attack aircraft in combat and at the same time they were getting better ground-attack planes. These developments affected and hampered the German ground forces in their operations.[39] Also, almost the whole bomber force in the air armies were equipped with the Pe-2, a fast and light bomber aircraft. Their fighter units had started receiving new fighters such as the La-5FN and the Yak-9, which were a great improvement on the fighters one year earlier. It is important to note that the new fighters had 12.7mm instead of 7.62mm machine-guns when equipped with MGs. Thus the Red Air Force had La-5FN, Yak-1b, Yak-7B, Bell P-39 and Yak-9 as fighters, Il-4, A-20 and Pe-2 as bombers and the excellent Il-2 Type 3 for ground attack.

AIRCRAFT AGAINST TANKS

It has often been claimed that the Luftwaffe was a force dedicated to tactical ground support, but actually it had few aircraft suited to that role. Rather, the main components of the Luftwaffe were fighters, medium bombers and reconnaissance units. Only the Ju-87 could be regarded as suitable for tactical ground support. However, this type usually made up less than 10 per cent of the aeroplane inventory of the Luftwaffe. Generally the Luftwaffe conceived its aim to attain air superiority and to conduct interdiction, though this was often designed to support army operations.

Yet even if the Ju 87 had excellent accuracy compared with level-flight bombers, it had certain drawbacks. It had poor survivability unless air superiority had been established. Also, it was vulnerable to AA fire. Additionally, even though its bombing accuracy was excellent, it was not certain to hit enemy tanks, except in isolated lucky instances. The Russian Sturmovik was a more sturdy, survivable aircraft, less dependent on air superiority and weak enemy AA defences on the ground. To improve its ability to destroy enemy tanks, the Ju 87 was fitted with a pair of 37mm cannons fitted under the wings.[40] This gave the Luftwaffe a dedicated tank hunter. This conversion started in early 1943 and the model was called Ju 87G. The other aircraft used by the Luftwaffe at Kursk as a tank hunter was the Henschel Hs 129.

The Henschel Hs 129 was intended to be a dedicated aircraft for tactical ground support but it did not prove the success Luftwaffe had hoped for. The first prototype flew on 26 May 1939 and production started in June 1940.[41] This first production was very limited because of the low power output of the engines. A new engine was needed, which was finally found. The first of these new (Hs 129B-1) were produced in December 1941. Later minor modifications appeared (Hs 129B-2 and B-3).

To provide anti-tank capability an underbelly pod with a 30mm cannon was mounted on the aircraft. Later it was also tried with 37 and 75mm guns. These Henschels with 30mm cannon and the Junkers Ju 87G were the main anti-tank weapons for the Luftwaffe. The Henschel also had difficulties surviving in a hostile environment. For most of the war the Luftwaffe used cannons as the main weapon against tanks. It was not until late 1944 that rockets were used, when the Focke-Wulf Fw 190F-8 was thus equipped.[42] Given the poor results by allied rocket armed fighters against German tanks in Western Europe in 1944[43] it seems that the late German introduction of rockets for anti-tank purposes was a minor disadvantage.

Except for these few aircraft equipped with cannons for tank-hunting the Germans had to try to use bombs against tanks. Here follows the description of a such an attack by an Fw-190F pilot:

Against the enemy tanks and armoured vehicles we usually made skip-bombing attacks, running at speeds of around 485km/h at between 4 and 10 metres above the ground and releasing the bomb just as the tank disappeared beneath our engine cowling. The 250kg bombs used during these attacks would either skip off the ground and into the tank or else smash straight into the tank. The bombs were fused with a one-second delay to give us time to get clear before they went off. It was a very accurate form of attack and we used it often against tanks caught in open country.[44]

The Red Air Force could use the Stormoviks for tank hunting. It had two 23mm cannons and usually carried RS-82 or RS-132 rockets. Some Stormoviks (Il-2 Type 3M) had 37mm (NS-37) instead of 23mm cannons. These were mounted in a gondola under the wings, each with 50 rounds. Because of the extra weight of these cannons compared to the 23mm cannons, the underwing rocket rails were deleted.[45] Stormoviks thus adapted had quite demanding flight characteristics compared with a normal Stormovik, which was one reason for the limited production of these tank hunters with 37mm cannons. There was another fighter aircraft equipped with a 37mm cannon, the Bell P-39 Airacobra.[46] These could also be used for tank hunting. In addition to cannons and rockets the Soviet forces had a new anti-tank bomb, the PTAB-2.5 or 1.5.

This was a hollow-charge bomb and is described as very effective.[47] Aircraft could carry 200 of these small bombs.[48] But were these bombs really effective against tanks? The 16th Air Army dropped 23,315 of these bombs and used 4,000 RS-82 rockets during the defensive phase, while 2nd Air Army dropped 69,000 of the PTABs and used 7,448 RS-82 rockets between 5 July and 14 July.[49]

Between them these two Air Armies dropped 100,000 of PTAB bombs on German Panzer forces and the effect was quite limited since the Red Army claimed that just 3,147 tanks and assault guns were disabled by all Soviet forces (tanks, assault guns, anti-tanks guns, anti-tank mines and so on).

NOTES

1. M.N. Kozhevnikov, *The Command and Staff of the Soviet Army Air Force in the Great Patriotic War 1941–1945* (Moscow, 1977; trans. US Air Force, Washington, DC), p. 115.
2. W. Murray, *Luftwaffe – Strategy for Defeat 1933–45* (Grafton, London, 1988), p. 221.
3. O. Groehler, *Geschichte des Luftkriegs 1910 bis 1980* (Militärverlag der DDR, Berlin, 1981), p. 363.
4. *Sovetskie Voenno-Vozdushnye Sily v Velikoy Otechestvennoy Voine 1941–1945* (Voenizdat, Moscow, 1968), pp. 176f.

5. H. Boog, *Die Deutsche Luftwaffenführung 1935–1945* (Deutsche Verlags-Anstalt, Stuttgart, 1982), pp. 178–80.

6. According to Groehler 654 sorties against Gorki, 420 against Saratov and 110 against Yaroslavl. The losses were 41 aircraft, whether this is Soviet claims or reported German losses is unclear. O. Groehler, *Geschichte des Luftkriegs*, p. 392.

7. W. Dierich, *Kampfgeschwader 55 'Greif'* (Motorbuch Verlag, Stuttgart, 1994), pp. 304–8.

8. M.N. Kozhevnikov, *The Command and Staff of the Soviet Army Air Force in the Great Patriotic War*, p. 120.

9. W.C. Green and W.R. Reeves, *The Soviet Military Encyclopedia Abridged English-Language Edition*, Vols A–F (Westview Press, Boulder, CO, 1993), pp. 21–2, 33, 36.

10. G.A. Koltunov and B.G. Soloviev, *Kurskaya Bitva* (Voenizdat, Moscow, 1970), p. 77. *Voenno-Istoricheskii Zhurnal*, no. 6, 1968, *Dokumenty i Materialy: Kurskaya Bitva v Tsifrakh (period Oborony)*, p. 63. *16-ya Vozdushnaya* (Moscow, 1973), p. 90. They show different numbers of reconnaissance aircraft, the Air Army history gives 22 while Koltunov and Soloviev and VIZh only 4.

11. G.A. Koltunov and B.G. Soloviev, *Kurskaya Bitva*, p. 77. M.N. Kozhevnikov, *The Command and Staff of the Soviet Army Air Force in the Great Patriotic War*, p. 126. Both these sources give 320, while in *Voenno-Istoricheskii Zhurnal*, no. 6, 1968, *Dokumenty i Materialy: Kurskaya Bitva v Tsifrakh (period Oborony)*, p. 63, the number of bombers is 480. The difference could be explained by the lower number representing operational and the higher on hand but the problem is that all sources have similar numbers for the air armies.

12. K.S. Moskalenko, *Bitva Na Kurskoy Duge* (Nauka, Moscow, 1975), p. 124.

13. 1st Air Army had 1,322 aircraft on 10 July, 5th Air Army had 470 aircraft on 5 July and 15th Air Army had 995 aircraft on 10 July. O. Groehler, *Geschichte des Luftkriegs*, p. 371. G.A. Koltunov and B.G. Soloviev, *Kurskaya Bitva*, p. 76.

14. O. Groehler, *Geschichte des Luftkriegs*, p. 376.

15. Dr A. Price, *Luftwaffe Handbook 1939–1945* (second ed.) (Ian Allan, Shepperton, 1986), pp. 13f.

16. E. Klink, *Das Gesetz des Handels, Die Operation 'Zitadelle' 1943* (Deutsche Verlags-Anstalt, Stuttgart, 1966), pp. 337f.

17. O. Groehler, *Geschichte des Luftkriegs*, p. 364. R.P. Hallion, *Strike from the Sky* (Shrewsbury, 1989), p. 250.

18. C. Shores, *Duel for the Sky* (Doubleday, New York, 1985), p. 145.

19. G. Aders and W. Held, *Jagdgeschwader 51 'Mölders'* (Motorbuch Verlag, Stuttgart, 1993), pp. 135f.

20. W. Dierich, *Kampfgeschwader 55 'Greif'*, p. 309.

21. Not including any claim from army units. Almost all independent Flak belonged to the Luftwaffe.

22. M.N. Kozhevnikov, *The Command and Staff of the Soviet Army Air Force in the Great Patriotic War*, pp. 134–6.

23. G.A. Koltunov and B.G. Soloviev, *Kurskaya Bitva*, p. 365. *16-ya Vozdushnaya* (Voenizdat, Moscow, 1973), p. 106. *Sovetskie Voenno-Vozdushnye Sily v Velikoy Otechestvennoy Voine*, p. 186. Strangely, when *Grif Sekretnosti Snyat* by Krivosheev (ed.) was published, a lower loss figure was presented compared with what had been presented during the Soviet period. The book states that 459 aircraft were lost during the defensive phase. *Grif Sekretnosti Snyat* (Voenizdat, Moscow, 1993), p. 370.

24. *Sovetskie Voenno-Vozdushnye Sily v Velikoy Otechestvennoy Voine 1941–1945*, p. 184.

25. *Voenno-Istoricheskii Zhurnal*, no. 7, 1968 *Dokumenty i Materialy: Kurskaya Bitva v Tsifrakh (period Kontrnastupleniya)*, pp. 82–3.

26. M.N. Kozhevnikov, *The Command and Staff of the Soviet Army Air Force in the Great Patriotic War*, pp. 134–6.

27. Ibid., pp. 137 and 142.
28. Central Front 5–11 July, Voronezh Front 5–23 July and Steppe Front 9 July–23 July.
29. M.N. Kozhevnikov, *The Command and Staff of the Soviet Army Air Force in the Great Patriotic War*, p. 127.
30. Ibid., p. 135.
31. O. Groehler, *Geschichte des Luftkriegs*, p. 370. M.N. Kozhevnikov, *The Command and Staff of the Soviet Army Air Force in the Great Patriotic War*, pp. 137 and 142.
32. I.V. Timokhovich, *Operativnoe Iskusstvo Sovetskikh VVS v Velikoy Otechestvennoy Voine* (Voenizdat, Moscow, 1976), p. 201.
33. I.V. Timokhovich, *Sovetskaya Aviatsiya v Bitve pod Kurskom* (Voenizdat, Moscow, 1959), p. 71. In Moskalenko's memoirs the number of sorties are 10,821 for the period from 5 to 17 July. K.S. Moskalenko, *Ha Yugo-Zapadnom Napravlenii 1943–1945* (*Kniga 2*) (Izdatelstvo Nauka, Moscow, 1973), p. 68.
34. Calculated with help of other info. 28,160 missions of which frontal aviation made 75 per cent and 2nd Air together with 17th Air made 15,250. This gives us 21,120 minus 15,250.
35. N.M. Komorokhov (ed.), *17-ya Vozdushnaya Armiya v Boyakh ot Stalingrada do Veny* (Voenizdat, Moscow, 1977), p. 61.
36. Dr A. Price, *Luftwaffe Handbook*, p. 125.
37. O. Groehler, *Geschichte des Luftkriegs*, p. 331.
38. Even of Fw 190F there were few, thus Ju-87 Stuka was still the main aircraft for ground-attack support.
39. W. Schwabedissen, *The Russian Air Force in the Eyes of German Commanders* (Arno Press, New York, 1960), p. 169.
40. A.J. Barker, *Stuka Ju-87* (Chartwell Books, London, 1980), pp. 34 and 57.
41. P. Stachura, D. Bernad and D. Haladéj, *Henschel Hs 129* (MBI, Praha, 1993), pp. 6 and 10.
42. M. Griehl and J. Dressel, *Flugzeuge gegen Panzer*, Waffen-Arsenal Sonderband 16 (Podzun-Pallas, Friedberg, 1990), pp. 45–7.
43. It seems that the reputation for allied rocket-armed fighter-bombers (e.g. the Typhoon) as an effective killer of German tanks is mainly based on wildly exaggerated claims by the pilots. Comparing the efforts made with the actual number of German tanks destroyed by aircraft, the results were almost negligible. See I. Gooderson, *Allied Fighter-Bombers versus German Armour in North-Western Europe 1944–1945: Myths and Realities, Journal of Strategic Studies*, Vol. 14, no. 2 (June, 1991) and A. Price, *Tanks for the Memories*, Air International, June 1998, pp. 340f.
44. A. Price, *Focke-Wulf FW-190 in Combat* (Sutton Publishing, Stroud, 1998), p. 141. It should be emphasized that allied air units in the West were consistently too optimistic about accuracy and effectiveness of their attacks against most targets and in particular tanks. There is no reason to believe that the Germans were considerably more accurate.
45. H-H. Stapfer, *Il-2 Stormovik in action* (Squadron/Signal Publications, Carrollton, 1995), p. 41.
46. B. Gunston, *Allied Fighters of World War II* (Salamander, London, 1981), p. 98; William Green, *War Planes of Second World War; Fighters, Vol. 3* (MacDonald, London, 1968), pp. 170–1. Late 1943 Yak-9T appeared with 37mm cannon between the cylinder blocks.
47. *Sovetskie Voenno-Vozdushnye Sily v Velikoy Otechestvennoy Voine 1941–1945*, p. 180.
48. K.S. Moskalenko (ed.), *Bitva na Kurskoy Duge* (Nauka, Moscow, 1975) p. 82.
49. I.V. Timokhovich, *Sovetskaya Aviatsiya v Bitve pod Kurskom* (Voenizdat, Moscow, 1959), pp. 49 and 71.

6

Chronology of the Offensive

The Kursk salient was attacked by 9th Army from the north and 4th Panzer Army and Army Detachment Kempf from the south. These attacking forces fought two separate battles but German success in one of them could affect the other. German success in either of these could force the Red Army to divert forces to meet the more serious threat. Had the German forces broken through somewhere, it could of course have had a profound impact on the battle in other sectors.

Northern Sector

From east to west the following divisions attacked early in the morning, 216th ID, 78th Assault, 86th ID, 292nd ID, 6th ID, 20th PD, 31st ID, 7th ID and 258th ID. Only one division of the Soviet 48th Army was attacked, the 16th Rifle Division. There were six further rifle divisions assaulted during the morning, 8th RD, 148th RD, 81st RD, 15th RD, 132nd RD and 280th RD.

The German XXIII Corps (216th ID and 78th Assault Division) attacked towards Maloarkhangelsk to secure the right flank of the attacking forces but it did not succeed in penetrating the defence although a breach did occur between 148th RD and 81st RD. Both these divisions suffered heavy casualties, thus forcing Central Front to insert the 74th Rifle Division between them.[1] XXXXI Panzer Corps (86th ID and 292nd ID) had Ponyri as its goal and XXXXVII Panzer Corps (6th ID and 20th PD) strove towards Olkhovatka. The 292nd ID took Ozerki and 86th ID captured Ochki during the day.[2] Finally, XXXXVI Panzer Corps was to secure the right flank of the attacking forces. The furthest advance during the first day was 8km into the defence line of Central Front.[3]

84

Southern Sector

Here four Corps attacked, Corps Raus, III Panzer, II SS-Panzer, and XXXXVIII Panzer Corps. Their assault was mainly directed against two armies from the Voronezh Front, 6th Guards and 7th Guards. The 6th Gds Army had seven rifle divisions of which four (375th RD, 52nd GRD, 67th GRD and 71st GRD) were in forward positions to meet the initial assault. The 52nd GRD was hit so hard by II SS-Panzer Corps that it was split into two parts, one retreating northwest and one northeast.[4] The SS-Divisions reached Bykovka during the first day (a depth of 8km).[5] This caused parts of the Soviet second echelon (51st GRD) to be involved in the fighting.

The XXXXVIII Panzer Corps attacked with its three armoured divisions in the centre and one infantry division advancing on each flank. The attack mainly hit 71st GRD from 6th Gds Army and partly 100th RD from 40th Army. The spearheads of XXXXVIII Panzer Corps managed to advance 7–9 kilometres during this first day. Cherkasskoye was almost completely in German hands. Part of Großdeutschland's Panzer Regiment was unlucky early in the morning, when it advanced into an undiscovered minefield. Twenty-five tanks and assault guns from Großdeutschland were disabled due to mines on 5th July.[6]

If the two attacking corps of 4th Panzer Army had succeeded in making considerable progress during the first day, elements of Army Detachment Kempf were not so lucky. The attack from the bridgehead at Mihailovka towards Stary Gorod failed[7] and 6th Panzer Division was transferred to III Panzer Corps' right flank instead, since it was believed no success would come from further attacks from the bridgehead.[8] The right flank of III Panzer Corps together with Corps Raus had created several bridgeheads across the Northern Donets during the day.

Voronezh Front ordered its reserves to move forward during the day. The 35th Guards Rifle Corps and 2nd Guards Tank Corps were sent to the left flank. The 1st Tank Army moved forward behind 6th Gds Army to take up positions immediately behind its second echelon, along the line Melovoe–Syrtsev–Iakovlevo.[9] Covering the left flank at Iakovlevo was 5th Gds Tank Corps. Furthermore, the commander of 40th Army was ordered to strengthen his left flank to prevent any breach from occurring between his forces and 6th Guards Army.

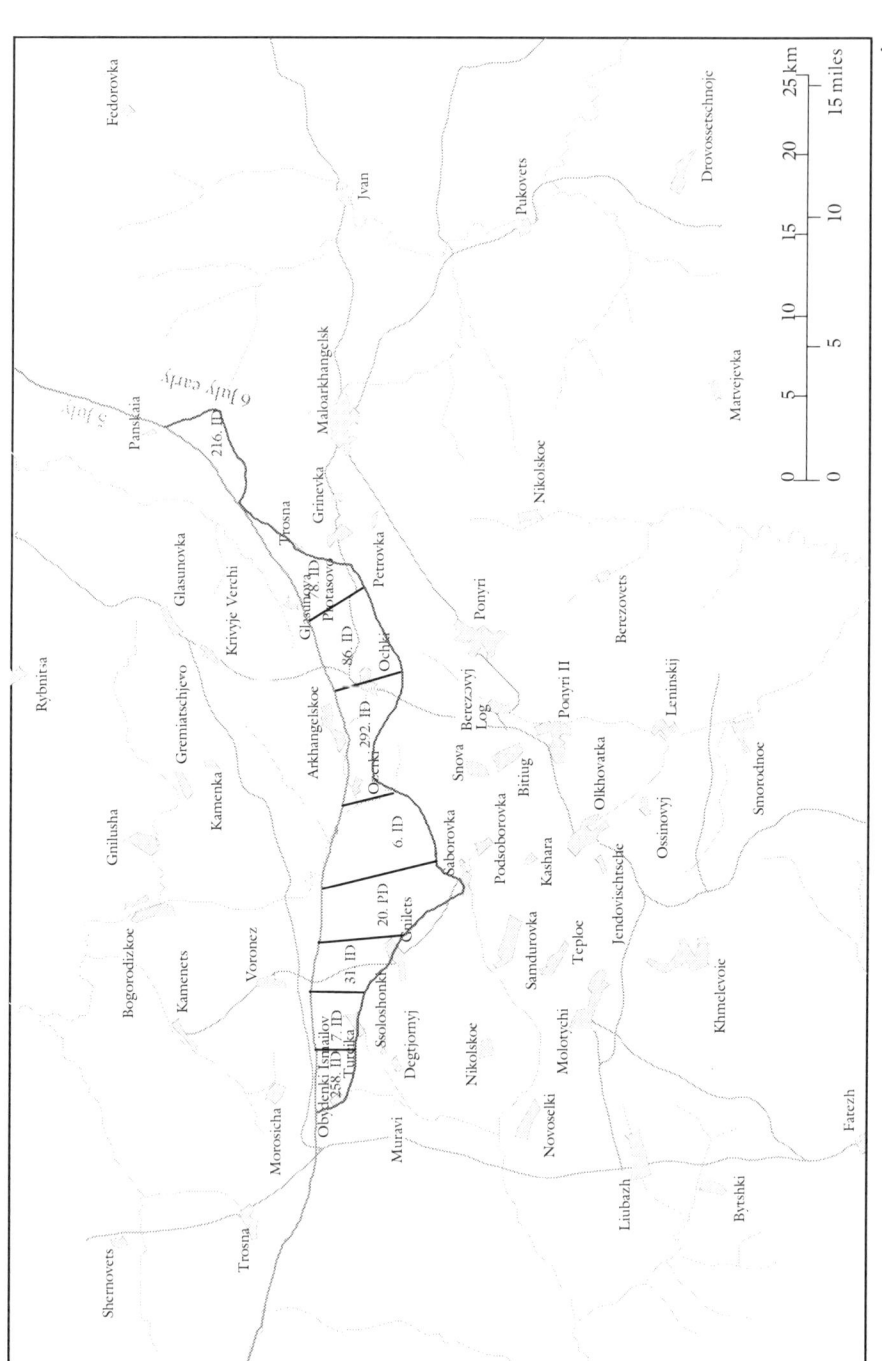

Map 3. 9th Army attacks, 5–6 July

6 JULY

Northern Sector

The Central Front staged a counterattack with the aim of restoring the front line to the same positions it had had on 4 July. The 17th Guards Rifle Corps (6th GRD, 70th GRD and 75th GRD), 16th Tank Corps and 19th Tank Corps had moved forward to perform a synchronized attack. However, 19th Tank Corps was unable to attack before 18.30 since minefields had to be cleared beforehand.[10] The counterattack was supported by 900 guns, 637 mortars and 200 MRLs. The 70th Army had moved 175th RD forward to strengthen their forces on the right. The German left wing was attacked by 148th and 74th Rifle Division. The German forces repelled the Soviet assault, with heavy losses for the attackers. For example, of 50 tanks available to 107th Tank Brigade from 16th TC no less than 46 were disabled by enemy fire.[11] The Germans also started to push the Soviet units back and by the evening of 6 July 13th Army's second defensive belt had been reached in the centre. The 78th Assault Division on the right of XXIII Corps took Protasovo but the attacks on the left wing of the corps stalled.[12]

The Central Front also had to commit 3rd Tank Corps and 307th RD to stop the enemy advance. The 307th RD relieved 81st RD, which had suffered heavy casualties, 2,518 during two days of fighting.[13] In Ponyri, 307th RD took up defensive positions and was reinforced with several GHQ units, for example 129th Tank Brigade and 1422nd SU Regiment. The total number of guns the division had under its control was 380. No division in the Red Army at any time during the war had more. The Germans ordered 2nd Panzer and 9th Panzer Division forward and 9th Panzer joined the attack towards Olkhovatka (XXXXVII Panzer Corps) with a frontal drive on 17th Guards Rifle Corps (whose orders were to attack in the opposite direction).

Southern Sector

The II SS-Panzer Corps continued to push north towards Teterevino with Das Reich and Leibstandarte. At the end of the day they had advanced to the area between Pokrovka and Luchki, forcing 5th Guards Tank Corps to withdraw.[14] Luchki was cleared by Das Reich.[15] The XXXXVIII Panzer Corps' main line of attack, with three divisions, from right to left 167th ID, 11th PD, and GD, was during this day towards the northeast. The corps took Novo Cherkasskoye and Olkhovka and reached the outskirts of Dubrova and Lukhanino. The main enemy forces encountered during the day were 3rd Mechanized Corps: 52nd, 67th and 90th Guards Rifle Divisions. The 3rd Panzer Division attacked to the north and managed to take Zavidorka but the spearhead of the division had to abandon the village because the main part of the division failed to provide the needed support.

The III Panzer Corps enlarged the bridgeheads across the Northern Donets and took control over Generalovka, Krutoi Log and Razumnoe.[16] Even though Corps Raus made some progress during the day it was obvious that the corps was too weak for its task. The 198th ID was ordered forward to reinforce Raus. During the day, Army Detachment Kempf had fought against five rifle Divisions (81st Gds, 78th Gds, 73rd Gds, 213th and 72nd Gds).

On the evening of this day, the Voronezh Front had committed all its reserves except for three rifle divisions in the rear belt of defence for 7th Guards Army. During the evening Stavka decided that 2nd Tank Corps, 10th Tank Corps and 5th Guards Tank Army should reinforce the Voronezh Front. These forces comprised almost 1,000 tanks and assault guns. To improve the air support for the next day, it was decided that the Voronezh Front's Air Army would support the fighting against 4th Panzer Army while the Southwestern Front's Air Army would support 7th Guards Army against Kempf.

7 JULY

Northern Sector

To reinforce the offensive, two further panzer divisions joined the fighting. The 2nd PD relieved 6th ID, which was taken out of the front line, and 18th PD was inserted on the right flank of XXXXI Panzer Corps to support XXXXVII Panzer Corps which now represented the *Schwerpunkt*. The 4th Panzer Division moved forward from its reserve position to be available next day.

The Soviet 70th Army further strengthened its right flank by moving 140th RD towards Samodurovka. The division was subjected to heavy attacks during the day and finally was forced to withdraw from its positions. The 13th Army did not insert any new divisions and the tank corps went over to the defence and was ordered to dig in behind the Rifle Divisions.[17]

The German attacks against Ponyri did not succeed in throwing 307th RD out of the town. XXXXI Panzer Corps only managed to take the

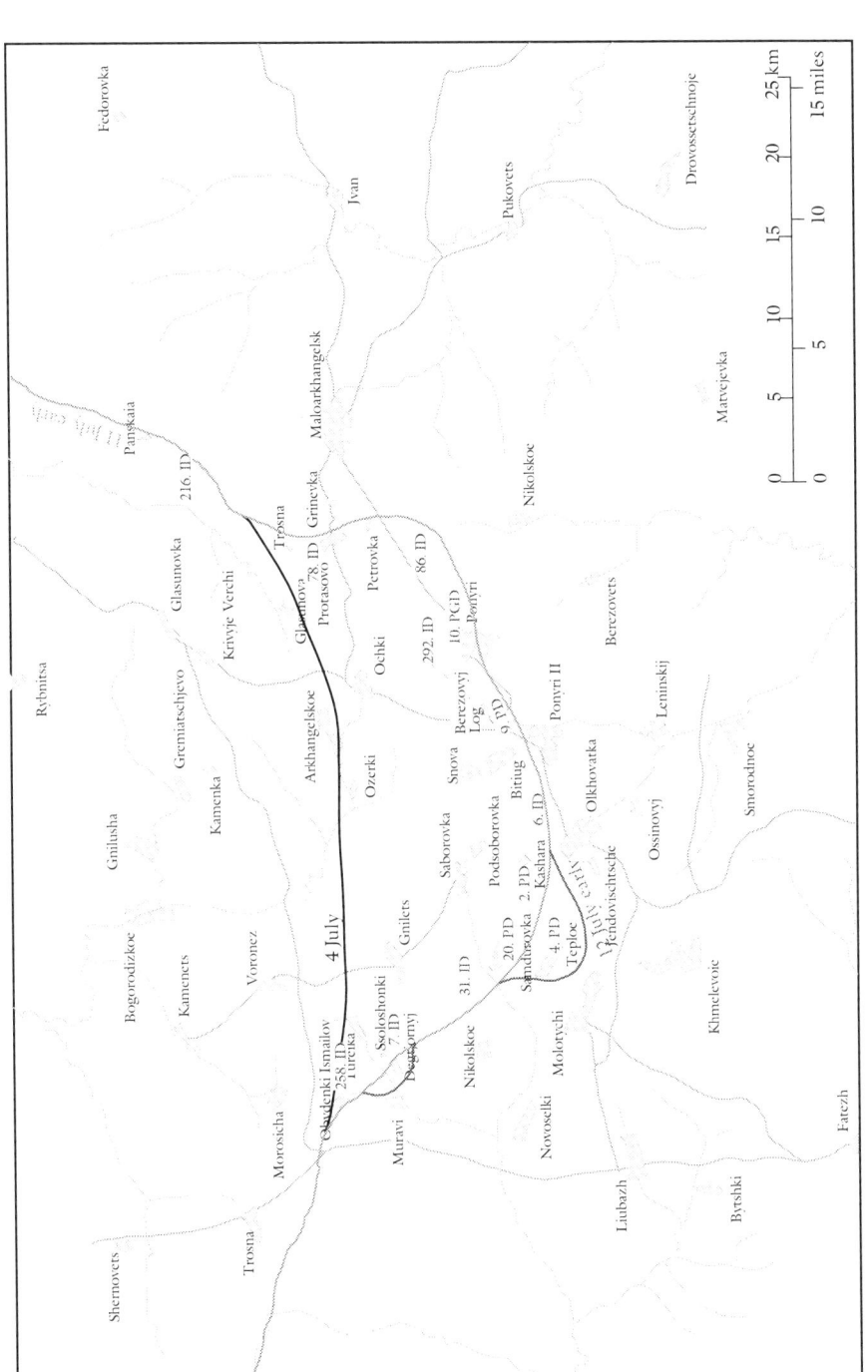

Map 4. 9th Army attacks, 11–12 July

northern part of the town. Neither did XXXXVII Panzer Corps succeed in breaking through to Olkhovatka, although 17th Gds Rifle Corps was pushed back slightly. It lost part of Bitiug during the day. The corps was reinforced with 43rd and 58th Tank Regiments to support it during the hard fighting.[18]

Southern Sector

On this day Teterevino was taken by II SS-Panzer Corps,[19] thus bringing the advance to a depth of 28km. The main push by XXXXVIII Panzer Corps was on its right to help II SS-Panzer Corps to secure its left flank. Lukhanino was attacked in the afternoon by 3rd Panzer Division in an attempt to clear that area of 90th Guards Rifle Division. Part of Großdeutschland attacked towards Syrtsev to help 3rd Panzer in its operations. At the end of the day 1st Tank Army held a line running from Lukhanino–Krasnaia Dubrova–Malenkie Maiacki–Greznoe.

The III Panzer Corps succeeded in taking Sevriukovo, which forced 7th Gds Army to move 111th RD and 270th RD into blocking positions against any advances towards the north.[20]

During the day the Voronezh Front shifted units from 38th and 40th Army to help in defending the road towards Oboyan. These forces included 309th Rifle Division plus three AT brigades, two artillery regiments and a tank regiment. In the evening, the 10th Tank Corps arrived in the Prokhorovka area. Also the Voronezh Front ordered several counter-strokes to be made against the flanks of 4th Panzer Army next day. The following units were to participate: 2nd, 6th, 10th, 2nd Gds, 5th Gds Tank Corps plus 161st RD and 71st GRD (under command of 40th Army).

8 JULY

Northern Sector

Model realized that more forces were needed to achieve a breakthrough. Among the newly committed units was the 4th Panzer Division, which was inserted in the line between 2nd PD and 20th PD to attack towards the hills south of Samodurovka. Also a special corps was created to improve the possibilities for the offensive, Lieut-General von Esebeck took control of 31st Infantry and 20th Panzer Division as Group von Esebeck to improve fighting on the right flank for XXXXVII Panzer Corps.[21] But this was to no avail, since only minor advances were made during the day. Even so the Central Front had to commit 9th Tank Corps during the afternoon to meet these attacks.[22] The 292nd ID, fighting around Ponyri, reported 11 counterattacks against its positions. This unit had to defend grimly, rather than continue its own offensive. The 307th RD had been reinforced with 51st Tank Brigade (3th TC), 103rd Tank Brigade (3rd TC) and 27nd Guards Heavy Tank Regiment for these attacks. Also, 18th Guards Rifle Corps mounted several counterattacks against XXIII Corps.

Southern Sector

To secure the left flank II SS-Panzer Corps began to attack towards Sukho-Solotino and Greznoe. Two Tank Corps attacked II SS-Panzer Corps' right flank during the day, the first in the morning towards Kalinin by 5th Gds Tank Corps against Das Reich. This was beaten back. At midday 2nd Gds Tank Corps advanced towards Nechaevka (south of Luchki) but was spotted by air reconnaissance. Flying tank-hunters were called in and these aircraft dispersed the attacking corps and forced it to withdraw.[23]

The 3rd Panzer Division continued during this day fighting in and around Lukhanino and Syrtsev. The main part of Großdeutschland tried to clear Verkhopenoye of Red Army forces, which however kept control of the northern part of town. The 11th Panzer Division reached the outskirts of Krasnaya Polyana. On the opposite side 6th Tank Corps and 3rd Mechanized Corps from 1st Tank Army were engaged.

None of the counterattacks mounted by the Voronezh Front against 4th Panzer Army produced any significant results. The 10th Tank Corps was even forestalled by the enemy and had to defend itself supported by 183rd RD.

During the day, 6th Panzer Division took Melekhovo. The 7th Panzer Division provided flank protection to the east for III Panzer Corps. The advance to Melekhovo resulted in a very narrow projection northwards. It was necessary to widen it, thus forcing the corps temporarily to discontinue advances to the north.

9 JULY

Northern Sector

During this day no new attacks were performed by the Germans. Rather, they spent most of the day preparing for attacks to be conducted the following day.[24] Soviet forces mounted counterattacks trying to push the Germans back to the starting line. These attacks failed to achieve any gains.

Southern Sector

Leibstandarte reached Sukho–Solotino and Totenkopf arrived at the river Psel while Das Reich secured the right flank at Teterevino.[25] During the day III Panzer Corps with 6th PD and 19th PD secured its left flank by pushing 81st GRD and 92nd GRD back, while Stary Gorod, Blizhniaia Igumenka and Dalniaia Igumenka were taken. Thus the positions were greatly improved for continuation of the offensive in a northerly direction. 7th Panzer Division still provided flank protection to the east for III Panzer Corps but in the evening the first columns from 198th ID began to relieve some of the units of 7th PD.[26]

The XXXXVIII Panzer Corps continued the advance towards Oboyan but with less force since one of their panzer divisions was not available. This was the 3rd Panzer Division, which was still preoccupied with the task of clearing the area around Lukhanino and Syrtsev. The corps nevertheless managed to push almost 10 kilometres to the north. Several units of 3rd Mechanized Corps had to be taken out of the front line because of the considerable losses they had suffered.[27] In the evening, the 204th Rifle Division, which had been transferred from 38th Army, arrived to defend the Oboyan region. Also 5th Guards Tank Corps was ordered to shift towards the Oboyan region (Orlovka) and hand over its present area to 69th Army. This army was inserted between 6th and 7th Guards Armies to control the following divisions: 183rd RD, 93rd GRD, 89th GRD, 375th RD, 81st GRD, 92nd GRD, 94th GRD, 305th RD and 107th RD plus 2nd Guards Tank Corps.[28] Another tank corps, the 10th, was also transferred to defend the approach to Oboyan from its present location on the Psel River.

This day saw Stavka order three armies from the Steppe Front (27th, 53rd and 5th Guards) to move forward to take up positions in the rear. The 27th Army was directed to the Kursk fortified region for defence, 53rd Army to the Seim River at Solntsevo and 5th Guards Army to the Psel River.

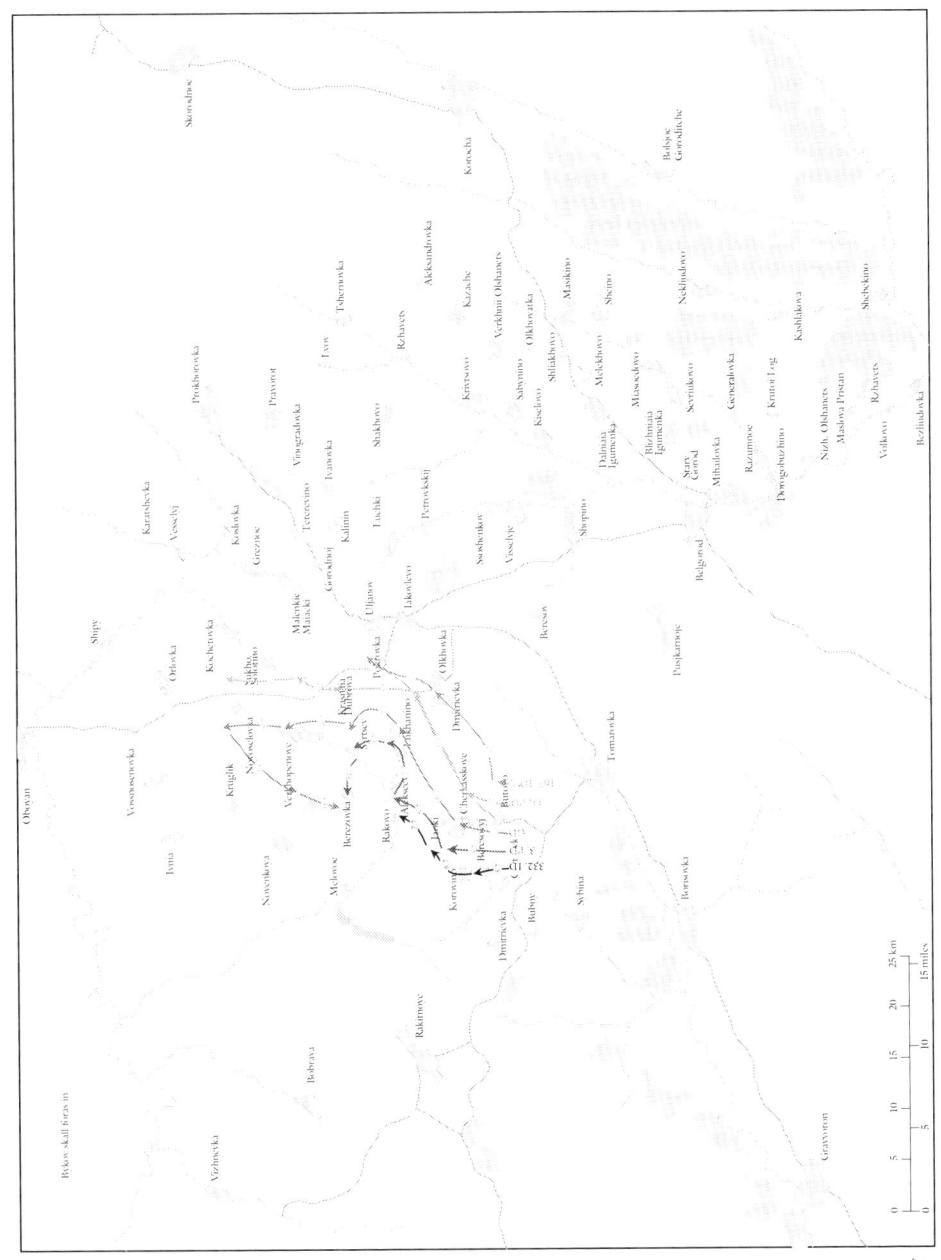

Map 5. XLVIII Panzer Corps attacks, 5–10 July

10 JULY

Northern Sector

The flank problem had been solved for XXXXVII Panzer Corps, enabling 20th PD and 31st ID to return to their respective Corps. Von Esebeck received a new assignment to take command of the main assault group within XXXXVII Panzer Corps. It was composed of units from 2nd PD, 4th PD and 20th PD and was to attack towards Olkhovatka. All available Luftwaffe resources supported this assault.[29] The enemy was well entrenched and prepared however, thus only minor gains were made. Teploe was taken during the morning and after hard house to house fighting the panzer grenadiers from 4th Panzer Division cleared the village of the enemy.[30] 10th Panzergrenadier Division was ordered to relieve 292nd ID from the front line and two divisions, 12th Panzer and 36th Motorized Infantry, moved forward as new reserves. The German command was planning to let 5th and 8th Panzer Division move to this sector of the front and to attack along the road from Trosna to Fatezh in the hope that this would improve the possibilities of a successful offensive.[31]

Southern Sector

Totenkopf was able to establish a bridgehead over the River Psel after hard fighting. On this day Totenkopf suffered 430 casualties, its highest losses during Zitadelle. Leibstandarte began to attack towards Prokhorovka but only minor advances were made during the day.[32] The III Panzer Corps was regrouping its forces to continue the advance to the north.

The Panzer Corps on its left, XXXXVIII, had to secure its left flank. This forced Großdeutschland to turn around and attack towards the southwest during the day. By doing this it was hoped that 3rd Panzer Division would be freed for the advance towards Oboyan. It was intended to move the LII Corps forward to cover the left flank of XXXXVIII Panzer Corps.

The Soviet 1st Tank Army had in its composition for 11th July the following major units: 6th, 10th and 31st Tank Corps, 3rd Mech Corps, 5th Gds Tank Corps, 204th RD and 309th RD. It was ordered to prepare, together with 6th Gds Army and 5th Gds Tank Army, to counterattack on 12th July. The goal was the line Pokrovka–Iakovlevo. Not all units were especially ready for this task. As mentioned earlier 3rd Mechanized Corps had suffered heavy losses but this also applied to 6th Tank Corps, which was down to 35 operational tanks.[33]

11 JULY

Northern Sector

Field Marshal von Kluge released both 12th PD and 36th Motorized ID for Model to use in attacks towards Olkhovatka. Only a battlegroup from 12th Panzer Division advanced forward during the day and was ready behind the attacking divisions of XXXXVII Panzer Corps. Yet no success for exploitation appeared during this day.

Southern Sector

Leibstandarte continued to press on against Prokhorovka, where 9th Gds Airborne Division had to be put in the front line to prevent the enemy from reaching Prokhorovka. Totenkopf could not attack out of its bridgehead over the Psel during the day, since the bridging equipment for heavy weapons (Panzers) had been delayed due to enemy artillery fire. When a bridge finally was ready in the afternoon the roads had been turned into mud by heavy rains causing the vehicles to get stuck on the riverbanks.[34]

After hard fighting, Berezovka fell to 3rd Panzer Division. The attack was supported by part of Großdeutschland attacking from north.

On this day III Panzer Corps made its greatest advance, 6th Panzer Division with 503rd Heavy Tank Battalion in the lead penetrating 305th Rifle Division's front and captured Olkhovatka. At dusk the spearheads had taken Kazache, but 6th Panzer did not stop because of the darkness. It continued the advance during the night.[35] Simultaneously 19th Panzer Division forced 89th GRD over the Northern Donets and took control of Kiselovo.[36]

12 JULY

Northern Sector

No offensive attacks were made by the Germans, since Army Group Centre had to react to the Soviet offensive against the 2nd Panzer Army, which began this day. This offensive forced the army group to begin regrouping some of the forces belonging to 9th Army to sectors held by 2nd Panzer Army. Early in the morning both 12th Panzer Division and 36th Motorized Infantry Division were ordered to move out towards the

Soviet offensive spearheads.[37] All plans for further offensive action by 9th Army had to be shelved.

Southern Sector

Almost all armoured forces on the Voronezh Front were attacking the 4th Panzer Army's spearheads with the purpose of destroying them. Two new Tank Corps, 18th and 29th from 5th Gds Tank Army, made a frontal attack against Leibstandarte which brought enormous tank losses for these two Corps.[38] Totenkopf was attacking out of its bridgehead but made only minor advances into 33rd Gds Rifle Corps defensive line. The corps counter-attacked with 95th Guards and 42nd Guards Rifle Division against Totenkopf's left flank.[39]

During the day the Red Army mounted several attacks against the units of XXXXVIII Panzer Corps. Among them was an attack by 32nd Guards Rifle Corps, 13th GRD and 66th GRD, against 11th Panzer Division. However the most successful of these was on the left flank towards Verkhopenoye.

Early on 12 July 6th Panzer established a bridgehead over the Northern Donets at Rzhavets which was secured at dawn.[40] Both flanks of the division had to be secured during the day, causing the advance to be temporarily halted. During the day 7th Gds Army mounted several counterattacks[41] against Corps Raus, which had the effect of tying down a large part of 7th Panzer Division in support of Corps Raus.

13 JULY

Northern Sector

No further offensive efforts were made by the Germans. Most of the forces were ordered early in the morning to go over to a defensive posture. Other units, for example 18th and 20th Panzer Division, were withdrawn and moved to meet the Soviet offensive directed at Orel.[42]

Southern Sector

Totenkopf attacked out of its bridgehead towards the northeast to outflank the Prokhorovka position, but heavy Soviet counterattacks on Totenkopf's left flank forced the division to transfer units to the threatened sector, thus stalling the advance.

Several attacks of battalion and regimental strength occurred during the day against 11th Panzer Division. On the left flank the 3rd Panzer Division together with the 332nd Infantry Division tried to clear the area northwest of Berezovka.

When 6th Panzer Division received air support for the attack in the morning, one He 111H made a navigation error and dropped its bombs on 6th Panzer Division. The division took 64 casualties, 13 of them being officers. The losses included two regimental commanders and four battalion commanders, the Heinkel having hit a command post.[43] The division tried to clear Aleksandrovka of the Red Army, while 7th PD on the left attacked towards Krassnoye Anamya.

14 JULY

Northern Sector

No further offensive efforts were made by the Germans.

Southern Sector

South of Prokhorovka, Das Reich was attacking to the east, trying to establish contact with III Panzer Corps, which was attacking in a westerly direction. By these attacks the German command hoped to shorten their lines and be able once again to start their advance against Oboyan.

Again many attacks were launched against 11th Panzer Division, many being broken up by artillery fire. Both 332nd Infantry and 3rd Panzer Division were still working to clear the area northeast of Berezovka.

15 JULY

Northern Sector

No further offensive efforts were made by the Germans.

Southern Sector

The 7th Panzer Division attacked to the west in order to establish contact with Das Reich. Heavy rains delayed Das Reich's advance but at noon the division managed to establish contact with the 7th Panzer Division at Mal. Iablonovo.[44]

Finally, 3rd Panzer Division was able to clear the area northeast of Berezovka and identify the new Soviet defence line west of Novenkoya. For 11th Panzer Division the front line was calmer on this day, only minor exchanges of fire occurring. The Panthers managed to destroy 16 enemy tanks in a small attack. 1st Tank Army was ordered to go over to defence after three days of unsuccessful attacks against XXXXVIII Panzer Corps.

Late that evening Totenkopf was ordered to withdraw from the bridgehead on the northern side of the Psel. The withdrawal was due to be completed on the night between 17 and 18 July.[45]

16 JULY

Northern Sector

No further offensive efforts were made by the Germans.

Southern Sector

Army Group South had concluded that an attack along the shortest route to Oboyan offered the best prospects for success. This new plan was called 'Roland' and it included the regrouping of the II SS-Panzer Corps further to the west.[46] This had become feasible now that contact had been established with III Panzer Corps. This was now subordinated to 4th Panzer Army.[47] The day was mainly spent in regrouping. The Red Army too spent the day without much offensive action. The 1st Tank Army was taken out of the line and placed in the Voronezh Front's second echelon.[48]

17 JULY

Northern Sector

No further offensive efforts were made by the Germans.

Southern Sector

The II SS-Panzer Corps was regrouping for 'Roland' when orders arrived that Leibstandarte and Das Reich were to move to Belgorod instead. This effectively ended the German offensive.

98

NOTES

1. *Journal of Slavic Military Studies*, no. 4, December 1993, *Documents: The Defense Battle for the Kursk Bridgehead, 5-15 July 1943*, pp. 683–5.
2. E. Klink, *Das Gesetz des Handelns, Die Operation 'Zitadelle' 1943* (Deutsche Verlags-Anstalt, Stuttgart, 1986), p. 247.
3. Wehrwissenschaftliche Rundschau Jahrgang 15 (1965), G. Heinrici and W. Hauck, *Zitadelle (III)*, p. 588. *Journal of Slavic Military Studies*, no. 3, September 1993, *Documents: Collection of Materials for the Study of War Experience No.11 – The Battle of Kursk July 1943*, p. 503. K. Rokossovsky, *A Soldier's Duty* (Progress Publishers, Moscow, 1970), p. 197.
4. *Journal of Slavic Military Studies*, no. 4, December 1993, *Documents: The Defense Battle for the Kursk Bridgehead, 5-15 July 1943*, p. 658.
5. It was the Leibstandarte. S. Stadler, *Die Offensive gegen Kursk 1943, II SS-Panzerkorps als Stosskeil im Grosskampf* (Munin Verlag, Osnabrück, 1980), pp. 42–5.
6. BA-MA RH 10/64 Tagesmeldungen 6.7.1943 Operationsabteilung, Hgr. Süd meldet Ausfälle an Pz und Stug 5.7.
7. *Journal of Slavic Military Studies*, no. 4, December 1993, *Documents: The Defense Battle for the Kursk Bridgehead, 5-15 July 1943*, p. 658.
8. W. Paul, *Brennpunkte, Die Geschichte der 6.Panzerdivision (1.leichte) 1937–45* (Biblio Verlag, Osnabrück, 1993), p. 305. E. Klink, *Gesetz des Handelns*, pp. 213–15.
9. *Journal of Slavic Military Studies*, no. 4, December 1993, *Documents: The Defense Battle for the Kursk Bridgehead, 5-15 July 1943*, p. 659.
10. Ibid., pp. 686–7.
11. *Journal of Slavic Military Studies*, no. 1, March 1994, *Documents: Tank forces in Defense of the Kursk Bridgehead and Operational Maskirovka According to Voronezh Front Experience, July–August 1943*, p. 87.
12. W. Haupt, *Die Schlachten der Heeresgruppe Mitte 1941–1944* (Podzun-Pallas, Friedberg, 1983), p. 212.
13. M.A. Kozlov (ed.), *V Plameni Srazhenii* (Voenizdat, Moscow, 1973), p. 112.
14. *Journal of Slavic Military Studies*, no. 1, March 1994, *Documents: Tank forces in Defense of the Kursk Bridgehead and Operational Maskirovka According to Voronezh Front Experience, July–August 1943*, p. 96. *Journal of Slavic Military Studies*, no. 4, December 1993, *Documents: The Defense Battle for the Kursk Bridgehead, 5–15 July 1943*, p. 661.
15. S. Stadler, *Die Offensive gegen Kursk 1943*, p. 51.
16. *Journal of Slavic Military Studies*, no. 4, December 1993, *Documents: The Defense Battle for the Kursk Bridgehead, 5–15 July 1943*, p. 662.
17. *Journal of Slavic Military Studies*, no. 1, March 1994, *Documents: Tank forces in Defense of the Kursk Bridgehead and Operational Maskirovka According to Voronezh Front Experience, July–August 1943*, p. 88. *Journal of Slavic Military Studies*, no. 4, December 1993, *Documents: The Defense Battle for the Kursk Bridgehead, 5–15 July 1943*, pp. 688–9.
18. *Journal of Slavic Military Studies*, no. 4, December 1993, *Documents: The Defense Battle for the Kursk Bridgehead, 5–15 July 1943*, p. 688.
19. S. Stadler, *Die Offensive gegen Kursk 1943*, p. 60. O. Weidinger, *Division Das Reich, Band IV, 1943* (Munin Verlag, Osnabrück, 1986), p. 176.
20. *Journal of Slavic Military Studies*, no. 4, December 1993, *Documents: The Defense Battle for the Kursk Bridgehead, 5–15 July 1943*, p. 666.
21. E. Klink, *Das Gesetz des Handelns*, p. 253.
22. K. Rokossovsky, *A Soldier's Duty*, p. 201.

23. S. Stadler, *Die Offensive gegen Kursk 1943*, pp. 65–7. O. Weidinger, *Division Das Reich*, pp. 182–5. *Journal of Slavic Military Studies*, no. 4, December 1993, *Documents: The Defense Battle for the Kursk Bridgehead, 5–15 July 1943*, p. 668.
24. W. Haupt, *Die Schlachten der Heeresgruppe Mitte 1941–1944*, p. 217. E. Klink, *Das Gesetz des Handelns*, pp. 254, 257–8.
25. O. Weidinger, *Division Das Reich*, pp. 187–1. E. Klink, *Das Gesetz des Handelns*, p. 224.
26. G. Graser (ed.), *Zwischen Kattegat und Kaukasus, Weg und Kämpfe der 198.Infanterie-Division 1939–1945* (Selbstverlag, Tübingen, 1961), p. 249.
27. *Journal of Slavic Military Studies*, no. 1, March 1994, *Documents: Tank forces in Defense of the Kursk Bridgehead and Operational Maskirovka According to Voronezh Front Experience, July–August 1943*, pp. 98–9. *Journal of Slavic Military Studies*, no. 4, December 1993, p. 670.
28. *Journal of Slavic Military Studies*, no. 4, December 1993, p. 674.
29. E. Klink, *Das Gesetz des Handelns*, p. 259.
30. D. von Saucken, *4 Panzer Division, Teil II der Divisionsgeschichte* (Selbstverlag, Coburg, 1968), p. 6.
31. E. Klink, *Gesetz des Handelns*, p. 260.
32. R. Lehmann, *The Leibstandarte*, Vol. III (J.J. Fedorowicz Publishing, Winnipeg), pp. 227–30.
33. *Journal of Slavic Military Studies*, no. 1, March 1994, *Documents: Tank forces in Defense of the Kursk Bridgehead and Operational Maskirovka According to Voronezh Front Experience, July–August 1943*, p. 101.
34. W. Vopersal, *Soldaten, Kämpfer, Kameraden*, Band 3 (Selbstverlag, Osnabrück, 1987), pp. 374–9.
35. W. Paul, *Brennpunkte, Die Geschichte der 6.Panzerdivision*, pp. 309–10.
36. *Journal of Slavic Military Studies*, no. 4, December 1993, *Documents: The Defense Battle for the Kursk Bridgehead, 5–15 July 1943*, p. 678.
37. W. Haupt, *Die Schlachten der Heeresgruppe Mitte 1941–44*, p. 223.
38. R. Lehmann, *The Leibstandarte*, Vol. III, pp. 234–8.
39. A.S. Zhadov, *Chetyre Goda Voiny* (Voenizdat, Moscow, 1978), p. 93.
40. As a ruse the 6th Panzer Division used two T-34s captured earlier during the fighting. These two led a German column to capture the bridge during the darkness. W. Paul, *Brennpunkte, Die Geschichte der 6.Panzerdivision*, p. 311.
41. *Journal of Slavic Military Studies*, no. 4, December 1993, *Documents: The Defense Battle for the Kursk Bridgehead, 5–15 July 1943*, p. 679.
42. W. Haupt, *Die Schlachten der Heeresgruppe Mitte 1941–44*, p. 223.
43. W. Paul, *Brennpunkte, Die Geschichte der 6 Panzerdivision*, pp. 314–15.
44. S. Stadler, *Die Offensive gegen Kursk 1943*, p. 127. O. Weidinger, *Division Das Reich*, Band IV *1943*, pp. 212–13.
45. V. Vopersal, *Soldaten, Kämpfer, Kameraden*, Band 3 (Selbstverlag, Bielefeld, 1987), p. 407.
46. S. Stadler, *Die Offensive gegen Kursk 1943*, pp. 134–5. R. Lehmann, *The Leibstandarte*, Vol. III, pp. 246–7.
47. W. Paul, *Brennpunkte, Die Geschichte der 6.Panzerdivision*, p. 318.
48. *Journal of Slavic Military Studies*, no. 1, March 1994, *Documents: Tank forces in Defense of the Kursk Bridgehead and Operational Maskirovka According to Voronezh Front Experience, July–August 1943*, p. 103.

7

Prokhorovka

In many accounts of the battle of Kursk the tank battle at Prokhorovka is regarded as the moment when the German offensive on the southern side of the Kursk salient ran out of steam. Considering the importance conferred to the action at Prokhorovka it is remarkable that the battle is not clearly defined. It is not entirely evident which units took part, the geographical limits are not clear and, finally, it is not obvious how many days should be attributed to the battle. On top of that, the number of tanks given by some authors is pure fiction.[1]

Usually the tank battle at Prokhorovka is regarded as a clash between the Soviet 5th Guards Tank Army, commanded by Pavel Rotmistrov and the German II SS-Panzer Corps, commanded by Paul Hausser. However, a closer look at the map reveals several ambiguities in this picture.

PROKHOROVKA: THE TRADITIONAL SOVIET VIEW

Soviet accounts of the battle usually state that the total number of tanks that took part in the battle were either 1,200 (700 Soviet and 500 German) or 1,500 (800 Soviet and 700 German).[2] The difference occurs because what is included in the battlefield varies. With the lower numbers it is II SS-Panzer Corps versus the main part of 5th Guards Tank Army. For the higher numbers the whole 5th Guards Tank Army must be included, while on the German side III Panzer Corps has to be added.

Part of 5th Guards Mechanized Corps was sent to reinforce 69th Army, which was fighting against the German III Panzer Corps. The latter threatened to cut off several units of the 69th Army. The units sent from 5th Guards Mechanized Corps were 11th and 12th Guards Mechanized Brigades, reinforced with the 26th Tank Brigade from the 2nd Guards Tank Corps.[3] This force had about 100 tanks and met a force from III

101

Panzer Corps (6th and 19th Panzer Division) with 200 tanks according to Soviet estimates.[4]

The remainder of 5th Guards Tank Army met II SS-Panzer Corps, which was believed to have 500 tanks of which 100 were of newer types (Tiger, Ferdinand and Panther).[5] According to Rotmistrov, the Germans lost 350 tanks and 10,000 men during 12 July.[6] In another book Rotmistrov states that the Germans lost on that day 400 tanks (including 70 Tigers), 88 guns, 70 mortars, 83 MGs, more than 300 motor vehicles and 3,500 men when fighting the 5th Guards Tank Army.[7] More modest claims can be found in the Soviet General Staff study where it is estimated that the Germans lost in five days of battle – from 12 to 16 July inclusive – 300 tanks, 20 assault guns, more than 200 guns, 500 motor vehicles and more than 4,500 soldiers.[8]

Soviet losses were 300 tanks and self-propelled guns from their tank army during 12 July,[9] a figure including both retrievable losses and total write-offs. Rotmistrov wrote that 29th Tank Corps lost 60 per cent of its tanks and 18th Tank Corps lost 30 per cent, while 5th Guards Mechanized Corps' losses were small.[10]

THE GERMAN SIDE OF THE STORY

To begin with the smaller force, when Zitadelle began the three Panzer divisions of the III Panzer Corps had 299 tanks (6th – 106, 7th – 112 and 19th – 81).[11] The corps also had a heavy Tank battalion of 45 tanks. So if 6th and 19th Panzer Division between them had had 200 operational tanks on 12 July it would have been a remarkable achievement indeed.

TABLE 7.1: OPERATIONAL TANKS AND ASSAULT GUNS WITH ARMY DETACHMENT KEMPF, 11–15 JULY 1943[12]

	11 July	12 July	13 July	14 July	15 July
6th Panzer Division	23	no report	12	14	15
7th Panzer Division	54	39	41	no report	23
19th Panzer Division	16	15	25	28	28
503rd Panzer Bn	23	no report	no report	no report	9
905th Assault Gun Bn	28	29	29	27	27
228th Assault Gun Bn	no report	19	no report	no report	14
393rd Assault Gun Bty	9	9	4	5	4

Note: Figures refer to the number of operational tanks and assault guns on the *morning* of the indicated dates.

102

Unfortunately reports giving the number of tanks operational with the German units are not available for all units on 12 July, but for the 11 July such reports can be found. On this day 116 tanks were operational among the units subordinated to III Panzer Corps.

Of the assault gun units only the 228th Assault Gun Battalion was part of III Panzer Corps. If the strength for 12 July is used, it can be concluded that the corps probably had no more than 135 tanks and assault guns available for the Prokhorovka battle.

The III Panzer Corps took its bridgehead over the Northern Donets River during the night between 11 and 12 July. Since the Soviet forces staged several counterattacks during 12 July, both against III Panzer Corps and Corps Raus, most of 12 July was spent by the Germans in consolidating their positions.[13] The following day the Germans began attacking out of the bridgehead and at this time it was probably not more than 100 tanks and assault guns that participated.

Around the village of Prokhorovka the Germans committed the II SS-Panzer Corps. Of its three divisions Totenkopf to the left was attacking across the Psel River, while Leibstandarte in the centre attacked towards Prokhorovka and Das Reich covered Leibstandarte's right flank. Note that Totenkopf mainly faced units of Zhadov's 5th Guards Army, not Rotmistrov's 5th Guards *Tank* Army. That the Corps had 500 tanks and assault guns during 12 July is the Soviet version but according to German documents it had the following number:

TABLE 7.2: II SS-PZ CORPS' OPERATIONAL TANKS AND ASSAULT GUNS,
11–16 JULY 1943[14]

	11 July	12 July	13 July	14 July	15 July	16 July
1st SS-Pz.Gr.Div.	77	no report	70	78	85	96
2nd SS-Pz.Gr.Div.	95	103	107	115	99	103
3rd SS-Pz.Gr.Div.	122	121	74	73	77	93

Note: Figures refer to number of operational tanks and assault guns on the *evening* of the indicated dates.

Thus, on the evening before 12 July the II SS-Panzer Corps had 294 tanks and assault guns operational of which 15 were Tigers (no Panthers or Ferdinands, not even in workshops). When the Zitadelle offensive started, the II SS-Panzer Corps had 494 tanks and assault guns available (almost all were operational), of which 42 were Tigers (no Panthers or Ferdinands). Not even at the beginning of operation Zitadelle did the II SS-Panzer Corps possess as many tanks as the Soviets believed they had

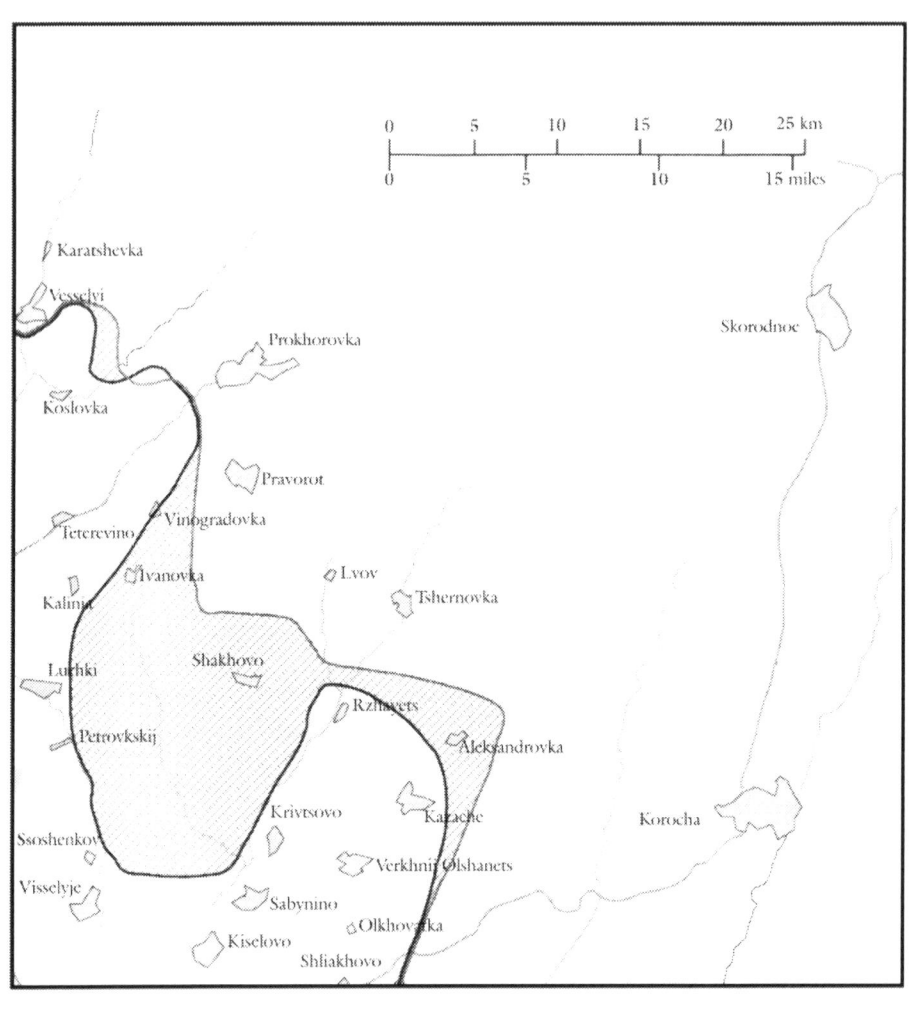

Map 6. German territorial gains in the Prokhorovka area, 12–15 July

at the time of Prokhorovka, which was a week later. Note too that on 16 July the corps had 292 tanks and assault guns operational, only two less than on 11 July.

The Leibstandarte claimed to have destroyed 192 tanks on 11 and 12 July, while Das Reich claimed 75 tanks on 12 July and Totenkopf claimed 77 tanks.[15] The three SS-Divisions lost 8,095 men – killed, wounded and missing in action – during Zitadelle but of these casualties only a fraction occurred during the period from 11 July to 15 July.

TABLE 7.3: II SS-PZ CORPS' MANPOWER LOSSES, 11–16 JULY 1943[16]

	11 July	12 July	13 July	14 July	15 July	16 July
1st SS-Pz.Gr.Div.	323	279	325	100	120	103
2nd SS-Pz.Gr.Div.	211	243	61	287	114	224
3rd SS-Pz.Gr.Div.	430	316	160	175	65	89
Corps Troops:	1	4	1	2	0	4

Note: Figures include killed, wounded and missing.

If 11 July is not included, II SS-Panzer Corps lost 2,672 men. On 12 July alone the II SS-Panzer Corps lost 842 men. Evidently Rotmistrov's claim is too high and it is important to remember that Totenkopf fought mainly against units from 5th Guards Army, typically 52nd GRD and 95th GRD. For neither of the SS divisions was 12 July the worst day in terms of casualties.[17]

THE SIZE OF THE ARMOURED CLASH AT PROKHOROVKA

As indicated above, the number of tanks on the Soviet side depends on what is included in the 'Battle at Prokhorovka'. In Chapter 3 the strength of 5th Guards Tank Army was 793 tanks (501 T-34, 261 T-70 and 31 Churchill) and 57 self-propelled guns (SU). How these armoured vehicles were distributed among the units in 5th Guards Tanks Army can provide a picture of how they were deployed on the battlefield.

For the battle at Prokhorovka, the 2nd Tank Corps and 2nd Guards Tank Corps were subordinated to the 5th Guards Tank Army. Before operation Zitadelle began, the 2nd Tank Corps had 195 T-34 and 2nd Guards Tank Corps had 135 T-34 and 63 T-70, but on the morning of 12 July these corps had no more than a total of 187 tanks in their composition

TABLE 7.4: SOVIET TANKS AND SP GUNS IN 5TH GUARDS TANK ARMY, 12 JULY 1943

	T-34	T-70	Churchill	Total Tanks	SU	Total Tanks and SU
5th Gds Mech Corps	159	48	0	207	16	223
18th Tank Corps	96	63	31	190	0	190
29th Tank Corps[18]	122	70	0	192	20	212
53rd Gds Tank Reg	32	7	0	39	0	39
1549th SU Reg	0	0	0	0	12	12
Total:	409	188	31	628	48	676

Note: Figures do not include 2nd Tank Corps, 2nd Guards Tank Corps or 1529th SU Regiment.[19]

according to Soviet sources.[20] From the numbers presented above, it can be deduced that the 2nd Tank Corps and 2nd Guards Tank Corps had 92 T-34 and 73 T-70 or a total of 165, figures which do not fit precisely with the total of 187 given by Soviet sources. A possible explanation for the discrepancy is that the figure of 793 tanks in 5th Guards Tank Army refers to operational vehicles, while Table 7.4 may include tanks in need of repair. If this is true, the units listed in Table 7.4 would have had 606 tanks operational, not 628.

However, the number of T-70 available to 2nd Tank Corps and 2nd Guards Tank Corps is actually higher than the number on hand on 5 July. Either the units had received T-70 tanks as replacements or some of the information presented by the Soviet sources is incorrect, but it has not been possible to establish the precise reasons for this contradiction. The total number of tanks seems to be correct though, the problem lying mainly in getting a clear picture as to how the tanks were distributed.

Rotmistrov wrote in his memoirs that 2nd Tank Corps had few tanks left and had to be reinforced with the 10th Anti-Tank Brigade to enable it to fulfil its mission of protecting the flanks of 29th and 2nd Guards Tank Corps.[21] According to this the corps played no major part in the battle. Consequently, on 12 July three Corps attacked elements of II SS-Panzer Corps. They were 18th, 29th and 2nd Guards.

It seems that against the German III Panzer Corps, at least 150 Soviet tanks were newly committed on 12 July, while at least 450 tanks were hurled against II SS-Panzer Corps. Also a further 100 joined in against the II SS-Panzer Corps on 13 July, on the northern side of the Psel. As we have written earlier 2nd Tank Corps and 2nd Guards Tank Corps had 187 tanks together and, if we assume that at least 120 belonged to 2nd Guards Tank Corps (80 versus II SS and 40 versus III Panzer), these

106

TABLE 7.5: DISTRIBUTION OF 5TH GUARDS TANK ARMY ATTACKING UNITS

	Tanks and Assault Guns	Date	Engaged Against
18th Tank Corps	190	12 July	Leibstandarte, partly Totenkopf
29th Tank Corps	212	12 July	Leibstandarte
1549th SU Regiment	12	12 July	Leibstandarte
1529th SU Regiment	? (9)	12 July	Leibstandarte
2nd Gds Tank Corps (-)	?(80)	12 July	Das Reich
53rd Gds Tank Regiment	39	12 July	III Panzer Corps
96th Tank Brigade (69th Army)	?(20)	12 July	III Panzer Corps
26th Gds Tank Brigade (2nd GTC)	?(40)	12 July	III Panzer Corps
5th GMC (11th and 12th GMB)	96	12 July	III Panzer Corps
5th GMC (10th GMB and 24th GTB)	113	13 July	Totenkopf

Notes: The date refers to when the formation entered the battle of Prokhorovka. The 1447th SU Regiment (part of 5th Guards Mechanized Corps) with 16 SU has not been included since it has not been possible to establish where and when it was committed.

figures will be obtained. The 96th Tank Brigade had 61 T-34 when it started the battle as reserve with the 6th Guards Army and here it has been assumed that 20 tanks were still operational.

Depending on how one prefers to define the battle at Prokhorovka, it involved from 294 German (II SS-Panzer Corps) and 616 Soviet AFV (those engaging II SS-Panzer Corps) up to a maximum of 429 German and 870 Soviet AFV. If looking closer at the engagement involving the II SS-Panzer Corps, which most western historians seem to equate with the battle at Prokhorovka, it can be concluded that Rotmistrov committed 18th and 29th Tank Corps together with the majority of 2nd Guards Tank Corps against units of the II SS-Panzer Corps on 12 July. During 13 July, about half of 5th Guards Mechanized Corps was also thrown into the fighting. The 2nd Tank Corps, which had a flanking task, tied up parts of Das Reich. On the German side Leibstandarte bore the brunt of the fighting against 5th Guards Tank Army units on 12 July. Totenkopf, which disposed of no less than 122 of the 294 tanks available to the II SS-Panzer Corps on the 12th, mainly fought against 5th Guards Army. However one defines the battle, it is impossible to say that the numerical ratio was approximately even.

The result of Prokhorovka

First the extent of the battle of Prokhorovka must be defined. Our definition is that the clash started on 12 July and ended on 16 July. It involved II SS-Panzer Corps and III Panzer Corps on the German side, while the Red Army had three armies involved in the fighting (69th Army, 5th Guards Tank Army and 5th Guards Army).

It we take a look at how the front lines changed during these five days one could interpret it as some sort of success for the Germans, since the two corps were finally able to shorten their flanks (right flank for II SS and left for III Pz) by capturing a large area south of Pravorot. However, if we compare the outcome with the German orders for the battle, which stated that Prokhorovka was the target, it is clear that the Germans fell short of their goals. The Red Army had hoped to push the II SS-Panzer Corps back and crush it. This failed completely, but at least the 5th Guards Tank Army prevented the Germans from taking Prokhorovka.

The II SS-Panzer Corps suffered 2,672 casualties during this period. During the period 5–20 July the III Panzer Corps had casualties similar to the II SS-Panzer Corps. On the assumption that III Panzer Corps had similar losses during this period we have to add 2,790 casualties for this corps,[22] giving 5,462 casualties for eight divisions[23] during five days of intensive fighting. This is neither abnormal nor very high.

The manpower losses for the Red Army are more difficult to establish. On the Southern sector the Red Army incurred, on average, 7,576 casualties per day. If we assume that during this period the daily losses of the forces involved in the Prokhorovka fighting (69th, 5th Guards and 5th Guards Tank Army) were half of that, or 3,788, they would have lost 18,940 men.[24]

One Soviet account states that 5th Guards Tank Army alone took 14,000 casualties during the defensive fighting up to 23 July.[25] Thus 18,940 casualties for the three armies cannot be considered an exaggeration, but rather a quite modest estimate.

Tank losses have often been described as equally severe for both sides but this does not match the reality. The German losses in destroyed tanks were very small compared to the losses suffered by the Red Army. The II SS-Panzer Corps lost 36 tanks and assault guns between 5 and 23 July of which at least 19 were destroyed before Prokhorovka.[26] Accordingly, the II SS-Panzer Corps cannot have lost more than 17 during Prokhorovka.

The III Panzer Corps, which had less armour than II SS-Panzer Corps, seems to have had higher losses. During the period from 11 to 20 July, it lost 37 tanks and assault guns,[27] but not all units of the corps took part in the Prokhorovka battle.

Rotmistrov's 5th Guards Tank Army reported that it had lost 222 T-34, 89 T-70, 12 Churchill and 11 assault guns up to 16 July.[28] These were total write-offs. This gives a total of 334 destroyed Soviet tanks and assault guns,[29] which can be compared to, at most, 54 German tanks and assault guns destroyed. This means that Soviet tank losses were at least six times higher. In fact, since more German units are included in this calculation than actually took part in the Prokhorovka battle, while not all Soviet units are included, the real ratio was even higher.

Losses for the German forces were not particularly severe during this period, but added to the losses suffered previously they were not insignificant. No German unit was withdrawn from the front for refitting. On the Soviet side the 2nd Guards Tank Corps was withdrawn to be refitted.

Against this background it is hard to see Prokhorovka as a decisive German defeat.[30] In fact some publications even claim that the commander of the II SS-Panzer Corps, Paul Hausser, was relieved of his command due to the German 'defeat' at Prokhorovka. It is strange that such a mistake should have occurred, since he remained in command of the II SS-Panzer Corps until 28 June 1944, when he was given command of 7th Army in Normandy.

NOTES

1. In one book it is stated that II SS Panzer Corps had 600 tanks and III Panzer Corps had 360 tanks which gives a total of 960. F. Kurowski, *Der Panzerkrieg* (Moewig Verlag, München, 1980), p. 371. Bryan Perrett writes that the SS-Panzer Corps had 700 tanks. B. Perrett, *A History of Blitzkrieg* (Robert Hale, London, 1983), p. 159. Another author presents an even higher figure, he writes that 900 tanks (including Panthers and Elefants) in Hausser's Corps met 5th Guards Tank Army. R. Edwards, *Panzer, A Revolution in Warfare, 1939–1945* (Arms & Armour, London, 1989), p. 182.
2. G.A. Koltunov and B.G. Soloviev, *Kurskaya bitva* (Voenizdat, Moscow, 1970), p. 174.
3. P.A. Rotmistrov, *Stal'naya gvardiya* (Voenizdat, Moscow, 1984), p. 195.
4. Koltunov and Soloviev, p. 174.
5. Ibid.
6. Rotmistrov, *Stal'naya gvardiya*, p. 197.
7. V.P. Morozov (ed.), *Kurskaya Bitva* (Tsentralmo-Chernozemnoe, Voronezh, 1973) in which P.A. Rotmistrov has written a chapter (*Vstrechnoe srazhenie*), p. 155.
8. *Journal of Slavic Military Studies*, Vol. 7, no. 1, March 1994. Documents: *Tank forces in Defense of the Kursk Bridgehead and Operational Maskirovka According to Voronezh Front Experience, July–August 1943*, p. 109.
9. Koltunov and Soloviev, p. 175.
10. Rotmistrov, *Stal'naya gvardiya*, p. 198.
11. These were available and, of course, almost all of them were operational. See also Table 3.15.
12. BA-MA RH 20-8/97. KTB Ia AOK 8 Panzerlage. Command tanks are included in the figures.
13. W. Paul, *Brennpunkte, die Geschichte der 6.Panzerdivision (1.leichte) 1937–1945* (Biblio Verlag, Osnabrück, 1993), pp. 310–14.

14. BA-MA RH 21-4/118. KTB Ia Tagesmeldungen und Nachmeldeungen 'von' II.SS-Pz.Korps 'zu' Pz.A.O.K.4.
15. BA-MA RS 2-2/25: II.SS.Pz.Korps Anlagen. BA-MA RS 2-2/18 Tagesmeldung von 13.7.1943 LSSAH. W. Vopersal, *Soldaten, Kämpfer, Kameraden* (Selbstverlag, Bielafeld, 1987), p. 390.
16. Gen.Kdo II. SS-Pz.Korps, der Korpsarzt, reports from 11 July to 2 August (BA-MA RS 2-2/17).
17. The corps as a whole suffered its highest casualties on 5 July, the second worst day was 6 July and the third worst day was 11 July. Leibstandarte suffered its highest casualties on 5 and 6 July, Das Reich on 5 and 14 July and Totenkopf on 10 and 11 July. BA-MA RS 2-2/17: Gen.Kdo.II.SS-Pz.Korps, Meldungen der Korpsarzt.
18. R.G. Foerster (ed.), *Gezeitenwechsel im Zweiten Weltkrieg?* (E.S. Mittler & Sohn, Berlin, 1996), p. 122.
19. Letter from Charles Sharp to the authors.
20. P.Ya. Egorov *et al.*, *Dorogami Pobed* (*Boevoi put 5-i Gvardeiskoy Armii*) (Voenizdat, Moscow, 1969), p. 28. In a study made during the War the Red Army wrote that 2nd TC and 2nd GTC had almost 200 tanks left. *Journal of Slavic Military Studies*, Vol. 7, no. 1, March 1994, p. 104.
21. Rotmistrov, *Stal'naya gvardiya*, p. 189.
22. II SS-Panzer Corps had 8,095 casualties from 5 to 20 July. Of these 2,661, or 32.9 per cent, occurred between 12 and 16 July. If the same percentage is applied to III Pz.Corps, which suffered 8,489 casualties from 5 to 20 July, it would have lost 2,790 men from 12 to 16 July. Figures according to reports from Der Korpsarzt, II. SS-Pz.Korps (BA-MA RS 2-2/17) and KTB AOK 8 Ia, Personelle Verluste für die Zeit 5.7 – 20.7 1943 (BA-MA RH 20-8/97).
23. 1st SS, 2nd SS, 3rd SS, 6th Pz, 7th Pz, 19th Pz, 167th Inf and 168th Inf.
24. During the fighting in the south (5 to 23 July), Soviet casualties were 143,950 (Krivosheyev, *Grif Sekretnosti Sniat*, Voenizdat, Moscow, 1993), p. 188.
25. Koltunov and Soloviev, p. 385. It is not stated which units are included but we can assume that it includes 18th TC, 29th TC, 5th GMC, 2nd TC, 2nd GTC and probably 9th Guards Airborne Rifle Division.
26. Gen.Kdo II. SS-Pz.Korps, 23.7.43 (BA-MA RS 2-2/18) and Pz.AOK 4 O.Qu Anlage 11 zum KTB, Tätigkeitsberichte von der Abteilungen (BA-MA RH 21-4/450).
27. Pz.AOK 4 O.Qu Anlage 11 zum KTB, Tätigkeitsberichte von der Abteilungen (BA-MA RH 21-4/450) and Heeresgruppe Süd Totalverluste (BA-MA RH 10/64).
28. R.G. Foerster (ed.), *Gezeitenwechsel im Zweiten Weltkrieg?*, p. 121.
29. The total losses for the Defensive Fighting according to G.A. Koltunov and B.G. Soloviev (p. 385) are 427 tanks and assault guns. In an article in *Voenno-Istoricheskij Zhurnal* (no. 8/93, N.G. Andronikov, *Gitlerovskii 'Fakel' byl nogashen na ognennoi duge*, p. 2) the losses are 439 from 12 to 24 July.
30. Roger Edwards writes about Prokhorovka that it was '… a terrifying defeat for 4th Panzer Army'. R. Edwards, *Panzer, A Revolution in Warfare, 1939–1945* (Arms & Armour, London, 1989), p. 182.

8

The Cost of the Battle

Many estimates concerning the losses suffered by the opponents during the battle have been published, but surprisingly little substantial information has been presented. The lack of hard facts concerning the Soviet losses is of course attributable to the fact that Soviet archives have been classified, nor has it been *comme il faut* in Soviet literature to present information on losses suffered by the Red Army. More difficult to accept is the lack of any reliable information on German losses, since this was available from archival records long ago.

Yet even if correct information is available, the issue of how to define the battle at Kursk remains. Thus, any figures on losses must be accompanied by information as to which units and to which period of time they apply, or else they become quite meaningless.

GERMAN MANPOWER LOSSES

Various figures on German losses have been presented, which have in common that they originate from Soviet sources. The fact that information on losses taken from the opposing side is usually inaccurate has often been compounded by historians not distinguishing between casualties and killed, and also not always distinguishing between damaged and destroyed equipment. Kursk is no exception to this pattern.

One example of what can happen is provided by John Erickson. In his book *The Road to Berlin* he writes that the Russians claimed that at Kursk 70,000 German officers and men were killed, 2,952 tanks and 195 assault guns were destroyed, along with 844 field guns, 1,392 planes and over 5,000 lorries.[1]

But a few important words have disappeared somewhere. The Soviet General Staff did produce a series called 'Collection of Materials for the Study of War Experience', which is highly informative. In this one can read that during the period of their offensive, the Kursk–Orel and Belgorod–Kharkov German groupings lost a total of 70,000 men killed *and wounded*, and 2,952 tanks, 195 self-propelled guns, 844 field guns, 1,392 aeroplanes and more than 5,000 motor vehicles were *damaged or destroyed*.[2]

Now this is considerably different since soldiers killed in action usually constituted less than one in four of the number of wounded for the Germany Army during offensive operations. Even if soldiers who died from wounds are added to those killed in action, the number of wounded is still about three times as large as the number of killed. Similarly, during offensive operations, the number of tanks damaged considerably exceeded the number destroyed.

If we assume that the Soviet estimate of 70,000 killed and wounded apply to the forces of 9th Army, 4th Panzer Army and Army Detachment Kempf, and that the period of offensive operations was from 5 to 11 July in the Army Group Centre sector and from 5 to 23 July in the South, the Soviet estimate on German manpower losses is not remarkably off the mark. The German 9th Army suffered 22,273 casualties from 5 July to 11 July according to the data presented in Table 8.1. For the period from 4 to 20 July casualties amounted to 15,960 for Army Detachment Kempf while Hoth's 4th Panzer Army suffered 18,594 casualties,[3] for a total of 34,454 in Army Group South. If this is combined with the information on 9th Army it can be concluded that casualties for the offensive period (5–11 July in the north and 4–20 July in the south) amounted to 56,827. If the Soviet estimate is compared to this figure, it is about 24 per cent too high. Such an error is not uncommon. Rather, when compared to allied estimates on German losses in Normandy[4] or the Ardennes for example, which were far higher than reality, it is a relatively sober estimate.

As can be seen in Table 8.1, 9th Army's losses were most severe on the first day of the offensive and subsequently loss rates declined. Compared to the ration strength of the army at the beginning of the offensive, losses up to 9 July (inclusive) constituted about 5 per cent, while losses for the entire month constituted about 10 per cent of the ration strength at the beginning of the month.

On the southern side of the salient 4th Panzer Army (see Table 8.3) and Army Detachment Kempf (see Table 8.2) enjoyed somewhat greater success and the offensive operations continued until 15 July. Fighting continued along the front line reached by the Germans for about a week, until the Germans began evacuating the bulge they had driven into the Kursk salient. The casualties suffered by Army Group South were slightly greater than those in the 9th Army sector. This was a consequence of the

COST OF THE BATTLE

TABLE 8.1: CASUALTIES SUFFERED BY THE GERMAN 9TH ARMY

	Killed in Action	Wounded in Action	Missing in Action	Total
4 July	11	61	0	72
5 July	1,086	5,922	215	7,223
6 July	569	2,351	76	2,996
7 July	486	2,204	171	2,861
8 July	580	2,456	184	3,220
9 July	371	1,405	85	1,861
10 July	496	1,996	68	2,560
11 July	281	1,176	23	1,480
5–11 July	3,880	17,571	822	22,273
12–20 July	1,299	5,011	704	7,014
21–31 July	1,103	4,805	440	6,348

Sources: Armeearzt AOK 9 Q.U. 10.7.1943, 19.7.1943, 25.7.1943 and 1.8.1943 (BA-MA RH 20-9/441) and Wehrmacht Verlustwesen file BA-MA RW 6/v. 564.

greater commitment and longer duration of the offensive. On the other hand, Soviet casualties were considerably greater on the southern sector as will be shown later.

The infantry divisions suffered more severe casualties than the panzer divisions. The divisions of 42nd Corps were an exception since the corps did not take part in the operation, but stood guarding the quiet front line along the Donets. It has been written that the losses suffered by the German infantry divisions were unusually high, and the 106th, 168th and 320th Infantry Divisions losses have been cited as examples, with numbers almost identical to those in Table 8.2.[5] The same author also stated that such losses as were suffered by the German infantry divisions in Zitadelle were much higher than those suffered by Allied divisions in northwest Europe in 1944. It is said that it took the worst-hit British divisions six months to reach the level of losses suffered by the German divisions during the offensive towards Kursk. This has also been echoed in a recent book on Zitadelle.[6] However, the facts do not agree with this conclusion.

In Normandy (6 June to 22 August) British and Canadian forces suffered 83,825 casualties and employed 16 divisions (British, Canadian and Polish).[7] This equates to an average of 5,329 casualties for each division. Of course, part of the losses would fall upon GHQ troops, but the infantry, which was almost exclusively found in divisions, endured the vast majority. Also the average is calculated by including all divisions, including those landing rather late on the continent. Thus a number of

113

TABLE 8.2: CASUALTIES SUFFERED BY ARMY DETACHMENT KEMPF, 4–20 JULY 1943

		Killed in Action	Wounded in Action	Missing in Action	Total
42nd Corps	39th Inf.Div.	18	48	3	69
	161st Inf.Div.	23	110	0	133
	282nd Inf.Div.	25	68	0	93
	Corps Troops	1	21	0	22
Total		67	247	3	317
Corps Raus	106th Inf.Div.	566	2,667	44	3,277
	320th Inf.Div.	472	2,140	426	3,038
	198th Inf.Div.	135	609	17	761
	Corps Troops	6	72	0	78
Total		1,179	5,488	487	7,154
3rd Pz. Corps	6th Pz.Div.	273	1,523	25	1,821
	7th Pz.Div.	235	1,219	33	1,487
	19th Pz.Div.	266	1,758	94	2,118
	167th Inf.Div.	50	222	1	273
	168th Inf.Div.	420	2,132	71	2,623
	Corps Troops	27	140	0	167
Total		1,271	6,994	224	8,489

Sources: KTB AOK 8 Ia (BA-MA RH 20-8/97)
Comments: The 167th Infantry Division alternated between 4th Panzer Army and Army Detachment Kempf during Zitadelle, thus it is included in both Tables 8.2 and 8.3.

divisions must have lost considerably more than 5,329 during the two-and-a-half months of fighting in Normandy. Information on individual allied divisions in certain operations confirms this pattern. Among US divisions it can be mentioned that the 4th Infantry Division lost 5,400 men during June 1944,[8] the 90th Infantry Division suffered over 4,000 casualties from 3 to 14 July,[9] the 30th Infantry Division suffered 3,300 casualties from 7 to 15 July[10] and the 83rd Infantry Division suffered no less than 5,000 casualties during the 12-day period ending on 14 July.[11] Also the VIII Corps had over 10,000 casualties between 3 and 14 July 1944, which was the price for an advance of 11 km.[12] Several other examples could be cited from the fighting during July 1944.[13]

For British and Commonwealth units information is more scarce,[14] but the 3rd Canadian Division suffered 2,831 casualties from 6 to 12 June 1944 (two-thirds of them after D-Day).[15] The 15th (Scottish) Division endured

2,720 losses during operation Epsom (26–30 June).[16] Seen against this background, the German losses, while certainly not marginal, cannot be regarded as extreme. The probable explanation for this erroneous statement is that the author believed that the loss figures for German divisions refer only to killed, a common error.

TABLE 8.3: CASUALTIES SUFFERED BY 4TH PANZER ARMY, 4–20 JULY 1943

		Killed in Action	Wounded in Action	Missing in Action	Total
II SS Pz. Corps	Leibstandarte	495	2,301	100	2,896
	Das Reich	456	1,849	23	2,328
	Totenkopf	531	2,228	43	2,802
	Corps Troops	5	64	0	69
Total		1,487	6,442	166	8,095
XXXXVIII Pz. Corps	Großdeutschland	364	1,859	68	2,291
	11th Pz.Div.	241	1,539	45	1,825
	3rd Pz.Div.	235	1,154	27	1,416
	167th Inf.Div.	128	721	14	863
	Corps Troops	22	124	0	146
Total		990	5,397	154	6,541
LII Corps	57th Inf.Div.	30	112	1	143
	255th Inf.Div.	132	752	13	897
	332nd Inf.Div.	393	2,402	123	2,918
Total		555	3,266	137	3,958

Sources: KTB Abt. Qu XXXXVIII Pz.Korps (NARA T314, Roll 1169);[17] Anlagenheft vom 21.7 bis 26.7.1943 zum KTB Nr 6 LII. A.K. Ia (BA-MA RH 24-52/159); Gen.Kdo. II. SS-Pz.Korps, der Korpsarzt, Meldungen 11.7 - 2.8.1943 (BA-MA RS 2-2/17).

Comments: The 167th Infantry Division alternated between 4th Panzer Army and Army Detachment Kempf during Zitadelle, thus it is included in both Tables 8.2 and 8.3.

As discussed earlier, the term 'the battle at Kursk' can be interpreted in at least two ways. If it is seen as part of a larger operation, ending with the reduction of the Orel salient and the Soviet recapture of Kharkov, it can be interesting to present losses for Army Groups Centre and South during July and August 1943. As is shown in Table 8.4, the overall casualties for Army Groups Centre and South amounted to 340,949 men during July and August. However, this applies to a longer period of time and to a larger part of the front than is covered by what can strictly be called 'the battle at Kursk'.

TABLE 8.4: GERMAN CASUALTIES, JUNE–SEPTEMBER 1943

	Army Group North	Army Group Centre	Army Group South	Army Group A
June	8,980	13,613	6,785	4,556
July	18,275	92,485	85,787	9,537
August	26,056	80,445	82,232	8,903
September	10,934	48,070	56,222	13,983

Note: Figures include killed, wounded and missing, but non-combat losses are not included.
Source: BA-MA RH 2/1343.

It is, however, possible to obtain more precise information on the overall German casualties during the fighting around Orel, Kursk, Belgorod and Kharkov during July and August. On the German side, the armies involved were the 2nd Pz, 9th, 2nd, 4th Pz and Army Det Kempf. Usually Soviet literature considers that these operations began on 5 July and ended with the capture of Kharkov on 23 August. From Table 8.5 it can be derived that those German armies involved suffered about 203,000 casualties between 5 July and 23 August.[18]

Another interesting observation that can be gleaned from Table 8.5 is that the periods 1–10 July and 10–20 July are not the worst for Army Detachment Kempf and 4th Panzer Army. Rather the latter part of August took a greater toll of those two armies. For the 9th Army the first period in the table is clearly the worst, but the losses suffered by 2nd Panzer Army, its neighbour in the Orel salient, were even worse between 21 and 31 July. This indicates that operation Zitadelle was only the beginning of the summer fighting in 1943.

SOVIET MANPOWER LOSSES

Reliable information on Soviet losses has been lacking since the battle was fought. Indeed, even unreliable information has been scarce too. There have been available some German estimates and figures on how many prisoners the Wehrmacht took. According to von Manstein, Army Group South took 24,000 prisoners up to 13 July.[19] For the entire battle (probably meaning up to 18 July) von Manstein claimed that Army Group South had taken 34,000 prisoners and estimated that the enemy lost 17,000

TABLE 8.5: GERMAN CASUALTIES ON THE EASTERN FRONT FOR EACH ARMY,
1 JULY–31 AUGUST 1943

	1–10 July	11–20 July	21–31 July	1–10 August	11–20 August	21–31 August
18th Army	1,761	2,428	11,575	8,922	5,946	4,785
16th Army	584	852	945	1,011	2,801	2,467
3rd Panzer Army	1,240	761	705	747	522	607
4th Army	545	1,017	1,073	6,675	21,453	9,335
2nd Panzer Army	1,059	10,120	34,749	8,162	7,399	–
9th Army	20,189	8,258	8,908	4,336	6,756	4,663
2nd Army	213	303	200	1,219	1,426	4,112
4th Panzer Army	9,977	5,725	7,449	1,202	10,164	14,545
Army Det. Kempf	9,628	7,987	5,270	2,009	11,359	12,111
1st Panzer Army	984	7,408	7,088	4,092	5,495	6,133
6th Army	737	7,378	11,295	5,050	1,683	3,439
17th Army	986	1,907	4,406	3,344	2,193	1,128

Note: Figures include killed, wounded and missing, but non-combat losses are not included.

Source: 10-day reports from the Wehrmacht Verlustwesen (BA-MA RW 6/v. 558).

Comments: Reports were compiled 4 days after the end of the period they apply to (i.e. on the 4th, 14th and 24th each month). When units occasionally reported too late the unreported losses were included in the next report. Thus it may for example be that some of the losses suffered by 4th Panzer Army and Army Detachment Kempf at the beginning of the Soviet offensive against Kharkov in August is included in the period 10–20 August.

The German 2nd Panzer Army HQ was withdrawn to the Balkans in August and most of its combat units were assigned to the 9th Army, hence the lack of figures for 21–31 August.

soldiers killed and twice that number wounded.[20] This would have meant that the Red Army forces on the southern sector must have suffered 85,000 casualties.

Today more information has become available from Russia, including substantial information on losses suffered by the Red Army. The most comprehensive work on Soviet casualties probably is G.F. Krivosheyev's *Grif Sekretnosti Sniat*, which drew upon archival records to provide much valuable information on Soviet losses during World War II (and other wars). It also contains information on Soviet strength for a large number of operations, including Kursk and much other valuable information.

This work has not escaped criticism since its publication. Possibly the most important has been articulated by B.V. Sokolov.[21] He not only criticizes *Grif Sekretnosti Sniat* for its lack of clarity concerning methodology and sources used. He also presents several cases of inconsistency within the book and with other kinds of sources. The argumentation certainly has some merit and Sokolov's conclusion is that the casualty figures presented in *Grif Sekretnosti Sniat* are too low. One example of unexplained inconsistencies concerns Zitadelle. According to *Grif Sekretnosti Sniat* the Central Front possessed 738,000 men on 5 July and 645,300 men on 12 July,[22] a decrease of 92,700 men. In the meantime quoted losses amounted only to 33,897, despite the fact that the order of battle shows only minimal changes (adding one brigade and losing two).[23] Where the remaining 58,803 men have gone to warrants an explanation.

Another strange aspect with the casualty figures presented in *Grif Sekretnosti Sniat* concerns the southern sector. The Steppe Front was created on 9 July by the renaming of the Steppe Military District and none of the subordinated units at that time under the Steppe Front's command was deployed at the front (5th Guards Army and 5th Guards Tank Army had been transferred to the Voronezh Front).[24] It was not until 18 July that the Steppe Front took command over front-line units, 69th Army and 7th Guards Army.[25] So how could this front have suffered the same level of casualties as the Voronezh Front?

One plausible explanation is that, both during and after the fighting, units' reports of casualties were filed with the front command to which they belonged for the moment and that these subordinated units were the only ones included in the accounted for total. For example, on 24 July the Voronezh Front reported that it had suffered 100,932 casualties between 4 and 22 July,[26] yet when the Voronezh Front filed a battle report upon the defensive phase (4 to 23 July) on 23 August 1943 the front reported 74,500 casualties from 4 to 23 July.[27] Clearly, better knowledge about Soviet reporting methods is needed.

The information from *Grif Sekretnosti Sniat* will still be used, but the reader should regard the information on Soviet losses with some scepticism. They should be regarded similarly with respect to sectors north and south of the Kursk bulge. These are the losses that Russian researchers acknowledge today.

As can be seen from Table 8.6, von Manstein's estimate that the enemy suffered 17,000 killed and 34,000 missing on the Army Group South sector was pretty accurate (Krivosheyev's total in killed and missing is 54,994 while the Germans estimated it to be 51,000). He did, however, underestimate the number of enemy soldiers wounded.

Soviet losses in the operation were about 3.4 times higher than German losses. In the Army Group Centre sector Soviet losses were about 1.5 times higher than German losses, but Army Group South had a much more favourable loss ratio. On this sector Soviet losses were 4.6 times higher than German losses. The reasons for this great difference may be that

COST OF THE BATTLE

TABLE 8.6: CASUALTIES SUFFERED BY THE RED ARMY DURING OPERATION ZITADELLE

	Killed and Missing	Wounded	Total
Central Front, 5–11 July	15,336	18,561	33,897
Voronezh Front, 5–23 July	27,542	46,350	73,892
Steppe Front, 9–23 July	27,452	42,606	70,058
Total	70,330	107,517	177,847

Source: G.F. Krivosheyev, *Grif Sekretnosti Sniat*, p. 188.

Army Group South enjoyed a better numerical ratio, at least initially. This does usually by itself give a better loss ratio, but it also resulted in a higher advance rate, which in turn resulted in more Soviet units being cut off. Accordingly, the number of prisoners becomes greater, as is indicated by the fact that Army Group South took 34,000 prisoners, a number exceeding the overall losses on the Central Front.

TABLE 8.7: CASUALTIES SUFFERED BY THE RED ARMY DURING MAJOR OPERATIONS
IN SUMMER 1943

	Killed and Missing	Wounded	Total
Kursk defensive operations, 5–23 July	70,330	107,517	177,847
Orel offensive operations, 12 July–18 Aug	112,529	317,361	429,890
Belgorod–Kharkov offensive operations, 3–23 Aug	71,611	183,955	255,566
Smolensk offensive operations, 7 Aug–2 Oct	107,645	343,821	451,466
Donbass offensive operations, 13 Aug–22 Sept	66,166	207,356	273,522
Chernigov–Poltava, 26 Aug–30 Sept	102,957	324,995	427,952
Total	531,238	1,485,005	2,016,243

Source: G.F. Krivosheyev, *Grif Sekretnosti Sniat*, pp. 188–93.

If the Soviet definition of the battle at Kursk is accepted, including the Orel and Belgorod–Kharkov operations too, losses for the battle would be 254,470 killed and missing, and 608,833 wounded, giving an overall total of 863,303 casualties. The losses for the major Soviet operations are given in Table 8.7. As can be seen, the defensive part of the battle was actually the least costly. It should also be emphasized that, far from all losses suffered by the Red Army during the summer of 1943 being inflicted within the context of the operations listed in Table 8.7, other operations such as the diversionary attack at the Mius initiated on 17 July are not included.[28]

Tank and assault gun losses

In a battle called the greatest tank battle of all history, tank losses are of course of paramount interest. Unfortunately erroneous statements on German tank losses have plagued this battle. The example presented at the beginning of this chapter is but one. Other authors state even higher losses. Two Russians have recently claimed that the Germans lost 2,644 tanks on the southern sector (up to 15 July) and 928 on the northern sector.[29] This is taken from a Soviet archival document, which also gives Soviet losses amounting to 651 tanks on the Central Front sector and 890 tanks being destroyed among the Voronezh Front units. This would indicate that the Germans lost far more tanks than the Red Army. This is not at all the case however. It is an error of methodology to search among Russian records for information on German losses.[30] It seems that these figures on German losses stem from Soviet unit after-action reports, a notoriously unreliable source for such data.[31] Another problem with these figures is that it is not clear whether the number of German tanks lost refer to tanks put out of action or to total write-offs.

Another figure commonly presented in Soviet literature is 1,500 German tanks destroyed in the Orel–Kursk–Kharkov area between 5 July and 23 August.[32] This seems to refer to total write-offs, but it is still too high since the Germans on the *entire* eastern front lost 1,331 tanks and assault guns from 1 July to 31 August,[33] where, for example, the fighting along the Mius, in the Donbass and on the Smolensk axis and the resultant tank losses have also been included in the overall total.

However, there are German documents that do give an accurate picture of the extent of German losses. As shown in Table 8.8, 88 German tanks and assault guns were destroyed among the units in 9th Army up to 14 July.

For the whole of July losses were, of course, higher. The entire Army Group Centre lost 311 tanks, StuPz IV and Ferdinands, as is shown in Table 8.9. Also, the independent Sturmgeschütz battalions lost 60 assault guns.[34] This would indicate losses during Zitadelle constituted a minor part of the overall losses for Army Group Centre during July. This is not really surprising. First, two panzer divisions, 5th and 8th, were committed to the defence of the Orel salient and took no part in Zitadelle. These two

TABLE 8.8: DESTROYED TANKS IN ARMY GROUP CENTRE, 5–14 JULY 1943

	Pz III	Pz IV	Tiger I	StuG
2nd Panzer Division		14		
4th Panzer Division		6		
9th Panzer Division		2		
12th Panzer Division		1		
18th Panzer Division	2	9		
20th Panzer Division	1	3		
505th Panzer Abteilung			4	
177th StuG Abteilung				1
185th StuG Abteilung				3
189th StuG Abteilung				1
244th StuG Abteilung				5
245th StuG Abteilung				2
904th StuG Abteilung				2
909th StuG Abteilung				3
656th Pz Jäger Regiment				19
216th StuPz Abteilung				10

Source: BA-MA RH 10/65.

TABLE 8.9: TANK LOSSES AMONG UNITS IN ARMY GROUP CENTRE DURING JULY 1943

	Pz III	Pz IV	Pz VI	StuG	StuPz IV	Ferdinand	BefPz	Total
2nd Panzer Division	13	29	0	0	0	0	3	45
4th Panzer Division	3	15	0	0	0	0	1	19
5th Panzer Division	11	43	0	0	0	0	1	55
8th Panzer Division	14	24	0	0	0	0	3	41
9th Panzer Division	7	18	0	0	0	0	0	25
12th Panzer Division	0	13	0	0	0	0	1	14
18th Panzer Division	14	12	0	0	0	0	1	27
20th Panzer Division	3	20	0	0	0	0	1	24
505th Panzer Abteilung	0	0	5	0	0	0	0	5
216th StuPz Abteilung	0	0	0	0	17	0	0	17
656th Pz Jäger Regiment[35]	0	0	0	0	0	39	0	39

Note: Figures refer to total write-offs.
Source: Pz. Offz. b. Chef Gen.St.d.H. Bb. Nr. 562/43 g.Kdos, v. 14.8.1943 (BA-MA RH 10/48).
Commentary: Note that 5th and 8th Panzer Division, which did not take part in Zitadelle, but in the defence of the Orel bulge, were among the units that suffered highest losses.

divisions lost 96 tanks during July. Also, it must be emphasized that with-drawal operations usually meant greater tank losses for the Germans than offensive operations. Generally far more German tanks were damaged rather than destroyed by enemy fire. If the vehicle could be towed away it could usually be repaired and sent into action again. When withdrawing this was of course much more difficult, resulting in the loss of even lightly damaged tanks. Thus, it is quite realistic to expect that most losses for Army Group Centre were not suffered during Zitadelle, but during the withdrawal from the Orel salient.

Army Group South presents a different pattern. All its panzer divi-sions were committed from the beginning of the operation and it held its advanced positions for a longer period than Army Group Centre. Thus it could be expected that losses would be greater during the offensive period, but smaller subsequently.

According to documents from the Inspector-General of Panzer Troops, the number of tanks that had been completely destroyed in the Army Group South sector up to 17 July is shown in Table 8.10.

TABLE 8.10: DESTROYED TANKS IN ARMY GROUP SOUTH, 5–17 JULY 1943

	Flamm.Pz	Pz III	Pz IV	Panther	Tiger I	StuG
3rd Panzer Division		6	3			
11th Panzer Division		2	3			
Großdeutschland		3	16			1
LAH*		1	9		1	1
Das Reich		1	6		1	1
Totenkopf		2	8		1	1
6th Panzer Division	3	9	13			
7th Panzer Division		8	2			
19th Panzer Division		8	19			
503rd Panzer Abteilung					3	
10th Panzer Brigade				44		
911th StuG Abteilung						3
905th StuG Abteilung						5
228th StuG Abteilung						1
393rd StuG Bttr						5

Note: LAH* = Leibstandarte Adolf Hitler (also used is LSSAH, Leibstandarte SS Adolf Hitler).
Source: BA-MA RH 10/64.

Thus, Army Group South lost 190 tanks and assault guns between 5 and 17 July. Probably losses did not increase drastically for the remainder of July. It is known that 65 Panthers were lost by 10th Panzer Brigade during July,[36] which means that two-thirds of all Panther losses were

COST OF THE BATTLE

incurred before 18 July. The Panther did at this stage suffer from many teething troubles, among them many poor gaskets and an inadequate cooling system. This made the tank very flammable, and indeed two Panthers of the 10th Panzer Brigade succeeded in completely destroying themselves by fires in the engine room, before the beginning of the offensive.[37] Such incidents could also have occurred on exercises in units being formed and trained in Germany even though it may perhaps have been more likely to occur during the heat of battle. However the tank was certainly very difficult to knock out by enemy anti-tank guns. Up to 7 July only two Panthers had been pierced by Soviet gunfire.[38] This suggests that many Panthers were lost quite unnecessarily and probably minor improvements might have reduced losses drastically. Also, between 1 and 20 July, 16 Panthers were returned to Germany for major repairs.[39] Yet it was not only a question of the tank possessing weaknesses requiring major repairs. The Panther was also subject to several minor problems, which, while relatively easy to repair, still caused the vehicles to require time in workshops. For example, during the night between 12 and 13 July it was reported that 93 Panthers were in short-term repair (in this case that meant operational within four days).[40]

The 503rd s. Panzer Abteilung had only lost seven Tigers between 5 July and 18 August.[41] This does not suggest that actions after the offensive phase of the fighting during July were particularly costly. Similarly, the condition of the panzer divisions on 1 August does not indicate that losses after 17 July were excessive.[42]

Losses of aircraft

German aircraft losses are not as difficult to establish as tank losses. Even though damaged aircraft were sometimes cannibalized for spare parts, the proportion of immediately destroyed to merely put out of action is much higher for aircraft than for tanks, at least for the Germans at Kursk. The daily aircraft losses for the German air units participating in Zitadelle have been established from archival sources and are presented in Table 8.11.

TABLE 8.11: GERMAN AIRCRAFT LOSSES AND SORTIES DURING ZITADELLE

	Losses Suffered by Luftflotte 6 (supporting 9th Army)	Losses Suffered by 8th Fliegerkorps (supporting 4th Pz and Kempf)	Number of Sorties Luftflotte 6	Number of Sorties 8th Fliegerkorps
4–15 July	94	99	12,823	14,398

Source: E. Klink, *Das Gesetz des Handelns*, pp. 337–8.

Thus, the German air forces operating in the vicinity of Kursk lost 193 aircraft shot down while performing a total of 27,221 sorties. Of course, further aircraft may have been written off when damaged machines were cannibalized for spare parts. It is also not clear from the source whether the figures above refer to aircraft lost due to all causes or lost due to enemy action. The difference can be quite significant. For example, during 1942 the Luftwaffe lost 4,151 aircraft due to enemy action, plus another 497 that were brought home damaged but were not repaired. At the same time 3,163 were lost without any influence from the enemy and a further 1,791 were damaged but not repaired.[43] Accordingly, about half the German aircraft losses were not caused by the enemy.

It would however not be prudent to assume that the proportion of aircraft destroyed due to enemy action and not due to enemy action was identical at Kursk. First of all the opposition facing the Luftwaffe was tougher than in 1942 and, secondly, the better weather during July was less likely to have caused flying accidents than the conditions during autumn and winter.

Two sets of figures concerning the overall losses on the eastern front might also be interesting. Williamson Murray states that the Luftwaffe lost 1,030 planes (351 fighters, 273 bombers, 202 dive bombers and 204 other aircraft) on the eastern front during July and August 1943.[44] Tony Wood and Bill Gunston on the other hand put Luftwaffe losses on the eastern front at 911 planes in July and 785 in August.[45] Possibly, the difference between these figures can be explained by Murray's figure referring to combat losses, while the other set of numbers concern losses due to all causes. Whatever the cause for this difference, it is quite clear that Soviet claims to have shot down 3,700 German planes in air combat in the Orel–Kursk–Kharkov area between 5 July and 23 August[46] are very exaggerated.

Losses of other equipment

Concerning other kinds of equipment it has only been possible to present scattered information. The II SS-Panzer Corps submitted a report on 23 July with detailed information on equipment losses.[47] This report gave losses (including destroyed but not damaged and repairable equipment) as 5 Panzer III, 23 Panzer IV, 3 Tiger, 5 StuG, 2 15cm heavy infantry guns, 2 10.5cm field howitzers, 16 7.5cm PAK 40 (towed), 2 7.5cm PAK (SP), 3 per cent of all machine-guns, 3.5 per cent of all 5cm AT guns, 3 per cent of all motorcycles, 4 per cent of all cars and trucks, 4 per cent of all towing vehicles, 8 per cent of all armoured personnel carriers (SPW).

Even though the precautions discussed in Appendix 14 should be observed when using this report on destroyed equipment, a number of interesting conclusions can be drawn from it. The loss of 36 tanks and assault guns is indicated, a figure far below the common estimates on the losses suffered by II SS-Panzer Corps. But also it is interesting to note that 16 towed AT guns of 7.5cm calibre were destroyed. This is testimony to the German practice of pushing the anti-tank guns as far forward as possible. For all other types of equipment the losses were negligible. This is perhaps typical of offensive operations, since the tanks and the infantry thrust forward, with most other weapons supporting from behind. During defensive operations, the situation can be different.

There exists a report from 2nd Panzer Army which provides infor-mation on its losses during July, thus covering an important part of the defensive operation in the Orel bulge.[48] This shows the following equipment losses (total write-offs): 83 3.7cm AT guns, 52 5cm AT guns, 26 7.5cm AT guns, 35 7.5cm AT guns (SP), 29 7.62cm AT guns (captured Russian pieces, 8 of them SP), 45 other types of anti-tank guns (mainly captured pieces), 210 5cm mortars, 179 8cm mortars, 3 12cm mortars (captured Russian), 95 field howitzers (of 10.5 and 15cm calibre), 3 heavy artillery guns (one each of 10cm and 17cm calibre plus one 21cm howitzer), 59 infantry support guns (of 7.5 and 15cm calibre), 11 Nebelwerfers, 37 artillery pieces of captured types, 32 AA guns, 1,891 machine-guns and 45 tanks.

Evidently the amount of artillery pieces lost according to this report was much higher than for II SS-Panzer Corps, while the number of tanks lost was not that much greater. This does of course reflect differences in force structure, but also the postures of the forces and the fact that the Red Army gained terrain in the Orel sector, while the II SS-Panzer Corps drove Soviet units out of their positions and thereafter made an orderly withdrawal.

Panzengrenadier Division Großdeutschland filed a report on its losses (complete write-offs) of other vehicles during Operation Zitadelle. The division lost 32 motorcycles, 28 cars, 31 trucks, 9 non-armoured half-tracks, 4 SPWs (Sdkfz 250 and 251) and 1 Marder II.[49]

SOVIET EQUIPMENT LOSSES

German estimates have been available from a variety of sources. According to von Manstein, the Red Army forces facing 4th Panzer Army and Army Detachment Kempf had lost 1,800 tanks, 267 artillery pieces and 1,080 AT guns up to 13 July.[50]

125

During 1943 the Red Army lost (total write-offs) 23,500 tanks and assault guns.[51] Between 1 January and 30 June 1943, 5,747 tanks and assault guns were completely lost to the Red Army.[52] This would indicate a total loss of 17,753 tanks and assault guns during the second half of 1943. Over the same period the German combat units reported the destruction of 30,668 tanks and assault guns.[53] The German high command did reduce this by 50 per cent to compensate for double counting and repairable vehicles and accordingly settled for a total of 15,334 tanks and assault guns destroyed. Compared with the figures presented above the German high command was a little too drastic in its reduction of claims. Instead of reducing by 50 per cent, 42 per cent would have been more accurate. For the period 1 July to 31 August the claims of the combat units were 16,250 tanks and assault guns, which accordingly were reduced to 8,125 by the high command.[54] If the 42 per cent reduction is applied, it would indicate 9,400 tanks and assault guns destroyed. This is an extremely high number, but some support is evident from the fact that all Soviet tank armies were withdrawn at the end of August for refit, despite the urgent need for such units for exploitation during the German retreat.[55]

For various Soviet units useful information on losses does exist. Rodin's 2nd Tank Army was committed on 6 July and had 456 tanks on hand.[56] Of these 30.7 per cent were completely lost before 15 July and another 16.7 per cent were damaged but repairable.[57] This would indicate that 140 tanks were completely destroyed or captured, while 76 were damaged but repairable. Table 8.12 lists the daily losses for 2nd Tank Army.

Also, some Soviet documents have been made available to Western researchers. According to a report from the deputy commander of staff of the tank and mechanized forces of the Red Army 2,924 tanks and assault

TABLE 8.12: LOSSES IN 2ND TANK ARMY DURING THE DEFENSIVE PHASE, JULY 1943[58]

	3rd Tank Corps		16th Tank Corps		11th Gds Tank Brig		Overall	
	All losses	Destroyed	All losses	Destroyed	All losses	Destroyed	All losses	Destroyed
6 July	3	–	88	69	–	–	91	69
7 July	14	7	35	20	–	–	49	27
8 July	45	32	3	1	1	–	49	33
9 July	8	5	–	–	–	–	8	5
10 July	8	4	1	–	–	–	9	4
11 July	–	–	1	–	–	–	1	–
12 July	–	–	2	–	–	–	2	–
14 July[59]	–	–	4	–	–	–	4	–
Total	78	48	134	90	1	–	213	138

guns were committed on the Voronezh Front sector (including reserves from the Steppe front) from the beginning of the battle until 20 July, of which 1,254 were irretrievably lost.[60] If these figures for the Voronezh Front tank losses are used, the front would have suffered 43 per cent complete losses among its tanks. This is slightly lower than the percentage given below for 1st Tank Army.

Katukov's 1st Tank Army had 634 tanks at the beginning of Zitadelle.[61] After ten days of defensive fighting it was down to 321 tanks, thus 51 per cent of initial strength was written off.[62]

Another interesting set of figure concerns the 5th Guards Tank Army. A document signed by the chief of staff of the 5th Guards Tank Army, Major-General Baskakov reveals that 222 T-34, 89 T-70, 12 Churchill lend-lease tanks and 11 assault guns were irretrievably lost between 12 and 16 July.[63] This makes for a total of 334 tanks and assault guns, indicating that it lost about 40 per cent of its tanks. This would then be quite similar to 1st Tank Army, despite the fact that 1st Tank Army had been fighting for about a week when the 5th Guards Tank Army entered the combat.

For the Central Front one author states that the tank losses between 5 and 15 July amounted to 651 vehicles lost irretrievably.[64] If to this is added the numbers given above for the Voronezh Front the Red Army would have lost 1,905 tanks completely destroyed or captured by the enemy. However, Krivosheyev's book states that the total losses of the defensive phase at Kursk were 1,614 tanks and assault guns (see Table 8.13).

According to a report filed by the Voronezh Front on 24 July 1943 regarding losses, the front lost from 4 July to 16 July: 1,605 guns of all calibres, 1,734 mortars, 4,381 machine-guns, 1,634 heavy machine-guns,

TABLE 8.13: EQUIPMENT LOSSES OF THE RED ARMY DURING MAJOR OPERATIONS IN SUMMER 1943

	Small Arms Weapons	Tanks and Assault Guns	Guns and Mortars
Kursk defensive operations, 5–23 July	70,800	1,614	3,929
Orel offensive operations, 12 July–18 Aug	60,500	2,586	892
Belgorod-Kharkov offensive operations, 3–23 Aug	21,700	1,864	423
Smolensk offensive operations, 7 Aug–2 Oct	33,700	863	234
Donbass offensive operations, 13 Aug–22 Sept	37,900	886	814
Chernigov–Poltava, 26 Aug–30 Sept	48,000	1,140	916
Total	272,600	8,953	7,208

Source: G.F. Krivosheyev, Grif Sekretnosti Sniat, p. 370.

35,026 sub-machine-guns, 40,520 rifles, 3,247 anti-tank rifles. The units also lost from 16 July to 22 July: 108 guns of all calibres, 162 mortars, 399 machine-guns, 161 heavy machine-guns, 872 sub-machine-guns, 1,612 rifles and 212 anti-tank rifles.[65] The losses of guns and mortars thus equals 3,609. If we compare it to the losses reported in *Grif Sekretnosti Sniat* it would mean that only 320 guns and mortars were lost by the Central Front during the German offensive. That is too low in our opinion. But we do not know for certain that the weapon losses reported by the Voronezh Front were write-offs. The weapons are only listed as losses, while for vehicles the report separates those put out of action and those irretrievably lost. Perhaps future research will clarify this matter.

NOTES

1. J. Erickson, *The Road to Berlin* (Grafton, London, 1985), p. 148.
2. See *Journal of Slavic Military Studies*, Vol. 6, no. 4 (December 1993), p. 692. These claims were first included in a declaration signed by Stalin on 24 July 1943 concerning the defeat of the German offensive: more than 70,000 soldiers and officers killed and 2,952 tanks, 195 self-propelled guns and 844 field guns damaged and destroyed, 1,392 air planes and more than 5,000 motor vehicles destroyed. (Notice the changes the Red Army make to these claims in their General Staff Study 'Collection of War Experience'.) *Rysskii Arkhiv: Velikaya Otechestvennaya 4(4), Kurskaya Bitva, Dokumenti i Materiali 27 Marta–23 Avgusta 1943 goda* (Terra, Moscow, 1997), pp. 63–4.
3. See Table 8.2 for casualties suffered by Army Detachment Kempf, 4–20 July and Table 8.3 for casualties suffered by 4th Panzer Army, 4–20 July.
4. The allies estimated that the Germans had lost 210,000 men as prisoners, while the 240,000 were killed or wounded in the period 6 June to 22 August (according to B.L. Montgomery, *Normandy to the Baltic* (Hutchinson, London, 1946), p. 112). According to German documents from the Army High command medical section, published in H. Jung, *Die Ardennen Offensiv* (Musterschmitt, Göttingen, 1971), pp. 280–8, casualties 1 June–31 August 1944 in the OB (Oberbefehlshaber West – encompassing France, Belgium and the Netherlands) West sector amounted to 23,019 killed in action, 67,240 wounded in action and 198,616 missing. The figures from German sources refer to events in southern France as well as on the main front in Normandy.
5. John Ellis, *Brute Force* (André Deutsch, London, 1990), p. 108.
6. Robin Cross, *Citadel – The Battle of Kursk* (Michael O'Mara Books, London, 1993), p. 233.
7. L.F. Ellis, *Victory in the West*, Vol. I (HMSO, London 1962), p. 493 and Appendix IV.
8. Martin Blumenson, *Breakout and Pursuit*, Office of the Chief of Military History, Dept. of the Army, Washington, DC, 1961, p. 86.
9. Ibid., pp. 71, 127.
10. Ibid., p. 142.
11. Ibid., p. 132.
12. Ibid., p. 127.
13. The following examples are taken from Martin Blumenson's *Breakout and Pursuit*:

83rd Infantry Division suffered 'almost 1,400 casualties' on 4 July (p. 84); 4th Infantry Division suffered 2,300 casualties 6–15 July (p. 130), while 9th Infantry Division lost 2,500 men 10–20 July (p. 145).

14. We have not had the opportunity to search in British archives for such information. In published literature it is however scarce.

15. C.P. Stacey, *The Victory Campaign: The Operations in NW Europe 1944–1945* (The Queen's Printer and Controller of Stationery, Ottawa, 1960), p. 140.

16. Ibid., p. 149.

17. Versorgungslageberichte des Gen.Kdo. XXXXVIII. Pz.Korps Abt. Qu. vom 2.7. 1943 bis 30.10.1943, Anlageband 3 zum KTB nr 2 (National Archives and Records Administration, Washington DC, Microfilm publication T314), roll 1169. The frames used are: 000752, 000755, 000758, 000761, 000765, 000768, 000770, 000777, 000788, 000791, 000794. These present a casualty compilation for the period 4 July to 10 July and daily losses for the period 11 July to 20 July. Figures are lacking for the entire corps for 18 July and for the 11th Panzer Division for 17 July. Note that the Großdeutschland division began to pull out of the line on the night 16–17 July and there are no casualty reports for GD after 16 July. For the missing dates, estimates have been made, using the average for the five-day period 16–20 July.

18. Adding together the losses for Army Detachment Kempf, 4th Panzer Army, 2nd Army, 9th Army and 2nd Panzer Army for the period 1 July to 20 August and half the losses for the period 21 August to 31 August.

19. Erich von Manstein, *Verlorene Siege* (Athenäum-Verlag, Bonn, 1958), p. 501.

20. Ibid., p. 504.

21. See *Journal of Slavic Military Studies*, Vol. 9, no. 1 (March 1996), pp. 152–93, and B.V. Sokolov, 'The Battle for Kursk, Orel, and Charkov: Strategic Intentions and Results – A Critical View of the Soviet Historiography', in Jürgen G. Foerster (ed.), *Gezeitenwechsel im Zweiten Weltkrieg?* (Mittler & Sohn, Hamburg, 1996), pp. 69–88. Also see Niklas Zetterling and Anders Frankson, 'Analysing WWII East Front Battles', *Journal of Slavic Military Studies*, Vol. 11, no. 1 (March 1998).

22. G.F. Krivosheyev, *Grif Sekretnosti Sniat* (Voenizdat, Moscow, 1993), pp. 188–9.

23. Ibid.

24. Stavka Directive, issued on 9 July 1943, quotes subordinated units as 27th Army with 4th Guards Tank Corps, 53rd Army with 1st Mechanized Corps, 47th Army with 3rd Guards Mechanized Corps, 4th Guards Army with 3rd Guards Tank Corps, 52nd Army with 3rd, 5th, 7th Guards Cavalry Corps. *Rysskii Arkhiv: Velikaya Otechestvennaya 4(4), Kurskaya Bitva, Dokumenti i Materiali 27 Marta–23 Avgusta 1943 goda*, p. 48.

25. Stavka Directive, issued on 16 July 1943. *Rysskii Arkhiv: Velikaya Otechestvennaya 4(4), Kurskaya Bitva*, p. 58.

26. Voronezh Front reports about losses, 24 July 1943 in *Rysskii Arkhiv: Velikaya Otechestvennaya 4(4), Kurskaya Bitva*, pp. 272–3.

27. Report by General Staff Officer over Defence Operation 4 to 23 July 1943 in *Rysskii Arkhiv: Velikaya Otechestvennaya 4(4), Kurskaya Bitva*, pp. 375–93.

28. The Red Army suffered 2,864,661 casualties 1 July–30 September 1943 (Krivosheyev, *Grif Sekretnosti Sniat*, p.147).

29. Viktor V. Muchin and Igor N. Venkov in Jürgen G. Foerster (ed.), *Gezeitenwechsel im Zweiten Weltkrieg?*, pp. 238–44.

30. Except possibly for information found in German documents captured by the Soviets during, or immediately after the war. See also N. Zetterling and A. Frankson, 'Analysing WWII East Front Battles', pp. 176–203, for a more comprehensive discussion on the problems associated with reports concerning casualties and losses.

31. Another example is a report filed by the Voronezh Front on 24 July 1943 where they claim to have disabled 4,728 German tanks and assault guns during the defensive operation. Of these they estimate that 2,500 to 3,000 were destroyed. *Rysskii Arkhiv: Velikaya Otechestvennaya 4(4), Kurskaya Bitva*, pp. 269–70.

32. See, for example, *Geschichte des Zweiten Weltkrieges*, Vol. 7 (Deutscher Militärverlag, East Berlin, 1975–85, p. 214; A. Vasilevkiy, *Delo Vsey Zhizni* (Politzdat, Moscow, 1976), p. 346; G.K. Zhukov, *Vospominaniya u Razmyshleniya*, Tom 3 (Novosti, Moscow, 1974), p. 72.

33. BA-MA RH 10/77.

34. Pz. Offz. b. Chef Gen.St.d.H. Bb. Nr. 562/43 g.Kdos, v. 14.8.1943 (BA-MA RH 10/48).

35. The 653rd Battalion lost 13 up to 29 July and 654th Battalion lost 25. BA-MA RH 10/246.

36. Anlage 2 zu Gen.Insp.d.Pz.Truppen, Führer-Vortrag, H.Qu, OKH., den 26.8.43, T78, R623, F000445.

37. Bergung der Pz.Kpfw. V ('Panther') im Zuge der Absetzbewegung ab 18.7.43, Abt. V den 20. Juli 1943 (BA-MA RH 21-4/450).

38. T.N. Dupuy *et al.*, *Breakthrough Operations* (Hero, Dunn Loring, VI), p. 141. This book contains a long section covering the fighting in XXXVIII Panzer Corps sector. It is essentially a translation into English of the reports from the subordinated units to Corps HQ. Thus it is an excellent, almost minute by minute, coverage of the fighting from the German perspective.

39. Bergung der Pz.Kpfw. V ('Panther') im Zuge der Absetzbewegung ab 18.7.43, Abt. V den 20. Juli 1943 (BA-MA RH 21-4/450).

40. 12.7-13.7 Nachtmeldung Pz.A.O.K 4 O.Qu. Anlage zu KTB, Aktennotiz 13.7.1943 (BA-MA RH 21-4/450).

41. Der Panzeroffizier beim Chef Gen.St.d.H. Nr. 574/43 g.Kdos. 19.8.1943, BA-MA RH 10/60.

42. See Chapter 10 and Appendix 14.

43. KTB OKW, Vol. II, p. 1322.

44. W. Murray, *Luftwaffe – Strategy for Defeat 1933–45* (Grafton, London, 1988), p. 224.

45. T. Wood and B. Gunston, *Hitler's Luftwaffe* (Leisure Books, Turnhout, 1984), p. 80.

46. B.V. Sokolov, *The Battle for Kursk, Orel, and Charkov: Strategic Intentions and Results – A Critical View of the Soviet Historiography*, pp. 78–9.

47. Gen.Kdo. II. SS-Pz.Korps 23.7.1943 (BA-MA RS 2-2/18).

48. Pz.AOK 2, Abt. Ia, Waffenausfälle in der Zeit vom 1.7.1943–31.7.1943 einschl (BA-MA RH 21-2/v.796b).

49. BA-MA RH 24-23/126 Panzergrenadier Division Großdeutschland Zustands-bericht vom 1.8.1943.

50. Von Manstein, *Verlorene Siege*, p. 501.

51. G.F. Krivosheyev, *Voina Broni i Motorov* (article in *Voenno-Istoricheskij Zhurnal*, no. 4, 1991), p. 40.

52. Edwin Bacon, 'Soviet Military Losses in World War II', *Journal of Slavic Military Studies*, Vol. 6, no. 4 (December 1993), p. 623. The exact losses for each month were: January 1,516, February 1,570, March 1,937, April 361, May 283 and June 80.

53. Panzerverluste Ost seit 1.Juli 1943 (BA-MA RH 10/77).

54. Panzerverluste Ost seit 1.Juli 1943 (BA-MA RH 10/77).

55. V.A. Pronko, 'Die Sowjetische Strategie im Jahre 1943', in J. Förster (ed.), *Stalingrad* (R. Piper, München, 1993), p. 322. Also Zhukov writes on page 449 in his memoirs that the tank units needed replenishment with material and trained effectives since the bitter fighting had severely undermanned them, he points to this problem again

on page 480. G.K. Zhukov, *The Memoirs of Marshal Zhukov* (Natraj, New Dehli, 1985).

56. G.A. Koltunov and B.G. Soloviev, *Kurskaya bitva* (Voenizdat, Moscow, 1970), p. 70.

57. 'Tank forces in the Kursk Bridgehead,' *Journal of Slavic Military Studies*, Vol. 7, no. 1 (March 1994), p. 112.

58. M. Kolomiets and M. Svirin, *Kurpskaya Duga* (EksPrint, NV Moscow, 1998), p. 22. The authors have written that on the morning of 6 July the 2nd Tank Army had 607 tanks of which 455 were operational. We have chosen to use the strength for the 2nd Tank Army presented in G.A. Koltunov and B.G. Soloviev, *Kurskaya bitva*, p. 70, because the loss percentage presented in 'Tank forces in the Kursk Bridgehead', *Journal of Slavic Military Studies*, Vol. 7, no. 1 (March 1994), does not at all fit the actual losses if 607 is used as the strength of the 2nd Tank Army.

59. Both in M. Kolomiets and M. Svirin, *Kurpskaya Duga*, p. 22 and 'Tank Forces in the Kursk Bridgehead', *Journal of Slavic Military Studies*, Vol. 7, no. 1 (March 1994), p. 112 they have given the last as dated 14 July not 13 July.

60. A report filed by Colonel Zaev on 23 July 1943 regarding losses suffered by the fronts during the period 5 to 20 July. Referred to in R.G. Foerster (ed.), *Gezeitenwechsel im Zweiten Weltkrieg?*, p. 129. This report does not correspond with a report filed by the Voronezh Front on 24 July 1943 where they report that 1,571 tanks and 57 assault guns had been write-offs between 4 and 22 July 1943. *Rysskii Arkhiv: Velikaya Otechestvennaya 4(4), Kurskaya Bitva*, pp. 272–3.

61. Based on archival records in *The International TNDM Newsletter*, Vol. 1, June 1997, no. 6, p. 27.

62. *Voenno-Istoricheskii Zhurnal*, no. 8, 1993, N.G. Andronikov, *Gitlerovskii 'Fakel' byl nogashen na ognennoi duge*, p. 2.

63. Report on irretrievable losses in 5th Guards Tank Army filed on 17 July 1943. Referred to in R.G. Foerster (ed.), *Gezeitenwechsel im Zweiten Weltkrieg?*, p. 121.

64. R.G. Foerster (ed.), *Gezeitenwechsel im Zweiten Weltkrieg?*, p. 238. This information is given by Igor N. Venkov (who has written that particular chapter). However he does not indicate what document he has used. Also the document gives losses in the Voronezh Front sector that are too low compared with the other documents cited (though this can be explained by the possibility that Venkov's figure only includes the Voronezh Front forces, not those committed from the Steppe Front which are included in the figures we have given in the text). Additionally he gives German tank losses which are quite absurd. Thus the figures given by him have lower credibility.

65. *Rysskii Arkhiv: Velikaya Otechestvennaya 4(4), Kurskaya Bitva*, pp. 272–3. Later when the Voronezh Front filed their battle report 23 August 1943 the losses are considerably lower: 672 guns all calibres, 622 mortars, 2,152 machine-guns, 588 heavy machine-guns, 12,434 sub-machine-guns, 27,800 rifles. This huge difference could be explained by the same reason as the changes of the Voronezh Front's personnel losses (see our discussion concerning Soviet manpower losses earlier in the chapter). *Rysskii Arkhiv: Velikaya Otechestvennaya 4(4), Kurskaya Bitva*, p. 387.

9

An Analysis of the Battle

Many conclusions of various kinds have been presented in the literature on operation Zitadelle, concerning, for example, the effectiveness of the Soviet anti-tank defences, the role of the tank as an offensive weapon and the ability of other weapons to destroy tanks. Also discussed are the skills of the opposing forces and the role of air power.

It is sometimes asserted that the Red Army calculated that a Soviet 76mm AT gun would put out of action two or three enemy medium tanks before it was itself destroyed.[1] However, this seems unlikely. According to von Manstein, the Soviet forces facing Army Group South lost 1,080 anti-tank guns up to 13 July.[2] Although based on reports from German units, it is likely that these figures are reasonably close to the truth. Since the Germans were advancing, they probably captured a significant number of AT guns.[3] Also, the very fact that they usually occupied the battlefield gave them better opportunities for estimating their success.

In the Army Group South sector, the Voronezh Front disposed of 7 AT brigades and 27 AT Regiments.[4] The numbers of AT guns deployed with 6th Guards Army, 7th Guards Army and Front reserves[5] was 1,529.[6] A further 692 AT guns were deployed with 38th and 40th Army.[7] Not all of these AT guns were in independent AT units. A large part of them belonged to the mobile corps and rifle divisions (which had a T/O&E strength of 48 AT guns).[8] Von Manstein's estimate concerns the situation until 13 July. If it is assumed that the Red Army, until 17 July inclusive, lost 1,000 AT guns, this is probably not an exaggeration.[9] It would, then, seem likely that about half of them, or 500, were 76mm guns.[10]

This can be compared with the Germans losses of about 190 tanks and assault guns on the southern side of the Kursk salient from 5 to 17 July.[11] Even if it is assumed that all those vehicles were destroyed by 76mm guns, the ratio still would not be 2.5 tanks destroyed for each one, but rather the opposite, 2.5 AT guns were lost for each tank destroyed. However, not all tanks were destroyed by 76mm AT guns, though the

76mm gun was probably the most common cause of German tank losses.

It is also illuminating to observe that, if the 76mm gun had the alleged effectiveness, only 63–95 guns would have been lost for the destruction of 190 German tanks and assault guns. It is unthinkable that von Manstein's estimate would have been that far from reality.[12]

In fairness, it must be said that the Soviet figures possibly include not only vehicles destroyed, but also those damaged but later repaired. Also it may include other armoured vehicles, such as half-tracks and armoured cars. Another factor to consider is that, according to the Soviet estimates on the effectiveness of the 76mm AT gun, the effectiveness was halved against heavier German tanks like the Panther and the Tiger. However, this probably did not have a significant impact, since the vast majority of the German tanks employed at Zitadelle, were neither of these.

These objections notwithstanding, the Soviet estimate of the effectiveness of the 76mm AT gun seems to have been considerably exaggerated, at least as regards to this operation.[13]

One arm that is often claimed to be a great menace to tanks is the air force. During Zitadelle it seems that few tanks were destroyed by air power. According to a Soviet study of the battle, enemy air forces accounted for only 2 per cent of the tanks destroyed among 1st Tank Army and 6.5 per cent among 2nd Tank Army.[14] If these percentages are representative for the Voronezh and Central Fronts respectively, the losses would have amounted to 42 Soviet tanks destroyed by air in the north and 58 in the southern sector. The Luftwaffe claimed to have destroyed 75 tanks in the north and 161 in the south.[15] It is important to note that the day which the Luftwaffe made most claims (84) in the south was 8 July, the day the flying tank-hunters went into action against 2nd Guards Tank Corps and forced it to withdraw. Thus the percentages for 1st Tank Army are perhaps not representative for all Soviet tank units in the south. During 1944 all Luftwaffe claims were in general reduced by 50 per cent by the German Military Intelligence when calculating enemy losses.[16] We have written earlier in Chapter 5, 'The Air War', about the effect that Soviet air-units had against tanks. Their impact was quite limited if we only look at actual losses. The main effect of air-strikes lies not with the losses they cause, but rather the disruption and insecurity they create, which affects deployment, regrouping and advances.

The shortage of infantry units affected the German ability to advance. Army Group South had to deploy mobile divisions to protect and secure its flanks, thus losing part of its offensive power. For example, 7th Panzer Division had to assist Corps Raus[17] to secure the flank of Army

Detachment Kempf. This occurred within all Panzer Corps in Army Group South. Also to break through several prepared defence lines must cause losses and fatigue. The number of infantry divisions assigned to this task was clearly insufficient, since the mobile infantry battalions (Panzergrenadiers) were tied up in clearing areas instead of advancing forward.

In the northern sector eight infantry divisions and one Panzer division with support units assaulted on 5 July. This indicated a large part of the forces was held back in the two main attacking corps.[18] When trying to break through enemy lines it is important to attack with a heavy blow. In this respect Army Group Centre was perhaps too optimistic. Here we can take into account the different reactions of the Central Front and the Voronezh Front. In the north a large counterattack was mounted on 6 July to re-establish the front line, while in the south they tried to create a solid defensive position. Would Central Front have been willing to conduct a counterblow, if it had been attacked by the full force from Army Group Centre? About this one can only surmise, but Army Group South attacked with full force on the first day while Army Group Centre did not.[19]

Some authors have stated that the German panzer units were given orders not to assist disabled tanks, but to continue forward. It is said that this was a virtual death warrant for the crews of the stricken tanks.[20] This seems to be a considerable exaggeration. First, it is clear that the vast majority of the damaged German tanks were recovered.[21] The majority of them were repaired within a few days.[22] It seems quite unlikely that the tanks would have been repaired, but that the crews would have been killed or wounded. Indeed, a look into the German documents indicates the opposite, that the survivability of the crews was better than that for the tanks.[23]

The 503rd s.Pz.Abteilung provides an indication of the survivability of tank crews. This battalion fought with III Pz.Corps during Zitadelle and suffered casualties of 25 killed, 68 wounded and one missing during July 1943.[24] This can be compared with the fluctuations of the number of operational Tigers with the battalion shown in Appendix 6. On 21 July the battalion was down to four operational tanks and, given the previous fluctuations, the likelihood is that each of the 45 Tigers the battalion had when Zitadelle began must have been in workshops at least once. Since the Tiger had a crew of five, the battalion must have had 225 soldiers who fought inside the tanks. This does not support the 'death warrant' theory.

Often German tank attacks during Zitadelle are described as in wedge formations with Tigers at the tip and the lighter Panther and Pz IV tanks at the sides. This seems largely to be a myth too. Even if the Germans had intended to use such a formation, they had too few operational Tigers to use it except in isolated instances. Occasionally, descriptions of German panzer wedges gives the impression that entire corps were formed into a single wedge-attack formation. This is not consistent with German command and control procedures. Divisions were given individual objects and each attacked as a single group. Also, terrain features often restricted the attack formations, making it impossible to form wedges of corps size. Finally, German tactical methods emphasized the importance of individual initiative, even at the lowest level, which would have been restricted if such a large formation had been adopted.

The ability to repair damaged tanks was of great importance in this operation. At midnight on 10 July, the 4th Panzer Army had 462 tanks and assault guns in workshops.[25] Up to that moment 64 tanks and assault guns had been destroyed.[26] Thus, destroyed tanks only accounted for, at most, 12 per cent of those put out of action (due to enemy action, mechanical breakdown or other causes).[27]

It is often argued that defence is the stronger form of combat, an expression usually attributed to von Clausewitz. Certainly, defensive posture gives certain advantages, but there are also drawbacks with defence. One is that it is much easier to recover damaged tanks if the battlefield is controlled. This is can be illustrated by the fact that from 1 October 1943 to 31 January 1944, the German tank maintenance companies on all fronts repaired 8,702 tanks and assault guns.[28] Another 453 were repaired in the rear areas.[29] During the same period 2,945 were permanently lost.[30] This means that 25 per cent of all tanks put out of action were actually lost, a percentage twice as high as in the Zitadelle example cited above.

Since the forces employed in Zitadelle had enjoyed a long lull before the offensive began, they had had ample time to ensure that their vehicles were in good mechanical condition. Also they had received deliveries of brand new tanks. The German forces in the autumn and winter of 1943/44 on the other hand had to operate with already worn equipment and had less time to carry out repairs and overhauls. Therefore it seems likely that the Zitadelle forces were less prone to being plagued by mechanical breakdowns.[31] Consequently, it would be expected that the percentage of repairable vehicles would be smaller during Zitadelle.

The major reason for the lower percentage of complete write-offs during Zitadelle is the fact that the Germans were advancing, which gave them better opportunities to recover their damaged vehicles.[32] During the retreats in late 1943 and the beginning of 1944, this was more difficult. In addition, when retreating they probably lost vehicles which had no worse fault than being out of fuel or which were just stuck in mud.

Perhaps it should be added that the core factor is not whether a force was attacking or defending, but rather whether it was losing or taking ground. If the defender successfully holds his positions, he will probably be able to recover his damaged vehicles relatively easily.

Another advantage which the defender is often said to enjoy is that it is more costly to attack than to defend. Indeed, Charles B. MacDonald has even written on the fighting by the US 110th Infantry Regiment in the Ardennes, 16–19 December 1944:

> To those casualties in the race for Bastogne would have to be added those incurred by the 28th Division's 110th Infantry and its attached and supporting units. The 110th Infantry lost 2,750 officers and men wounded, captured and killed ... It was impossible to ascertain with accuracy what the fight cost the Germans, but losses of forces on the attack almost always exceeded those of forces on the defence.[33]

If this assertion that forces on the attack almost always lost more than those on the defence was true, Zitadelle would constitute a major exception. In Chapter 8 it was shown that Soviet casualties were more than three times higher than German manpower losses.

However, it seems that Zitadelle was not a single isolated exception. In fact, almost every German offensive operation on the eastern front resulted in casualties that were far greater on the Soviet side.[34] Indeed, it seems that the Germans usually inflicted greater casualties than they suffered themselves when they attacked on other fronts too. Thus it is no surprise that the German casualties in the engagement described by MacDonald were substantially smaller than the American losses.[35]

If all other factors are equal for the attacker and the defender, it is undoubtedly the defender who has an advantage. There are however many more factors that affect the ratio between attacker and defender casualties. One of the most important is the amount of firepower available. Usually the attacker has concentrated superior firepower to the sector where he has chosen to make his effort. Yet perhaps even more important is how skilfully firepower is used and how well it is combined with manoeuvre. This, of course, applies both to the defender and the attacker.

On the eastern front the Germans had a considerable skill superiority, especially on the tactical level. This far outweighed any advantages inherent in defensive posture. At Kursk the Germans had to rely on the skill of their junior officers and their men to do the work. Given Soviet numerical preponderance, lack of surprise and an operational plan that was known to the enemy, this was almost their only advantage. How much that advantage was worth is evident from the loss ratios. This German superiority is of course nothing new, and has been the subject of many publications.[36]

On the southern side of the Kursk salient the Germans used a more classical 'Blitzkrieg' attack, committing their panzer divisions from the very beginning. This enjoyed more success than the piecemeal commitment of tank forces that was chosen by Model. Of course, it must also be noted that the German forces in the south had more tanks and this was a major reason for the greater success. In fact, despite the extensive Soviet defences, they failed to halt the Germans, who advanced 32 km during the first three days. After that, the long flanks slowed down the German forces and during the following five days the advance rate was reduced, but during the first week of the offensive, the Germans averaged 6.4 km/day. This advance rate can be compared with the first week of operation Cobra, the US breakout in Normandy 25–31 July 1944. During this period the US forces advanced 8.1 km/day.

In fact, despite its marginally slower advance rate, the German advance is the more impressive, since it was made without the vast numerical superiority the US forces enjoyed. During the first three days the advance rate was actually higher in Zitadelle than it was in Cobra. The fact that the German advance rate became slower after the initial push is explained by the fact that the Soviet defences had much greater depth than the German defences in Normandy. Also, in Normandy there were no reserves available, while the Red Army had new armies to commit to stem the German advance.

However, there was one German reserve that could have been used in operation Zitadelle, XXIV Panzer Corps. According to von Manstein, this was the one card left for Army Group South when the battle reached its culminating point on 13 July. In his memoirs von Manstein includes two divisions in corps, 17th Panzer Division and 5th SS-Panzergrenadier Division 'Wiking'. According to von Manstein this was perhaps the force needed to alter the scales in German favour. However, the Army Group did not get approval from Hitler to use it. Instead he ordered that the offensive should be broken off.[37]

Could two divisions have changed the outcome of this huge battle? One author[38] writes that the size of the battle itself is enough to show that one panzer corps was too small a reinforcement. He also states that the Soviet forces, which had at this time begun their counteroffensive, had been reinforced by two tank armies and five combined armies from the strategic reserves. Hence, it would be naive of Manstein to think that one corps would have given the Germans victory.

But he misses one central point, that for the Germans there were two battles, one in the north and one in the south. Soviet reinforcements for an offensive against Orel had no effect on Manstein's possibilities to continue his offensive as long as his resources were not taken away to be used in the Orel sector. Also on the southern sector, the Red Army had used all of the Voronezh Front's reserves and was forced to reinforce it with one tank army (5th Guards Tank Arms), one combined army (5th Guards Army) and two tank corps (2nd and 10th) to stop the offensive.[39]

Consequently, the Soviets had already committed large forces to halt the southern attack but again Manstein had the possibility to change the direction of the main attack. He planned to focus the attack towards the northwest towards Oboyan instead of continuing to push northeast. Both 5th Guards Tank Army and 5th Guards Army had entered the fighting to stop the German forces' expansion to the east. By keeping the offensive going Manstein would still have had the initiative and the Voronezh Front would have had to react to his moves. The attacker often has the advantage of initial surprise, which means that if the defender has not correctly identified the direction of the attack, he must shift his forces to meet it. By shifting his main point of attack, Manstein could have taken some ground initially and perhaps gained momentum in the attack before the Soviets had moved forces to meet it.

Also, when he wrote his memoirs, Manstein seems to have forgotten that 23rd Panzer Division had been attached to XXIV Panzer Corps on 7 July, when it was still near Stalino as reserve for 6th Army and 1st Panzer Army. The division started to move north towards Kharkov and reached Merefa about 60 km south of Kharkov.[40] Thus, the corps had three divisions.

General Walther Nehring, a very experienced panzer commander, commanded this corps.[41] The tank strength of 17th Panzer Division was 4 Panzer II, 29 Panzer III, 32 Panzer IV and 2 T-34, of which 84 per cent were operational.[42] The division had no armoured infantry battalion, but four motorized infantry battalions.[43] The SS-Wiking was a somewhat stronger division since it had five motorized infantry battalions and the artillery regiment had four battalions. The panzer battalion in Wiking had 4 Panzer II, 24 Panzer III, 17 Panzer IV and 6 Sturmgeschütz on 3 July 1943 and all of them were operational.[44] The 23rd Panzer Division was similar to 17th Panzer Division in strength. On 1 July it had one panzer battalion in its regiment with 33 Panzer IV and 17 Panzer III on hand (same T/O&E as 17th PD).[45] The regimental HQ had 6 Panzer III and an assault gun company with seven Sturmgeschütz 33Bs was attached to the regiment, while it had an armoured infantry battalion in one of its two panzergrenadier regiments.

Together, these three divisions had only 181 tanks and assault guns, but that was not the most important factor. Of greater importance was that together they had 13 mobile infantry battalions.[46] As shown in Chapter 3, casualties incurred by the divisions were mostly suffered by the infantry (Panzergrenadiers). Here Manstein had the possibility to insert 13 'fresh' battalions in the front line and let some of the weary ones have a rest. This would have enhanced the possibilities of continuing the offensive. Also it would have allowed Manstein to change the *schwerpunkt* from Prokhorovka to Oboyan. If that had been done the offensive would have again hit 1st Tank Army and 6th Guards Army hard. These two armies had suffered severely during the first week of the German offensive. The 6th Guards Army for example took 30,000 casualties during the defensive phase of the battle at Kursk.[47]

What the consequences of such an employment might have been is of course impossible to determine. It could hardly have turned Zitadelle, including 9th Army, into a success. Perhaps it could have enabled von Manstein to destroy parts of the Soviet 38th and 40th Armies, and to inflict further losses on 6th Guards Army and 1st Tank Army.

As events turned out, 4th Panzer Army was not reinforced but weakened. Großdeutschland moved to Army Group Centre, Leibstandarte to Italy and some other divisions (Totenkopf and Das Reich, for example) moved down to the area of the Mius to repel the Soviet attack there. Also the 23rd and 17th Panzer Divisions were ordered to the Mius sector.

If von Manstein had used XXIV Panzer Corps in the Zitadelle offensive, this would also have weakened the forces available to repel the Soviet attack at the Mius.

The start of operation Zitadelle was delayed several times by Hitler. The question comes to mind as to which side benefited most from this? Of course the Red Army was able to prepare their field defences to a much greater extent. Since the Soviet Union had much larger arms-production than Germany during 1943 a delay might well have been advantageous for the Red Army, or perhaps not?

On 1 April 1943 the Red Army had 4,882 tanks and 94 assault guns in front-line strength while on 1 July it had increased this to 9,831 tanks and 368[48] assault guns, thus an increase of almost 105 per cent.[49] The Germans, on the other hand, had 2,103 tanks and assault guns on 10 April on the Eastern Front and this had increased to 3,523 tanks and assault guns by 30 June.[50] This gives an increase of 67 per cent. In this calculation we have not taken into account that the Stavka Reserves were also increased (see Tables 1.3 and 2.3 regarding the Steppe Military District). The Germans had no equivalent to the Stavka reserves. Thus in pure numbers (quantity) the Red Army was clearly the winner but how about quality?

As we have written in Chapter 4, the Red Army had no new tanks and very few new assault guns ready for the summer. Thus the improvement of quality was the increased percentage of T-34s though the light tanks were still present in large numbers (30 per cent of all the tanks initially available in the Kursk Salient were light tanks). For the Germans it was quite different because on 10 April they had 982[51] tanks and assault guns armed with cannons that had no problem with Soviet tanks. By 30 June the Eastern Front had a further 1,113 tanks and assault guns armed with cannons which had no problem with Soviet tanks.[52] Thus their numbers had increased to 2,095.

The improved anti-tank capability the Germans possessed at Zitadelle was negated by the increase of numbers on the Soviet side. Especially important was the huge Stavka Reserve of 2,688 tanks and assault guns, but the Red Army had even more forces in reserve in the interior military districts,[53] since according to Soviet accounts they had moved forward 1,500 tanks and assault guns as reinforcements to stop the German offensive. A further 1,800 tanks and assault guns moved forward from reserves to support their own offensive operations against Orel and Belgorod–Kharkov. The total number of tanks and assault guns committed to the fighting around Kursk (5 July–23 August) by the Red Army was more than 8,000.[54]

Clearly, the Red Army had the advantage of the delay in more field-works and the possibility to create large reserves. Further, the Red Army gained more time to prepare for its own offensive operations, not only around Kursk but also for the offensives launched against 6th Army and 1st Panzer Army for example.

The summer fighting during July and August 1943 was probably the most intense fighting on the eastern front so far, if we use the Germans' expenditure of ammunition as a yardstick. During 1942 the expenditure of ammunition was highest during the month of September, 160,645 tons.[55] In July 1943 the expenditure was 236,915 tons, in August 254,648 tons.[56] During the autumn it slowly decreased to become equal to the highest expenditure of 1942.

NOTES

1. See, e.g., J.F. Dunnigan, *The Russian Front* (Arms & Armour Press, London, 1978), p. 103. On this page one can also read that Soviet anti-tank brigades 'shattered division after division of German tank troops'. Considering the losses the German panzer

divisions actually suffered, this is a gross exaggeration.

2. Von Manstein, *Verlorene Siege* (Athenäum-Verlag, Bonn, 1958), p. 501. Probably some of these anti-tank guns were actually artillery pieces from the rifle divisions.

3. As it seems, the Soviet AT guns were deployed in well-camouflaged nests, without immediately available transport. This might often have caused them to fight in a situation where they either repulsed the enemy attack, or were destroyed themselves.

4. See Order of Battle in Appendix 1. The numbers refer to the entire Voronezh Front, but the majority of those AT units were deployed with the 6th and 7th Guards armies. Also many of the units assigned to 40th and 38th Armies were sent to parry the advances made by 4th Panzer Army. The following units from 40th Army and 38th Army were deployed to stop the German advance, 29th and 32nd AT Brigade, 4th, 12th, 222nd, 869th, 1244th AT Regiment.

5. Front reserves included 1st Tank Army, 69th Army and 35th Guards Rifle Corps.

6. G.A. Koltunov and B.G. Soloviev, *Kurskaya bitva* (Voenizdat, Moscow, 1970), p. 69. We have not included the 76mm regimental guns which we estimate to have been 264 based on T/O&E.

7. G.A. Koltunov and B.G. Soloviev, *Kurskaya bitva*, p. 69. We have not included the 76mm regimental guns which we estimate to have been 156 based on T/O&E.

8. Charles C. Sharp, *Soviet Order of Battle in World War II*, Vol. X, '*Red Swarm*' (George F. Nafziger, West Chester, OH, 1996), p. 141.

9. The Voronezh Front reported it had lost 1,605 guns of all calibres up to 16 July. *Rysskii Arkhiv: Velikaya Otechestvennaya 4(4), Kurskaya Bitva, Dokumenti i Materiali 27 Marta – 23 Avgusta 1943 goda* (Terra, Moscow, 1997), pp. 272–3.

10. If anything, the larger and heavier 76mm gun must have been more likely to be lost if the enemy advanced and captured the defender's positions.

11. BA-MA RH 10/65. See also Chapter 8 for a more detailed discussion on the German tank losses.

12. It should be observed that his estimates on Soviet casualties, if anything, were too low, see Chapter 8.

13. Given the size of the tank forces committed, this operation is not an obscure little example. Rather it is a an operation which traditionally has been regarded as an example of the effectiveness of the Soviet defences against German tanks.

14. 'Tank Forces in Defence of the Kursk Bridgehead', *Journal of Slavic Military Studies*, Vol. 7, no. 1, (March 1994), p. 114.

15. E. Klink, *Das Gesetz des Handelns, Die Operation 'Zitadelle' 1943* (Deutsche Verlags-Anstalt, Stuttgart, 1986), pp. 337–8. For those claims made in the north only those up to 11 July are included because on the 12 July and thereafter many of the Luftwaffe claims concerned Bryansk and the Western Front.

16. BA-MA RH 2/2101 Fremde Heere Ost (IIc) 10.10.1944 Sow.russ.Panzer- und Sturmgeschütz-Verluste 1944.

17. This corps from the start clearly had insufficient forces for its mission.

18. The 2nd Panzer Division, 9th Panzer Division and 18th Panzer Division in the attacking corps. The 9th Army had a further three divisions in reserve, thus nine divisions moved forward and six remained behind.

19. In the planning for the summer campaign 1943, N. Vatutin and his staff (Voronezh Front) wanted to make a pre-emptive blow instead of waiting for the Germans to attack. Thus they were showing a more offensive attitude.

20. See for example G. Jukes, *Kursk – The Clash of Armour* (Ballantine, New York, 1969), p. 76. Also see R. Cross, *Citadel* (Michael O'Mara Books, London, 1993), p. 153 and M. Healy, *Kursk 1943* (Osprey, London, 1992), p. 29.

21. An example of this is the II SS-Panzer Corps, which lost 36 tanks and assault guns

during the Zitadelle offensive (Gen.Kdo. II. SS-Pz.Korps 23.7.1943, BA-MA RS 2-2/18), but the number of damaged tanks must have been considerably greater, since on 10 July, the corps had 173 tanks in workshops, the vast majority being at divisional repair facilities (BA-MA RH 21-4/450).

22. For example, II SS-Panzer Corps, during the night between 12 and 13 July, had 122 tanks and assault guns that were expected to be repaired within four days (PzAOK 4 O.Qu Anlage zu KTB, Aktennotiz 13.7.1943, BA-MA RH 21-4/450).

23. The monthly reports submitted from the panzer divisions to the Inspector-General of Panzer Troops usually contain two parts. One is a form that is filled with data on tanks and other heavy weapons operational and in workshops. The other part is a graphic presentation of the structure of the division, which usually also contains the manpower situation for each battalion. Almost invariably the manpower strength of the tank battalions is diminished less than the tank strength after intensive combat. At Zitadelle this system of reporting was quite new and the reporting is incomplete, but according to what we have found, Zitadelle does not present a different pattern from other parts of the war. Also a report concerning the tank forces that fought in the Orel salient during July shows that most panzer divisions had a surplus of tank crews on 1 August 1943, after their tank losses during July (Pz. Offz. b. Chef GenStdH Bb. Nr. 562/43 g.Kdos. v. 14.8.1943, BA-MA RH 10/48). This also contradicts the theory that crews of damaged tanks would have little chance of surviving.

24. BA-MA RH 10/220.

25. Versorgungslageberichte des Gen.Kdo. XXXXVIII. Pz.Korps Abt. Qu. vom 2.7.1943 bis 30.10.1943, Anlageband 3 zum KTB nr 2 (National Archives, Washington, DC, Microfilm Publication T314, Roll 1169, Frame 000749)and PzAOK 4 O.Qu Anlagen zum KTB, BA-MA RH 21-4/450.

26. Ibid.

27. In fact there were probably more than 462 tanks and assault guns that had been damaged (either due to enemy action or mechanical breakdown) since during the period 5–10 July there were certainly a considerable number of tanks that were repaired.

28. H.B. Müller-Hillebrand, *German Tank-Strength and Loss Statistics*, MS P-059 (manuscript at National Archives, Washington, DC, 1950), p. 16.

29. Ibid.

30. Ibid., Appendix 2.

31. The Panthers employed at Zitadelle probably did not correspond to this pattern, since they suffered from teething troubles, several of which were rectified later.

32. A comparison can be made with 7th and 11th Panzer Division. During the first ten days of July during the German offensive 7th Panzer lost 10 Panzers as total losses and 11th Panzer lost 3 Panzers as total losses, while during the first ten days of August during the Soviet offensive towards Belgorod–Kharkov 7th Panzer lost 29 Panzers as total losses and 11th Panzer lost 38 Panzers as write-offs. During July they were advancing while during August they were retreating. The size of manpower casualties for July is similar to August for both divisions. BA-MA RH 21-4/450-451. Pz.A.O.K.4. O.Qu Anlage 11 zum KTB Tätigkeitsberichte v.d. Abteilungen.

33. C.B. MacDonald, *The Battle of the Bulge* (Weidenfeld & Nicolson, London, 1984), pp. 296–7.

34. In fact, we have not found any operation that deviates from this pattern, but we cannot completely exclude the possibility that there may exist exceptions.

35. The US units in the example given by MacDonald faced elements from three German divisions, the 26th, the 2nd Panzer and Panzer-Lehr. These three divisions suffered losses of 1,012, 255 and 329 respectively during the period 16–23 December, giving

a total of 1,596. Note that these losses refer to a period twice as long as that given by MacDonald. In reality, German casualties were therefore lower. Figures are taken from the most reliable source available in print, T.N. Dupuy, *Hitler's Last Gamble* (Airlife, Shrewsbury, 1995), pp. 473 and 475. It should be noted that principally all statements on German losses given in MacDonald's book are based on US after-action reports and witnesses, two sources of very low reliability for such information. MacDonald's book may have a value as a source for the actions by US units. It is however utterly unreliable when it comes to information on strength and losses of German units.

36. See for example T.N. Dupuy, *Numbers Predictions and War* (HERO, Arlington, 1985), pp. 95–110 and N. Zetterling, 'Loss Rates on the Eastern Front during World War II', *Journal of Slavic Military Studies*, Vol. 9, no. 4 (December 1996), pp. 895–906.

37. E. Von Manstein, *Verlorene Siege* (Athenaeum-Verlag, Bonn, 1958), pp. 501–4.

38. B. Solowjow, *Wendepunkt des Zweiten Weltkrieges, Die Schlacht bei Kursk* (Paul-Rufenstein, Köln, 1984), pp. 118f.

39. The size of the reserves moved forward was 295,000 soldiers, 5,300 guns and mortars and 1,500 tanks and assault guns. This large force not only includes 5th Guards Army, 5th Guards Tank Army, 2nd Tank Corps and 10th Tank Corps but also 27th Army and 53rd Army. *Rysskii Arkhiv: Velikaya Otechestvennaya 4(4), Kurskaya Bitva*, p. 406.

40. E. Rebentisch (ed.), *Zum Kaukasus und zu den Tauern, die Geschichte der 23. Panzer-Division 1939–1945* (Selbstverlag, Esslingen, a. N., 1963), pp. 215f and 544.

41. Nehring had been one of the earliest advocates of tanks in the German Army and had been chief of staff to Guderian during the campaigns in Poland and France. During operation Barbarossa he commanded 18th Panzer Division and from March 1942 to December 1942 he served in Africa, much of the time as commander of the Afrika Korps. He was wounded in August 1942 and after periods of vacation he received command of XXIV Panzer Corps in February 1943. Nehring became one of the most highly decorated German soldiers. He received the Knight Cross with the Oak Leaves and Swords. This was only awarded to 159 soldiers of the Army, Navy, Air Force and Waffen-SS – see W. Paul, *Panzer-General Walther K. Nehring* (Motorbuch, Stuttgart, 1986).

42. PzAOK 1 Ia, 3.7.43, BA-MA RH 21-1/98.

43. Ibid.

44. Report to the Inspector-General of Panzer Troops, Stand 1.7.1943 (BA-MA RH 10/316) and PzAOK 1 Ia, 3.7.43, BA-MA RH 21-1/98.

45. Report to the Inspector-General of Panzer Troops, Stand 1.7.1943 (BA-MA RH 10/159).

46. Initially Army Group South had 44 mobile infantry battalions. Another 13 would mean an increase of almost 30 per cent.

47. G.A. Koltunov and B.G. Soloviev, *Kurskaya bitva*, p. 385.

48. Of these 368 assault guns 64 per cent were heavy or medium. *Istoriya Vtoroi Mirovoi Voiny 1939–45*, Vol. 7 (Voenizdat, Moscow, 1976), p. 97.

49. *Istoriya Vtoroi Mirovoi Voiny 1939–45*, Vol. 7, p. 97.

50. See Appendix 9 – Number of German Tanks and Assault Guns on the Eastern Front, April to December 1943.

51. Based on Appendix 9, adjusted for the fact that 53 of 589 Stug III had a short 7.5cm cannon.

52. Based on Appendix 9; 89 Ferdinands and 19 Stug III Long have been added, the extra Stug III Long adjusting for the fact that Stug III with short 7.5cm on 30 June stood at 19 less than on 10 April.

53. For example, Moscow Military District.

54. *Rysskii Arkhiv: Velikaya Otechestvennaya 4(4), Kurskaya Bitva*, pp. 406–7. *Istoriya Vtoroi Mirovoi Voiny 1939–45*, Vol. 7, p. 109.

55. F. Hahn, *Waffen und Geheimwaffen des deutschen Heeres 1933–45*, Band 2 (Bernard & Graefe Verlag, Koblenz, 1987), p. 227.

56. Ibid., p. 239.

10

The Consequences of the Battle

Whether Kursk was a decisive battle or not depends on what is implied by 'decisive'. Certain basic facts can sometimes demonstrate that a battle produced losses or a situation from which one side could not recover. This can hardly apply to Kursk, since neither German nor Soviet casualties or equipment losses were particularly high. During Zitadelle German manpower losses amounted to 56,827 men killed, wounded or missing.[1] This can be compared with the overall combat losses for Germany on the eastern front during 1943, amounting to 1,601,454 men.[2] Thus, casualties suffered during Zitadelle constituted only about 3 per cent of the total for 1943. Similarly, Soviet casualties suffered during Zitadelle amounted to 177,847 men,[3] which is only 2.3 per cent of the 7,857,503 casualties suffered during 1943 by the Red Army.[4] Evidently, manpower losses in Zitadelle were quite small for both powers, and cannot be seen as decisive, at least not in the context of the struggle on the eastern front. For the Germans, comparison can also be made with the 89,480 replacements that arrived on the eastern front during July 1943,[5] which were more than sufficient to cover the losses suffered during Zitadelle, though not losses sustained elsewhere on the same front. If we only take into account the reserves moved forward by the Red Army during Operation Zitadelle we find that the Red Army in fact increased its strength in the Kursk salient; 295,000 soldiers from Stavka reserves moved into the Kursk Bulge, though not all of them were fully committed to battle.[6] Thus the Red Army had larger forces in the front line after the German offensive than before in terms of manpower. A further 363,000 soldiers from the Stavka reserves moved forward to assist the offensive against Orel and Belgorod–Kharkov.[7]

Another possibility is of course that equipment losses might have been decisive, particularly as regards tanks. German tank losses during the battle did not exceed 300 and this includes assault guns.[8] This can be compared with two other figures. During the period July–December

1943, the German monthly tank and assault gun losses were on average 640.[9] The other relevant comparison to be made is with German tank and assault gun production, which on average amounted to 908 during the latter half of 1943.[10] During July 511 tanks and 306 assault guns left the factories in Germany.[11] Evidently, German tank losses were not extraordinarily high during Zitadelle nor were they impossible to replace.

It is also illuminating to look at how the number of German tanks fluctuated during 1943. As can be seen in Figure 10.1,[12] German tank strength rose considerably from April to July. Thereafter a drop can be seen until in October the tank strength began to rise again. In December the number of tanks is actually slightly greater than it had been at the beginning of July.

It could of course be inferred from Figure 10.1 that a trend was reversed by Zitadelle and certainly there is some truth to this. However, what is remarkable in the figure is the long period of build-up before Zitadelle. Also it must not be forgotten that the quality of the tanks on the eastern front steadily rose, which is indicated by the growth in the number of Tigers, Panthers and late-model Panzer IV (see Appendix 9 for exact

FIGURE 10.1: GERMAN TANKS ON THE EASTERN FRONT, APRIL–DECEMBER 1943

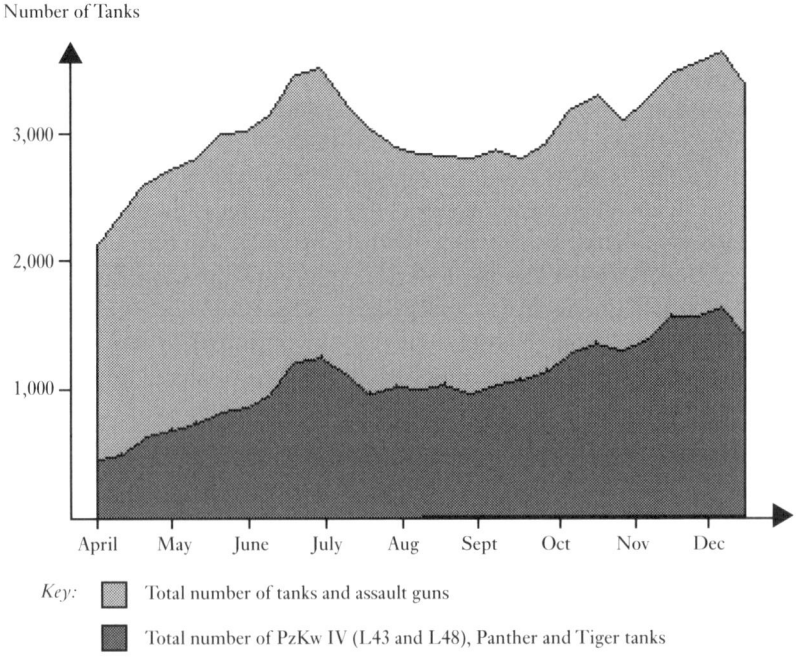

Number of Tanks

Key:
Total number of tanks and assault guns

Total number of PzKw IV (L43 and L48), Panther and Tiger tanks

numbers). Thus it can be argued that the *Ostheer* was better equipped with tanks at the end of the year than it had been before Zitadelle.

Losses do not provide the only factor governing the status of the panzer force in Russia. Equally important is the number of new tanks sent to the eastern front.

TABLE 10.1: GERMAN TANKS AND ASSAULT GUNS SENT TO THE EASTERN FRONT DURING 1943

	Replacement tanks	Replacement assault guns	Tanks sent with complete companies and battalions	Assault guns sent with complete companies and battalions	Total	Total German production
January	163	68	0	41	272	387
February	118	47	0	0	165	460
March	129	135	0	62	326	577
April	194	154	0	62	410	618
May	218	51	0	31	300	1,094
June	188	59	231	93	571	789
July	122	73	58	62	315	817
August	123	111	164	93	491	754
September	93	129	45	154	421	946
October	230	73	71	104	478	1,069
November	262	138	154	180	734	728
December	367	149	34	62	612	1,133

Note: Not included are tanks and assault guns sent with divisions to the eastern front. During October the 1st, 14th and 24th Panzer divisions were sent to the east from the west, while 16th and 25th Panzer divisions plus the Leibstandarte arrived in November. All these divisions had received new tanks before they arrived (but not necessarily the full complement of two battalions). No other Panzer divisions arrived during the second half of 1943.

Sources: Pz – Fertigung (Planung) und Zuführung (BA-MA RH 10/67) and StuG – Fertigung (Planung) und Zuführung (BA-MA RH 10/67); Müller-Hillebrand, Das Heer, Vol. III, Anhang B.

The figures in Table 10.1 can be compared with the losses suffered on the eastern front during the second half of 1943, which are shown in Table 10.2. Unfortunately, the source does not provide any information on how the losses are divided between July and August, but, considering the information presented in Table 8.8, we can conclude that losses in those two months were rather similar in magnitude.

Comparing the information from Tables 10.1 and 10.2 indicates that the fluctuations in tanks sent to the eastern front were more significant than the fluctuations in losses. Thus it is not possible to conclude from Figure 10.1 that operation Zitadelle was a turning point in the war.

147

TABLE 10.2: GERMAN TANK AND ASSAULT GUN LOSSES ON THE EASTERN FRONT,
JULY–DECEMBER 1943

1 July– 31 August	September	October	November	December
1,331	513	585	748	664

Note: Figures refer to total write-offs.
Source: BA–MA RH 10/77.

Guderian prophesied that Zitadelle would lead to tank losses that could not be replaced during 1943.[13] In fact, German tank production during July alone surpassed the losses suffered during Zitadelle.[14] In retrospect, it seems clear that he was wrong, unless of course one assumes that had Zitadelle not been launched the Red Army would have stood idle during the rest of the summer. From what is known of the Soviet planning and operational considerations this seems implausible.

For the Red Army the tank losses were worse than for the Germans. In fact, Soviet production did not suffice to keep up with losses. During the third quarter of 1943 production amounted to 5,761 tanks and assault guns.[15] This can be compared with the fact that during six major operations alone, irretrievable losses amounted to 8,953 tanks and assault guns during the third quarter.[16] During Zitadelle, the Orel and the Belgorod–Kharkov operations losses amounted to 6,064, according to Krivosheyev, thus during these 50 days of fighting around Kursk the Red Army lost 121 tanks, including assault guns, per day as write-offs.[17] This trend continued for the rest of 1943. On 1 July, the Red Army had a tank strength of 9,888 in the front armies and 2,688 in Stavka reserves.[18] Six months later the Red army had less than half that number in their field units and Stavka reserves.[19] During those six months 11,890 tanks and assault guns had been produced.[20] It must be emphasized that when a force suffers such extensive losses as the Red Army armoured forces did during the second half of 1943, production of tanks will not suffice to replace losses. There will also be delays before the new tanks are issued to combat units owing to the need for training new crews.[21]

One important effect of operation Zitadelle failing to reach its goals was that the Red Army now knew that they could withstand a German summer offensive. This probably had a positive effect on its self-confidence, thus the Red Army became more secure and confident in its conduct of operations. Manstein's backhand blow had taught them not to overextend their offensives and now the officers and soldiers in the Red Army knew that the Germans were not invincible during the summer.[22]

Also the way the Red Army launched their offensive operations during the summer of 1943 can be seen as a forerunner of summer 1944.

It has also been written that Zitadelle marked a shift in the balance of forces on the eastern front. During the Stalingrad counteroffensive, the Red Army is said to have enjoyed numerical parity, while during Zitadelle the numerical superiority is purported to have been 1.5 to 1 in the Soviet favour, which should have increased further to 2 to 1 in the battles along the Dniepr.[23] This is all wrong however. The Red Army enjoyed a far better numerical ratio than equality during the Stalingrad offensive. The myth of equality is fostered by Soviet literature that claims that the 1.106 million men of the Southwest, Don and Stalingrad Fronts were opposed by 1.011 million men from the Axis powers.[24] But the Axis forces on the sector covered by those three Soviet fronts, comprising 1.106 million men, did not amount to one million men. Rather the Red Army was opposed by around half a million men.[25] This produces a force ratio quite consistent with the fact that the overall force ratio on the eastern front was 6.03 million Red Army soldiers[26] versus 2,932,329 German[27] and 648,000 satellite[28] troops. Similarly, the 1.5: 1 force ratio at Kursk (derived from 1,300,000 Soviet and 900,000 German troops) is highly dubious, since it does not include Soviet reserves committed during the battle and it also overstates the size of the German forces. During the defensive phase of the battle of Kursk the Red Army committed 1,630,000 soldiers, 27,000 guns and mortars, 5,000 tanks and assault guns, and 3,000 aircraft from the three Fronts – Voronezh, Central and Steppe.[29] Thus it is not possible to portray the period from the Soviet Stalingrad offensive to the battles along the Dniepr as one of changing force ratios on the eastern front.

Consequently, neither is it possible to claim that Zitadelle produced an outcome which was decisive to the war in the east. It is questionable whether any single battle did produce decisive results in this vast conflict. At the beginning of June 1944 it was quite clear that Germany was fighting a hopeless war. The *Ostheer* had shrunk in size by about half a million men since the previous summer[30] and the threat of an allied amphibious assault somewhere along the shores of western Europe loomed ever larger. The allied bomber offensive at last began to hit targets that were vital to the German war effort, especially sorely felt being the bombings of the synthetic fuel plants. But what of the casualties incurred by the Germans up to June 1944? The fighting in Russia was clearly the most important, because 92 per cent of all casualties since 1 June 1941 had been suffered by units fighting the Red Army.[31] Using documents on monthly casualties on the eastern front it is possible to draw up a graph on the accumulated personnel losses, as in Figure 10.2. This shows a steady increase in

FIGURE 10.2: ACCUMULATED GERMAN CASUALTIES ON THE EASTERN FRONT,
22 JUNE 1941–31 MAY 1944

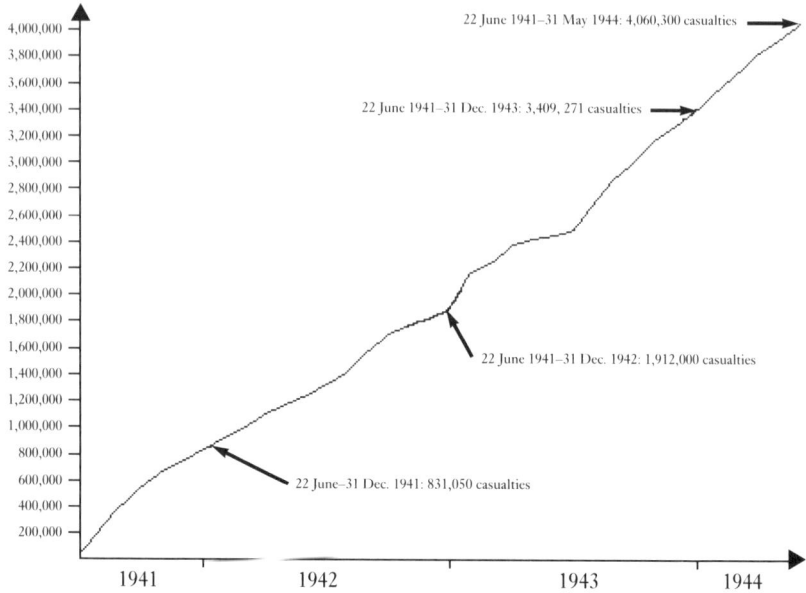

Note: Casualties include killed, wounded and missing. Note that many of the wounded
did return; the forces on the eastern front did not suffer a net loss of 4 million men
during the period covered by the figure.
Source: BA-MA RW 6/v. 552, BA-MA RW 6/v. 553 and BA-MA RH 2/1343.

accumulated German casualties without any distinctive or sudden rises in
losses. In fact, this graph displays a rather even attrition which may
gradually have worn the German forces down. It is also prudent to look
at the ratio between killed, wounded and missing. Another document[32]
shows marginally higher (1.5 per cent higher) casualties for the period
1 June 1941 to 31 May 1944 (751,769 killed in action, 2,826,958 wounded
and 541,505 missing) on the eastern front.[33] This marginal discrepancy is
to be expected since the document was compiled at a later date and has
corrections included. Interestingly the number of missing (and thus the
upper limit of the number of prisoners taken by the Red Army) amounts
to only about 13 per cent of the total losses suffered. This indicates that
it was not any particular hauls of prisoners that dominated the operations
in the east (at least not prisoners taken by the Red Army). However, it can
be argued that an operation may be decisive not because of what happened,
but because of what did not happen. When moving into these fields facts
tend to be replaced by speculations. We have previously argued that the

150

CONSEQUENCES OF THE BATTLE

war of attrition was not a foregone conclusion, due to the much greater casualties suffered by the Red Army (see Chapter 8), but this does not mean that a possible German success at Kursk would have made much of a difference. To argue that Germany might still have swung the balance during the summer of 1943, more than a successful conclusion for them of Zitadelle is required. Such a line of argument would readily be lost in the realms of fantasy.

NOTES

1. See Chapter 8 and Appendix 14 for a more thorough discussion of German casualties.
2. BA-MA RH 2/1343.
3. G.F. Krivosheyev, *Grif Sekretnosti Sniat* (Voenizdat, Moscow, 1993), p. 188.
4. Ibid., pp. 146f.
5. BA-MA RH 2/1343.
6. *Rysskii Arkhiv: Velikaya Otechestvennaya 4(4), Kurskaya Bitva, Dokumenti i Materiali 27 Marta–23 Avgusta 1943 goda* (Terra, Moscow, 1997), p. 406.
7. Notice that in the offensive against Orel forces from two more Fronts joined in, Bryansk with 433,600 and the left wing of the Western Front with 211,500. Thus the Red Army committed 46 per cent of its front-line strength of 1 July and 59 per cent of its Stavka Reserves of 1 July to the summer fighting around Kursk (5 July to 23 August). *Rysskii Arkhiv: Velikaya Otechestvennaya 4(4), Kurskaya Bitva*, pp. 406–7.
8. See Chapter 8 for a more thorough discussion of German tank losses.
9. BA-MA RH 10/77.
10. B. Müller-Hillebrand, *Das Heer*, Vol. III (Mittler & Sohn, Frankfurt am Main, 1969), Anhang B, foldout tables after page 272. The number of tanks was 590, while assault guns amounted to 318.
11. Ibid.
12. See Appendix 9 for the exact figures and for the sources used.
13. Guderian, *Panzer Leader* (Futura, London, 1982), p. 307.
14. During July 202 Panthers, 65 Tigers, 244 Panzer IV and 306 StuG were produced (see B. Müller-Hillebrand, *Das Heer*, Vol. III Anhang B).
15. *Journal of Slavic Military Studies*, Vol. 6, no. 4 (December 1993), E. Bacon, 'Soviet Military Losses in World War II', p. 619.
16. See Table 8.16.
17. Krivosheyev, *Grif Sekretnosti Sniat*, p. 370.
18. See Table 1.2.
19. Front-line forces had 5,254 tanks and assault guns while Stavka reserves had 389 tanks and assault guns. *Istoriya Vtoroi mirovoi voiny 1939–1945*, Vol. 8 (Voenizdat, Moscow, 1976), pp. 45 and 52. Another source states the front-line strength to be 5,347 tanks and assault guns. *Voennoe Iskusstvo, Vtoraya Mirovaya Voina*, Vol. 2 (Nauka, Moscow, 1966), p. 11.
20. *Journal of Slavic Military Studies*, Vol. 6, no. 4 (December 1993), E. Bacon, p. 619.
21. By summer 1944 the Red Army had started to recruit women to their tank and assault gun units because of a shortage of trained crews. Mostly as drivers, they had got their skills while working at tank production facilities. S. Zaloga, J. Kinnear, A. Aksenov and A. Koschchavtsev, *Stalin's Heavy Tanks 1941–1945, The KV and IS Heavy Tanks* (Concord Publications, Hongkong, 1997), p. 62.

151

22. The summer of 1942 was still in their memories. After a successful winter campaign in 1941/42 they had suffered a serious débâcle. Now they had again fought a successful winter campaign in 1942/43.

23. R. Cross, *Citadel – The Battle of Kursk* (Michael O'Mara Books, London, 1993), p. 252.

24. See for example the tables on pages 44 and 45 of *Geschichte des Zweiten Weltkrieges*, Vol. 6 (Deutscher Militärverlag, East Berlin, 1975–85).

25. The ration strength of 6th Army amounted to 298,573 men on 19 November 1942 (see M. Kehrig, *Stalingrad*, Anlage 14 (Deutsche Verlagsanstalt, Stuttgart, 1974), p. 671). For the Rumanian 3rd Army the authorized strength was 152,000 (Kehrig, *Stalingrad*, Anlage 9, p. 667), thus real strength most likely was lower. The German 4th Panzer Army had 42,215 men in German divisions and the Rumanian divisions subordinated to them had an authorized strength of 80,700 men, additionally there were 24,000 troops in corps and army units, resulting in a total strength of the army of 146,915 (Kehrig, *Stalingrad*, Anlage 9, p. 667). Thus, since ration strength and authorized strength has been used, it is most likely that actual strength was lower. Only those three armies faced the Soviet offensive and their front sectors corresponded quite well with the sectors occupied by the Soviet Southwest, Stalingrad and Don Fronts. This is also evident from Soviet sources, such as the map volume (map number 46) of *Geschichte des Großen Vaterländichen Krieges der Sowjetunion*.

26. *Geschichte des Zweiten Weltkrieges*, Vol. 6, p. 44.

27. OKH Org. Abt. (I) Nr. I/4325/43 g.Kdos. H.Qu., den 18.9.43. (National Archives, Microfilm Publication T78, Roll 411, Frame 6379596). The figure applies to 1 October 1942 but it had shrunk to 2,908,800 by 1 January 1943.

28. OKH Org. Abt. (I) Nr. 4493/42 g.Kdos. H.Qu., den 21.9.42. (BA-MA RH 2/429). The figure applies to 10 September 1942 but only marginal changes occurred up to the beginning of Uranus.

29. G.A. Koltunov and B.G. Soloviev, *Kurskaya bitva*, p. 354.

30. 1 July 1943 the *Ostheer* numbered 3,138,000 men and on 1 June 1944 it numbered 2,620,000 men (National Archives Microfilm Publication T78, Roll 414, Frame 6383128 and OKH Org. Abt. Nr. I/20737/11 g.Kdos. 24. November 1944, BA-MA RH 2/1341).

31. Personelle blutige Verluste des Feldheeres, Berichtigte Meldung für die Zeit 1.6.1944 bis 10.1.1945. Den Heeresarzt im OKH GenStdH/Gen Qu Az 1335 c/d (IIb) found in National Archives Microfilm Publication T 78 Roll 414, Frame 6383235.

32. Ibid.

33. The sector north of Leningrad is not included in 'the eastern front'.

Appendix 1:
Soviet Order of Battle

(*Source*: Boevoy Sostav Sovetskoy Armii, chast III)

CENTRAL FRONT, 1 JULY 1943

13TH ARMY
17th Guards Rifle Corps
  6th, 70th, 75th Guards Rifle Division
18th Guards Rifle Corps
  2nd, 3rd and 4th Guards Rifle Division
15th Rifle Corps
  8th, 74th, 148th Rifle Division
29th Rifle Corps
  15th, 81st, 307th Rifle Division

Army Troops
FIELD ARTILLERY
4th Breakthrough Artillery Corps
5th Breakthrough Artillery Division
  16th Lt.Art.Bde., 24th Cannon Bde., 9th How.Bde., 86th Hvy. How.
  Bde., 100th Super Hvy.How.Bde., 1st Mtr.Bde.
12th Breakthrough Art.Div.
  46th Lt.Art.Bde., 41st Cannon Bde., 32nd How.Bde., 89th Hvy. How.
  Bde., 104th Super Hvy.How.Bde., 11th Mtr.Bde.
5th Guards Rocket Art.Div.
  16th, 22nd, 23rd Guards Rocket Art.Bde.
19th Guards Cannon Regt., 476th Mtr.Regt., 477th Mtr.Regt., 6th Guards
Rocket Art.Regt., 37th Guards Rocket Art.Regt., 65th Guards Rocket
Art.Regt., 86th Guards Rocket Art.Regt., 324th Guards Rocket Art.Regt.

ENGINEERS
275th Eng.Bn.

OTHERS
1st AA Div. (1042nd, 1068th, 1085th, 1090th AA Regt.), 25th AA Div. (1067th, 1356th, 1362nd, 1368th AA Regt.), 1287th AA Regt., 874th Anti-Tank Regt., 129th Tank Bde, 27th Guards Tank Regt., 30th Guards Tank Regt., 43rd Tank Regt., 58th Tank Regt., 237th Tank Regt., 1442nd SU Regt., 49th Armoured Train Bn.

48TH ARMY

42nd Rifle Corps
16th, 202nd, 399th Rifle Division
73rd, 137th, 143rd, 170th Rifle Division

Army Troops
FIELD ARTILLERY
1168th Cannon Regt., 479th Mtr.Regt.

ENGINEERS
313th Eng.Bn.

OTHERS
16th AA Div. (728th, 1283rd, 1285th, 1286th AA Regt.), 461st AA Regt., 615th AA Bn., 2nd Anti-Tank Bde., 220th Guards Anti-Tank Regt., 45th Tank Regt., 193rd Tank Regt., 229th Tank Regt., 1454th SU Regt., 1455th SU Regt., 1540th SU Regt., 37th Armoured Train Bn.

60TH ARMY

24th Rifle Corps
112th Rifle Division, 42nd, 129th Rifle Brigade
30th Rifle Corps
121st, 141st, 322nd Rifle Division
55th Rifle Division, 248th Rifle Brigade

Army Troops
FIELD ARTILLERY
1156th Cannon Regt., 128th Mtr.Regt., 138th Mtr.Regt., 497th Mtr. Regt., 98th Guards Rocket Art.Regt., 286th Guards Rocket Art.Bn.

ENGINEERS
59th Eng.Sapper Brigade, 317th Eng.Bn.

OTHERS
  221st Guards AA Regt., 217th AA Regt., 1178th Anti-Tank Regt., 150th Tank Bde., 58th Armoured Train Bn.

65TH ARMY

18th Rifle Corps
  69th, 149th, 246th Rifle Division
27th Rifle Corps
  60th, 193rd Rifle Division, 115th Rifle Brigade
37th Guards Rifle Division, 181st, 194th, 354th Rifle Division

Army Troops
FIELD ARTILLERY
  143rd Guards Mtr.Regt., 218th Mtr.Regt., 478th Mtr.Regt., 94th Guards Rocket Art.Regt.

ENGINEERS
  14th Eng.-Mine Bde., 321st Eng.Bn.

OTHERS
  29th Guards Tank Regt., 40th Tank Regt., 84th Tank Regt., 255th Tank Regt., 120th AT Regt., 543rd AT Regt., 235th AA Regt.

70TH ARMY

28th Rifle Corps
  132nd, 211th, 280th Rifle Division
  102nd, 106th, 140th, 162nd, 175th (NKVD) Rifle Division

Army Troops
FIELD ARTILLERY
  1st Guards Art.Div. (1st Guards Cannon Art.Bde., 2nd Guards How.Art.Bde., 3rd Guards Lt.Art.Bde.), 136th Mtr.Regt.

ENGINEERS
  169th Eng.Bn., 371st Eng.Bn., 386th Eng.Bn.

OTHERS
  3rd Destroyer Bde. (from 2nd Destroyer Div.), 240th Tank Regt., 251st Tank Regt., 259th Tank Regt., 378th AT Regt., 12th AA Div. (836th, 977th, 990th AA Regt.), 581st AA.Reg.

2ND TANK ARMY

3rd Tank Corps
  50th, 51st, 103rd Tank Bde., 57th Motorized Rifle Bde., 881st AT

Regt., 234th Mtr.Regt., 121st AA Regt., 74th MC Bn., 728th AT Bn.
16th Tank Corps
107th, 109th, 164th Tank Bde., 15th Motorized Rifle Bde., 1441st SU
Regt., 614th AT Regt., 226th Mtr.Regt., 51st MC Bn., 729th AT Bn.

Army Troops

FIELD ARTILLERY
None

ENGINEERS
357th Eng.Bn.

OTHERS
11th Guards Tank Bde., 87th MC Bn.

FRONT RESERVES

9th Tank Corps
23rd, 95th, 108th Tank Bde., 8th Motorized Rifle Bde., 730th AT Bn.
19th Tank Corps
79th, 101st, 102nd Tank Bde., 26th Motorized Rifle Bde.
115th, 119th, 161st Fortified Sectors

Support Troops

FIELD ARTILLERY
68th Cannon Art.Bde., 21st Mtr.Bde., 84th Guards Rocket Art.Regt.,
92nd Guards Rocket Art.Regt., 323rd Guards Rocket Art.Regt.

ENGINEERS
1st Guards Special Purposes Eng.Bde., 6th Mine Eng.Bde., 12th
Guards Mine Bn., 120th Eng.Bn., 257th Eng.Bn., 9th Pontoon Bn.,
49th Pontoon Bn., 50th Pontoon Bn., 104th Pontoon Bn.

OTHERS
1541st SU Regt., 4th Destroyer Bde. (from 2nd Destroyer Div.), 14th
Destroyer Bde., 40th Armoured Train Bn., 1st AT Bde., 13th AT Bde.,
130th AT Regt., 563rd AT Regt., 10th AA Div. (802nd, 975th, 984th,
994th AA Regt.), 997th AA Regt. (from 12th AA Div.), 325th AA Regt.,
1259th AA Regt., 1263rd AA Regt., 13th Guards AA Bn., 27th AA Bn.,
31st AA Bn.

6TH GUARDS ARMY

22nd Guards Rifle Corps
  67th, 71st, 90th Guards Rifle Division
23rd Guards Rifle Corps
  51st, 52nd, 375th Guard Rifle Division
89th Guards Rifle Division

Army Troops

FIELD ARTILLERY
  27th Cannon Art.Bde., 33rd Cannon Art.Bde., 628th Cannon Art.
  Regt., 263rd Mtr.Regt., 295th Mtr.Regt., 5th Guards Rocket Art.
  Regt., 16th Guards Rocket Art.Regt., 79th Guards Rocket Art.Regt.,
  314th Guards Rocket Art.Regt.

ENGINEERS
  205th Eng.Bn., 540th Eng.Bn.

OTHERS
  96th Tank Bde., 230th Tank Regt., 245th Tank Regt., 1440th SU Regt.,
  60th Armoured Train Bn., 27th AT Bde., 28th AT Bde., 493rd AT
  Regt., 496th AT Regt., 611th AT Regt., 694th AT Regt., 868th AT
  Regt., 1008th AT Regt., 1240th AT Regt., 1666th AT Regt., 1667th
  AT Regt., 26th AA Div. (1352nd, 1357th, 1363rd, 1369th AA Regt.),
  1487th AA Regt.

7TH GUARDS ARMY

24th Guards Rifle Corps
  15th, 36th, 72nd Guards Rifle Division
25th Guards Rifle Corps
  73rd, 78th, 81st Guards Rifle Division
213th Rifle Division

Army Troops

FIELD ARTILLERY
  109th Guards Cannon Art.Regt., 161st Guards Cannon Art.Regt.,
  265th Guards Cannon Art.Regt., 290th Mtr.Regt.

ENGINEERS
  60th Eng.Sapper Bde., 175th Eng.Bn., 329th Eng.Bn.

OTHERS
  27th Guards Tank Bde., 201st Tank Bde., 262nd Tank Regt., 148th

Tank Regt., 167th Tank Regt., 1529th SU Regt., 1438th SU Regt., 34th Armoured Train Bn., 38th Armoured Train Bn., 30th AT Bde., 114th Guards AT Regt., 115th Guards AT Regt., 1669th AT Regt., 1670th AT Regt., 5th AA Div. (670th, 743rd, 1119th, 1181st AA Regt.), 162nd Guards AA Regt., 258th Guards AA Regt.

38TH ARMY

167th, 180th, 204th, 232nd, 240th, 340th Rifle Division

Army Troops

FIELD ARTILLERY

111th Guards How.Art.Regt., 112th Guards Cannon Art.Regt., 491st Mtr.Regt., 492nd Mtr.Regt., 66th Guards Rocket Art.Regt., 441st Guards Rocket Art.Bn (from 314th Guards Rocket Art.Regt.)

ENGINEERS

235th Eng.Bn., 268th Eng.Bn., 1505th Mine Eng.Bn., 108th Pontoon Bn.

OTHERS

180th Tank Bde., 192nd Tank Bde., 29th AT Bde., 222nd AT Regt., 483rd AT Regt., 1658th AT Regt., 1660th AT Regt., 981st AA Regt. (from 9th AA Div.), 1288th AA Regt.

40TH ARMY

100th, 161st, 184th, 206th, 219th, 237th, 309th Rifle Division

Army Troops

FIELD ARTILLERY

36th Cannon Art.Bde., 29th How.Art.Bde. (–), 76th Guards Cannon Art.Regt., 493rd Mtr.Regt., 494th Mtr.Regt., 9th Mtn.Mtr.Regt., 10th Mtn.Mtr.Regt.

ENGINEERS

14th Eng.Bn.

OTHERS

86th Tank Bde., 59th Tank Regt., 60th Tank Regt., 32nd AT Bde., 4th Guards AT Regt., 12th AT Regt., 869th AT Regt., 1244th AT Regt., 1663rd AT Regt., 1664th AT Regt., 9th AA Div. (800th, 974th and 993rd AA Regt.), 1488th AA Regt.

69TH *ARMY*

107th, 111th, 183rd, 270th, 305th Rifle Division

Army Troops

FIELD ARTILLERY
496th Mtr.Regt.

ENGINEERS
328th Eng.Bn.

OTHERS
1661st AT Regt., 225th Guards AA Regt., 322nd AA Bn.

1ST TANK ARMY

3rd Mechanized Corps
1st, 3rd, 10th Mech.Bde., 1st Guards Tank Bde., 49th Tank Bde., 35th AT Regt., 265th Mtr.Regt., 58th MC Bn., 405th Guards Rocket Art.Bn.
6th Tank Corps
22nd, 112th, 200th Tank Bde., 6th Motorized Rifle Bde., 1461st SU.Regt., 538th AT Regt., 270th Mtr.Regt., 85th MC Bn.
31st Tank Corps
100th, 237th, 242nd Tank Bde.

Army Troops

FIELD ARTILLERY
316th Guards Rocket Art.Regt.

ENGINEERS
71st Eng.Bn., 267th Eng.Bn.

OTHERS
8th AA Division (797th, 848th, 978th and 1063rd AA Regt.)

FRONT RESERVES

2nd Guards Tank Corps
4th, 25th, 26th Guards Tank Bde., 4th Guards Motorized Rifle Bde., 47th Guards Tank Regt., 1500th AT Regt., 273rd Mtr.Regt., 1695th AA Regt., 755th AT Bn.
5th Guards Tank Corps
20th, 21st, 22nd Guards Tank Bde., 6th Guards Motorized Rifle Bde., 48th Guards Tank Regt., 1499th AT Regt., 454th Mtr.Regt., 1696th AA Regt.

35th Guards Rifle Corps
92nd, 93rd, 94th Guards Rifle Division.

Support Troops

FIELD ARTILLERY

1528th How.Art.Regt (from 29th How.Art.Bde.), 522nd Super Hvy.How.Art.Regt., 1148th Super Hvy.How.Art.Regt., 12th Mtr. Bde., 469th Mtr.Regt., 36th Guards Rocket Art.Regt., 80th Guards Rocket Art.Regt., 97th Guards Rocket Art.Regt., 309th Guards Rocket Art.Regt., 315th Guards Rocket Art.Regt.

ENGINEERS

4th Mine Eng.Bde., 5th Mine Eng.Bde., 42nd Special Purposes Eng. Bde., 6th Pontoon Bde., 13th Guards Mine Bn., 6th Pontoon Bn., 20th Pontoon Bn.

OTHERS

Separate Tank Regt. (unnumbered), 14th AT Bde., 31st AT Bde., 1076th AT Regt., 1689th AT Regt., 22nd Guards AA Bn.

STEPPE FRONT (STEPPE MILITARY DISTRICT),
1 JULY 1943

4TH GUARDS ARMY

20th Guards Rifle Corps
5th, 7th, 8th Guards Airborne Rifle Division
21st Guards Rifle Corps
68th, 69th, 80th Guards Rifle Division
3rd Guards Tank Corps
3rd, 18th, 19th Guards Tank Bde., 2nd Guards Motorized Rifle Bde., 1436th SU-Regt., 73rd MC Bn., 1496th AT Regt., 266th Mtr.Regt., 1701st AA Regt., 749th AT Bn., 324th Guards Rocket Art Bn.

Army Troops

FIELD ARTILLERY

466th Mtr.Regt., 96th Guards Rocket Art.Regt.

ENGINEERS

48th Eng.Bn.

OTHERS

452nd, 1317th AT Regt., 27th AA Div. (1354th, 1358th, 1364th, 1370th AA Regt.)

5TH GUARDS ARMY

32nd Guards Rifle Corps
  13th, 66th Guards Rifle Division, 6th Guards Airborne Rifle Division
33rd Guards Rifle Corps
  95th, 97th Guards Rifle Division, 9th Guards Airborne Rifle Division
10th Tank Corps
  178th, 183rd, 186th Tank Bde., 11th Motorized Rifle Bde., 1450th SU
  Regt., 77th MC Bn., 727th AT Bn., 287th Mtr.Regt., 1693rd AA Regt.
42nd Guards Rifle Division

Army Troops
FIELD ARTILLERY
  308th Guards Rocket Art.Regt.

ENGINEERS
  256th, 431st Eng.Bn.

OTHERS
  301st, 1322nd AT Regt., 29th AA Div (1360th, 1366th, 1372nd, 1374th
  AA Regt.)

27TH ARMY

71st, 147th, 155th, 163rd, 166th, 241st Rifle Division

Army Troops
FIELD ARTILLERY
  480th Mtr.Regt., 47th Guards Rocket Art.Regt.

ENGINEERS
  25th, 38th Eng.Bn.

OTHERS
  680th, 1070th AT Regt., 93rd Tank Bde., 39th Tank Regt., 23rd AA
  Div. (1064th, 1336th, 1342nd, 1348th AA Regt.)

47TH ARMY

21st Rifle Corps
  23rd, 218th, 337th Rifle Division
23rd Rifle Corps
  29th, 30th, 38th Rifle Division

Army Troops
FIELD ARTILLERY
  460th Mtr.Regt., 83rd Guards Rocket Art.Regt.

ENGINEERS
91st Eng.Bn.

OTHERS
269th, 1593rd AT Regt., 21st AA Div (1044th, 1334th, 1340th, 1346th AA Regt.)

53RD ARMY

28th Guards, 84th, 116th, 214th, 233rd, 252nd, 299th Rifle Division

Army Troops

FIELD ARTILLERY
461st Mtr.Regt., 89th Guards Rocket Art.Regt.

ENGINEERS
11th, 17th Eng.Bn.

OTHERS
232nd, 1316th AT Regt., 34th, 35th Tank Regt., 30th AA Div (1361st, 1367th, 1373rd, 1375th AA regt.)

5TH GUARDS TANK ARMY

5th Guards Mechanized Corps
10th, 11th, 12th Guards Mechanized Bde., 24th Guards Tank Bde., 4th Guards A/C Regt., 2nd Guards MC Bn., 1447th SU Regt., 104th Guards AT Regt., 285th Mtr.Regt., 737th AT Bn., 409th Guards Rocket Art.Bn.
29th Tank Corps
25th, 31st, 32nd Tank Bde., 53rd Motorized Rifle Bde., 1446th SU Regt., 38th A/C Bn., 75th MC Bn., 108th AT Regt., 271st Mtr.Regt., 747th AT Bn.

Army Troops

FIELD ARTILLERY
678th How.Art.Regt., 76th Guards Rocket Regt.

ENGINEERS
377th Eng.Bn.

AIR UNIT
994th Light Bomber Regiment

OTHERS
689th AT Regt., 53rd Guards Tank Regt., 1549th SU Regt., 1st Guards MC Regt., 6th AA Div (146th, 366th, 516th, 1062nd AA Regt.)

162

FRONT RESERVES

35th Rifle Corps
(HQ only)
3rd Guards Cavalry Corps
    5th, 6th Guards Div., 32nd Cavalry Div., 144th Guards AT Regt., 3rd Guards AT Bn., 64th Guards Mtr.Bn., 1731st AA Regt.
5th Guards Cavalry Corps
    11th, 12th Guards Div., 63rd Cavalry Div., SU Reg. (unnumbered), 150th Guards AT Regt., 5th Guards AT Bn., 72nd Guards Mtr.Bn., 585th AA Regt.
7th Guards Cavalry Corps
    14th, 15th, 16th Guards Cavalry Div., 145th Guards AT Regt., 7th Guards AT Bn., 57th Guards Mtr.Bn., 1733rd AA Regt.
4th Guards Tank Corps
    12th, 13th, 14th Guards Tank Bde., 3rd Guards Motorized Rifle Bde., 1451st SU Regt., 76th MC Bn., 756th AT Regt., 264th Mtr.Regt., 752nd AT Bn., 120th Guards AA Regt.
3rd Guards Mechanized Corps
    7th, 8th, 9th Guards Mechanized Corps, 35th Guards Tank Bde., 1st Guards MC Bn., 1510th AT Regt., 129th Mtr.Regt., 743rd AT Bn., 334th Guards Rocket Art.Bn., 1705th AA Regt.
1st Mechanized Corps
    19th, 35th, 37th Mechanized Bde., 219th Tank Bde., 57th MC Bn., 75th AT Regt., 294th Mtr.Regt.
2nd Mechanized Corps
    18th, 34th, 43rd Mechanized Bde., 33rd Tank Bde., 68th MC Bn., 79th AT Regt., 468th Mtr.Regt., 734th AT Bn., 410th Guards Rocket Art Bn., 1706th AA Regt.

Support Troops

ENGINEERS
    8th Eng.Sapper Bde., 27th Special Purposes Eng.Bde., 7th, 19th, 40th Ponton Bn., 246th, 247th, 248th, 250th, 284th Eng.Bn.

OTHERS
    78th MC Bn., 11th AA Div. (804th, 976th, 987th, 996th AA Regt.)

REINFORCEMENT FROM SOUTHWESTERN FRONT

2nd Tank Corps
26th, 99th, 169th Tank Bde., 58th Motorized Rifle Bde., 83rd MC Bn., 1502nd AT Regt., 269th Mtr.Regt., 1698th AA Regt., 307th Guards Rocket Art.Bn.

REINFORCEMENT FROM STAVKA RESERVES

18th Tank Corps
110th, 170th, 181st Tank Bde., 32nd Motorized Rifle Bde., 36th Guards Tank Regt., 1000th AT Regt., 736th AT Bn., 292nd Mtr.Regt., 1694th AA Regt.

AIR ARMIES SUPPORTING THE SOVIET FORCES

2nd Air Army (Voronezh Front)
1st Bomber Air Corps (BAK): 1st Guards Bomber Division, 293rd Bomber Division
1st Attack Air Corps (ShAK): 266th, 292nd Attack Division
4th Fighter Air Corps (IAK): 294th, 302nd Fighter Division
5th Fighter Air Corps (IAK): 8th Guards Fighter Division, 205th Fighter Division
291st Attack Division
203rd Fighter Division
208th Night Bomber Division
385th, 454th Light Bomber Regiment
50th Reconnaissance Regiment
1554th, 1555th, 1605th Anti-Aircraft Artillery Regiment

5th Air Army (Steppe Front)
7th Combined Air Corps (SAK): 202nd bomber Division, 287th Fighter Division
8th Combined Air Corps (SAK): 4th Guards Attack Division, 26th Attack Division, 256th Fighter Division
3rd Fighter Air Corps (IAK): 265th, 278th Fighter Division
7th Fighter Air Corps (IAK): 259th, 304th Fighter Division
69th Guards Fighter Regiment
511th Reconnaissance Regiment

16th Air Army (Central Front)
3rd Bomber Air Corps (BAK): 241st, 301st Bomber Division
6th Combined Air Corps (SAK): 221st Bomber Division, 282nd Fighter Division

6th Fighter Air Corps (IAK): 273rd, 279th Fighter Division
2nd Guards, 299th Attack Division
1st Guards, 283rd, 286th Fighter Division
271st Nighter Bomber Division
16th Reconnaissance Regiment
1610th, 1611th, 1612th Anti-Aircraft Artillery Regiment

17th Air Army (Southwestern Front)
1st Combined Air Corps (SAK): 5th Guards Attack Division, 288th
Fighter Division
3rd Combined Air Corps (SAK): 290th Attack Division, 207th Fighter
Division
9th Combined Air Corps (SAK): 305th Attack Division, 295th Fighter
Division
244th Bomber Division
306th Attack Division
262nd Night Bomber Division
39th Reconnaissance Regiment
1613th, 1614th, 1615th Anti-Aircraft Artillery Regiment

Appendix 2:
German Order of Battle

(*Sources*: BA-MA RH 20-9/135, 21-4/133, 24-11/76)

4TH PANZER ARMY, 6 JULY 1943

LII CORPS

57th Infantry Division, 255th Infantry Division and 332nd Infantry Division

Corps Troops

FIELD ARTILLERY
  Arko 137, I/108th Field Art.Bn. (RSO), 3rd/731st 15cm Gun Battery, 1st Hvy.Rocket Art.Regt.

ENGINEERS
  677th Eng.Regt. for special purposes, 74th Eng.Bn., 217th Constr.Bn., 23rd and 80th Bridge Column Bn.

OTHERS
  226th Bicycle Security Bn. (minus 1 Coy.)

XXXXVIII PANZER CORPS

167th Infantry Division, 3rd Panzer Division, 11th Panzer Division and Großdeutschland Panzergrenadier Division

166

Corps Troops
FIELD ARTILLERY
Arko 132, Arko 144, 70th Art.Regt.Staff for special purposes, III/109th Howitzer Bn. (motorized), 101st Hvy.Field Art.Bn., 842nd 10cm Gun Bn., 911th Assault Gun Bn., 19th Lt.Art.Obsv.Bn.

ENGINEERS
515th Eng.Regt. for special purposes, 48th Eng.Bn. (motorized), 1st Eng.Training Bn., Bridging Staff 938 (Bridge Column Bn. 22nd, 609th, 639th, 649th, 676th and J.841), 81st Bridge Constr.Bn. (minus 4th Coy.)

OTHERS
616th Army AA Coy.

II SS-PANZER CORPS

SS-Totenkopf, SS-Das Reich and SS-Liebstandarte Panzergrenadier Divisions

Corps Troops
FIELD ARTILLERY
Arko 122, 861st Field Art.Bn. (RSO), III/818th Field Art.Bn. (RSO), Commander of Smoke Troops 3, 55th Rocket Art.Regt., 1st Lehr Rocket Art.Regt., SS-Corps Rocket Art Bn.

ENGINEERS
680th Eng.Regt. for special purposes, 627th Eng.Bn. (motorized), 666th Eng.Bn. (motorized), Bridging Staff 929 (Bridge Column Bn. 2/41st, 11th, 21st, 31st, 537th and J.840), Commander of Constr. Troops 8., 26th Bridge Constr.Bn., 508th Lt.Bicycle Road Constr.Bn., 410th Constr.Bn.

Army Troops
Higher Arko 312, Higher Constr.Staff 14, Commander for Constr.Forces 14, 155th Constr.Bn. (K), 305th Const.Bn., Bridging Staff 922 (Bridge Column Bn. 617, 2nd/413th)

ARMY-DETACHMENT KEMPF, 4 JULY 1943

III PANZER CORPS

168th Infantry Division, 6th Panzer Division, 7th Panzer Division and 19th Panzer Division

Corps Troops

FIELD ARTILLERY

Arko 3, 612th Art.Regt. for special purposes, 857th 21cm How.Bn., II/62nd Field Art.Bn., II/71st Hvy.Field Art.Bn., 228th Assault Gun Bn., 54th Rocket Art.Regt.

ENGINEERS

601st Eng.Regt. (motorized), 674th Eng.Regt. (motorized), 70th Eng.Bn. (motorized), 651st Eng.Bn. (motorized), 127.Eng Bn. (motorized) (minus 1 Coy.), 531st Bridge Constr.Bn., 925th Bridge Constr.Bn.

OTHERS

503rd Hvy Tank Bn., 99th AA Regt., 153rd AA Regt.

RAUS CORPS

106th Infantry Division and 320th Infantry Division

Corps Troops

FIELD ARTILLERY

Arko 153, I/77th Field Art.Bn., I/213th Field Art.Bn., II/54th Field Art.Bn., 31st Lt.Art.Obsv.Bn., 905th Assault Gun Bn., 393rd Assault Gun Battery, II/1st Hvy.Rocket-Launcher Regt., 52nd Rocket Art.Regt.

ENGINEERS

18th Eng.Regt. (motorized), 52nd Eng.Bn. (motorized), 923rd Bridge Constr.Bn., 41st Bridge Constr.Bn., 246 Constr.Bn.

OTHERS

4th AA Regt., 7th AA Regt., 48th AA Regt.

XXXXII CORPS

39th Infantry Division, 161st Infantry Division and 282nd Infantry Division

Corps Troops
FIELD ARTILLERY
Arko 107, 2nd/800th 15cm Gun Bty., 13th Art.Obsv.Bn.

ENGINEERS
620th Mtn.Eng.Regt. (motorized), 26th Constr.Regt., 219th Constr.Bn., 112th Constr.Bn. (U), 153rd Constr.Bn. (K)

OTHERS
Anti-Tank Bn. C., 560th Hvy.Anti-Tank Bn. (Nashorn), 18th Penal Bn.

Army Troops
Higher Arko 310, Commander of Smoketroops 1, 781st Art.Regt.Staff, 22nd Constr.Bde., 21st Bridge Constr.Bn., 538th, 676th Hvy.Road Constr.Bn.

9TH ARMY, 30 JUNE 1943

XX CORPS

45th Infantry Division, 72nd Infantry Division, 137th Infantry Division and 251st Infantry Division

Corps Troops
FIELD ARTILLERY
Arko 129, 860th Field Art.Bn., 15th Lt.Art.Obsv.Bn.

ENGINEERS
512th Eng.Regt.Staff, 4th Eng.Regt. staff for special purposes, 750th Eng.Bn., Bridge Column B 626, 44th Constr.Bn., 418th Constr.Bn., 80th Constr.Bn., 244th Constr.Bn. (K)

XXXXVI PANZER CORPS

7th Infantry Division, 31st Infantry Division, 102nd Infantry Division and 258th Infantry Division

Corps Troops

FIELD ARTILLERY

Arko 1, 609th Art.Regt.Staff for special purposes, 909th Assault Gun Bn., 430th Field Art.Bn., 611th 10cm Gun Bn., II/47th Mixed Art.Bn., 3rd/637th 21cm How.Bty., 3rd/620th 15cm Gun Bty., 1st Recoilless Gun Bn. (with 423, 433 and 443 Bty.), 18th Hvy.Mtr.Bn.

ENGINEERS

752nd Eng.Bn., Bridge Column B 12, 29, Bridging Staff 930, Commander of Constr.Forces 33, 584th Road Constr.Bn.

OTHERS

Group von Manteuffel (9th, 10th, 11th Jaeger Bn.)

XXXXVII PANZER CORPS

6th Infantry Division, 2nd Panzer Division, 9th Panzer Division and 20th Panzer Division

Corps Troops

FIELD ARTILLERY

Arko 130, 904th Assault Gun Bn., 245th Assault Gun Bn., II/63rd Hvy.Field Bn., II/67th Hvy.Field Bn., 637th 21cm How.Bn. (minus 3rd Bty.), 1st/620th 15cm Gun Bty, 2nd Hvy.Rocket-Launcher Regt.

ENGINEERS

678th Eng.Regt.Staff, 2nd Training Eng.Bn., 47th Eng.Bn. (motorized), 145th Bridge Constr.Bn., Bridging Staff 928 (Bridge Column B 47, 2nd 402nd, J 845)

OTHERS

505th Hvy.Tank Bn. (minus 3rd Coy.), 312th Panzer Coy. (Fkl)

XXXXI PANZER CORPS

86th Infantry Division, 292nd Infantry Division and 18th Panzer Division

Corps Troops
FIELD ARTILLERY
Arko 35, 69th Art.Regt.Staff, 177th Assault Gun Bn., 244th Assault Gun Bn., 616th Field Art.Bn., 425th Field Art.Bn., II/64th Field Art.Bn., 427th 10cm Gun Bn., II/61st Hvy.Field Art.Bn., 604th 21cm How.Bn., 2nd/620th 15cm Gun Bty., 53rd Rocket Art.Regt., 19th Hvy.Mtr.Bn.

ENGINEERS
104th Eng.Regt.Staff for special purposes, 42nd Eng.Bn. (motorized), Bridging Staff 932 (Bridge Column B 2/409, 606), 407th Constr.Bn.

OTHERS
656th Tank Destroyer Regt. (653rd Tank Destroyer Bn., 654th Tank Destroyer Bn., 216th Assault Tank Bn., 313th Panzer Coy. (Fkl), 314th Panzer Coy. (Fkl)

XXIII CORPS

216th Infantry Division, 383rd Infantry Division, 87th Grenadier Regiment (from 36th ID) and 78th Assault Division

Corps Troops
FIELD ARTILLERY
Arko 112, 109th Art.Regt.Staff, 41st Art.Regt.Staff, 774th Art. Regt.Staff, 185th Assault Gun Bn., 189th Assault Gun Bn., II/59th Field Art.Bn., 426th Field Art.Bn., 851st Field Art.Bn., 79th 10cm Gun Bn., 4th/69th 10cm Gun Bty., 422nd Mixed Art.Bn., 848th Hvy.Field Art.Bn., II/66th Hvy.Field Art.Bn., 859th 21cm How.Bn., 1st, 2nd/635th 21cm How.Bty., 1st/817th 17cm Gun Bty., 22nd Lt.Art.Obsv.Bn., 51st Rocket Art.Regt.

ENGINEERS
623rd Eng.Regt.Staff, 746th Eng.Bn., 85th Mtn.Eng.Bn., Bridge Column B 88, 78th Road Constr.Bn., 811th Armoured.Eng.Coy., 813th Armoured Eng.Coy.

OTHERS
8th Jaeger Bn., 13th Jaeger Bn.

Army Troops
442nd Divisional Staff for special purposes, Commander of Smoke Troops 4, 654th Eng.Bn., 751st Eng.Bn., 42nd Bridge Constr.Bn., 539th Bridge Constr.Bn., Bridge Column B 1/430th, 535th, Commander of Constr.Forces 42, 544th Road Constr.Bn., 576th Road Constr.Bn., 580th Road Constr.Bn., Higher Constr.Staff 10, 889th Sec.Bn.

ARMY GROUP CENTRE RESERVE

4th Panzer Division, 12th Panzer Division, 10th Panzer Grenadier Division

LUFTWAFFE, 4 JULY 1943

VIIITH AIR CORPS (from Luftflotte 4) supporting Army Group South

Kampfgeschwader 3 (Staff, I Group, II Group, III Group)
Kampfgeschwader 27 (Staff, I Group, II Group, III Group)
Kampfgeschwader 55 (Staff, II Group, III Group)
Kampfgeschwader 100 (I Group)
Jagdgeschwader 3 (II Group, III Group)
Jagdgeschwader 52 (Staff, I Group, II Group, III Group)
Sturzkampfgeschwader 2 (Staff, I Group, II Group, III Group, 10./2.)
Sturzkampfgeschwader 77 (Staff, I Group, II Group, III Group)
Schlachtgeschwader 1 (II Group, 4./1.)
Schlachtgeschwader 2 (4./2., 8./2.)

1ST AIR DIVISION (from Luftflotte 6) supporting Army Group Centre

Kampfgeschwader 1 (I Group)
Kampgeschwader 4 (Staff, II Group)
Kampfgeschwader 51 (Staff,II Group, III Group)
Kampfgeschwader 53 (Staff, I Group, II Group, III Group)
Jagdgeschwader 51 (Staff, I Group, III Group, IV Group)
Jagdgeschwader 54 (I Group)
Sturzkampfgeschwader 1 (Staff, I Group, II Group, III Group, 10./1.)
Sturzkampfgeschwader 3 (III Group)
Schlachtgeschwader 1 (Staff, I Group, 8./1.)
Zerstörergeschwader 1 (I Group, 10./1.)

Notes: Kampf – Bomber
Jagd – Fighter
Sturzkampf – Dive bomber
Schlacht – Ground attack
Zerstörer – Heavy fighter
(See page 77 above for a description of how a Geschwader was organized.)

Appendix 3:
Soviet Tank Units Facing
Army Group South

This appendix presents the Soviet tank units deployed to halt the advance of 4th Panzer Army and Army Detachment Kempf.

Forces committed initially

Initially the Red Army deployed the 6th and 7th Guards Armies in the forward defensive belt and the 1st Tank Army in reserve, covering the approaches to Oboyan. Also the 2nd Guards and 5th Guards Tank Corps were held in reserve by the Voronezh Front.

The following tank units were with the 6th Guards Army:
    230th and 245th Tank Regiments (total of 74 tanks)
    96th Tank Brigade (61 T-34)
    1440th SU Regiment (20 SU-76)

The following tank units were with the 7th Guards Army:
    148th and 167th Tank Regiments (total of 78 tanks)
    262nd Heavy Tank Regiment (21 KV-1)
    27th Guards Tank Brigade and 201st Tank Brigade (total of 125 tanks)
    1529th SU Regiment (10 SU-122)
    1438th SU Regiment (12 SU-122)

Total number of AFVs amounted to 359 tanks and 42 SUs on 5 July.

Further forces committed

Date	Unit	Enemy against which directed	Number of AFVs Tanks	SU	Accumulated AFV strength
6 July[1]	1st Tank Army	XXXXVIII Pz. Korps	634	–	1,035
6 July[2]	2nd Guards Tank Corps	II SS-Pz. Korps	198	–	1,233
6 July[3]	5th Guards Tank Corps	II SS-Pz. Korps	219	–	1,452
7 July[4]	180th Tank Brigade	XXXXVIII Pz. Korps	61	–	1,513
7 July[5]	192nd Tank Brigade	II SS-Pz. Korps	61	–	1,574
8 July	2nd Tank Corps	II SS-Pz. Korps	195	–	1,769
8 July[6]	86th Tank Brigade	II SS-Pz. Korps	53	–	1,822
8 July[7]	59th Tank Regiment	II SS-Pz. Korps	35	–	1,857
8 July[8]	10th Tank Corps	XXXXVIII Pz. Korps	210	–	2,067
9 July[9]	60th Tank Regiment	XXXXVIII Pz. Korps	21	–	2,088
12 July	18th Tank Corps[10]	II SS-Pz. Korps	190	–	2,278
12 July	29th Tank Corps[11]	II SS-Pz. Korps	192	20	2,490
12 July	5th Guards Mech Corps[12]	II SS-Pz. Korps	207	16	2,713
12 July	53rd Guards Tank Regiment[13]	II SS-Pz. Korps	39	–	2,752
12 July	1549th SU Regiment[14]	II SS-Pz. Korps	–	12	2,764

Note that the Soviet units did not necessarily spend all the time fighting the German units indicated above. For example, the 31st Tank Corps (part of 1st Tank Army) fought against the II SS-Panzer Corps between 7 and 9 July,[15] while the 5th Guards Tank Corps was transferred to the sector where XXXXVIII Pz. Korps were fighting during the night between 10 and 11 July.[16] Also part of 5th Mechanized Corps was committed against III Panzer Corps.

Included in the table above are only units committed, not tanks that may have arrived as replacements. Thus the real number of tanks was even higher, which is also indicated by a Soviet document stating that up to and including the 12th, 2,924 tanks and assault guns had been committed on the Voronezh front sector.[17]

NOTES

1. *Tankovye voiska v oborone kurskogo platsdarma* from S*bornik materialov po izucheniiu optya voiny* (Voenizdat, Moscow, 1944), translated by Harold S. Orenstein, published in *Journal of Slavic Military Studies*, Vol. 7, no. 1 (March 1994), p. 94.
2. Ibid., pp. 94–9.
3. Ibid.
4. Ibid., p. 97.
5. Ibid., pp. 98–9.
6. Ibid., p. 99.
7. Ibid.
8. Ibid.
9. Ibid., p. 100.
10. See Chapter 7.
11. See Chapter 7.
12. See Chapter 7.

13. See Chapter 7.
14. See Chapter 7.
15. *Tankovye voiska* ..., pp. 97–102.
16. Ibid., p. 102.
17. See Karl-Heinz Frieser in Jürgen G. Foerster (ed.), *Gezeitenwechsel im Zweiten Weltkrieg?* (Mittler & Sohn, Hamburg, 1996), p. 124, note 44.

Appendix 4:
The Panther Tank in Zitadelle

The Panther tank played a major, though mixed, role in Zitadelle. One of the chief reasons for the delay seems to have been the desire to employ this new tank in the offensive that was supposed to result in a victory that was to be like a beacon for the world. Perhaps this was the most important effect the tank had on the battle.

Much has been written about the flaws exhibited by the Panther due to its hurried development and testing. Indeed there were flaws. Already on the approach march to the deployment area for the battle two Panthers caught fire and each became a complete loss.[1] This behaviour continued during the battle. Between 5 and 9 July another four were completely destroyed by fires in the engine room caused by self-ignition (i.e. nothing attributable to enemy action).[2] Thus six Panthers had succeeded in destroying themselves by 9 July. Of the 28 Panthers which had been completely destroyed up to 10 July (inclusive),[3] about a quarter were not attributable to enemy action. This is, of course, exceptional, though not in a positive sense. Less serious damage was of course also widespread. During the first five days of the battle, the two tank repair companies of the 39th Panzer Regiment (the parent HQ for the two Panther battalions employed in Zitadelle) received 81 Panthers which had been damaged by other than enemy action.[4] This included vehicles requiring completely new engines and tanks with defects in hydraulic systems, steering and transmission.

Another frequent problem was defective seals and gaskets. This was particularly serious since it resulted in leaks of fuel, oil and hydraulic fluids. To this was added an engine with an inefficient cooling system, which made the engine prone to overheating. The complete loss of the six Panthers due to self-ignition up to 9 July was probably the result of these deficiencies. But these defects probably did not only result in spontaneous

177

ignition. A hit in the engine compartment was very likely to lead to the complete loss of the vehicle due to fire. These defects were later rectified, but during Zitadelle many, possibly the majority of the Panthers destroyed, were lost unnecessarily.

It was not only technical deficiencies that bedevilled the Panther formations. They seem to have received no training as units. This resulted in the units taking insufficient care of flank protection. Since the Panther was practically invulnerable frontally, the protection of the more vulnerable flanks was very important to avoid unnecessary losses. Also the units seem not to have been properly led. Contrary to German practice, attacks were conducted without situation briefings. Not even company commanders were always clearly informed of the objectives and attack directions. Also the units had not been given the opportunity to test their radio equipment, causing communications within the Panther battalions to be unsatisfactory. Many radio sets malfunctioned during the battle.[5]

Guderian made a visit at the front and discussed their experiences with the men in the Panther units. His report is illuminating. He emphasized that the employment of the Panther did not mean that the proven principles of tank tactics should be discarded. He also stated that other heavy weapons should not be pulled out just because Panthers were attacking. This suggests a considerable measure of overconfidence. Another problem was that there had been no training exercises with units greater than platoons, which resulted in improper employment of the Panther. Drivers, gunners and commanders had received insufficient training.[6]

But the employment of the Panther was not entirely negative. During Kursk it also proved to be a very potent weapon. Up to 15 July XXXXVIII Panzer Corps destroyed or captured 559 enemy tanks.[7] Of these, the Panthers destroyed 269.[8] Thus, Panthers knocked out almost half the Soviet tanks destroyed deployed against XXXXVIII Panzer Corps. The ranges at which the Panther achieved its kills were equally impressive. On average the distance was 1,500 to 2,000 metres and occasionally KV tanks were destroyed at 3,000 metres.[9] This anti-tank capability, particularly applicable to the Panthers, was only equalled by the Ferdinands in 9th Army.

There exists differing information relating to the number of Panthers operational during Zitadelle. Three such sets of figures are presented here:

1. According to Tagesmeldungen (daily reports) and Nachmeldungen (supplementary reports) from the operations section of XXXXVIII Pz.Korps staff to 4th Panzer Army[10] the following number of Panthers were operational:

6 July	7 July	8 July	9 July	10 July	11 July	12 July	13 July	14 July	15 July	16 July	17 July	18 July
40	43	?	16	33	30	25	43	36	20	43	44	44

2. Another set of figures is presented by the Quartermaster section of the staff of XXXXVIII Panzer Corps in its daily reports:[11]

6 July	7 July	8 July	9 July	10 July	11 July	12 July	13 July	14 July	15 July	16 July	17 July	18 July
135	43	?	?	33	(38)	38	51	56	56	43	44	65

3. Finally let us look at a set of figures concerning the number of operational Panthers presented by Thomas L. Jentz in his excellent book about the Panther tank:[12]

6 July	7 July	8 July	9 July	10 July	11 July	12 July	13 July	14 July	15 July	16 July	17 July
166	40	?	16	10	30	25	43	36	20	43	44

The difference between these reports may be explained by the fact that they do not apply to the same time on the respective days, but all of them seem to refer to the status between 1700 and 2400 hours on the given date.

Most of the time, Panthers constituted about one-fifth of the operational tanks in XXXXVIII Panzer Corps.[13] If, as the figures above suggest, they accounted for around half the enemy tanks destroyed or captured they clearly were more efficient as tank killers than the other tanks in the corps.

NOTES

1. PzAOK 4, Abt. V, *Betr:* Bergung der Pz.Kpfw. V (Panther) im Zuge der Absetzbewegung ab 18.7.43, den 20. Juli 1943 (BA-MA RH 21-4/450).
2. Gen.Kdo. XXXXVIII. Pz.Korps O.U., den 11.7.1943, BA-MA RH 25-48/379.
3. BA-MA RH 10/64.
4. Gen.Kdo. XXXXVIII. Pz.Korps O.U., den 11.7.1943, BA-MA RH 25-48/379.
5. Thomas L. Jentz, *Panzer Truppen II* (Shiffer Military/Aviation History, Atglen Pennsylvania 1996), pp. 96f.
6. Ibid., p. 99.
7. T.N. Dupuy/G.P. Hayes/P. Martell/V.E. Lyons/J.A.C. Andrews, *A Study of Breakthrough Operations* (Hero, Dunn Loring, VI, 1976), p. 196. See also note 8.
8. Thomas L. Jentz, *Panzer Truppen II* (Shiffer Military/Aviation History, Atglen, PA, 1996), p. 96. Both the number of kills for the entire corps and for the Panthers are German claims, which may be exaggerated. However, what is of interest here is the ratio between Panthers and other tanks. There is no reason to believe that Panther

crews exaggerated more than other soldiers. If anything, the fire of Panthers was more likely to cause unrecoverable damage than that of other tanks. Also, the Germans were advancing, giving them control of the battlefield, which made it easier for them to get a clear picture of the outcome of combat.

9. Ibid.
10. BA-MA RH 21-4/118.
11. Versorgungslageberichte des Gen.Kdo. XXXXVIII. Pz.Korps Abt. Qu. vom 2.7.1943 bis 30.10.1943, Anlageband 3 zum KTB nr 2 (National Archives Microfilm Publication T314, Roll 1169, Frames 000729 – 000782).
12. Jentz, *Panzer Truppen II*, p. 132.
13. Derived from the Tagesmeldungen and Nachmeldungen, XXXXVIII Pz.Korps an PzAOK 4 (BA-MA RH 21-4/118).

Appendix 5:
Deliveries of New Tanks to the Eastern Front, June–August 1943

Pz. Kpfw. IV

Train dispatched	Number of tanks	Unit to which directed	Comments
12 June	15	5th Pz. Div.	
13 June	15	5th Pz. Div.	
13 June	15	5th Pz. Div.	
13 June	15	5th Pz. Div.	
22 June	15	2nd Pz. Div.	
22 June	14	2nd Pz. Div.	
27 June	3	2nd Pz. Div.	Did not arrive before 1 July
25 June	16	Leibstandarte	Did not arrive before 1 July
25 June	15	9th Pz. Div.	Did not arrive before 1 July
27 June	11	9th Pz. Div.	Did not arrive before 1 July
5 July	15	8th Pz. Div.	
6 July	15	8th Pz. Div.	
6 July	3	Großdeutschland	
9 July	12	8th Pz. Div.	
11 July	15	Army Group Centre	Replacements to be distributed among units
13 July	15	Army Group South	Replacements to be distributed among units
16 July	15	Army Group South	Replacements to be distributed among units
19 July	15	Army Group Centre	Replacements to be distributed among units
25 July	15	Army Group South	Replacements to be distributed among units (probably did not arrive before 1 August)
10 August	15	Army Group South	
11 August	15	Army Group South	
12 August	15	Army Group South	
12 August	8	Army Group South	
24 August	18	Army Group South	
25 August	7	Army Group South	

Note: Of the tanks dispatched 10–12 August, 12 were eventually delivered to 3rd Pz. Div., 5 to 6th Pz. Div., 10 to 7th Pz. Div., 8 to 11th Pz. Div., 8 to 19th Pz. Div. and 10 to Das Reich.

Pz. Kpfw. V Panther

Arrival date	Number of tanks	Unit to which directed	Comments
24–25 June	98	51st Pz. Abt.	2 of the tanks were recovery vehicles (Bergepanzer)
28 June	8	Regts.–Stab 39	Command tanks to the regimental staff
28–29 June	98	52nd Pz. Abt.	2 of the tanks were recovery vehicles (Bergepanzer)

Train dispatched	Number of tanks	Unit to which directed	Comments
13 July	6	Pz. Rgt. 39	
17 July	6	Pz. Rgt. 39	
18 July	96	51 Pz. Abt.	Did not arrive before 1 August

During August the only Panthers sent to the eastern front were those that arrived with the Panther battalion of Das Reich (96 Panthers), which had been training in Germany during July. The battalion entered combat with the parent division on 22 August.

Pz. Kpfw. VI Tiger

Train dispatched	Number of tanks	Unit to which directed	Comments
8 June	4	Pz.Abt.505	
9 June	2	Pz.Abt.505	
10 June	5	Pz.Abt.505	
19 June	14	Pz.Abt.505	The 3rd company of the battalion, which had not arrived when Zitadelle began
29 June	3	Großdeutschland	These probably did not arrive before 1 July
7 July	12	2nd SS-Pz.Abt.	(See note)
14 July	5	Leibstandarte	Arrived 25 July
20 July	16	2nd SS-Pz.Abt.	(See note)
28 July	13	2nd SS-Pz.Abt.	(See note)
31 July	4	2nd SS-Pz.Abt.	(See note)
16–19 August	12	Pz.Abt.503	
16–19 August	6	Großdeutschland	

APPENDIX 5

Note: It was intended already in 1942 that Waffen-SS corps should have a heavy tank battalion equipped with Tigers. However this was not accomplished at all until 1944 and then only for a minority of the Waffen-SS corps. Thus many of the Tigers sent to 2nd SS-Pz.Abt. did not remain with that unit. Also, of the 45 Tigers indicated as dispatched on 7, 20, 28 and 31 July to 2nd SS-Pz.Abt., only 27 were actually dispatched during July. The remaining 18 are those dispatched 16–19 August.

The figures above differ from those presented in Table 10.1. This is explained by the fact that it is difficult to pinpoint the exact date a tank arrived on the eastern front. As can be seen above, on several occasions tanks were dispatched at the end of a month, but did not arrive until the beginning of the following month. It is not clear within which months those tanks should be counted when making a compilation of the kind presented in Table 10.1. If one is looking at a longer period than a month, one might expect those effects to be cancelled out, and indeed this is what happens if a period of a couple of months is studied.

Sturmgeschütze

Train dispatched	Number of tanks	Unit to which directed
6 June	15	Großdeutschland
7 June	6	Großdeutschland
30 July	3	3rd Gebirgs Division
30 July	3	5th Jäger Division
30 July	3	28th Jäger Division
1 August	4	3rd Gebirgs Division
1 August	4	5th Jäger Division
1 August	4	28th Jäger Division
7 August	5	3rd Gebirgs Division
7 August	5	5th Jäger Division
7 August	5	28th Jäger Division
20 August	2	3rd Gebirgs Division
20 August	2	5th Jäger Division
20 August	2	28th Jäger Division

Unlike the case with Panzer IV, V and VI tanks, the number of StuG dispatched to the eastern front given in the table above do not fit well with the figures presented in Table 10.1. According to that table 59 StuG were sent as replacements to the eastern front during June 1943, in addition to three complete battalions with 31 StuG each. July saw 73 assault guns despatched as replacements and two battalions (31 each), while the figures for August were 111 replacements and three battalions (31 each). This is a discrepancy far too great to be explained in the same manner as for the tanks. Rather it is likely to be a result of the fact that the source used for this appendix was compiled by the Inspector-General of Panzer Troops, and not all assault gun units fell under the sphere of responsibility of that agency. In particular the GHQ assault gun battalions were part of the artillery, not the panzer troops and the majority of the assault guns on the eastern front were with such battalions. Hence the considerable discrepancy between this Appendix and Table 10.1.

Source: Verteilung der Pz.-Fahrz. Bd. ab Mai 1943 (BA-MA RH 10/349).

Appendix 6:
Daily Tank Strength in
Army Group South

This appendix gives the number of operational tanks among the tank units in Army Group South. Also, see Appendix 4 for the status of the Panthers during Zitadelle. The reader should be aware that tanks were continually repaired and the number of operational tanks was usually lowest at the end of the day. During the evening and night, more vehicles could be expected to return from the workshops to the combat units than were put out of action. Consequently a report issued at 2400 hours usually gives a higher number of operational tanks than a report compiled at 1900 hours.

TABLE A6.1: 3RD PZ.DIVISION

Date and Time	Pz II	Pz III 5cm/L42	Pz III 5cm/L60	Pz III 7.5cm	Pz IV L24	Pz IV L43 and 48	Pz VI	Bcf Wg	StuG	Flamm Pz
4 July	?	3	27	17	0	21	0	?	2	0
6 July (2400)	7		Total of 52 Pz III		0	21	0	1	2	0
8 July (2400)	6		Total of 47 Pz III		0	18	0	1	2	0
9 July (2230)	?	3	20	16	0	17	0	?	0	0
10 July (2045)	?	4	13	11	0	4	0	?	2	0
11 July (2045)	?	3	3	10	0	7	0	?	0	0
12 July (2400)	?		Total of 17 Pz III		0	15	0	5	2	0
13 July (2000)	?	3	13	13	0	11	0	?	1	0
14 July (2000)	?	2	2	9	0	11	0	?	1	0
15 July (1935)	?	2	9	10	0	11	0	?	2	0
16 July (1925)	?	3	3	11	0	9	0	?	1	0
17 July (2040)	?	3	14	11	0	11	0	?	1	0
18 July (1945)	?	3	14	15	0	11	0	?	2	0

Sources for 3rd Pz.Div.:
Versorgungslageberichte des Gen.Kdo. XXXXVIII. Pz.Korps Abt. Qu. vom 2.7.1943 bis 30.9.1943, Anlageband 3 zum KTB nr 2 (NARA T314, R1169, F000729-000757) and Tagesmeldungen PzAOK 4 Ia 4.7.43–18.7.43 (BA-MA RH 21-4/118).

TABLE A6.2: 11TH PZ.DIVISION (INCL. 911TH STUG.ABT.)

Date and Time	Pz II	Pz III 5cm/L42	Pz III 5cm/L60	Pz III 7.5cm	Pz IV L24	Pz IV L43 and 48	Pz VI	Bef Wg	StuG	Flamm Pz
4 July	?	8	42	0	0	22	0	?	22	8
6 July (2400)	5	Total of 46 Pz III		0	Total of 18 Pz IV		0	4	?	8
7 July (2400)	5	Total of 36 Pz III		0	Total of 18 Pz IV		0	2	?	9
8 July (2400)	5	Total of 23 Pz III		0	Total of 11 Pz IV		0	2	7	5
9 July (2230)	?	4	20	0	1	12	0	?	23	6
10 July (2045)	?	6	20	0	1	12	0	?	24	5
11 July (2045)	?	2	28	0	0	13	0	?	11	5
12 July (2010)	?	0	23	0	0	11	0	?	12	5
13 July (2000)	?	1	22	0	0	13	0	?	14	5
14 July (2000)	?	2	24	0	0	12	0	?	17	3
15 July (1935)	?	2	19	0	0	13	0	?	19	3
16 July (1925)	?	2	27	0	0	?	0	?	14	3
17 July (2040)	?	2	32	0	0	13	0	?	22	3
18 July (2400)	6	Total of 27 Pz III		0	Total of 15 Pz IV		0	2	15	3

Sources for 11th Pz.Div.:
Versorgungslageberichte des Gen.Kdo. XXXXVIII. Pz.Korps Abt. Qu. vom 2.7.1943 bis 30.9.1943, Anlageband 3 zum KTB nr 2 (NARA T314, R1169, F000729-000782) and Tagesmeldungen PzAOK 4 Ia 4.7.43–18.7.43 (BA-MA RH 21-4/118).

TABLE A6.3: GD PZ.GREN.DIVISION

Date and Time	Pz II	Pz III 5cm/L42	Pz III 5cm/L60	Pz III 7.5cm	Pz IV L24	Pz IV L43 and 48	Pz VI	Bef Wg	StuG	Flamm Pz
4 July	?	2	20		7	55	14	?	34	14
6 July	?	1	8		1	21	2	?	?	12
7 July (2400)	?	Total of 30 Pz III and Pz IV					1	?	?	?
8 July (2400)	?	Total of 39 Pz III and Pz IV					?	?	?	?
9 July (2230)	?	1	3		0	24	8	?	?	?
10 July (2400)	3	?	8		Total of 36 Pz IV		10	1	?	13
11 July (2400)	7	?	8		Total of 38 Pz IV		11	1	26	13
12 July (2400)	7	?	8		Total of 38 Pz IV		11	1	26	13
13 July (2000)	?	?	8		3	19	6	?	25	12
14 July (2000)	?	?	8		3	18	?	?	25	9
15 July (1935)	?	?	6		5	11	5	?	23	4
16 July (1925)	?	?	4		4	25	5	?	23	8
17 July (2040)	?	?	14		6	23	8	?	25	10
18 July (1945)	?	?	13		6	23	8	?	25	10

Sources for GD Pz.Gren.Div.:
Versorgungslageberichte des Gen.Kdo. XXXXVIII. Pz.Korps Abt. Qu. vom 2.7.1943 bis 30.9.1943, Anlageband 3 zum KTB nr 2 (NARA T314, R1169, F000729-000757) and Tagesmeldungen PzAOK 4 Ia 4.7.43–18.7.43 (BA-MA RH 21-4/118).

TABLE A6.4: 1ST SS-PZ.GREN.DIVISION

Date and Time	Pz II	Pz III 5cm/L42	Pz III 5cm/L60	Pz III 7.5cm	Pz IV L24	Pz IV L43 and 48	Pz VI	Bef Wg	StuG	Flamm Pz
4 July	4	0	11	0	0	79	12	9	34	0
5 July	4	0	12	0	0	77	7	9	23	0
6 July	?	?	?	0	0	?	?	?	16	0
8 July (1850)	4	0	10	0	0	40	1	6	20	0
9 July (1905)	4	0	4	0	0	32	4	5	22	0
10 July (1900)	4	0	4	0	0	41	4	6	20	0
11 July (1835)	4	0	5	0	0	47	4	7	10	0
12 July					No Report					
13 July (1935)	4	0	5	0	0	31	3	7	20	0
14 July (1800)	4	0	6	0	0	32	8	7	21	0
15 July (1840)	4	0	6	0	0	32	8	7	28	0
16 July (1835)	4	0	5	0	0	42	9	6	30	0
17 July (1915)	4	0	6	0	0	46	9	8	28	0
18 July (1925)	3	0	7	0	0	55	9	8	28	0

Sources for 1st SS-Pz.Gren.Div.:
Tagesmeldungen PzAOK 4 Ia 4.7.43–18.7.43 (BA-MA RH 21-4/118).

TABLE A6.5: 2ND SS-PZ.GREN.DIVISION

Date and Time	Pz II	Pz III 5cm/L42	Pz III 5cm/L60	Pz III 7.5cm	Pz IV L24	Pz IV L43 and 48	Pz VI	Bef Wg	StuG	T-34
4 July	0	1	47	0	0	30	12	8	33	18
5 July	0	1	52	0	0	27	11	8	21	16
7 July (0230)	0	1	47	0	0	16	7	6	14	15
8 July (morning)	0	0	43	0	0	25	6	7	7	14
9 July (19.05)	0	0	31	0	0	13	1	7	26	7
10 July (1900)	0	0	33	0	0	15	1	7	26	7
11 July (1835)	0	0	34	0	0	18	1	7	27	8
12 July (1835)	0	0	42	0	0	18	2	6	27	8
13 July (1935)	0	0	43	0	0	20	1	8	24	11
14 July (1800)	0	0	41	0	0	25	4	8	25	12
15 July (1840)	0	0	37	0	0	17	2	7	23	13
16 July (1835)	0	0	37	0	0	18	5	7	25	11
17 July (1915)	0	0	36	0	0	24	9	6	25	17
18 July (1925)	0	0	36	0	0	24	9	7	28	17

Sources for 2nd SS-Pz.Gren.Div.:
Tagesmeldungen PzAOK 4 Ia 4.7.43–18.7.43 (BA-MA RH 21-4/118) and SS-Pz. Gren.Div 'Das Reich' nr 891/43 geh. Div.Gef.St. 7.7.43 (BA-MA RS 2-2/18).

TABLE A6.6: 3RD SS-PZ.GREN.DIVISION

Date and Time	Pz II	Pz III 5cm/L42	Pz III 5cm/L60	Pz III 7.5cm	Pz IV L24	Pz IV L43 and 48	Pz VI	Bef Wg	StuG
4 July	0	59	0	0	5	42	11	8	28
5 July	0	57	0	0	7	40	10	7	?
6 July	0	52	0	0	7	36	6	7	?
7 July (1900)	0	53	0	7	0	36	6	8	13
8 July (Morgenmeld)	0	53	0	0	7	36	6	8	13
8 July (1850)	0	52	0	0	7	28	5	7	13
9 July (1905)	0	47	0	0	7	20	2	5	12
10 July (1900)	0	48	0	0	7	21	2	5	21
11 July (1835)	0	54	0	0	4	26	10	7	21
12 July (1835)	0	53	0	0	4	26	10	7	21
13 July (1935)	0	32	0	0	3	14	0	5	20
14 July (1880)	0	28	0	0	3	14	5	7	16
15 July (1840)	0	28	0	0	3	17	7	6	16
16 July (1835)	0	30	0	0	4	23	9	7	20
17 July (1915)	0	31	0	0	4	25	7	7	20
18 July (1925)	0	30	0	0	4	25	7	7	20

Sources for 3rd SS-Pz.Gren.Div.:
Tagesmeldungen PzAOK 4 Ia 4.7.43–18.7.43 (BA–MA RH 21-4/118) and Tagesmeldung der SS-Pz.Gren.Div. 'Totenkopf' v. 7.7.1943 1900 (BA–MA RS 2-2/18).

TABLE A6.7: 6TH PZ.DIVISION

Date and Time	Pz II	Pz III 5cm/L42	Pz III 5cm/L60	Pz III 7.5cm	Pz IV L24	Pz IV L43 and 48	Pz VI	Bef Wg	StuG	Flamm Pz
9 July (morning)	7	0	24	12	0	14	0	3	0	10
10 July (morning)			12	1	0	7	0	2	0	?
11 July (morning)	2	2	11	?	0	6	0	2	0	?
12 July (morning)					No Report					
13 July (0500)			Total of 12 tanks of all types							
14 July (0500)	0	0	9	?	0	3	0	2	0	?
15 July (0500)	0	0	7	?	0	6	0	2	0	?
16 July (0500)	0	0	2	?	0	2	0	?	0	?
17 July (0500)	0	0	5	?	0	3	0	2	0	?
18 July (0500)	0	0	8	?	0	5	0	2	0	?
19 July (0500)	0	0	18	?	0	4	0	4	0	+ 1 T-34
20 July (0500)	0	0	7	?	0	5	0	4	0	?
21 July (0500)	0	0	8	?	0	4	0	4	0	?

Sources for 6th Pz.Div.:
KTB Ia AOK 8 Panzerlage (BA–MA RH 20-8/97).

TABLE A6.8: 7TH PZ.DIVISION

Date and Time	Pz II	Pz III 5cm/L42	Pz III 5cm/L60	Pz III 7.5cm	Pz IV L24	Pz IV L43 and 48	Pz VI	Bef Wg	StuG	Flamm Pz
9 July (morning)	4	0	16	1	3	12	0	3	0	0
10 July (morning)	?	?	21	4	1	17	0	6	0	0
11 July (morning)	0	0	19	5	1	25	0	4	0	0
12 July (morning)	0	0	24	2	1	9	0	3	0	0
13 July (0500)	0	0	28	0	1	9	0	3	0	0
14 July (evening)	0	0	11	0	1	10	0	2	0	0
15 July (0500)	0	0	11	?	?	10	0	2	0	0
16 July (0500)	0	3	10	?	?	9	0	1	?	0

Sources for 7th Pz.Div.:
KTB Ia AOK 8 Panzerlage (BA-MA RH 20-8/97), Anlage 2 zu Gen.Kdo. III. Pz.Korps Ia Nr. 1487/43 (BA-MA RH 24-3/88).

TABLE A6.9: 19TH PZ.DIVISION

Date and Time	Pz II	Pz III 5cm/L42	Pz III 5cm/L60	Pz III 7.5cm	Pz IV L24	Pz IV L43 and 48	Pz VI	Bef Wg	StuG	Flamm Pz
9 July (morning)	0	2	5	4	1	23	0	1	0	0
10 July (morning)	0	1	3	3	2	3	0	1	0	0
11 July (morning)	0	1	6	5	2	0	0	2	0	0
12 July (morning)	0	0	7	4	0	3	0	1	0	0
13 July (0500)	0	1	15	0	1	7	0	1	0	0
14 July (0500)	0	2	13	0	3	9	0	1	0	0
15 July (0500)	0	2	13	0	3	9	0	1	0	0
16 July (0500)	0	0	16	0	1	6	0	2	0	0
17 July (0500)	0	3	9	0	1	5	0	2	0	0
18 July (0500)	0	0	12	0	1	9	0	3	0	0
19 July (0500)	0	1	12	0	2	10	0	1	0	0
20 July (0500)	0	1	14	0	2	10	0	5	0	0
21 July (0500)	0	1	13	0	2	10	0	4	0	0

Sources for 19th Pz.Div.:
KTB Ia AOK 8 Panzerlage (BA-MA RH 20-8/97).

KURSK 1943

TABLE A6.10: OPERATIONAL TANKS IN NON-DIVISIONAL UNITS IN ARMY DETACHMENT
KEMPF

Date and Time	503rd Pz.Abt.	905th StuG.Abt.	228th StuG.Abt.	393rd StuG.Bty.
9 July (morning)	33	21	23	8
10 July (morning)	14	26	11	8
11 July (morning)	23	28	No Report	9
12 July (morning)	No Report	29	19	9
13 July (0500)	No Report	29	No Report	4
14 July (0500)	No Report	27	No Report	5
14 July (evening)	6	No Report	14	No Report
15 July (0500)	9	27	14	4
16 July (0500)	8	27	17	5
17 July (0500)	15	27	17	5
18 July (0500)	13	27	17	5
19 July (0500)	14	27	No Report	5
20 July (0500)	15	27	16	6
21 July (0500)	4	27	21	6

Sources for these four units:
KTB Ia AOK 8 Panzerlage (BA-MA RH 20-8/97), Anlage 2 zu Gen.Kdo. III. Pz.Korps
Ia Nr. 1487/43 (BA-MA RH 24-3/88).

Appendix 7:
The Condition of 8th Army,
30 August 1943

TABLE A7: CONDITION OF THE 8TH ARMY, 30 AUGUST 1943

Unit	Ration strength	Combat strength	Combat-ready tanks	Tanks in workshops	Assault guns combat ready	Assault guns in workshops	10.5 cm How	Wespe	15 cm How	Hummel	10 cm Gun	15 cm NbW	2 cm Flak	3.7 cm Flak	8.8 cm Flak	Med PAK	Hvy PAK	7.5 cm le.IG s.IG	15 cm s.IG	8 cm GrW	Hvy MG	Light MG	Rifles and MPs
6th Pz. Div.	9,777	3,883	6	48	0	0	23	0	12	6	4	0	18	0	6	13	17	16	15	12	96	333	9,922
Das Reich	13,592	5,692	22	138	22	6	24	12	8	4	4	0	37	6	12	34	28	25	12	80	103	1,388	13,363
Wiking	8,611	3,761	27	20	4	0	34	0	8	0	4	0	25	3	7	30	17	24	8	35	80	542	8,685
Totenkopf	8,976	4,805	31	124	15	17	10	12	8	6	4	0	38	8	12	30	25	27	18	83	92	1,140	15,849
3rd Pz.Div.	10,218	3,991	30	58	0	0	23	0	8	6	4	0	39	8	8	14	26	14	7	10	21	454	10,177
7th Pz.Div.	11,528	4,268	17	44	4	3	12	8	8	6	4	0	22	5	5	14	21	17	5	22	36	523	8,681
SS Cav. Div.	7,500	2,300	0	0	4	0	8	0	3	0	0	0	11	0	4	8	12	10	0	3	26	187	5,500
355th Inf. Div.	7,500	3,855	0	0	0	3	24	0	6	0	3	0	0	0	0	13	26	8	5	12	90	114	3,577
161st Inf. Div.	6,257	2,422	0	0	0	0	32	0	11	0	0	0	0	0	0	12	13	14	6	42	21	1,214	12,421
39th Inf. Div.	6,424	1,579	0	0	0	0	21	0	7	0	0	0	0	0	0	13	14	4	0	0	18	84	6,395
282nd Inf. Div.	8,711	2,669	0	0	0	0	12	0	6	0	0	0	0	0	0	2	4	4	0	13	38	238	11,914
293rd Inf. Div.	4,160	2,684	0	0	0	0	16	0	1	0	0	0	0	0	0	2	5	9	4	22	6	113	5,666
320th Inf. Div.	9,945	2,430	0	0	0	0	24	0	8	0	0	0	0	0	0	21	21	10	3	69	28	467	9,858
106th Inf. Div.	10,328	3,867	0	0	0	0	21	0	6	0	0	0	12	0	0	10	17	0	4	21	72	179	9,440
198th Inf. Div.	10,794	3,202	0	0	0	0	17	0	3	0	0	0	0	0	0	8	13	11	4	7	27	266	9,063
168th Inf. Div.	9,193	2,471	0	0	0	0	17	0	5	0	0	10	0	0	0	5	8	0	4	2	15	19	14,942
167th Inf. Div.	5,747	1,749	0	0	0	0	8	0	7	0	0	0	11	0	0	8	1	0	0	15	11	118	10,264
223rd Inf. Div.	7,787	4,717	0	0	0	0	27	0	6	0	0	0	0	0	0	16	24	18	0	50	89	297	9,069
503rd s.Pz.Abt.	1,092	355	25	17	0	0	0	0	0	0	0	0	0	0	0	0	0	0	0	0	0	108	765
560th s.Pz.Jäg.Abt.	648	312	13	18	0	0	0	0	0	0	0	0	6	0	0	0	0	0	0	0	0	57	522
905th StuG.Abt.	430	150	0	0	2	21	0	0	0	0	0	0	0	0	0	0	0	0	0	0	0	37	369
228th StuG. Abt.	470	165	0	0	4	26	0	0	0	0	0	0	3	0	0	0	0	0	0	0	0	55	404
393rd StuG.Bttr.			0	0	0	7	0	0	0	0	0	0	0	0	0	0	0	0	0	0	0	2	96

Notes: All the tanks belonging to 560th s.Pz.Jäg.Abt. are actually Nashorns. Of Totenkopf's 15cm s.I.G. 12 were self-propelled, as were all three with Das Reich. Of the 2cm Flak guns a few were usually quad-guns, but in no unit did the number of them exceed four. The Russian 7.62cm gun was present in two infantry divisions, 167th (12 pieces) and 223rd (4 pieces). Medium Pak refer to 5cm Pak 38 or similar. Heavy PAK refer to 7.5cm PAK 40 or similar.

Source: Übersicht über den Zustand der Divisionen und gep. Einheiten der 8. Armée, Anlage zu AOK 8 Ia Nr. 1511/43 g.Kdos. (BA–MA RH 20–8/91).

Appendix 8:
Examples of Causes of German Tank Losses

Two reports on tank losses appear in this appendix. They were submitted by 6th and 7th Panzer Division.[1] They present some information on the causes of tank losses (only total write-offs are included in the reports). It must be remembered that in the heat of battle, it can sometimes be difficult to determine if a tank has been hit by an AT round from a tank or from an anti-tank gun. When inspecting a tank at a later stage it can also be difficult to distinguish between these two weapons, since the Red Army employed 76mm guns mounted in tanks but also used them as towed anti-tank guns. Similarly the Soviet 45mm gun existed both as a tank gun and an AT gun. In the original documents, all cases which have here been termed 'hit by AT round' had been labelled *Paktreffer*. This would indicate that the tank had been hit by an anti-tank gun. However, in view of the difficulty of distinguishing between a hit from a 76mm AT gun and a hit from a 76mm tank gun, we opted for 'hit by AT round' instead.

6TH PZ.DIV.

Type of vehicle	Chassis number	Location	Damage
Pz II	24504	SE of Rzhavets	Hit by two AT rounds – vehicle burnt out
Pz III (7.5cm)	75232	2km NE of Aleksandrovka	Hit by AT round on left side of turret – vehicle burnt out
Pz III (7.5cm)	76314	2km NE of Aleksandrovka	Hit by AT round – blown up
Pz III (5cm/L60)	74154	2km S of Avdeevka	Hit in drive train – captured by Russians
Pz III (5cm/L60)	74191	1.5km N of Aleksandrovka	Hit by AT round – vehicle burnt out
Pz III (5cm/L60)	76502	2km NE of Aleksandrovka	Hit by AT round – vehicle burnt out
Pz III (5cm/L60)	76526	Eastern exit from Rzhavets	Hit by AT in engine room – vehicle captured by Russians
Pz IV (lang)	83503	2km NW of Aleksandrovka	Hit by AT round – vehicle burnt out
Pz.Bef.Wg. (267)	73631	Strelnikov, 30km NE of Belgorod	Bogged down in marsh. Recovery attempts unsuccessful, vehicle had to be blown up due to enemy pressure
Sfl.	29003	Klaivenovo	Hit by artillery round – impossible to tow the vehicle away
Sd.Kfz.232	85678	Krivtsovo, 24km NE of Belgorod	Hit by artillery round

7TH PZ.DIV.

Type of vehicle	Chassis number	Location	Damage
Pz II	28829	In transit to Germany	Hit in engine room
Pz II	28026	In transit to Germany	Damaged by mine
Pz II	28019	In transit to Germany	Hit by AT round
Pz III (5cm/L60)	74511	3km E of Myassoyedovo	Hit – burnt out
Pz III (5cm/L60)	73830	4km NE of Myassoyedovo	Hit by AT round
Pz III (5cm/L60)	74344	Malo Iablonovo	Hit by tank fire
Pz III (5cm/L60)	74499	Vypolskova	Hit by AT round
Pz III (5cm/L60)	73890	Vypolsovka – Krasnoye Snamya Road	Hit by AT round
Pz III (7.5cm)	76308	5km E of Myassoyedovo	Hit by AT round
Pz III (7.5cm)	74793	2km NE of Myassoyedovo	Hit – burnt out
Pz IV (L43)	82906	Malo Iablonovo	Hit by tank fire
Pz IV (L43)	82824	3–4km SE Sheina	Engine damage due to enemy fire, could not be towed away due to enemy activity
Pz IV (L43)	84011	6km S Sheina	Hit – burnt out. Could not be recovered due to enemy activity
Pz.Bef.Wg/L42	73743	At Myassoyedovo	Burnt out

NOTE

1. Anlage zu 6. Pz.Div. Abtlg. V Nr. 559/43 geh. v. 29.7.43 (BA–MA RH 21-4/450) and Anlage zu 7. Pz.Div. Gruppe V Nr. 289/43 geh. vom 23.7.43. (BA–MA RH 21-4/450).

Appendix 9:
Number of German Tanks and Assault Guns on the Eastern Front, April–December 1943

Date	Pz II	Pz 38 (t)	Pz III 50/L42	Pz III 50/L60	Pz III 75/L24	Pz IV 75/L24	Pz IV 75/L43 75/L48	Pz V	Pz VI	Flamm Pz	Bef Wg	StuG III	StuH III	StuPz IV
10 April	160	26	201	337	130	56	419		27	42	111	589	5	0
20 April	160	21	191	501	126	54	435		67	45	106	634	5	0
30 April	158	16	182	533	130	53	533		98	48	109	716	23	7
10 May	152	16	184	532	113	49	584		106	41	109	782	23	7
20 May	151	12	164	543	142	49	617		128	41	108	805	23	7
31 May	148	12	182	536	160	50	693		128	41	105	832	23	66
10 June	132	13	160	514	174	49	725		136	41	106	848	32	66
20 June	121	13	137	515	183	46	820		147	42	108	891	59	66
30 June	116	13	142	538	173	46	862	204	147	41	116	916	68	52
10 July	112	13	139	534	168	56	894	173	188	41	115	926	75	43
20 July	99	9	119	485	143	48	799	241*	184	45	120	910	68	48
31 July	99	13	116	488	124	45	665	134	175	38	114	885	67	44
10 August	92	13	101	403	100	37	674	189	167	33	104	866	56	45
20 August	89	10	99	365	91	38	649	178	177	27	102	894	65	45
31 August	87	10	99	342	87	40	635	225	181	26	99	861	63	43
10 September	100	10	97	333	82	32	574	200	187	25	108	922	75	43
20 September	89	13	96	329	79	32	584	269	175	23	109	947	74	43
30 September	88	13	88	298	68	32	578	266	214	22	109	914	64	42
10 October	87	12	79	266	56	25	598	330	220	36	121	967	80	42
20 October	74	11	64	272	51	25	769	297	218	40	139	1,094	71	40
31 October	74	10	56	254	44	22	817	316	227	37	148	1,160	75	36
10 November	66	7	57	225	46	22	822	258	218	40	145	1,096	75	21
20 November	65	9	43	226	43	24	808	337	247	36	144	1,183	75	21
30 November	75	12	37	199	37	20	872	419	278	34	141	1,246	69	21
10 December	68	12	29	174	41	21	831	457	271	26	135	1,386	70	0
20 December	64	10	29	164	41	19	933	432	267	25	151	1,422	72	0
31 December	62	13	24	135	37	19	822	349	232	21	135	1,441	66	0

Note: *This is probably a printing error in the original document, it is more likely that the correct figure is 141.

Sources: Panzer-Lage Ost (Nach Gen.Qu.), BA-MA RH 10/61 and StuG-Lage Ost (Nach Gen.Qu.), BA-MA RH 10/62.

Comments: a. Pz IV with the L43 and L48 guns have been lumped together due to the small differences in performance between the weapons. In the original documents they were separated however. On 10 April there were no Pz IV with the L48 weapon on the eastern front, but gradually they became more common. From late August, the L48-armed Pz IV were more numerous than the L43. At the end of the year, only 66 Pz IV L43 remained on the eastern front.

b. StuG III refers to assault guns with 7.5cm weapons. Almost all were armed with either the 7.5cm StuK L43 or the 7.5cm StuK L48 (the latter making up the majority). The latter had slightly superior armour-penetrating capabilities. A small number (on 10 April there were 53 on the eastern front, from then on the number declined) had the older 7.5cm StuK L24, with negligible anti-tank capabilities.

c. StuH III refers to the 10.5cm howitzer on Pz III chassis.

d. StuPz IV refers to the Brummbär (Grizzly Bear), armed with the very short 15cm weapon.

e. All figures include both operational vehicles and those in workshops.

Appendix 10:
Further Information on
German Casualties

The archival records contain much information on casualties, but this must be treated with great care since it can be misleading. First of all it must be realized that the conditions surrounding the initial compilation of casualty reports is not ideal. Usually reports refer to losses suffered during single days, and many of the units may still be involved in combat when the report is compiled. Other units may still not have been able to obtain a clear picture of the results of the engagements fought. Units may also not be able to report due to faltering communications. All this compelled units to send in complementary reports (Nachmeldungen) at some later date.

There exist methods to reduce the uncertainty caused by these phenomena. First of all the researcher can check reports from various levels in the military hierarchy and compare them. In the German Army such reports are usually to be found in division, corps and army files. Also the files of the German Wehrmacht Verlustwesen (≈ Armed Forces Casualty Department) can be useful. This latter was an agency within the OKW Allgemeine Heeresamt (≈ General Army Department) and was responsible for continuous monitoring of the losses suffered by the army (including Waffen-SS and Luftwaffe ground combat units). By comparing the compilations from higher headquarters with the combined losses for divisions and GHQ troops it is usually possible to check whether reports are complete. Furthermore, it is necessary to check reports compiled a couple of days after the end of the engagement, to allow for possible complementary reports and compilations covering longer periods of fighting.

If all these precautions are taken it is usually possible to find a number

KURSK 1943

of relevant reports, which should give an accurate picture of the losses suffered, but one cannot expect all of them to convey identical information. Yet it is also the fact that discrepancies between various documents are usually quite small, typically within a few per cent of each other. For situations however where the entire reporting system broke down, such as was the case with German Army Group Centre during the summer of 1944, it can be difficult to establish exact losses, although in this particular case documents do exist to establish German losses for this operation. The difficulties involved in studies of such operations may also raise some doubt on the detailed figures presented for Soviet defensive operations during 1941 in, for example, *Grif Sekretnosti Sniat*, where only a final figure is presented for an entire operation.

In previous chapters we have presented some information on German casualties. That information is far from being all the relevant data available from the archival records. Further casualty data from other archival sources exist that can be useful to the student of Zitadelle.

GENERAL SOURCES OF INFORMATION

Daily casualties according to Wehrmacht Verlustwesen

There exists a file (BA–MA RW 6/v. 564) which contains daily casualties suffered by the armies participating in Zitadelle. These compilations were made continuously during the battle, which means that complementary reports (Nachmeldungen) were added when they arrived. Usually such complementary reports were sent in a couple of days after the date to which they apply. Usually, but not always, such reports indicated when the losses had occurred. Thus the men at Wehrmacht Verlustwesen were meant to enter this information at the appropriate day but perhaps this was not always the case. This can be exemplified from study of the ten-day compilations on German casualties. These reports show the casualties suffered by each German combat army for the periods 1–10, 11–20 and 20–30 for each month. They were dated four days after the period to which they apply, consequently three reports were issued each month, on the 4th, 14th and 24th. So, if an army reported before the 14th that it had suffered 4,000 casualties between 1st and 10th, then it would be entered in the Wehrmacht Verlustwesen report dated 14th. If, sometime before the 24th, the army submitted a complementary report indicating that it had suffered an additional 1,500 casualties between 1st and 10th these 1,500 would be included in the compilation for 10th to 20th, together with

198

any casualties reported by the army pertaining to the latter period. It is possible that the same problem does occur in these daily reports but it is clear that efforts have been made to correct casualty figures on a day-by-day basis and these figures generally seem to be of good quality.

This file is quite unique, since Wehrmacht Verlustwesen did not normally make such detailed compilations for single operations. Rather, a continuous monitoring of the armies in action was made, but using the ten-day system mention above. It was a surprise therefore to find that it existed.[1]

TABLE A10.1: DAILY CASUALTIES OF ARMY DETACHMENT KEMPF,

4TH PANZER ARMY AND 9TH ARMY

	Army Detachment Kempf				4th Panzer Army				9th Army			
	KIA	WIA	MIA	Total	KIA	WIA	MIA	Total	KIA	WIA	MIA	Total
5 July	275	3,111	98	3,484	365	2,129	33	2,527	1,086	5,922	215	7,223
6 July	545	1,517	305	2,367	310	1,511	23	1,844	569	2,351	76	2,996
7 July	142	512	34	688	262	1,301	19	1,582	486	2,204	171	2,861
8 July	184	920	70	1,174	136	685	27	848	580	2,456	184	3,220
9 July	171	1,092	14	1,277	315	1,613	68	1,996	371	1,405	85	1,861
10 July	414	1,326	49	1,789	136	734	30	900	496	1,996	68	2,560
11 July	73	481	0	554	157	651	9	817	281	1,176	23	1,480
12 July	108	558	8	674	330	1,499	44	1,873	108	495	29	632
13 July	102	566	25	693	261	1,112	87	1,460	87	409	16	512
14 July	116	739	15	870	184	908	42	1,134	47	221	3	271
15 July	118	593	14	725	148	532	51	731	245	953	339	1,537
16 July	65	288	21	374	82	367	8	457	194	629	24	847
17 July	117	492	54	663	36	194	1	231	181	625	58	864
18 July	43	290	11	344	59	199	3	261	133	474	98	705
19 July	90	561	6	657	33	169	0	202	73	349	16	438
20 July	104	517	14	635	34	167	20	221	231	856	121	1,208
21 July	14	97	0	111	46	185	9	240	73	275	6	354
22 July	64	350	17	431	53	299	6	358	35	149	7	191
23 July	47	159	17	223	86	488	19	593	120	741	15	876
24 July	50	333	11	394	131	681	47	859	100	452	21	573
25 July	108	540	108	756	110	344	31	485	124	637	68	829
26 July	137	708	116	961	29	249	17	295	89	378	33	500
27 July	103	448	34	585	80	359	4	443	125	356	50	531
28 July	56	205	2	263	103	400	100	603	83	317	28	428
29 July	20	89	2	111	121	518	178	817	130	533	33	696
30 July	14	122	4	140	22	59	2	83	62	294	13	369
31 July	128	431	40	599	71	230	12	313	162	673	166	1,001
5–31:	3,408	17,045	1,089	21,542	3,700	17,583	890	22,173	6,271	27,326	1,966	35,563

Source: BA-MA RW 6/v. 564.

KURSK 1943

Ten-day reports from Wehrmacht Verlustwesen

This file (BA-MA RW 6/v. 558) contains reports presenting the losses for each army in action, which is valuable when putting Zitadelle in its perspective. From these, it is evident that Zitadelle was not the major cause of German manpower losses during the summer of 1943. Among other things it may be observed that the losses during July were more extensive for 2nd Panzer Army than for its southern neighbour, the 9th Army.

TABLE A10.2: TEN-DAY CASUALTIES SUFFERED BY GERMAN ARMIES ON THE EASTERN FRONT, JULY–SEPTEMBER 1943

		17th Army	6th Army	1st Pz Army	8th Army	4th Pz Army	2nd Army	9th Army	2nd Pz Army	4th Army	3rd Pz Army	16th Army	18th Army	Misc.	20th Mtn Army
1–10 July	KIA	166	127	183	1,370	1,577	41	3,511	199	108	232	84	322	43	41
	WIA	813	609	788	7,697	8,214	149	15,923	798	510	929	490	1,423	113	188
	MIA	7	1	13	561	186	23	755	62	35	79	10	16	11	3
	Total	986	737	984	9,628	9,977	213	20,189	1,059	653	1,240	584	1,761	167	232
11–20 July	KIA	342	1,294	1,400	1,280	1,400	77	1,523	1,410	195	161	158	472	51	43
	WIA	1,438	5,920	5,467	6,707	4,081	219	6,061	8,171	799	587	662	1,938	119	205
	MIA	127	164	541	154	244	7	674	539	23	13	32	18	19	4
	Total	1,907	7,378	7,408	8,141	5,725	303	8,258	10,120	1,017	761	852	2,428	189	252
21–31 July	KIA	885	1,986	1,177	799	910	33	1,612	6,734	230	143	167	2,392	80	89
	WIA	3,280	8,034	4,563	4,128	6,064	163	6,306	22,661	826	552	761	8,897	193	333
	MIA	241	1,275	1,348	343	475	4	990	5,354	17	10	17	286	0	9
	Total	4,406	11,295	7,088	5,270	7,449	200	8,908	34,749	1,073	705	945	11,575	273	431
1–10 Aug	KIA	574	861	868	460	192	266	934	1,187	1,202	162	181	1,996	196	186
	WIA	2,621	4,085	2,867	1,549	969	913	3,114	6,565	5,173	561	819	6,630	157	804
	MIA	149	104	357	334	41	40	288	1,410	300	24	11	296	0	6
	Total	3,344	5,050	4,092	2,343	1,202	1,219	4,336	9,162	6,675	747	1,011	8,922	353	996
11–20 Aug	KIA	408	218	963	1,889	1,251	313	1,154	1,137	3,684	77	573	1,190	71	187
	WIA	1,655	1,462	3,837	8,005	5,412	1,057	4,733	5,018	15,716	442	2,129	4,600	155	745
	MIA	130	3	695	1,465	3,501	56	869	1,244	2,053	3	99	156	0	16
	Total	2,193	1,683	5,495	11,359	10,164	1,426	6,756	7,399	21,453	522	2,801	5,946	226	948
21–31 Aug	KIA	199	524	1,113	2,147	4,215	694	809		1,646	98	445	977	88	87
	WIA	902	2,551	4,673	9,060	7,331	3,039	3,174		6,998	493	1,923	3,664	222	420
	MIA	27	364	347	904	2,999	379	680		691	16	93	144	0	7
	Total	1,128	3,439	6,133	12,111	14,545	4,112	4,663	0	9,335	607	2,461	4,785	310	514
1–10 Sept	KIA	320	419	624	1,754	388	850	1,263		1,271	81	163	323	143	78
	WIA	1,280	2,187	3,146	8,313	3,014	3,309	4,852		4,731	353	1,221	1,694	566	288
	MIA	81	260	384	535	282	524	709		378	9	0	28	14	15
	Total	1,681	2,866	4,154	10,602	3,684	4,683	6,824	0	6,380	443	1,384	2,045	723	381
11–20 Sept	KIA	523	379	481	837	513	273	827		1,683	127	174	680	91	23
	WIA	1,860	1,640	1,738	3,821	4,007	1,351	3,255		6,175	508	824	2,671	247	176
	MIA	89	410	522	389	719	95	264		826	37	6	310	17	2
	Total	2,472	2,429	2,741	5,047	5,239	1,719	4,346	0	8,684	672	1,004	3,661	355	201
21–30 Sept	KIA	371	870	1,068	768	204	819	495		541	382		379	49	67
	WIA	1,355	3,475	4,619	3,119	1,831	2,956	2,956		1,617	1,590		1,719	102	260
	MIA	103	689	3,163	456	254	867	867		179	205		11	4	2
	Total	1,829	5,034	8,850	4,343	2,289	4,642	4,318	0	2,337	2,177	0	2,109	155	329

200

Note: Army Detachment Kempf was renamed 8th Army during August. The latter name is used in the heading of this table. The 2nd Panzer Army HQ was transferred to the Balkans in August and its units subordinated to other army HQs.
Source: BA-MA RW 6/v. 558.

CASUALTIES IN EACH ARMY

2nd Panzer Army casualties, 10–19 July 1943

Table A10.2 indicated that 2nd Panzer Army suffered 10,120 casualties during the period 11–20 July while losses amounted to 34,749 during the last eleven days of the month. This is probably a result of late reporting from the 2nd Panzer Army, which was not included in the compilation for 11–20, but in the report for 21–31 instead. This thesis is supported by the daily casualties for 10–19 July as indicated by another compilation made by Wehrmacht Verlustwesen. As can be seen in Table A10.3, 2nd Panzer Army lost 19,884 men 11–19 July, or close to twice the number indicated in Table A10.2. This is the most serious discrepancy we have found. Comparing losses for Army Detachment Kempf, 4th Panzer Army and 9th Army from Tables A10.1 and A10.2 relatively small disagreements are found. It seems that the daily reports are the most accurate, since they usually were compiled at a later stage than the ten-day listings.

TABLE A10.3: 2ND PANZER ARMY CASUALTIES, 10–19 JULY 1943

	Killed in action	*Wounded in action*	*Missing in action*	*Total*
10 July	21	80	2	103
11 July	140	877	52	1,069
12 July	307	1,807	289	2,403
13 July	474	2,864	585	3,923
14 July	374	2,403	106	2,883
15 July	383	1,945	406	2,734
16 July	292	1,359	153	1,804
17 July	107	996	67	1,170
18 July	231	1,368	12	1,611
19 July	261	1,308	615	2,184

Source: BA-MA RW 6/v. 564.

Further information on 9th Army casualties

More detailed information on casualties among units subordinated to 9th Army can be found in the records. The information in Tables A10.4 to

A10.8 can provide a picture of where along the 9th Army front the fighting was most intense.

TABLE A10.4: 9TH ARMY CASUALTIES, 1–4 JULY 1943

	Officers				NCOs and enlisted men			
	KIA	WIA	MIA	Total	KIA	WIA	MIA	Total
GHQ Troops				0	2	10		12
6th Inf.Div.				0	1	14		15
7th Inf.Div.				0	2	8		10
31st Inf.Div.				0	4	22		26
45th Inf.Div.				0	9	36	2	47
72nd Inf.Div.	1			1	2	10		12
78th Inf.Div.				0	4	8		12
86th Inf.Div.				0	3	3		6
102nd Inf.Div.		1		1	6	17	1	24
137th Inf.Div.				0	6	18	1	25
216th Inf.Div.				0	8	25		33
251st Inf.Div.		1		1	9	19		28
258th Inf.Div.				0	1	2		3
292nd Inf.Div.				0	3	14		17
383rd Inf.Div.		1		1	5	18		23
Group Manteuffel		1		1	1	15		16
10th Pz.Gren.Div				0				0
2nd Pz.Div.				0				0
4th Pz.Div.				0				0
9th Pz.Div.				0				0
12th Pz.Div.				0				0
18th Pz.Div.				0				0
20th Pz.Div.		1		1	3	20		23
Gren.Rgt.87				0	2	5		7
NebelTr.				0				0
Total	1	5	0	6	71	264	4	339

Source: AOK 9, Abt. IIa Verluste (BA–MA RH 20-9/339).

TABLE A10.5: 9TH ARMY CASUALTIES, 5–10 JULY 1943

	Officers				NCOs and enlisted men			
	KIA	WIA	MIA	Total	KIA	WIA	MIA	Total
GHQ Troops	24	91	1	116	294	1,160	41	1,495
6th Inf.Div.	10	46	1	57	263	1,116	43	1,422
7th Inf.Div.	10	31		41	199	1,319	27	1,545
31st Inf.Div.	19	32		51	186	1,092	114	1,392
45th Inf.Div.	2	3	1	6	13	131	22	166
72nd Inf.Div.	1	4		5	7	56	3	66
78th Inf.Div.	19	42		61	347	1,507	105	1,959
86th Inf.Div.	8	22		30	304	1,199	20	1,523
102nd Inf.Div.		2	1	3	6	27	2	35
137th Inf.Div.	1	1		2	6	56	3	65
216th Inf.Div.	7	24	2	33	158	767	33	958
251st Inf.Div.				0	4	17	2	23
258th Inf.Div.	14	25		39	253	1,309	14	1,576
292nd Inf.Div.	11	33		44	404	1,437	128	1,969
383rd Inf.Div.	3	5	1	9	74	348	48	470
Group Manteuffel	1			1	22	64	15	101
10th Pz.Gren.Div.				0		31		31
2nd Pz.Div.	10	53		63	256	1,119	24	1,399
4th Pz.Div.	12	32	5	49	155	709	83	947
9th Pz.Div.	10	50	1	61	150	729	42	921
12th Pz.Div.		3		3	4	15		19
18th Pz.Div.	12	34	1	47	173	757	34	964
20th Pz.Div.	15	39	1	55	206	1,152	32	1,390
Gren.Rgt.87	6	1	1	8	17	92	21	130
NebelTr.				0				0
Total	195	573	16	784	3,501	16,209	856	20,566

Source: AOK 9, Abt. IIa Verluste (BA-MA RH 20-9/339).

TABLE A10.6: 9TH ARMY CASUALTIES, 11–20 JULY 1943

	Officers				NCOs and enlisted men			
	KIA	WIA	MIA	Total	KIA	WIA	MIA	Total
GHQ Troops	4	11	1	16	58	378	23	459
6th Inf.Div.	3	5		8	82	368	8	458
7th Inf.Div.	1	8		9	74	310	13	397
31st Inf.Div.	4	7		11	99	841	8	948
45th Inf.Div.	1	1		2	5	50	3	58
72nd Inf.Div.				0	9	32		41
78th Inf.Div.	13	15	1	29	214	597	26	837
86th Inf.Div.	15	29	2	46	209	765	385	1,359
102nd Inf.Div.	4	10	3	17	24	161	60	245
137th Inf.Div.	1	5		6	45	131	3	179
216th Inf.Div.	1	2		3	69	165	5	239
251st Inf.Div.				0	11	48	1	60
258th Inf.Div.	5	24		29	208	600	57	865
292nd Inf.Div.	6	14		20	86	253	34	373
383rd Inf.Div.	1	2		3	46	183	6	235
Group Manteuffel	2	1		3	52	241	16	309
10th Pz.Gren.Div.				0				0
2nd Pz.Div.		9		9	36	210	14	260
4th Pz.Div.	3	12	1	16	71	392	15	478
9th Pz.Div.	2	5		7	57	340	24	421
12th Pz.Div.		1		1	3	8		11
18th Pz.Div.				0				0
20th Pz.Div.	4	3		7	17	91	4	112
Gren.Rgt.87				0				0
NebelTr.				0				0
Total	70	164	8	242	1,475	6,164	705	8,344

Source: AOK 9, Abt. IIa Verluste (BA-MA RH 20-9/339).

TABLE A10.7: 9TH ARMY CASUALTIES, 21–31 JULY 1943

	Officers				NCOs and enlisted men			
	KIA	WIA	MIA	Total	KIA	WIA	MIA	Total
GHQ Troops	0	3		3	24	95	6	125
6th Inf.Div.	2	5		7	86	187	27	300
7th Inf.Div.	9	27	3	39	141	589	191	921
31st Inf.Div.	3	4		7	57	234	4	295
45th Inf.Div.	10	3		13	24	104		128
72nd Inf.Div.	1	6		7	18	81		99
78th Inf.Div.				0				0
86th Inf.Div.	1	5		6	15	96	4	115
102nd Inf.Div.	6	22	1	29	203	810	100	1,113
137th Inf.Div.	1			1	16	38	3	57
216th Inf.Div.	4	9		13	64	284	65	413
251st Inf.Div.		1		1	12	36	1	49
258th Inf.Div.	2	7	2	11	122	407	22	551
292nd Inf.Div.	9	20	2	31	160	533	201	894
383rd Inf.Div.	12	21	1	34	253	802	393	1,448
Group Manteuffel	2	6	1	9	88	252	98	438
10th Pz.Gren.Div.				0				0
2nd Pz.Div.				0				0
4th Pz.Div.	9	13		22	125	488	10	623
9th Pz.Div.				0				0
12th Pz.Div.				0				0
18th Pz.Div.				0				0
20th Pz.Div.				0				0
Gren.Rgt.87				0				0
NebelTr.	1	1		2	7	15		22
Total	72	153	10	235	1,415	5,051	1,125	7,591

Source: AOK 9, Abt. IIa Verluste (BA-MA RH 20-9/339).

TABLE A10.8: CASUALTIES AMONG UNITS SUBORDINATED TO 9TH ARMY,
5 JULY–21 AUGUST

	Officers				NCOs and enlisted men			
	KIA	WIA	MIA	Total	KIA	WIA	MIA	Total
GHQ Troops	31	72	2	105	413	1,770	70	2,253
6th Inf.Div.	21	59	2	82	560	2,026	146	2,732
7th Inf.Div.	23	82	4	109	541	2,793	247	3,581
14th Inf.Div.	4	16	0	20	95	473	71	639
26th Inf.Div.	3	13	3	19	138	474	10	622
31st Inf.Div.	31	57	0	88	470	2,146	173	2,789
36th Inf.Div.	6	1	1	8	17	92	21	130
45th Inf.Div.	3	7	1	11	48	299	25	372
72nd Inf.Div.	9	25	0	34	175	661	50	886
78th Inf.Div.	33	62	1	96	592	2,177	135	2,904
86th Inf.Div.	24	56	2	82	529	2,060	409	2,998
95th Inf.Div.	1	1	0	2	47	149	26	222
102nd Inf.Div.	14	45	5	64	408	1,721	252	2,381
110th Inf.Div.	1	5	0	6	14	46	4	64
129th Inf.Div.	1	1	0	2	25	62	5	92
134th Inf.Div.	2	7	0	9	81	255	25	361
137th Inf.Div.	3	6	0	9	75	248	11	334
183rd Inf.Div.	3	1	0	4	32	122	6	160
211th Inf.Div.	4	10	2	16	87	391	83	561
216th Inf.Div.	14	38	2	54	361	1,518	131	2,010
251st Inf.Div.	1	1	0	2	31	116	5	152
253rd Inf.Div.	2	0	0	2	10	30	0	40
258th Inf.Div.	36	74	6	116	669	2,594	148	3,411
292nd Inf.Div.	31	80	2	113	755	2,769	400	3,924
293rd Inf.Div.	1	6	0	7	34	215	67	316
296th Inf.Div.	1	4	0	5	50	161	6	217
299th Inf.Div.	0	9	0	9	50	223	7	280
321st Inf.Div.	2	11	3	16	44	187	6	237
339th Inf.Div.	1	0	0	1	11	31	0	42
383rd Inf.Div.	19	33	2	54	431	1,491	367	2,289
393rd Inf.Div.	1	0	0	1	7	29	0	36
707th Inf.Div.	0	1	0	1	9	15	21	45
10th Pz.Gren.Div.	0	6	0	6	0	31	0	31
20th Pz.Gren.Div.	0	4	0	4	31	136	1	168
2nd Pz.Div.	10	62	0	72	294	1,329	38	1,661
4th Pz.Div.	33	80	6	119	436	2,046	168	2,650
5th Pz.Div.	2	14	0	16	35	174	42	251
8th Pz.Div.	0	4	0	4	29	259	83	371
9th Pz.Div.	13	58	1	72	216	1,120	70	1,406
12th Pz.Div.	6	17	0	23	70	441	24	535
18th Pz.Div.	13	35	1	49	174	763	34	971
20th Pz.Div.	19	52	1	72	269	1,439	39	1,747
Total	422	1,115	47	1,584	8,363	35,082	3,426	46,871

Source: AOK 9, Abt. IIa Verluste (BA-MA RH 20-9/339).
Comment: Many of these units were subordinated to 9th Army during part of the period the table applies to. The losses indicated here are only those suffered while under 9th Army command.

Combat losses suffered by II SS-Panzer Corps

The role of II SS-Panzer Corps in the battle is probably the most frequently depicted part of operation Zitadelle. Its losses are therefore of particular interest and it is necessary to establish them with great precision. This is not the first occasion on which they have been published. Otto Weidinger[2] and Rudolf Lehmann[3] have previously published daily casualties for Das Reich and Leibstandarte, but to our knowledge daily losses for the Totenkopf have not previously been published. The losses suffered by corps troops were negligible compared to those incurred by the divisions.

TABLE A10.9: II SS-PANZER CORPS CASUALTIES, 5–20 JULY

	Leibstandarte				Das Reich				Totenkopf				Corps Troops			
	KIA	WIA	MIA	Total	KIA	WIA	MIA	Total	KIA	WIA	MIA	Total	KIA	WIA	MIA	Total
5 July	89	496	17	602	67	223	0	290	31	119	2	152	0	3	0	3
6 July	84	384	19	487	43	180	2	225	53	234	0	287	0	5	0	5
7 July	41	164	2	207	18	103	1	122	39	117	1	157	1	2	0	3
8 July	32	99	6	137	50	186	0	236	26	89	0	115	2	36	0	38
9 July	12	34	2	48	22	127	2	151	19	69	5	93	1	1	0	2
10 July	18	34	3	55	16	94	2	112	77	292	5	374	0	0	0	0
11 July	37	286	0	323	29	181	1	211	75	355	0	430	0	1	0	1
12 July	39	235	5	279	41	190	12	243	69	231	16	316	0	4	0	4
13 July	64	259	2	325	17	44	0	61	24	136	0	160	0	1	0	1
14 July	12	75	13	100	58	229	0	287	20	154	1	175	0	2	0	2
15 July	23	94	3	120	26	88	0	114	19	46	0	65	0	0	0	0
16 July	16	84	3	103	58	166	0	224	17	70	2	89	0	4	0	4
17 July	5	34	2	41	10	23	3	36	5	46	3	54	1	3	0	4
18 July	2	2	0	4	1	8	0	9	21	97	3	121	0	2	0	2
19 July	0	2	0	2	0	2	0	2	17	63	0	80	0	0	0	0
20 July	21	19	23	63	0	5	0	5	19	110	5	134	0	0	0	0
Total	495	2,301	100	2,896	456	1,849	23	2,328	531	2,228	43	2,802	5	64	0	69

Note: Losses are given as Killed in action (KIA), Wounded in action (WIA), Missing in action (MIA).
Source: Gen.Kdo. II. SS-Pz.Korps, der Korpsarzt (BA-MA RS 2-2/17), reports dated 11 July to 2nd August.

NOTES

1. The authors are indebted to Dr Rüdiger Overmans at the MGFA (Miltär-geschichtliches Forschungsamt) for providing us with this file.
2. O. Weidinger, *Division Das Reich*, Band IV, *1943* (Munin Verlag, Osnabrück, 1986), p. 217.
3. R. Lehmann, *The Leibstandarte III* (Fedorowicz Publishing, Winnipeg, 1990), pp. 215, 217, 220, 222, 224, 230, 234, 238, 240, 245–7.

Appendix 11:
Tank Data

TABLE A11: TANK DATA

	Weight	Horse-power	Road speed	Range	Ground pressure	Crew	Chassis armour			Turret* armour			MGs	Main gun ammo carried	Main armament
							Front	Side	Rear	Front	Side	Rear			
Pz III H	21.8	300	40	165	0.94	5	60/9	30/0	60/10	35/R	30/25	30/12	2	99	5cm KwK L42
Pz III L-M	22.7	300	40	155	0.95	5	70/9	30/0	50/10	77/R	30/25	30/12	2	92	5cm KwK 39
Pz III N	23	300	40	155	0.96	5	70/9	30/0	50/10	77/R	30/25	30/12	2	64	7.5cm KwK 37
Pz IV E	21	300	42	200	0.79	5	60/10	40/0	20/0	30/11	20/26	20/16	2	80	7.5cm KwK 37
Pz IV F2 L43	23.6	300	40	200	0.89	5	50/10	30/0	20/0	50/11	30/26	30/16	2	87	7.5cm KwK 40
Pz IV G L43	24	300	38	210	0.90	5	80/10	30/0	20/0	50/11	30/26	30/16	2	87	7.5cm KwK 40
Pz IV H L48	25	300	38	210	0.94	5	80/10	30/0	20/0	80/11	30/26	30/16	2	87	7.5cm KwK 40
Panther D	43	700	46	200	0.83	5	80/55	40/40	40/30	120/R	45/25	45/25	2	79	7.5cm KwK 42
Panther A	44.8	700	46	200	0.86	5	80/55	40/40	40/30	120/R	45/25	45/25	2	79	7.5cm KwK 42
Tiger I E	57	700	38	140	1.04	5	100/10	80/0	80/8	100/8	80/0	80/0	2	92	8.8cm KwK 36
StuG III G	23.9	300	40	155	1.00	4	80/21	30/0	50/10	80/10	30/11	30/0	2	54	7.5cm StuK 40
StuPz IV	28.2	300	40	210	1.06	5	80/12	30/0	20/10	100/40	50/15	30/25	0	38	15cm StuH 43
Ferdinand	65	2×300	30	150	1.23	6	200/12	80/0	80/0	200/25	80/30	80/20	0	50	8.8cm PAK 43
T-70	9.2	2×70	45	360	0.70	2	45/60	45/0	35/40	60/R	35/20	35/30	1	94	45mm M/1938
T-34 (mod. 1943)	30.9	500	53	465	0.71	4	60/60	45/40	45/45	70/R	52/30	52/35	2	100	76.2mm F-34
KV-I (mod. 1942)	48	550	43	250	0.83	6	110/30	130/0	75/R	120/25	120/25	90/25	4	114	76.2mm ZiS-5
SU-76	11.2	2×70	44	265	0.54	4	35/60	16/0	16/0	35/25	16/15	0/0	0	60	76.2mm ZiS-3
SU-122	30.9	500	47	400	0.71	5	45/50	45/0	45/45	45/60	45/20	45/10	0	40	122mm M-30S
SU-152	45.5	550	43	330	0.79	5	60/30	60/0	60/50	60/30	60/15	60/0	0	20	152mm ML-20S

Note: * Superstructure in the case of non-turreted vehicles.

The following units of measurement are used: Weight: metric tons; Road speed: km/h; Range: km; Ground pressure: kg/cm²; Ammo carried: number of complete main rounds; Armour: thickness in mm/angle in degrees, measured from vertical (R means rounded).

Appendix 12:
Tank and AT Gun Data

TABLE A12: TANK AND AT GUN DATA

Gun	Calibre	Length in calibres	Length of bore	Shell weight HE	Muzzle velocity HE	Shell weight AP	Muzzle velocity AP	AP — Armour pen at distance (m)				Shell weight APCR	Muzzle velocity APCR	APCR — Armour pen at distance (m)				
								500	1,000	1,500	2,000			100	500	1,000	1,500	2,000
5cm KwK L42	50	42	2.1	1.82	?	2.06	685	45	35	27	21	0.925	1,060	96	58	–	–	–
5cm KwK 39	50	60	3.0	1.82	550	2.06	835	67	52	40	31	0.925	1,180	130	72	38	–	–
7.5cm KwK 37	75	24	1.8	5.74	420	6.8	385	39	35	32	29	–	–	–	–	–	–	–
7.5cm KwK 40	75	43	3.22	5.74	550	6.8	740	89	78	68	60	4.10	920	126	108	87	69	–
7.5cm KwK 40	75	48	3.6	5.74	550	6.8	770	96	84	74	65	4.10	990	143	120	97	77	–
7.5cm KwK 42	75	70	5.25	5.74	700	6.8	935	141	126	112	101	4.75	1,120	194	174	149	127	106
8.8cm KwK 36	88	56	4.93	9.0	600	10.2	780	110	100	90	82	7.3	930	171	156	138	123	110
8.8cm PAK 43	88	71	6.25	9.4	750	10.2	1,000	185	165	148	132	7.3	1,180	237	217	193	171	151
10.5cm StuH	105	28	2.94	14.8	470	14.0	470	59	54	50	46	–	–	–	–	–	–	–
15cm StuH 43	150	12	1.8	38.0	240	–	–	–	–	–	–	–	–	–	–	–	–	–
45mm M/1938	45	46	2.07	2.1	750	1.43	760	49	39	32	26	0.85	1,070		60	37		
57mm ZIS-2	57	73	4.16	?	?	3.1	990	105	88	74	62	1.79	?					
76.2mm F-34	76.2	42.4	3.24	6.23	680	6.3	655	61	54	47	41	3.0	965		69	45		
85mm D-30	85	54.6	4.64	9.2	792	9.2	792	100	86	75	65	4.9	1,200		107	75		
122mm M-30S	122	22.7	2.77	24.9	515	(13.2)	(335)	(200)	(200)	(200)	(200)	–	–					
152mm ML-20S	152	28.8	4.38	43.7	655	48.7	600	105	97	89	82	–	–					

The following units of measurement are used: Calibre: mm; Length of bore: m; Shell weight: kg; Muzzle velocity: m/s; Armour penetration is against a plate of homogeneous armour at 30 degrees angle from vertical, and with a Brinell hardness of about 300. It should be noted that AP includes APC, APBC and APCBC ammo, which were the most commonly used types of conventional AP ammunition.

Note: The AP Round listed for the Soviet 122 mm gun is actually a HEAT round. The effectiveness of this kind of round is seriously degraded by spin. The penetration given in the table probably refers to a projectile fired statically, not from a gun with the spin resulting from the rifle of the barrel, which can easily halve penetration. Also a muzzle velocity of 335 m/s is not propitious for hitting a target, particularly if it is moving or at longer distance. Thus the performance of this gun in reality did not match the qualities indicated by the armour penetration capabilities given in the table, and hence the bracketed figures.

Appendix 13:
Armour-Penetration Capabilities

How to read: The first case given is the capabilities of the Soviet 76mm gun against the German Panther tank. The three letters F, S and R mean front, side and rear. Against the front armour of the Panther, the 76mm gun will not obtain penetrations, even at point blank range. Against the side of the Panther, the chances of obtaining a penetration is good up to a distance of 600m, as indicated by the continuous line. If the hit is at right angle, a penetration can be obtained up to about 1,200m, as indicated by the dashed line. Against the rear of the Panther, the 76mm gun will obtain penetrations up to 1,200m and 2,000m range respectively.

It has been assumed that the target is on horizontal ground. The chances of obtaining a penetration are considered good (the continuous line) when a hit at 30 degrees from a right angle will result in a penetration. Remember that there are always variations, for example in the hardening of the armour plates.

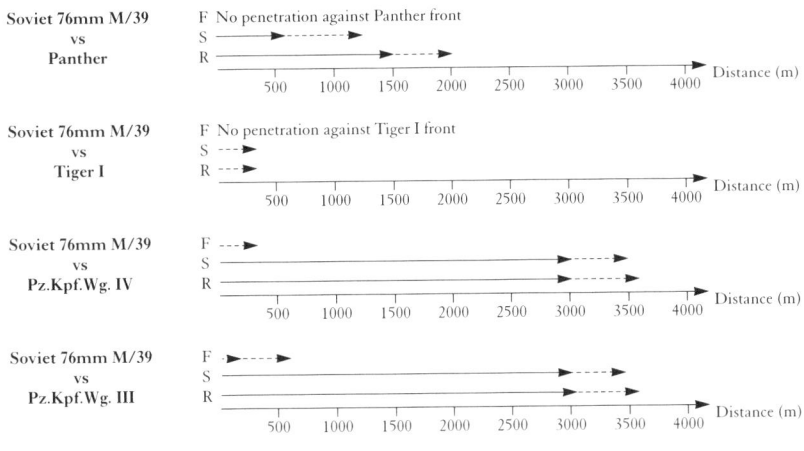

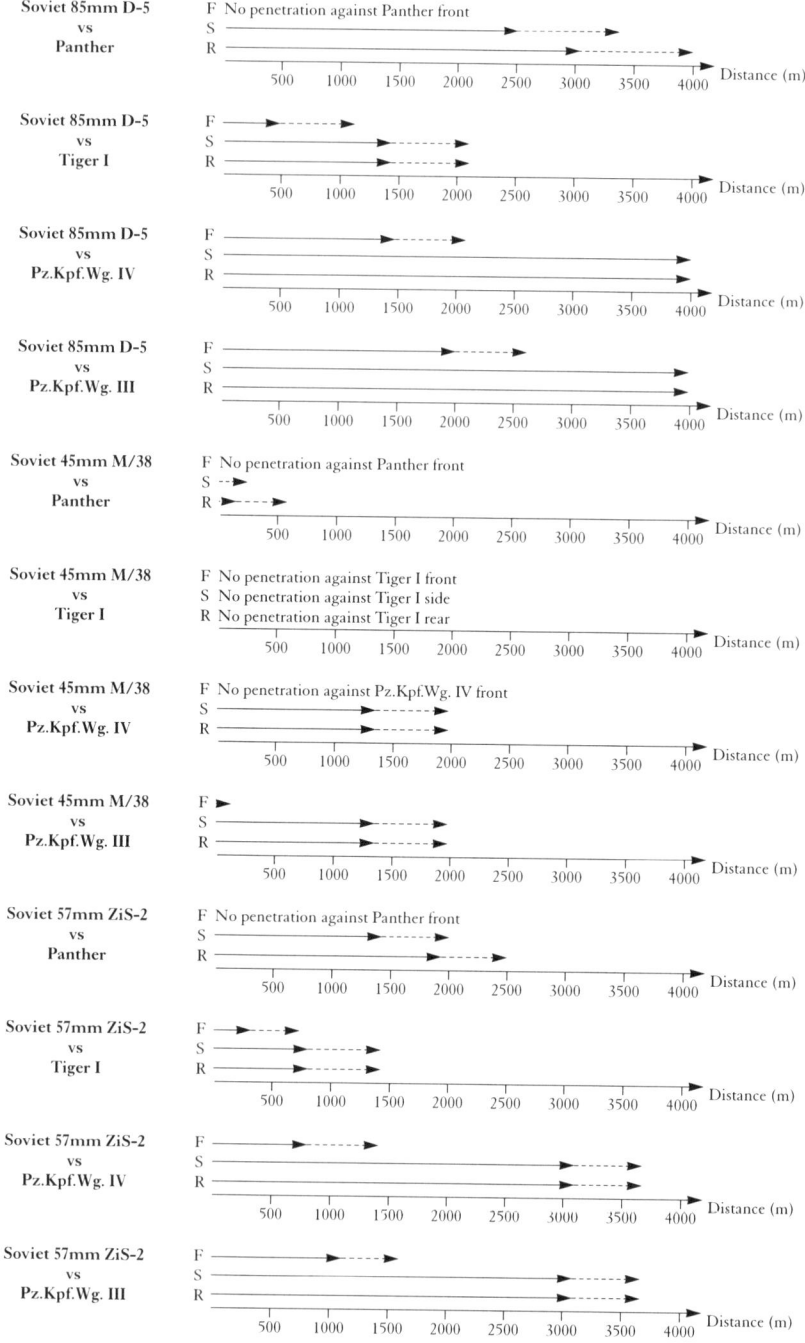

Soviet 85mm D-5
vs
Panther

F No penetration against Panther front
S
R

Distance (m)

Soviet 85mm D-5
vs
Tiger I

F
S
R

Distance (m)

Soviet 85mm D-5
vs
Pz.Kpf.Wg. IV

F
S
R

Distance (m)

Soviet 85mm D-5
vs
Pz.Kpf.Wg. III

F
S
R

Distance (m)

Soviet 45mm M/38
vs
Panther

F No penetration against Panther front
S
R

Distance (m)

Soviet 45mm M/38
vs
Tiger I

F No penetration against Tiger I front
S No penetration against Tiger I side
R No penetration against Tiger I rear

Distance (m)

Soviet 45mm M/38
vs
Pz.Kpf.Wg. IV

F No penetration against Pz.Kpf.Wg. IV front
S
R

Distance (m)

Soviet 45mm M/38
vs
Pz.Kpf.Wg. III

F
S
R

Distance (m)

Soviet 57mm ZiS-2
vs
Panther

F No penetration against Panther front
S
R

Distance (m)

Soviet 57mm ZiS-2
vs
Tiger I

F
S
R

Distance (m)

Soviet 57mm ZiS-2
vs
Pz.Kpf.Wg. IV

F
S
R

Distance (m)

Soviet 57mm ZiS-2
vs
Pz.Kpf.Wg. III

F
S
R

Distance (m)

214

APPENDIX 13

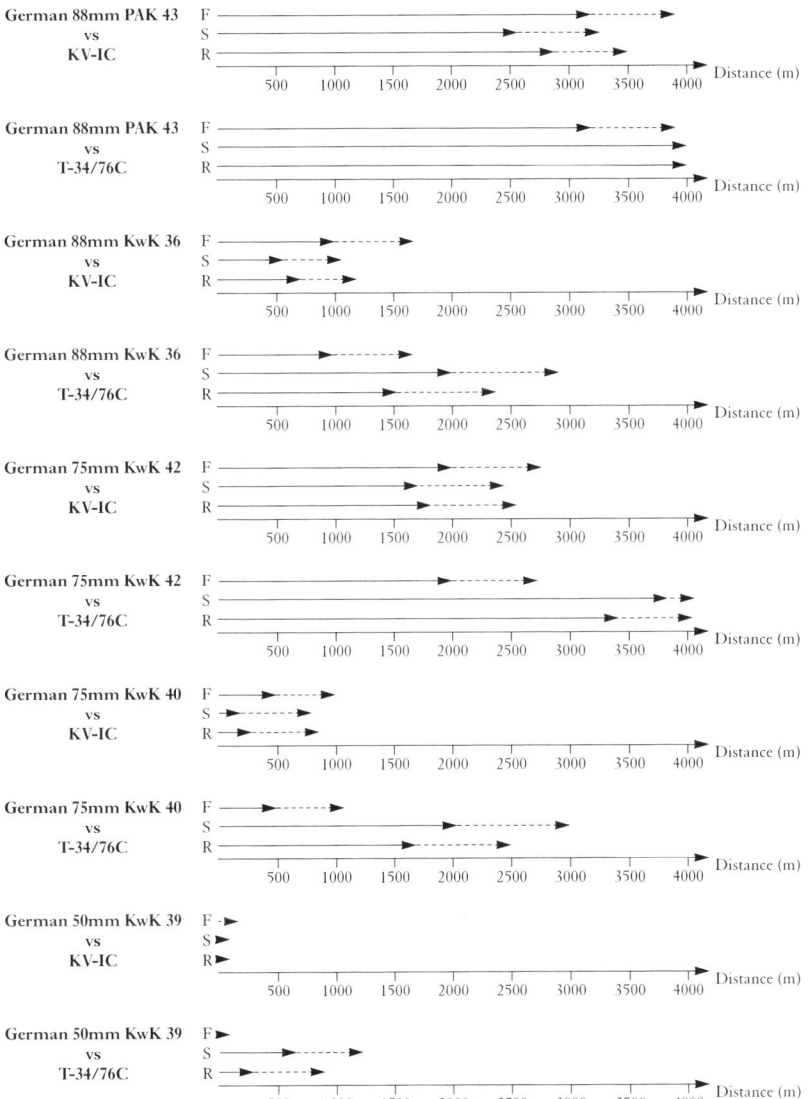

215

Appendix 14:
Information on German
Tank Losses

The major problem when trying to establish tank losses is that what actually happens to a tank put out of action can vary considerably. Unless the vehicle is blown to pieces, captured by the enemy or completely burnt out, it is quite often recovered. The percentage of recoverable tanks is usually far from negligible. Mines were laid extensively by the Red Army before Zitadelle and a considerable number of German tanks ran on to mines. However, only rarely does a mine destroy a medium or heavy tank. The number of German tanks damaged during Kursk probably exceeded the number actually destroyed by a considerable margin.

But this is not the only problem for the historian. When a tank is recovered it is usually examined to determine the extent and character of the damage. If the damage is considered slight the vehicle probably remains with the combat unit to be repaired. More severe damage will usually result in the vehicle being sent to rear echelon repair facilities. Really severe damage can result in the tank being sent back to the manufacturer or some other facility in safer areas. The problem is further compounded by the possibility of cannibalizing damaged tanks to repair others. Finally tanks under repair may be captured or destroyed by deeply thrusting enemy forces. The true fate of a tank may not be clear until some time has passed. Consequently it is not without risks to use reports submitted immediately after, or during, battle. Needless to say the information must originate from German archival documents.

But even if German archival documents, which are abundant with information on this subject, are used, this is a difficult subject and it can be useful first to set the upper limits of German tank losses. Table A14.1 gives monthly losses for various types of tanks and assault guns.

TABLE A14.1: GERMAN TANK LOSSES DURING SUMMER 1943 ON ALL FRONTS

	Pz II	Pz 38	Pz III	Pz IV	Pz V	Pz VI	Flamm.Pz	Bef.Pz	Elefant	StuG III	StuPz IV	Total
June	12	0	2	5	0	0	0	0	0	36	0	55
July	26	0	189	290	83	33	4	17	39	151	17	849
Aug	4	1	177	280	41	40	11	18	0	143	0	715
Sept	1	1	8	137	123	65	9	9	0	224	0	577

Note: Figures refer to total write-offs due to all causes for the entire German armed forces on all fronts.
Source: Müller-Hillebrand, *Das Heer*, Vol. III, p. 274.

On the eastern front losses during the period 1 July–31 August amounted to 1,331 tanks and assault guns, while losses during September were 513.[1] This means that during July/August 85 per cent of all tank losses occurred on the eastern front, while the corresponding percentage was 89 per cent during September.

Another approach is to check with the monthly reports on a division's status submitted to higher command echelons. The Inspector General of Panzer Troops began collecting such reports during the summer of 1943. Valuable information of the same kind can also be found in documents from Abteilung V of the staffs of the armies (this is the section concerned with motor vehicles and their maintenance).

One problem with these documents is that they seldom present identical information. In some reports on tank strength, command tanks are presented separately, sometimes not. Some reports contain information on special kinds of AFVs such as flame-thrower tanks, but sometimes that information is not included. Adding to the difficulties is the fact that tanks do suffer breakdowns. These are repaired and are occasionally delivered to combat units. This means that figures can differ slightly from hour to hour and thus two reports from the same date need not present identical information.

However, all this should not detract from the fact that the discrepancies are quite small, and almost irrelevant to the general picture when one studies an operation of the scope that Zitadelle encompasses.

For Table A14.2, which presents the number of tanks and assault guns among the Panzer divisions in 4th Panzer Army and Army Detachment Kempf, information from various sources have been compiled.

TABLE A14.2: NUMBER OF TANKS AND ASSAULT GUNS IN ARMY GROUP SOUTH
PANZER DIVISIONS, 1 JULY AND 1 AUGUST

		Pz II		Pz III		Pz IV		Pz VI		StuG		Flamm Pz		Bef.Pz		Total	
		O	R	O	R	O	R	O	R	O	R	O	R	O	R	O	R
Großdeutschland	1 July	1	2	22	2	62	0	14	1	34	1	14	0	9	0	156	6
	1 Aug	?	?	8	7	27	23	5	9	21	14	7	4	6	3	74	60
11th Pz.Div.	1 July	7	1	52	10	20	6	0	0	0	0	7	6	?	?	86	23
	1 Aug	2	6	33	23	23	5	0	0	0	0	4	9	?	?	62	43
3rd Pz.Div.	1 July	7	0	55	2	22	1	0	0	2	0	0	0	?	?	86	3
	1 Aug	?	?	16	41	8	14	0	0	?	?	0	0	?	?	24	55
Leibstandarte	1 July	7	0	12	1	63	3	11	2	33	0	0	0	?	?	126	6
	1 Aug	0	0	0	0	0	0	0	0	0	0	0	0	0	0	0	0
Das Reich	1 July	1	0	60	9	28	6	12	2	33	1	0	0	?	?	134	18
	1 Aug	?	?	39	28	16	5	3	18	27	5	0	0	?	?	85	56
Totenkopf	1 July	0	0	58	8	40	11	10	2	35	0	0	0	?	?	143	21
	1 Aug	0	0	49	24	9	50	10	18	49	21	0	0	?	?	117	113
6th Pz.Div.	1 July	13	0	49	3	26	2	0	0	0	0	13	0	?	?	101	5
	27 July	1	10	13	22	10	15	0	0	0	0	0	13	?	?	24	60
7th Pz.Div.	1 July	12	0	51	4	36	2	0	0	0	0	0	0	6	1	105	7
	1 Aug	6	1	42	0	28	4	0	0	0	0	0	0	5	0	81	5
19th Pz.Div.	1 July	2	0	38	0	38	0	0	0	0	0	0	0	?	?	81	0
	30 July	2	0	21	12	18	17	0	0	0	0	0	0	?	?	44	29

Sources: Monthly reports to the Inspector General of Panzer Troops[2] and reports from Abt. V of 4th Panzer Army.[3]

Comments: O refers to operational tanks at the time of the report.
R refers to tanks in workshops, estimated to be repaired usually within 3 weeks.
11th Pz.Div. includes the attached 911th StuG Battalion.
Leibstandarte left for Italy at the end of July and then handed over all its tanks and assault guns to Das Reich and Totenkopf.
On many occasions command tanks (Bef.Pz) are probably included in the numbers for the respective type of tank.

As can be calculated from Table A14.2, the Panzer Divisions of Army Group South had 57 fewer Panzer III at the end of the month compared with the beginning, while the number of Panzer IV had shrunk by 94. The number of Tigers had actually increased by nine and the number of StuG had increased by four, while there were minor decrements of flame-thrower tanks (three fewer) and command tanks (two fewer).

Clearly none of the Panzer divisions listed had suffered exceptional losses in tanks, even though some of them, in particular the 3rd and 6th, had several vehicles in workshops. But how many tanks had been delivered to the divisions to replace losses? The following numbers of tanks were sent from Germany to the units of Army Group South during July:[4]

1. 16 Panzer IV were sent to Leibstandarte on 25 June. Other information[5] suggests they did not arrive before the end of the month.
2. Three Panzer IV were sent to Großdeutschland on 6 July.
3. 15 Panzer IV were sent to Army Group South on 13 July as replacements.
4. 15 Panzer IV were sent to Army Group South on 16 July as replacements.
5. 12 Panzer IV were sent to Army Group South on 25 July as replacements, but they probably did not arrive during July.
6. Five Tigers were sent to the Leibstandarte on 14 July and arrived on 25 July.
7. 27 Tigers were sent to '2nd SS-Pz.Abt.' between 7 and 31 July. Since the forming of this unit was not completed, it seems that these tanks were sent to the eastern front instead. Of the vehicles sent in July, one-third were sent on 28 July or later and could not have arrived during July. Hence, at most, 18 could have arrived in July.
8. The delivery of Panzer III must have been quite small, since only 11 were produced in June and none from July onwards.[6]

The figures in Table A14.2 suggest that the Panzer and Panzer-grenadier divisions had 57 fewer Panzer III at the end of the month compared to the beginning of the month, while the number of Panzer IV had shrunk by 94 and the number of Tigers had increased by nine. Possibly as many as 23 Tigers and 46 Panzer IV did arrive during July. This would indicate a loss of 211 tanks of the main types in the divisions. However, vehicles in long-term repair (requiring more than three weeks before being repaired) are not included in Table A14.2. Since this number must have been greater at the end of July than at the beginning of July, the calculation is somewhat misleading.

For the panzer divisions of Army Group Centre, there exist information that can give some indication of the ratio between complete losses and vehicles in long-term repair. The panzer divisions that took part in the offensive by 9th Army and the Soviet offensive directed against the German-held Orel salient (thus including 5th and 8th Pz.Div. which had not taken part in Zitadelle) lost 250 tanks permanently during July.[7] Also 92 were in long-term repair at the end of the month.[8] If the same ratio between long-term repair and complete losses applied to the panzer divisions on the southern side of the Kursk salient, it would suggest that among those 211 missing tanks indicated above, 154 were total losses and 57 were in long-term repair. Two problems have to be mentioned though. First of all, in Table A14.2, long-term repair means more than three weeks, while for those figures presented above for Army Group Centre it means more than two weeks. This may mean that the ratio between vehicles in long-term repair and complete losses was smaller among the units in Army Group South. On the other hand, the majority of the tank losses sustained by Army Group Centre were probably incurred during the defensive operations in the Orel bulge, after 12 July,[9] that is, during a period of retreat, which would have resulted in greater difficulties when salvaging seriously damaged tanks. This might very well have resulted in a ratio between vehicles in long-term repair and complete losses that was greater among the units in Army Group South.

Another factor to consider is that part of the losses during July was sustained in operations other than Zitadelle. For example, Das Reich and Totenkopf were fighting along the Mius river during the last four days of the month, while Großdeutschland was sent to the Orel salient on 17 July. For these reasons it is perhaps more appropriate to estimate that during Zitadelle, at most 150 tanks were destroyed among the panzer and panzer grenadier divisions in Army Group South during July. This also lends credence to the figures presented in Table 8.10, since that table indicates that the panzer divisions among Army Group South lost 129 tanks and assault guns as total losses between 5 and 17 July.

Information on assault guns is of a slightly different character. The majority of the assault guns were deployed in independent battalions. The four panzer grenadier divisions in Army Group South also had one assault gun battalion each, but these are included in Table A14.2.

For the independent assault guns, the available documents present the following picture:[10]

TABLE A14.3: STRENGTH AND LOSSES AMONG INDEPENDENT ASSAULT GUN BATTALIONS

		177 StuG Abt	185 StuG Abt	189 StuG Abt	202 StuG Abt	228 StuG Abt	244 StuG Abt	245 StuG Abt	904 StuG Abt	905 StuG Abt	909 StuG Abt	911 StuG Abt
4 July	On hand	31	32	31	31	31	31	31	31	32	31	31
10 July	Operational	13	27	24	31	25	15	19	21	29	19	23
	In workshops	17	2	1		5	11	10	9		11	7
	Replacements*		2				4	2			2	
20 July	Operational	13	13	18	28	27	24	5	16	30	17	23
	In workshops	16	12	13	3	5	5	15	12	1	12	6
	Replacements*	3	5	2		2	3	3		3		
31 July	Operational	13	16	7	31	18	19	13	18	23	20	25
	In workshops	19	8	21		14	10	7	10	8	(14)?	12
	Replacements*		5	2		7	3	3				10

Note: *Replacements received since the previous date.
Source: StuG-Lage, BA-MA RH 10/62; BA-MA RH 21-4/450.

Table A14.3 suggests that 66 Sturmgeschütze were destroyed among those battalions listed in the table, with the exception of 909th StuG Battalion, for which the figures for 31 July seem unrealistic. Combining all these numbers would suggest that the units deployed for operation Zitadelle lost about 500 tanks (including assault guns) during the fighting in and around the Kursk and Orel salients during the entire month of July. Tables 8.8 and 8.10 indicate that the Germans lost 278 tanks and assault guns during their own offensive.

Also evident from the information presented above is that the German panzer and panzer grenadier divisions had *not* suffered such losses as to render them 'combat ineffective'. Especially the divisions of Army Group South were in relatively good shape, which lends support to von Manstein's judgement that all his panzer and panzer grenadier divisions, except one, were still capable of undertaking offensive operations at the end of Zitadelle.[11] Any notion of Zitadelle being 'the swansong of the German Panzerwaffe' is simply highly exaggerated.[12] Also it should be noted that German tank and assault gun production during July amounted to 817 vehicles, indicating that the losses of tanks during Zitadelle were far from unsustainable.

Another approach to the problem of German tank losses is to look at the number of tanks and assault guns on the eastern front on 1 July and 1 August to see how much it had changed and to compare this with the number of vehicles sent to the eastern front during July (see Appendix 5 and Table 10.1 for more detailed information). Table A14.4 gives the changes for the various types of tanks and assault guns on the eastern front during 31 July 1943:

TABLE A14.4: CHANGES IN THE NUMBER OF GERMAN TANKS AND ASSAULT GUNS
ON THE EASTERN FRONT FROM 1 JULY TO 1 AUGUST

Pz II	Pz 38(t)	Pz III 50/L42	Pz III 50/L60	Pz III 75/L24	Pz IV 75/L24	Pz IV 75/L43 75/L48	Pz V	Pz VI	Flamm Pz	Bef Wg	StuG III	StuH III	StuPz IV
–17	0	–26	–50	–49	–1	–197	–70	+28	–3	–2	–31	–1	–8

Source: See Appendix 9.

Here we see that the net loss was 387 tanks, while the number of Tigers actually increased. Simultaneously 39 Tigers, 12 Panthers and 150 Pz IV were dispatched to the eastern front, thus 588 must have been lost on the eastern front during July. Above is indicated a net loss of 40 assault guns. To this should be added the 39 Ferdinands destroyed during July, giving a net loss on the eastern front of 79 assault guns. During July 135 assault guns were sent to the eastern front,[13] thus indicating that the total losses would have been 214 assault guns. This latter figure is however not entirely reliable, since the source giving the number of assault guns sent to the eastern front is not entirely clear on whether it refers to vehicles sent or vehicles that had arrived. Anyway it does of course include more fighting than Zitadelle. In particular the operations in the Orel salient may have resulted in significant losses, since the Germans were retreating, thereby making it more difficult to recover damaged vehicles.

NOTES

1. Panzerverluste Ost seit 1. Juli 1943, BA–MA RH 10/77.
2. BA–MA RH 10/209, RH 10/149, RH 10/142, RH 10/312, RH 10/313, RH 10/314, RH 10/145, RH 10/146, RH 10/156.
3. BA–MA RH 21-4/450.
4. Verteilung der Pz.Fahrz.Bd. ab Mai 43 (BA–MA RH 10/349).
5. B. Müller-Hillebrand, *Das Heer*, Vol. III, p. 220.
6. Müller-Hillebrand, *Das Heer*, Vol. III, Anhang B.
7. Pz.Offz. b. Chef Gen.St.d.H. Bb. Nr. 562/43 g.Kdos, v. 14.8.1943 (BA–MA RH 10/48).
8. Pz.Offz. b. Chef Gen.St.d.H. Bb. Nr. 562/43 g.Kdos, v. 14.8.1943 (BA–MA RH 10/48).
9. Of the 250 completely lost tanks, 96 (38%) were lost by 5th and 8th Panzer Divisions (BA–MA RH 10/48), units that took no part at all in Zitadelle. Several of the panzer

divisions which took part in Zitadelle were sent to meet the Soviet offensive, and it seems inconceivable that all the other panzer divisions sent to meet the Soviets would have lost less than 29 tanks in the subsequent fighting.

10. StuG-Lage, BA-MA RH 10/62.
11. Von Manstein, *Verlorene Siege* (Athenäum Verlag, Bonn, 1958), p. 504.
12. Expressed for example by Geoffrey Jukes in *Kursk – The Clash of Armour* (Macdonald & Co., London, 1969), p. 103.
13. StuG – Fertigung (Planung) und Zuführung (BA-MA RH 10/67).

Appendix 15:
Ration Strength of the
4th Panzer Army

TABLE A15.1: TABULATED RATION STRENGTH

	20 June 1943		1 July 1943				10 July 1943		20 July 1943	
	Men	Horses	Men	Ost	Army	Horses	Men	Horses	Men	Horses
II SS-PzK										
Leibstandarte	24,953		24,555	1,238	2,369		24,240		To Italy	
Das Reich	20,110		20,654	1,576	660		22,524		To 6th Army	
Totenkopf	22,800		23,800	1,147	2,002		20,830		19,630	
Corps Troops	3,749		3,951	203	681		3,490		To 6th Army	
XXXVIII PzK										
Großdeutschland	21,745		21,167				21,475		To AG Centre	
3rd Pz.Div.			14,141				14,126	1,032	14,801	1,030
11th Pz.Div	16,959		17,151				16,520		15,149	150
Corps Troops			9,233				8,255	358	6,493	265
LII Korps:										
57th ID	13,362	6,269	15,974	1,342			13,787	6,686	13,787	6,686
255th ID	14,021	6,320	14,114	955			15,310	6,027	17,119	6,523
332nd ID	19,536	5,336	21,500	1,114			12,701	5,313	14,232	5,100
Directly subordinated to 4th Panzer Army										
167th ID	21,000	6,500	17,837	384			18,423	6,273	To Kempf	
Heeres-, Armee- und Versorg.Tr.	19,028	550	19,780	1,894			30,979	699	29,500	700
Sum	197,263	24,975	223,857	9,853	5,712	26,391	222,660	26,388	130,711	20,454

Source: Anlage 7 zum KTB, Meldungen (Beute, Verpflegungsstärken) von 1.7.1943 bis 31.12.1943 (BA–MA RH 21-4/422).

Comments: Ost refers to men from the occupied areas in the east that had been inducted as HiWi, to perform non-combat duties. *Army* refers to men belonging to the Army (as opposed to Waffen-SS) but temporarily subordinated to Waffen-SS units. These are included in the totals for the respective divisions. In the original document it is explicitly stated '*davon Ost*' and '*davon Heer*' in the headings for these columns.

Appendix 16:
Divisional Structure for
German Forces on 4 July 1943

5th SS-Panzergrenadier Division Wiking, 4 July 1943

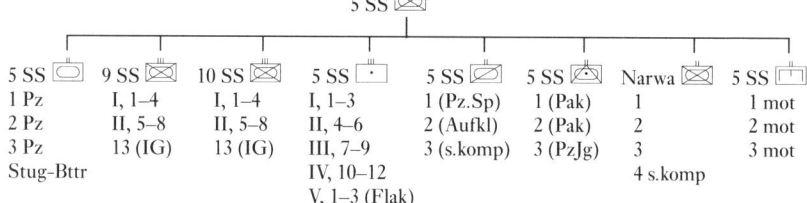

5 SS	9 SS	10 SS	5 SS	5 SS	5 SS	Narwa	5 SS
1 Pz	I, 1–4	I, 1–4	I, 1–3	1 (Pz.Sp)	1 (Pak)	1	1 mot
2 Pz	II, 5–8	II, 5–8	II, 4–6	2 (Aufkl)	2 (Pak)	2	2 mot
3 Pz	13 (IG)	13 (IG)	III, 7–9	3 (s.komp)	3 (PzJg)	3	3 mot
Stug-Bttr			IV, 10–12			4 s.komp	
			V, 1–3 (Flak)				

17th Panzer Division, 4 July 1943

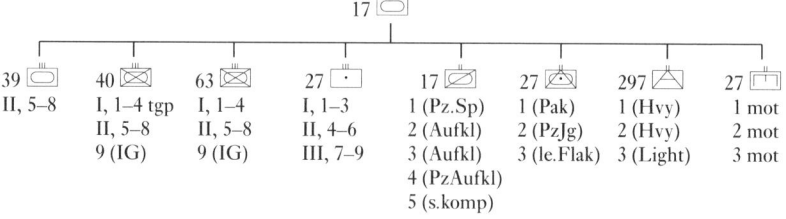

39	40	63	27	17	27	297	27
II, 5–8	I, 1–4 tgp	I, 1–4	I, 1–3	1 (Pz.Sp)	1 (Pak)	1 (Hvy)	1 mot
	II, 5–8	II, 5–8	II, 4–6	2 (Aufkl)	2 (PzJg)	2 (Hvy)	2 mot
	9 (IG)	9 (IG)	III, 7–9	3 (Aufkl)	3 (le.Flak)	3 (Light)	3 mot
				4 (PzAufkl)			
				5 (s.komp)			

23rd Panzer Division, 4 July 1943 (joined Corps 7 July 1943)

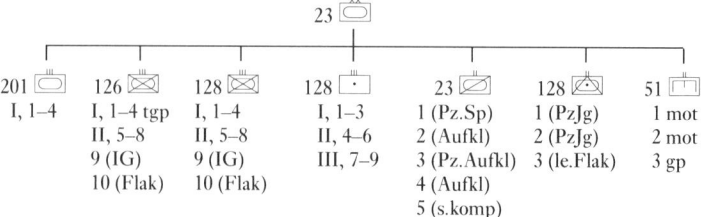

201	126	128	128	23	128	51
I, 1–4	I, 1–4 tgp	I, 1–4	I, 1–3	1 (Pz.Sp)	1 (PzJg)	1 mot
	II, 5–8	II, 5–8	II, 4–6	2 (Aufkl)	2 (PzJg)	2 mot
	9 (IG)	9 (IG)	III, 7–9	3 (Pz.Aufkl)	3 (le.Flak)	3 gp
	10 (Flak)	10 (Flak)		4 (Aufkl)		
				5 (s.komp)		

ARMY GROUP CENTRE: GRUPPE VON ESEBECK, 4 JULY 1943

4th Panzer Division, 4 July 1943

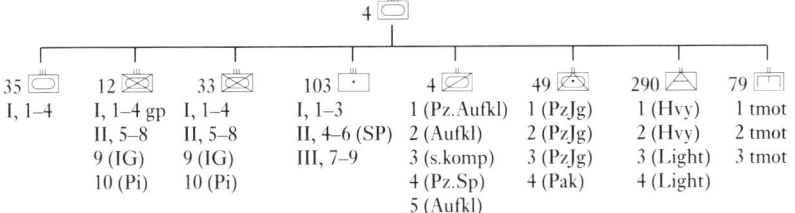

35	12	33	103	4	49	290	79
I, 1–4	I, 1–4 gp	I, 1–4	I, 1–3	1 (Pz.Aufkl)	1 (PzJg)	1 (Hvy)	1 tmot
	II, 5–8	II, 5–8	II, 4–6 (SP)	2 (Aufkl)	2 (PzJg)	2 (Hvy)	2 tmot
	9 (IG)	9 (IG)	III, 7–9	3 (s.komp)	3 (PzJg)	3 (Light)	3 tmot
	10 (Pi)	10 (Pi)		4 (Pz.Sp)	4 (Pak)	4 (Light)	
				5 (Aufkl)			

12th Panzer Division, 4 July 1943

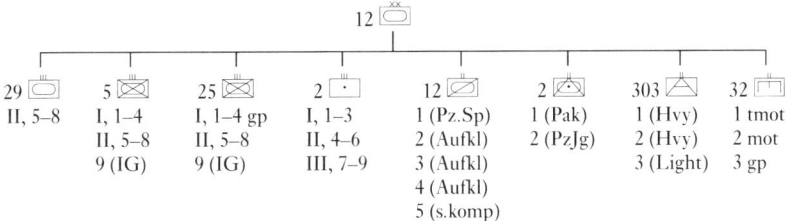

29	5	25	2	12	2	303	32
II, 5–8	I, 1–4	I, 1–4 gp	I, 1–3	1 (Pz.Sp)	1 (Pak)	1 (Hvy)	1 tmot
	II, 5–8	II, 5–8	II, 4–6	2 (Aufkl)	2 (PzJg)	2 (Hvy)	2 mot
	9 (IG)	9 (IG)	III, 7–9	3 (Aufkl)		3 (Light)	3 gp
				4 (Aufkl)			
				5 (s.komp)			

10th Panzergrenadier Division, 4 July 1943

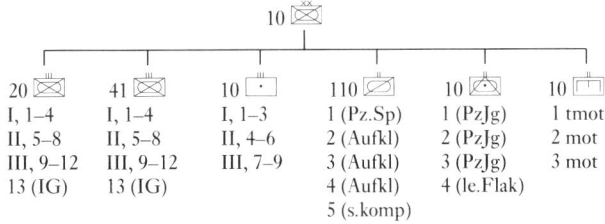

20	41	10	110	10	10
I, 1–4	I, 1–4	I, 1–3	1 (Pz.Sp)	1 (PzJg)	1 tmot
II, 5–8	II, 5–8	II, 4–6	2 (Aufkl)	2 (PzJg)	2 mot
III, 9–12	III, 9–12	III, 7–9	3 (Aufkl)	3 (PzJg)	3 mot
13 (IG)	13 (IG)		4 (Aufkl)	4 (le.Flak)	
			5 (s.komp)		

Key to Divisional Structure

I, 1–4 gp	I – First battalion, 1–4 – 1st to 4th company, gp – armoured with SPW
II, 5–8	II – Second battalion, 5–8 – 5th to 8th company
9 (IG)	9 – 9th company, IG – Infantry Gun
10 (Flak)	10 – 10th company, Flak – Anti-Aircraft guns
Aufkl	Reconnaissance M/C or Kübelwagens
Pz.Sp	Armoured Reconnaissance A/C or SPW 250/9
Pz.Aufkl	Armoured Reconnaissance SPW
s.komp	Heavy company (in anti-tank, mortars or machine-guns platoons, for example)
PzJg	Panzerjaeger (Marders)
Pak	Anti-tank guns (towed)
tgp	Partly armoured infantry battalion
gp	Armoured infantry battalion
Rdfr	Bicycles

Panzergrenadier Regiment – Motorized Infantry Regiment (sometimes one battalion is armoured)

Panzeraufklärungsabteilung = Reconnaissance battalion (if fully armoured every company except heavy has 'Pz')

Sources: BA-MA RH 10/154, BA-MA RH 10/159, BA-MA RH 10/316.

9th Army Divisional Structure on 4 July

9TH ARMY: XXXXVI PANZER CORPS, 4 JULY 1943

7th Infantry Division, 4 July 1943

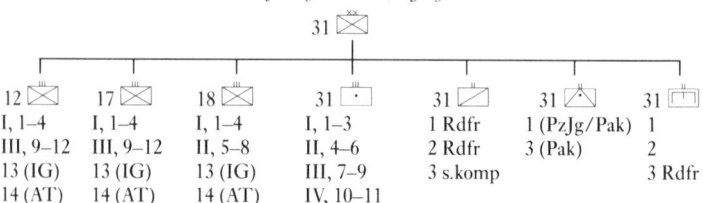

19	61	62	7	7	7	7
I, 1–4	I, 1–4	I, 1–4	I, 1–3	1 Rdfr	1 (Pak)	1
III, 9–12	III, 9–12	II, 5–8	II, 4–6	2 Rdfr	2 (Pak)	2
13 (IG)	13 (IG)	13 (IG)	III, 7–9	3 s.komp	3 (Pak)	3 Rdfr
14 (AT)	14 (AT)	14 (AT)	I/43, 1–3			

31st Infantry Division, 4 July 1943

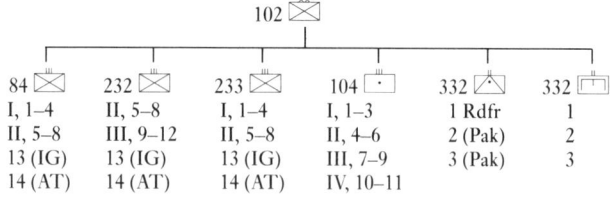

12	17	18	31	31	31	31
I, 1–4	I, 1–4	I, 1–4	I, 1–3	1 Rdfr	1 (PzJg/Pak)	1
III, 9–12	III, 9–12	II, 5–8	II, 4–6	2 Rdfr	3 (Pak)	2
13 (IG)	13 (IG)	13 (IG)	III, 7–9	3 s.komp		3 Rdfr
14 (AT)	14 (AT)	14 (AT)	IV, 10–11			

102nd Infantry Division, 4 July 1943

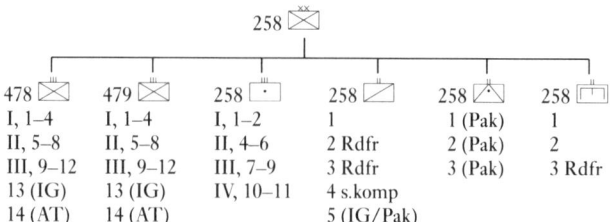

84	232	233	104	332	332
I, 1–4	II, 5–8	I, 1–4	I, 1–3	1 Rdfr	1
II, 5–8	III, 9–12	II, 5–8	II, 4–6	2 (Pak)	2
13 (IG)	13 (IG)	13 (IG)	III, 7–9	3 (Pak)	3
14 (AT)	14 (AT)	14 (AT)	IV, 10–11		

258th Infantry Division, 4 July 1943

258

478	479	258	258	258	258
I, 1–4	I, 1–4	I, 1–2	1	1 (Pak)	1
II, 5–8	II, 5–8	II, 4–6	2 Rdfr	2 (Pak)	2
III, 9–12	III, 9–12	III, 7–9	3 Rdfr	3 (Pak)	3 Rdfr
13 (IG)	13 (IG)	IV, 10–11	4 s.komp		
14 (AT)	14 (AT)		5 (IG/Pak)		

9TH ARMY: XXXXVII PANZER CORPS, 4 JULY 1943

2nd Panzer Division, 4 July 1943

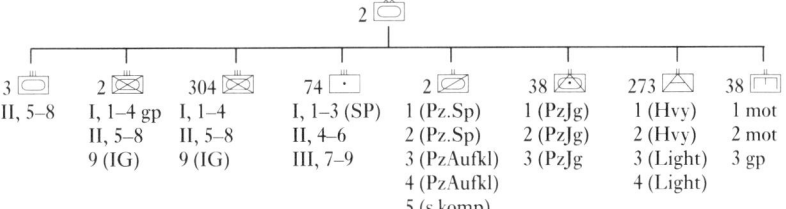

3	2	304	74	2	38	273	38
II, 5–8	I, 1–4 gp	II, 5–8	I, 1–3 (SP)	1 (Pz.Sp)	1 (PzJg)	1 (Hvy)	1 mot
	II, 5–8	9 (IG)	II, 4–6	2 (Pz.Sp)	2 (PzJg)	2 (Hvy)	2 mot
	9 (IG)		III, 7–9	3 (PzAufkl)	3 (PzJg)	3 (Light)	3 gp
				4 (PzAufkl)		4 (Light)	
				5 (s.komp)			

9th Panzer Division, 4 July 1943

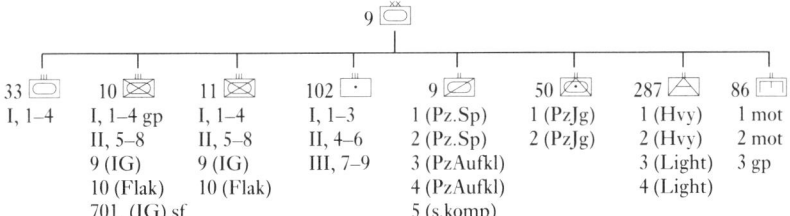

33	10	11	102	9	50	287	86
I, 1–4	I, 1–4 gp	I, 1–4	I, 1–3	1 (Pz.Sp)	1 (PzJg)	1 (Hvy)	1 mot
	II, 5–8	II, 5–8	II, 4–6	2 (Pz.Sp)	2 (PzJg)	2 (Hvy)	2 mot
	9 (IG)	9 (IG)	III, 7–9	3 (PzAufkl)		3 (Light)	3 gp
	10 (Flak)	10 (Flak)		4 (PzAufkl)		4 (Light)	
	701. (IG) sf			5 (s.komp)			

20th Panzer Division, 4 July 1943

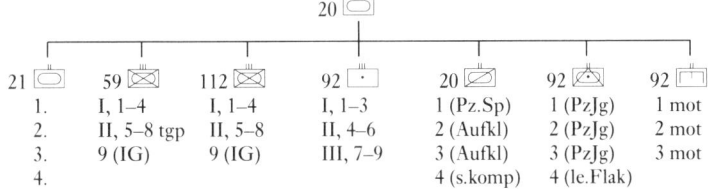

21	59	112	92	20	92	92
1.	I, 1–4	I, 1–4	I, 1–3	1 (Pz.Sp)	1 (PzJg)	1 mot
2.	II, 5–8 tgp	II, 5–8	II, 4–6	2 (Aufkl)	2 (PzJg)	2 mot
3.	9 (IG)	9 (IG)	III, 7–9	3 (Aufkl)	3 (PzJg)	3 mot
4.				4 (s.komp)	4 (le.Flak)	

6th Infantry Division, 4 July 1943

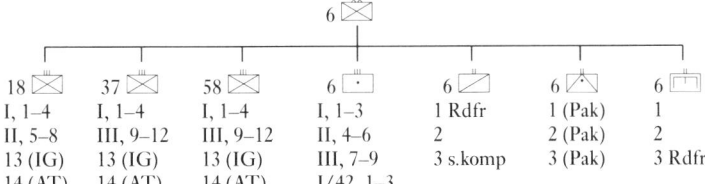

18	37	58	6	6	6	6
I, 1–4	I, 1–4	I, 1–4	I, 1–3	1 Rdfr	1 (Pak)	1
II, 5–8	III, 9–12	III, 9–12	II, 4–6	2	2 (Pak)	2
13 (IG)	13 (IG)	13 (IG)	III, 7–9	3 s.komp	3 (Pak)	3 Rdfr
14 (AT)	14 (AT)	14 (AT)	I/42, 1–3			

9TH ARMY: XXXXI PANZER CORPS, 4 JULY 1943

18th Panzer Division, 4 July 1943

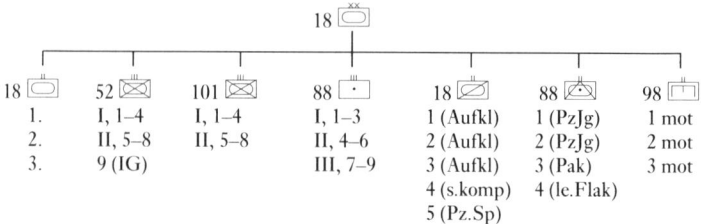

18	52	101	88	18	88	98
1.	I, 1–4	I, 1–4	I, 1–3	1 (Aufkl)	1 (PzJg)	1 mot
2.	II, 5–8	II, 5–8	II, 4–6	2 (Aufkl)	2 (PzJg)	2 mot
3.	9 (IG)		III, 7–9	3 (Aufkl)	3 (Pak)	3 mot
				4 (s.komp)	4 (le.Flak)	
				5 (Pz.Sp)		

86th Infantry Division, 4 July 1943

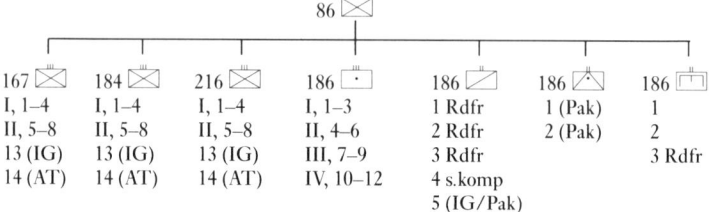

167	184	216	186	186	186	186
I, 1–4	I, 1–4	I, 1–4	I, 1–3	1 Rdfr	1 (Pak)	1
II, 5–8	II, 5–8	II, 5–8	II, 4–6	2 Rdfr	2 (Pak)	2
13 (IG)	13 (IG)	13 (IG)	III, 7–9	3 Rdfr		3 Rdfr
14 (AT)	14 (AT)	14 (AT)	IV, 10–12	4 s.komp		
				5 (IG/Pak)		

292nd Infantry Division, 4 July 1943

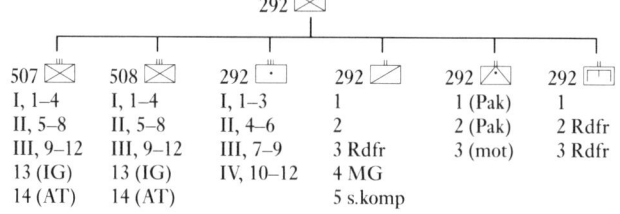

507	508	292	292	292	292
I, 1–4	I, 1–4	I, 1–3	1	1 (Pak)	1
II, 5–8	II, 5–8	II, 4–6	2	2 (Pak)	2 Rdfr
III, 9–12	III, 9–12	III, 7–9	3 Rdfr	3 (mot)	3 Rdfr
13 (IG)	13 (IG)	IV, 10–12	4 MG		
14 (AT)	14 (AT)		5 s.komp		

9TH ARMY: XXIII CORPS, 4 JULY 1943

78th Sturm Division, 4 July 1943

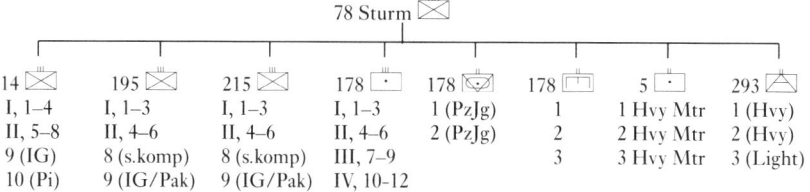

216th Infantry Division, 4 July 1943

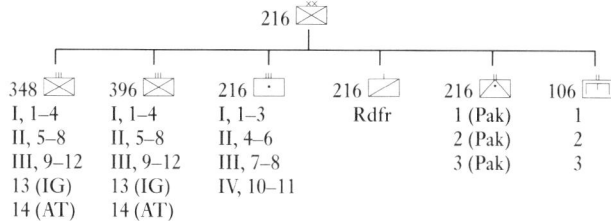

383rd Infantry Division, 4 July 1943

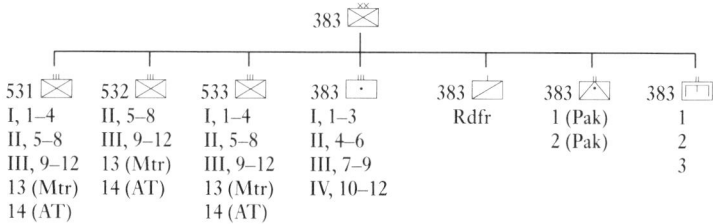

Sources: BA-MA RH 10/141, BA-MA RH 10/143, BA-MA RH 10/150, BA-MA RH 10/155, BA-MA RH 10/157, BA-MA RH 24-20/49, BA-MA RH 24-23/125, BA-MA RH 24-23/126, BA-MA RH 24-46/91.

Army Detachment Kempf Divisional Structure on 4 July 1943

ARMY DET. KEMPF: XXXXII CORPS, 4 JULY 1943

39th Infantry Division, 4 July 1943

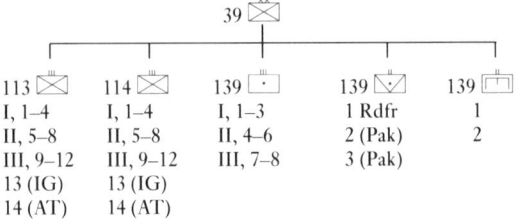

161st Infantry Division, 4 July 1943

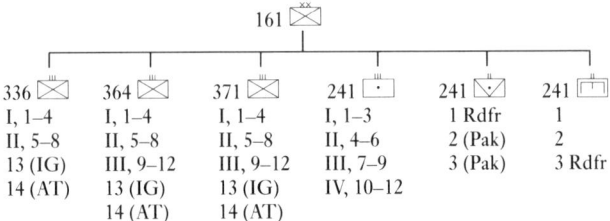

282nd Infantry Division, 4 July 1943

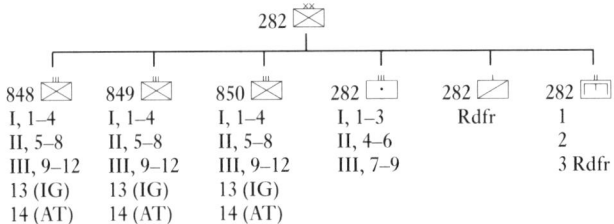

APPENDIX 16

ARMY DET. KEMPF: CORPS RAUS, 4 JULY 1943

106th Infantry Division, 4 July 1943

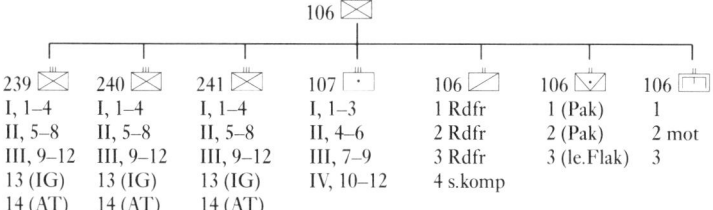

239	240	241	107	106	106	106
I, 1–4	I, 1–4	I, 1–4	I, 1–3	1 Rdfr	1 (Pak)	1
II, 5–8	II, 5–8	II, 5–8	II, 4–6	2 Rdfr	2 (Pak)	2 mot
III, 9–12	III, 9–12	III, 9–12	III, 7–9	3 Rdfr	3 (le.Flak)	3
13 (IG)	13 (IG)	13 (IG)	IV, 10–12	4 s.komp		
14 (AT)	14 (AT)	14 (AT)				

320th Infantry Division, 4 July 1943

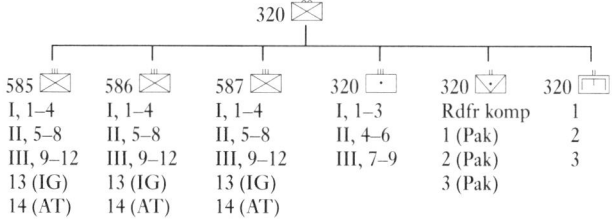

585	586	587	320	320	320
I, 1–4	I, 1–4	I, 1–4	I, 1–3	Rdfr komp	1
II, 5–8	II, 5–8	II, 5–8	II, 4–6	1 (Pak)	2
III, 9–12	III, 9–12	III, 9–12	III, 7–9	2 (Pak)	3
13 (IG)	13 (IG)	13 (IG)		3 (Pak)	
14 (AT)	14 (AT)	14 (AT)			

198th Infantry Division, 4 July 1943 (joined Corps 9 July 1943)

198

305	326	328	235	235	235
I, 1–4	I, 1–4	I, 1–4	I, 1–3	1 Rdfr	1 Rdfr
II, 5–8	II, 5–8	II, 5–8	II, 4–6	2 (Pak)	2
III, 9–12	III, 9–12	III, 9–12	III, 7–9	3 (Pak)	3
13 (IG)	13 (IG)	13 (IG)	IV, 10–12		
14 (AT)	14 (AT)	14 (AT)			

ARMY DET. KEMPF: III PANZER CORPS, 4 JULY 1943

6th Panzer Division, 4 July 1943

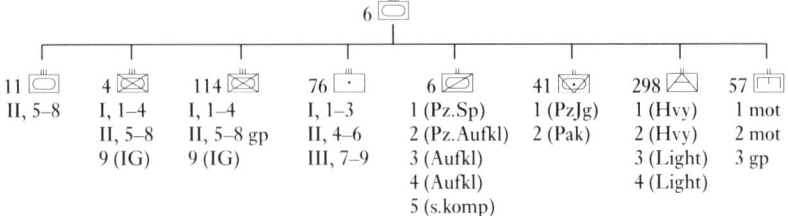

11	4	114	76	6	41	298	57
II, 5–8	I, 1–4	I, 1–4	I, 1–3	1 (Pz.Sp)	1 (PzJg)	1 (Hvy)	1 mot
	II, 5–8	II, 5–8 gp	II, 4–6	2 (Pz.Aufkl)	2 (Pak)	2 (Hvy)	2 mot
	9 (IG)	9 (IG)	III, 7–9	3 (Aufkl)		3 (Light)	3 gp
				4 (Aufkl)		4 (Light)	
				5 (s.komp)			

7th Panzer Division, 4 July 1943

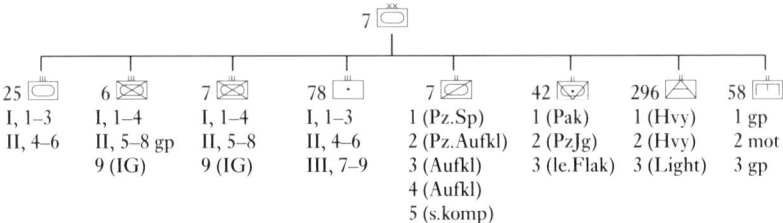

25	6	7	78	7	42	296	58
I, 1–3	I, 1–4	I, 1–4	I, 1–3	1 (Pz.Sp)	1 (Pak)	1 (Hvy)	1 gp
II, 4–6	II, 5–8 gp	II, 5–8	II, 4–6	2 (Pz.Aufkl)	2 (PzJg)	2 (Hvy)	2 mot
	9 (IG)	9 (IG)	III, 7–9	3 (Aufkl)	3 (le.Flak)	3 (Light)	3 gp
				4 (Aufkl)			
				5 (s.komp)			

19th Panzer Division, 4 July 1943

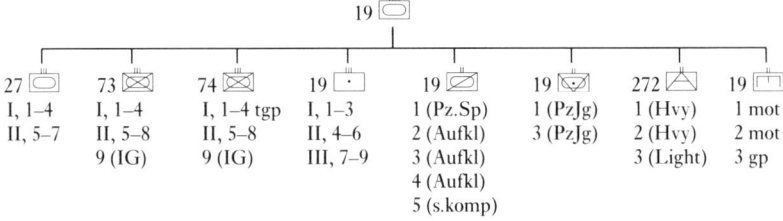

27	73	74	19	19	19	272	19
I, 1–4	I, 1–4	I, 1–4 tgp	I, 1–3	1 (Pz.Sp)	1 (PzJg)	1 (Hvy)	1 mot
II, 5–7	II, 5–8	II, 5–8	II, 4–6	2 (Aufkl)	3 (PzJg)	2 (Hvy)	2 mot
	9 (IG)	9 (IG)	III, 7–9	3 (Aufkl)		3 (Light)	3 gp
				4 (Aufkl)			
				5 (s.komp)			

168th Infantry Division, 4 July 1943

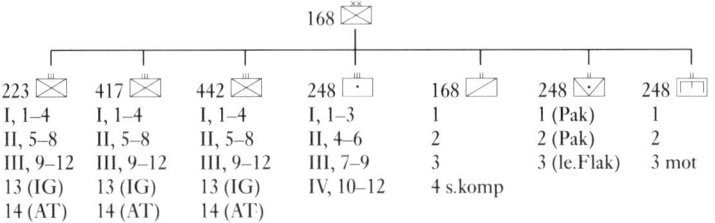

223	417	442	248	168	248	248
I, 1–4	I, 1–4	I, 1–4	I, 1–3	1	1 (Pak)	1
II, 5–8	II, 5–8	II, 5–8	II, 4–6	2	2 (Pak)	2
III, 9–12	III, 9–12	III, 9–12	III, 7–9	3	3 (le.Flak)	3 mot
13 (IG)	13 (IG)	13 (IG)	IV, 10–12	4 s.komp		
14 (AT)	14 (AT)	14 (AT)				

Sources: BA-MA RH 10/145, BA-MA RH 10/146, BA-MA RH 10/156, BA-MA RH 20-8/91, BA-MA RH 24-11/76.

4th Panzer Army Divisional Structure on 4 July 1943

4TH PANZER ARMY: LII CORPS, 4 JULY 1943

57th Infantry Division, 4 July 1943

57 ⊠

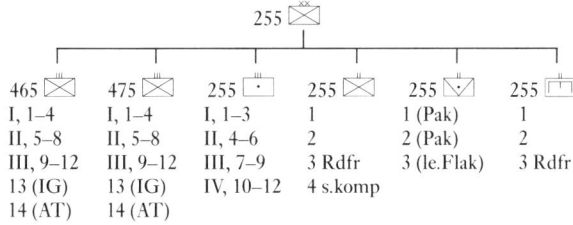

164 ⊠	199 ⊠	217 ⊠	157 ·	157	157 ∨	157 ⊡
I, 1–4	I, 1–4	II, 5–8	I, 1–3	1 Rdfr	1 (Pak)	1Rdfr
II, 5–8	II, 5–8	III, 9–12	II, 4–6	2 Rdfr	2 (Pak)	2
13 (IG)	13 (IG)	13 (IG)	III, 7–8	3 Rdfr	3 (le.Flak)	3
14 (AT)	14 (AT)	14 (AT)	IV, 10–12	4 s.komp		

255th Infantry Division, 4 July 1943

255 ⊠

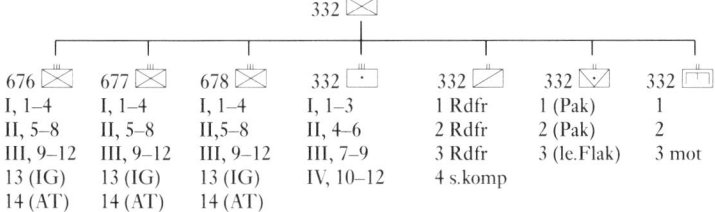

465 ⊠	475 ⊠	255 ·	255 ⊠	255 ∨	255 ⊡
I, 1–4	I, 1–4	I, 1–3	1	1 (Pak)	1
II, 5–8	II, 5–8	II, 4–6	2	2 (Pak)	2
III, 9–12	III, 9–12	III, 7–9	3 Rdfr	3 (le.Flak)	3 Rdfr
13 (IG)	13 (IG)	IV, 10–12	4 s.komp		
14 (AT)	14 (AT)				

332nd Infantry Division, 4 July 1943

332 ⊠

676 ⊠	677 ⊠	678 ⊠	332 ·	332	332 ∨	332 ⊡
I, 1–4	I, 1–4	I, 1–4	I, 1–3	1 Rdfr	1 (Pak)	1
II, 5–8	II, 5–8	II,5–8	II, 4–6	2 Rdfr	2 (Pak)	2
III, 9–12	III, 9–12	III, 9–12	III, 7–9	3 Rdfr	3 (le.Flak)	3 mot
13 (IG)	13 (IG)	13 (IG)	IV, 10–12	4 s.komp		
14 (AT)	14 (AT)	14 (AT)				

4TH PANZER ARMY: XXXXVIII PANZER CORPS, 4 JULY 1943

Panzergrenadier Division Großdeutschland, 4 July 1943

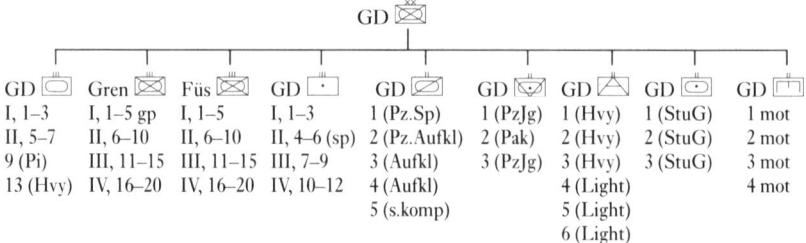

GD	Gren	Füs	GD	GD	GD	GD	GD	GD
I, 1–3	I, 1–5 gp	I, 1–5	I, 1–3	1 (Pz.Sp)	1 (PzJg)	1 (Hvy)	1 (StuG)	1 mot
II, 5–7	II, 6–10	II, 6–10	II, 4–6 (sp)	2 (Pz.Aufkl)	2 (Pak)	2 (Hvy)	2 (StuG)	2 mot
9 (Pi)	III, 11–15	III, 11–15	III, 7–9	3 (Aufkl)	3 (PzJg)	3 (Hvy)	3 (StuG)	3 mot
13 (Hvy)	IV, 16–20	IV, 16–20	IV, 10–12	4 (Aufkl)		4 (Light)		4 mot
				5 (s.komp)		5 (Light)		
						6 (Light)		

3rd Panzer Division, 4 July 1943

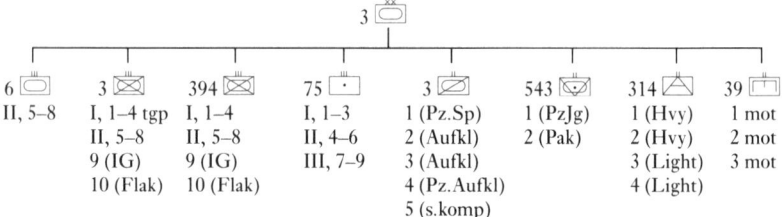

6	3	394	75	3	543	314	39
II, 5–8	I, 1–4 tgp	I, 1–4	I, 1–3	1 (Pz.Sp)	1 (PzJg)	1 (Hvy)	1 mot
	II, 5–8	II, 5–8	II, 4–6	2 (Aufkl)	2 (Pak)	2 (Hvy)	2 mot
	9 (IG)	9 (IG)	III, 7–9	3 (Aufkl)		3 (Light)	3 mot
	10 (Flak)	10 (Flak)		4 (Pz.Aufkl)		4 (Light)	
				5 (s.komp)			

11th Panzer Division, 4 July 1943

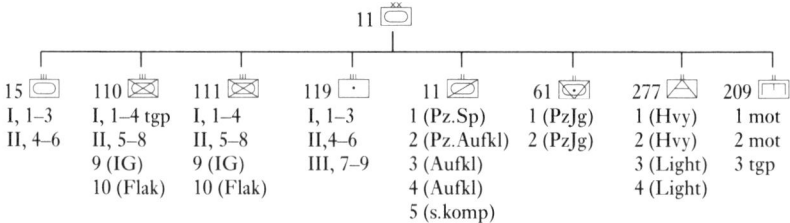

15	110	111	119	11	61	277	209
I, 1–3	I, 1–4 tgp	I, 1–4	I, 1–3	1 (Pz.Sp)	1 (PzJg)	1 (Hvy)	1 mot
II, 4–6	II, 5–8	II, 5–8	II,4–6	2 (Pz.Aufkl)	2 (PzJg)	2 (Hvy)	2 mot
	9 (IG)	9 (IG)	III, 7–9	3 (Aufkl)		3 (Light)	3 tgp
	10 (Flak)	10 (Flak)		4 (Aufkl)		4 (Light)	
				5 (s.komp)			

167th Infantry Division, 4 July 1943

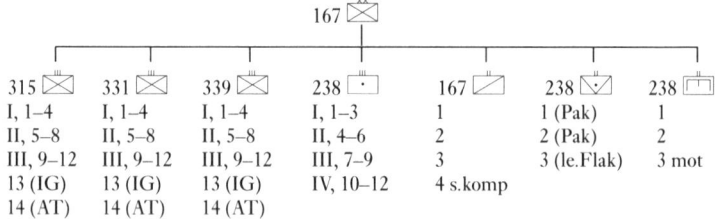

315	331	339	238	167	238	238
I, 1–4	I, 1–4	I, 1–4	I, 1–3	1	1 (Pak)	1
II, 5–8	II, 5–8	II, 5–8	II, 4–6	2	2 (Pak)	2
III, 9–12	III, 9–12	III, 9–12	III, 7–9	3	3 (le.Flak)	3 mot
13 (IG)	13 (IG)	13 (IG)	IV, 10–12	4 s.komp		
14 (AT)	14 (AT)	14 (AT)				

4TH PANZER ARMY: II SS-PANZER CORPS, 4 JULY 1943

1st SS-Panzergrenadier Division Leibstandarte SS Adolf Hitler, 4 July 1943

1 SS

1 SS	1 SS	2 SS	1 SS	1 SS	1 SS	1 SS	1 SS	1 SS	1 SS
II, 5–8	I, 1–5	I, 1–5	I, 1–3	1 (Aufkl)	1 (PzJg)	1 (Hvy)	1 (StuG)	1 gp	
9 (Pi)	II, 6–10	II, 6–10	II, 4–6 (SP)	2 (Aufkl)	2 (PzJg)	2 (Hvy)	2 (StuG)	2 mot	
13 (Hvy)	III, 11–15	III, 11–14 gp	III, 7–9	3 (Pz.Aufkl)	3 (PzJg)	3 (Hvy)	3 (StuG)	3 mot	
	16 (Flak)	15 (Flak)	10 (10cm K)	4 (Pz.Sp)		4 (Light)			
	17 (IG)	16 (IG)	11 (Nbw)	5 (s.komp)		5 (Light)			
	18 (Pak)	17 (Pak)				6 (Light)			
	19 (Aufkl)	18 (Aufkl)							
	20 (Pi)	19 (Pi)							

2nd SS-Panzergrenadier Division Das Reich, 4 July 1943

2 SS

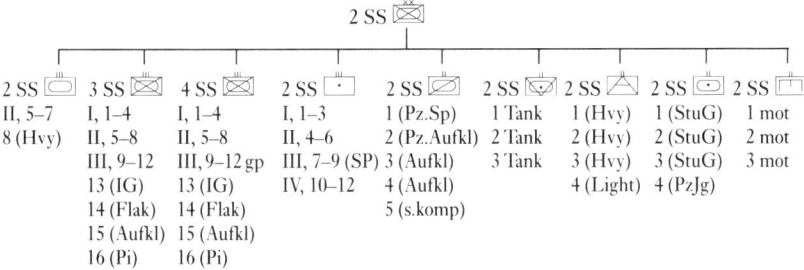

2 SS	3 SS	4 SS	2 SS	2 SS	2 SS	2 SS	2 SS	2 SS	2 SS
II, 5–7	I, 1–4	I, 1–4	I, 1–3	1 (Pz.Sp)	1 Tank	1 (Hvy)	1 (StuG)	1 mot	
8 (Hvy)	II, 5–8	II, 5–8	II, 4–6	2 (Pz.Aufkl)	2 Tank	2 (Hvy)	2 (StuG)	2 mot	
	III, 9–12	III, 9–12 gp	III, 7–9 (SP)	3 (Aufkl)	3 Tank	3 (Hvy)	3 (StuG)	3 mot	
	13 (IG)	13 (IG)	IV, 10–12	4 (Aufkl)		4 (Light)	4 (PzJg)		
	14 (Flak)	14 (Flak)		5 (s.komp)					
	15 (Aufkl)	15 (Aufkl)							
	16 (Pi)	16 (Pi)							

At this time, Das Reich had 14 Tiger I, 33 Panzer IV, 70 Panzer III and 26 T-34. This is too many tanks for four tank companies (I bn with 1st to 4th Company did not arrive until mid-August with Panthers). Hence, there existed an ad hoc unit, the Anti-Tank Battalion was used as a tank battalion (it had all the T-34 and some of the Pz III).

3rd SS-Panzergrenadier Division Totenkopf, 4 July 1943

3 SS

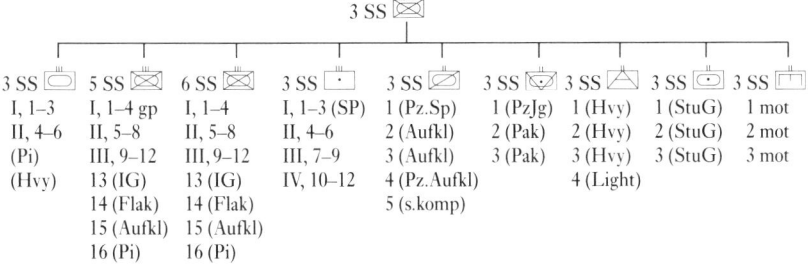

3 SS	5 SS	6 SS	3 SS	3 SS	3 SS	3 SS	3 SS	3 SS	3 SS
I, 1–3	I, 1–4 gp	I, 1–4	I, 1–3 (SP)	1 (Pz.Sp)	1 (PzJg)	1 (Hvy)	1 (StuG)	1 mot	
II, 4–6	II, 5–8	II, 5–8	II, 4–6	2 (Aufkl)	2 (Pak)	2 (Hvy)	2 (StuG)	2 mot	
(Pi)	III, 9–12	III, 9–12	III, 7–9	3 (Aufkl)	3 (Pak)	3 (Hvy)	3 (StuG)	3 mot	
(Hvy)	13 (IG)	13 (IG)	IV, 10–12	4 (Pz.Aufkl)		4 (Light)			
	14 (Flak)	14 (Flak)		5 (s.komp)					
	15 (Aufkl)	15 (Aufkl)							
	16 (Pi)	16 (Pi)							

Sources: BA-MA RH 10/142, BA-MA RH 10/149, BA-MA RH 10/209, BA-MA RH 10/312, BA-MA RH 10/313, BA-MA RH 10/314, BA-MA RH 24-52/151, BA-MA RH 26-167/29, BA-MA RH 26-255/114, BA-MA RH 26-332/21.

Bibliography

COMMENTS ON SOURCES USED

When we began working on this book in 1995 we were already acquainted with many of the published works available, since we had previously written an article about the operation. For this project we began to use archival records but we have had the opportunity to use German material only, although we have previously asserted that Soviet material should be used for the Red Army and German material for the Wehrmacht. It might be claimed that our study would suffer thereby. As it has not been possible for us to use Soviet archives, our analysis of the Red Army has had to be based on published works and articles made by other researchers and authors. Hence, our analysis cannot be considered a definitive analysis of Operation Zitadelle. Yet, except perhaps for the most trivial of subjects, is there ever any really definitive analysis? Rather, this work should be regarded as a step towards making a correct evaluation of the results and effects of this heavy fighting.

Archival material

As we started to study the German archives we were amazed by the wealth of information on this operation they contained. This information had previously been used by very few when writing about Operation Zitadelle. Thus some of our findings will appear to be completely new. Our main resource has been the files belonging to the Inspector of the Panzer forces. However, using archival material is not entirely free from trouble.

One problem that may be encountered is the difficulty of understanding what is actually written because of the abbreviations, formalities and practices used in the German Army when filling out reports during the war. Also different reports can give quite different numbers. Usually this is caused by the chaos war brings.

238

It is important to understand the terms the German Army used, since otherwise material can be misinterpreted. We have tried to clarify some aspects of this in an article published in the *Journal of Slavic Military Studies*. We have already explained some of the terms used by the German Army in the chapters of this book and so as not to repeat ourselves too much we will clarify here only the terminology used for tank forces. To be able to make a correct analysis of the German Panzers, one has to understand their way of reporting.

First we have the terms:
- *Soll* gives the number of tanks/assault guns the unit should have according to its T/O&E.
- *Ist* represents the number of tanks/assault guns the unit actually holds.
- *Einsatzbereit* is the number of operational tanks/assault guns.
- *Instandsetzung* gives the number of tanks/assault guns in the work-shops.

The T/O&E strength is a pure guideline. The Germans strove to equip their units according to the T/O&E but it was far from always possible. Occasionally it could also occur that a unit received a higher allotment of equipment than it was supposed to have. An example is 2nd Panzer Division, which had a T/O&E strength of 64 Panzers on 1 July yet held 99 Panzers at the start of Zitadelle.

The tanks a unit has are divided into two kinds, operational and repair objects. As we have shown in Appendices 4 and 6 the number operational can vary greatly from day to day. It is important to remember it is not only the enemy that can cause a tank to become non-operational. During combat the wear and tear also increases, due perhaps to more cross-country driving and rougher driving when trying to avoid becoming a target. Operational strength of a unit is the available tank strength at a specified moment and may change as soon the unit enters combat or the workshops get time to repair vehicles. Thus the operational tank strength can be a very blunt instrument by which to analyse the tank strength of a unit unless we have strength figures over a longer period of time. Reports for one day only give the situation for that day and nothing more, since operational tank strength can change rapidly from one moment to another. In many reports the Germans use the term 'Panzerlage', which also gives the number of operational tanks.

The tanks under repair are usually divided into two categories, short- and long-term. In the divisional reports to the inspector of the Panzer forces, short-term meant that vehicles are almost always repairable within three weeks, but in other reports it was occasionally two weeks. Long-term applied to vehicles not listed in the monthly divisional reports to the inspector of the Panzer forces.

Also we must be aware that a diminution of numbers on hand did not always represent total losses (write-offs). Units sometimes sent away tanks which needed extensive repairs and these were thus removed from the lists. Other causes could be that older vehicles were sent to the rear to be modified or rebuilt (to become Marders for example).

Finally, it is important to understand fully the numbers one is working with when using archive material so as to avoid misinterpretation. Also one must be careful to determine what is included or omitted from a report. Differences are to be noted if such exist between reports, and an effort made to find out the cause if possible.

Published works

We have decided to give a short one-line summary of each book listed in the Bibliography, because not everybody understands Russian and German and it is not always clear what a book is about.

In the list will be found some works that we have not actually used as a reference in our chapters. We have chosen to list them to assist anyone who wants to study the operation. This applies mainly to unit histories.

One category, of course, covers memoirs. On the German side only one of the field commanders wrote his memoirs, Erich von Manstein. However, we do not recommend the English translation, since it is an abridged version and this applies especially to the chapter about Operation Zitadelle. The German chapter which deals with Zitadelle contains over 400 per cent more pages, so to use the English translation in research on Zitadelle should be regarded as inadequate.

On the Soviet side all the higher commanders, except Vatutin, and some of the army commanders wrote memoirs. The most useful of them is that of Marshal G.K. Zhukov. Of course, all these memoirs have a great deal of political material in them but, irrespective of this, one can gain insight into their way of thinking.

There are also works that deal with the entire war on the eastern front. Useful for studies of the Soviet side are John Erickson's two books, *The Road to Stalingrad* and *The Road to Berlin*, while Earl F. Ziemke's and Magna E. Bauer's book *Moscow to Stalingrad* is also good. In Ziemke's earlier book *Stalingrad to Berlin* there is only limited use of Soviet sources, but it is still good for the German side. The German *Militärgeschichtliches Forschungsamt* has been working on an official German history of the war, *Das Deutsche Reich und der Zweite Weltkrieg,* for several years. This is a very ambitious work of a high standard, using a wide variety of sources. As far as we know they have reached volume 6, which ends with the events in March 1943. However, our research does appear to have revealed some discrepancies in numbers and narratives of operations to those given in Richard Overy's *Russia's War.*

Several battle histories have been published and of these we can recommend two, *Das Gesetz des Handels, Die Operation Zitadelle 1943* by Ernst Klink and *Kurskaya Bitva* by G.A. Koltunov and B.G. Solovev. The former is an account based on German archival material, including German intelligence reports. It is a good book. The latter is a Soviet account of the battle. When reading it one must remember that much of the information on the Germans is very unreliable. Other books in which we have found statements that conflict with our evidence are *Citadel, the Battle of Kursk* by Robin Cross, *Kursk 1943* by Mark Healy and *Kursk –The Clash of Armour* by Geoffrey Jukes.

Nor, for the same reason, when studying the German Panzer forces can we recommend *Panzer, A Revolution in Warfare, 1939–1945* by Roger Edwards and *Knights of the Black Cross* by Bryan Perrett. Several officers have written memoirs, of which a few have been translated into English, but we give the small warning that, though many write highly of von Mellenthin's book, *Panzer Battles*, it contains several inaccuracies. Probably these are caused by the lack of archival material or a diary when writing the memoirs and relying on his memory of the events. We have not used von Mellenthin as source unless his statements are corroborated by other sources. Using Guderian's *Panzerleader* together with Nehring's *Die Geschichte der deutschen Panzerwaffe 1916 bis 1945* will create a solid base to make a deeper analysis of the German Panzer forces. Nehring, however, does not always agree with his former commander.

For German order-of-battle research we recommend Georg Tessin's *Verbände und Truppen der Deutschen Wehrmacht und Waffen-SS.* It is very useful to confirm the existence of units but one should be aware that even if a subordinated unit to a division exists it does not necessarily need to be with its parent division. Other helpful reference works on the German Army are *Das Heer* by B.Müller-Hildebrand, *Panzertruppen* edited by Thomas L. Jentz, *Die Panzergrenadiere* by F.M. von Senger und Etterlin and *Die Gepanzerten und Motorisierten Deutschen Grossverbände 1935–1945* by Rolf Stoves.

For the order of battle for the Red Army the use of *Boevoy Sostav*

Sovetskoy Armii is a must. There a Soviet OoB is listed for the first of every month. One disadvantage is that the work is only available on microfiche. Charles Sharp's book *The Soviet Order of Battle in World War II* is very helpful for T/O&E organization of Soviet units. A good study of Soviet offensive methods during 1942 and 1943 is David Glantz's *From the Don to the Dnepr*.

Owing to the recent political changes, much new archival material has become available from Russian archives. Hopefully this will improve our knowledge and understanding of the war on the eastern front. In *Rysskii Arkhiv: Velikaya Otechestvennaya 4(4), Kurskaya Bitva, Dokumenti i Materiali 27 Marta – 23 Avgusta 1943 goda* several archival documents have been published which deal with the battles around Kursk. Sometimes parts of these documents have been included or referred to in Soviet memoirs. Now we have the possibility to see entire documents, although the work does not contain all the information one had hoped for on the battle.

ARCHIVES

Bundesarchiv-Militärarchiv Freiburg (BA-MA)

OKH (Army High Command)
BA-MA RH 2/60
- OKH, Gen.St.d.H./Org.Abt.Nr.I/2000/44 geh. H.Qu.den 25.4.1994. Festlegung der Stärkebegriffe.
BA-MA RH 2/340K
- *Zahlenmäßige Übersicht über die Verteilung der AOK, Gen.Kdos., Divn. und Heerestruppen, Stand 15.6.1942.*
BA-MA RH 2/429
- Überschlägige Kräfteberechnung für das Jahr 1943 und ihre Auswirkung auf die Kampfkraft der Ostfront. OKH Org.Abt. den 8.8.1942.
- Gen.St.d.Heeres/Org.Abt. den 20.9.1942.
BA-MA RH 2/1326
- OKH Gen.St.d.H./Gen.Qu.Abt. H. Vers./Qu. 1 Nr 1/0740/41 g.Kdos. den 20. Juni 1941.
- General der Artillerie beim Ob. d. H. (Ia) Nr 132/41 g.K.Chef.S. den 20. Juni 1941.
BA-MA RH 2/1343
- Charts on losses and replacements on the eastern front compiled by OKH.

BA-MA RH 2/1341
- OKH Org.Abt. I Nr. I/18280/44 g.Kdos H.Qu., den 23. Juli 1944.

BA-MA RH 2/2101
- Fremde Heere Ost (IIc) 10.10.1944 Sow.russ.Panzer- und Sturmgeschütz-Verluste 1944.

General Inspector for Armoured Forces
BA-MA RH 10/48
- Pz.Offz b. Chef Gen.std.H.Bb Nr 562/43 g.Kdos v.14.8.1943.

BA-MA RH10/60
- Entwicklung der Panzerlage bei Pz.Abt. 51 und 52 (Panther)18.8.1943.

BA-MA RH 10/61
- Pz-Lage Ost (Nach Gen.Qu.) 1943.

BA-MA RH 10/62
- StuG-Lage.

BA-MA RH 10/63
- PAK-Lage Ost.

BA-MA RH 10/64
- Hgr.Süd meldet Ausfälle an Pz. und Stug.

BA-MA RH 10/65
- Hgr.Mitte meldet Ausfälle an Pz. und Stug.

BA-MA RH 10/77
- Panzerverluste Ost seit 1.Juli 1943.

BA-MA RH 10/101
- Der General Inspekteur der Panzertruppen: Freie Gliederung 1944.

BA-MA RH 10/114
- Der General Inspekteur der Panzertruppen 15.1.45: Deutsche Panzer-verluste im Osten in der Zeit vom 22.6.41 bis 31.12.44.

BA-MA RH 10/141
- Divisional Report 2. Panzer Division 1.7.1943/1.9.1943.

BA-MA RH 10/142
- Divisional Report 3. Panzer Division 30.6.1943/1.8.1943/31.8.1943.

BA-MA RH 10/143
- Divisional Report 4. Panzer Division 4.7.1943/31.7.1943/31.8.1943.

BA-MA RH 10/145
- Divisional Report 6. Panzer Division 1.7.1943/1.9.1943.

BA-MA RH 10/146
- Divisional Report 7. Panzer Division 1.7.1943/1.8.1943/1.9.1943.

BA-MA RH 10/148
- Divisional Report 9. Panzer Division 1.7.1943/1.8.1943/1.9.1943.

BA-MA RH 10/149

- Divisional Report 11. Panzer Division 1.7.1943/1.8.1943/1.9.1943.
BA-MA RH 10/150
- Divisional Report 12. Panzer Division 1.7.1943/1.9.1943.
BA-MA RH 10/155
- Divisional Report 18. Panzer Division 1.7.1943/1.8.1943/1.9.1943.
BA-MA RH 10/156
- Divisional Report 19. Panzer Division 1.7.1943/1.9.1943.
BA-MA RH 10/157
- Divisional Report 20. Panzer Division 1.7.1943/1.8.1943/1.9.1943.
BA-MA RH 10/159
- Divisional Report 23. Panzer Division 1.7.1943/1.8.1943.
BA-MA RH 10/209
- Divisional Report Großdeutschland 1.8.1943/1.9.1943.
BA-MA RH 10/220
- Meldung s.Pz.Abt. 503. 1.7.1943./1.8.1943/1.9.1943.
BA-MA RH 10/246
- Meldung 656. PzJg.Rgt 4.7.1943.
- Verluste 656.sPzJg Reg. 1.7.1943-1.8.1943.
- Meldung Pz.Jg. Abt. 616.(SF) 1.7.1943/1.8.1943.
BA-MA RH 10/306
- 814.Panzer Engineer Kompanie Meldung 1.10.1943.
BA-MA RH 10/312
- Divisional Report 1.SS-PzGr Division 1.7.1943.
BA-MA RH 10/313
- Divisional Report 2.SS-PzGr Division 1.7.1943/1.8.1943/1.9.1943.
BA-MA RH 10/314
- Divisional Report 3.SS-PzGr Division 1.7.1943/1.8.1943/1.9.1943.
BA-MA RH 10/316
- Divisional Report SS-Wiking Division 1.7.1943./1.8.1943./1.9.1943.
BA-MA RH 10/348
- Oberkommando des Heeres H.Qu.OKH den 2.März 1944, des Solls an Panzerschreck und Panzerfaust.
BA-MA RH 10/349
- Verteilung der Pz.Fahrz. Bd. ab Mai 43.

1st Panzer Army
BA-MA RH 21-1/98
- Pz.A.O.K.1 Ia Meldung 3.7.1943.

2nd Army
BA-MA RH 20-2/494

- Anlage 1 zu A.O.K.2. Ia Kampfstärkemeldung 4.7.1943.
- A.O.K.2.a Ia 6.7.1943: Gefechtstärke der Gr.Btl stand 5.7.1943.

2nd Panzer Army
BA-MA RH 21-2/509
- Meldung 6.6.1943 Pz.A.O.K.2.
BA-MA RH 21-2/v.796b.
- Pz.A.O.K.2.Abt. Ia.Waffenausfälle in der Zeit vom 1.7.1943–31.7 einschl.

4th Panzer Army
BA-MA RH 21-4/118
- KTB Ia Tagesmeldungen und Nachmeldungen v. II.SS-Pz-Korps z. Pz.A.O.K.4.
BA-MA RH 21-4/133
- Kriegsgliederung Pz.A.O.K. 4.6.7.1943.
BA-MA RH 21-4/422
- Pz.A.O.K. 4, Anlage 7 zum KTB Meldungen (Beute, Verpflegungs-stärken) von 1.7.1943 bis 31.12.1943.
BA-MA RH 21-4/450
- Pz.A.O.K.4.O.Qu. Anlage 11 zum KTB Tätigkeitsberichte v.d. Abteilungen.
- 12.7-13.7 Nachtmeldung Pz.A.O.K.4.O.Qu. Anlage zu KTB, Akten-notiz 13.7.1943.
- Bergung der Pz.Kpfw. V ('Panther') im Zuge der Absetzbewegung ab 18.7.43, Abt. V den 20. Juli 1943.
BA-MA RH 21-4/451
- Pz.A.O.K.4 O.Qu. Anlage 11 zum KTB Tätigkeitsberichte v.d. Abteilungen.

8th Army (Army Detachment Kempf)
RH 20-8/91,
- Meldung XXXXII.Korps. 1.7.1943.
BA-MA RH 20-8/97
- KTB AOK 8 Ia Personelle Verluste für die Zeit vom 5.7-20.7.1943.
- KTB Ia AOK 8 Panzerlage.

9th Army
BA-MA RH 20-9/135
- Kriegsgliederung Gruppe Weiss 30.6.1943.
BA-MA RH 20-9/339

- AOK 9 Abt. IIa Verluste.

BA-MA RH 20-9/446

- A.O.Kraft O.U. An gep.kfz sind eingetroffen.

Corps

BA-MA RH 24-3/148

- III.PzK. Ic an Armee-Abt. Kempf Ic. Gesamtbeute des III.PzK. Juli 1943.

BA-MA RH 24-11/76

- Meldung Korps Raus.
- Gliederung der Artillerie und Flak beim Gen.Kdo Raus 2.7.1943.

BA-MA RH 24-11/77

- Meldung 22.7.1943 Gen.Kdo.zbV Raus Ia. Beutemeldung.

BA-MA RH 24-20/49

- Gliederung der Artillerie des XX.A.K Stand vom 9.7.1943.
- Gen.Kdo. XX.AK./Abt. IIa Verlustmeldung Juli 1943.

BA-MA RH 24-23/125

- Meldung XXIII.AK. Juli 1943.

BA-MA RH 24-23/126

- Abt Ia Meldung von 3.7.1943.
- Meldung 10.Pzgr Div 1.8.1943.
- Panzergrenadier Division Großdeutschland Zustandsbericht vom 1.8.1943.

BA-MA RH 24-23/371

- Gen.Kdo. XXIII.AK. Abt IIa Verlustmeldung Juli 1943.

BA-MA RH 24-46/91

- Gen.Kdo. XXXXVI.PzK. KTB nr 7
- Meldung 4.Panzer Division 3.7.1943.
- Kriegsgliederung der Stossgruppe Oberst von Manteuffel Stand 1.6.1943.
- XXXXVI.Pzkorps Abt. IIb K.gefStd 25.10.43. Personelle Verluste durch Feind einwirkung in der Zeit vom 1.6 bis 15.8.1943.

BA-MA RH 24-46/98

- Fernschreiben von XXXXVI.PzK. an gruppe Weiss 3.7.1943.

BA-MA RH 24-52/159

- Anlageheft vom 21.7 bis 26.7.1943 zum KTB Nr. 6 LII.A.K.Ia.

BA-MA RH24 - 52/316

- Meldung 255.ID vom 28.6.1943.

LII.AK. 42241/5. (old diary number)

- Anlageheft Nr.1 vom 6.7.43 bis 10.7.43 zum Kriegstagebuch Nr.6.

LVII.PzK. 54633/7 (old diary number)

- Fernschreiben an Pz.A.O.K.1 Ia 4.7.1943.
BA-MA RS 2-2/17
- Gen.Kdo.II.SS-Pz.Korps der Korpsarzt.
BA-MA RS 2-2/18
- Gen.Kdo.II.SS-Pz.Korps 23.7.1943.
- Tagesmeldung von 13.7.1943 LSSAH.
BA-MA RS 2-2/25
- II.SS.Pz.Korps Anlagen.

Divisions
BA-MA RH 26-6/52
- Anlageband V zum Kriegstagenbuch Nr. 7 6.ID.
BA-MA RH 26 - 36/31
- 36.ID KTB Nr. 7 vom 1.7 - 30.9.1943.
BA-MA RH 26-167/29
- Anlagenband Kriegstagebuch des Div. Kdos der 167.ID.
BA-MA RH 26-332/21
- 332.ID.Ia Meldung an Gen.Kdo. röm. 48.PzK. Juli 1943.
BA-MA RH 27-2/43
- 2.PzD KTB Anlageband 1b.
BA-MA RH 27 - 9/15(a)
- 9.Panzer.Div/Pz.Reg 33. 1.7.1943.
- Fernschreiben an Gen.Kdo. XXXXI.PzK. West 3.7.1943.
- Tagesmedlung 9.PzD I.a 9.7.1943.
BA-MA RH 27 - 11/72
- 11.PD KTB Anlageband.
BA-MA RH 27 - 11/73
- 11.PD KTB Anlageband.
BA-MA RH 27 -11/74
- 11.PzD KTB Anlageband.
BA-MA RH 27-19/14
- Anlagenband 5 zum KTB Nr 2 19. Pz.Div.
BA-MA RH 27-20/164
- 20.PzD KTB Anlageband Teil 7.

National Archives and Records Administration, Washington, DC

Microfilm Publications
T 78 roll 411
- OKH Org. Abt. (I) Nr. I/4325/43 g.Kdos. H.Qu., den 18.9.43. (Frame 6379596).

T 78 roll 414
- OKH/Gen.St.d.H./Org.Abt. Nr. I/18941/44 g.Kdos, v. 7.9.44 (Frame 6383112-4).
- Personelle blutige Verluste des Feldheeres, Berichtigte Meldung für die Zeit 1.6.1944 bis 10.1.1945. Den Heeresarzt im OKH Gen.St.d.H./ Gen.Qu.Az. 1335 c/d (Iib) (Frame 6383235).

T 312 roll 317
- AOK 9/O.Qu., Beilage zum KTB, Tätigkeitsbericht der Abteilung IVa, vom 27.6. bis 4.7.1943 (Frame 7885270).

T 312 roll 1665
- KTB AOK 2, Ia, Fernschreiben 5.7.43, *Betr*: Kampfstärken (Frame 001099f).

T 314 roll 1169
- Versorgungslageberichte des Gen.Kdo. XXXXVIII. Pz.Korps Abt. Qu. vom 2.7.1943 bis 30.10.1943, Anlageband 3 zum KTB Nr. 2. The frames used are: 000752, 000755, 000758, 000761, 000765, 000768, 000770, 000777, 000788, 000791, 000794.

Müller-Hillebrand, H.B., *German Tank-Strength and Loss Statistics* (Manuscript at National Archives, Washington, DC, MS # P-059).

PUBLISHED WORKS

Books

Aders, G. and W. Held, *Jagdgeschwader 51 'Mölders'* (Motorbuch, Stuttgart, 1993).
    Unit history of the Jagdgeschwader 51.
Ananyev, I.M., *Tankovye Armii v nastuplenii* (Voenizdat, Moscow, 1988).
    General history about the use of Soviet tank armies in operations.
Arkhipova, T.I. (ed.), *Kurskaya Bitva* (Tsentralno-Chernozemnoe, Voronezh, 1968).
    A collection of essays dealing with different aspects of Kursk.
Armstrong, Richard, *Red Army Tank Commanders, the Armoured Guards* (Schiffer, Atglen, 1994).
    Personal portraits of six Tank Army commanders, Katukov and Rotmistrov among them.

Babadzhanyan, A.Kh, N.-K. Popel, M.A. Shalin and I.M. Krauchenko, *Lyuki Otkryli v Berline* (Voenizdat, Moscow, 1973).
Unit history of the 1st Guards Tank Army.

Barker, A.J., *Stuka Ju-87* (Bison, London, 1980).
A short history about the Ju-87.

Bellamy, Chris, *Red God of War, Soviet Artillery and Rocket Forces* (Brassey's, London, 1986).
Deals with methods used and developed by the Soviet artillery.

Blumenson, Martin, *Breakout and Pursuit* (Office of the Chief of Military History, Dept. of the Army, Washington, DC, 1961).
US Army in Operation Cobra.

Boevoy Sostav Sovetskoy Armii, chast III (Voenizdat, Moscow, 1972).
Monthly Order of Battle for Red Army, the first of every month.

Boog, H., *Die Deutsche Luftwaffenführung 1935–1945* (Deutsche Verlags-Anstalt, Stuttgart, 1982).
History of the Luftwaffe High Command.

Bryja, Marcin, *Artyleria niemiecka 1933–45* (Wyadawnictwo Militaria, Warzaw, 1996).
Technical directory of all guns, mortars and rocket artillery in the Hitler war machine.

Buchner, Alex, *Das Handbuch der Deutschen Infanterie 1939–1945* (Podzun-Pallas, Friedberg, 1989).
The organization and equipment of the German infantry.

Bunke, Erich, *Der Osten blieb unser Schicksal 1939–1944* (Selbstverlag, Wietze, 1991).
Memoirs of a member of the AT battalion in the 31st Infantry Division.

Chamberlain, Peter, Hilary Doyle, and Thomas Jentz, *Encyclopedia of German Tanks of World War Two* (Arms & Armour Press, London, 1978).
Technical directory of all armoured vehicles in the Hitler war machine.

Chistyakov, I.M. (ret.), *Po Prikazu Rodiny – Boevoi put 6-i Gvardeiskoy Armii v Velikoi Otechestennoi Voine 1941–1945* (Voenizdat, Moscow, 1971).
Unit history of 6th Guards Army.

Cross, Robin, *Citadel, the battle of Kursk* (Michael O'Mara Books, London, 1993).
Concerning the German offensive operation.

Dierich, Wolfgang, *Kampfgeschwader 55 'Greif'* (Motorbuch, Stuttgart, 1994).
Unit history of Kampfgeschwader 55.

—, *Die Verbände der Luftwaffe 1935–1945* (Motorbuch, Stuttgart, 1976).

Short unit histories of Luftwaffe units.

Doyle, H. and T. Jentz, *Panther Variants 1942–45* (Osprey, London, 1997).
A short history of all the variants of the Panther tank.

Dragunskii, D.A., *Gody v Brone* (Voenizdat, Moscow, 1973).
Officer in 1st Mech Bde (3rd Mechanized Corps).

Dupuy, T.N., G.P. Hayes, P. Martell, V.E. Lyons and J.A.C. Andrews, *A Study of Breakthrough Operations* (Hero, Arlington, VA, 1976).
A report which contains a translation of the war diary of 48th Panzer Corps 4–15 July 1943.

Dupuy, T.N., *Numbers, Predictions and War* (Hero, Arlington, VA, 1985).
The analysis of historical battles.

—, *Hitler's Last Gamble* (Airlife, Shrewsbury, 1995).
An analysis of the Ardennes offensive of 1944.

Edwards, Roger, *Panzer, A Revolution in Warfare, 1939–1945* (Arms & Armour, London, 1989).
A general history of the German Panzer forces.

Egorov, P.Ya, I.V. Krivoborsky, N.K. Ivlev and A.I. Rogalevich, *Dorogami Podeg – Boevoi put 5-i Gvardeiskoy Armii* (Voenizdat, Moscow, 1969).
Unit history of 5th Guards Tank Army.

Ellis, John, *Brute Force* (André Deutsch, London, 1990).
A general history of the war from the viewpoint of the production of war material.

Ellis, L.F., *Victory in the West*, Vol. I (HMSO, London, 1962).
The Western Front 1944–45.

Engelmann, Joachim, *Zitadelle 1943, Die grösste Panzerschlacht im Osten* (Podzun-Pallas, Friedberg, undated).
A photo-history of the offensive.

—, *Das Buch der Artillerie 1939–1945* (Podzun-Pallas, Friedberg, 1983).
Photo-history of the German artillery.

Erickson, John, *The Road to Berlin* (Grafton, London, 1983).
Deals with Red Army during the last years of the war on the eastern front.

Erickson, J. and D. Dilkes, *Barbarossa – The Axis and the Allies* (Edinburgh University Press, Edinburgh, 1994).
Deals with several aspects concerning the eastern front.

Foerster, R.G. (ed.), *Gezeitenwechsel im Zweiten Weltkrieg?* (Mittler & Sohn, Berlin, 1996).
A collection of essays about the spring and summer of 1943.

Förster, Jörgen (ed.), *Stalingrad* (R. Piper, München, 1993), p. 322.
A collection of essays about Stalingrad and the eastern front in the winter of 1942/43.

Gätzschmann, Kurt, *Panzerabteilung 51 Heerestruppe, II. / Panzerregiment 33, 9.Panzerdivision 1943–1945* (Selbstverlag, 1984).
Unit history of 51st Panzer battalion (Panthers).

Geschichte der 3.Panzer-Division Berlin–Brandenburg 1935–1945 (Selbstverlag, Berlin, 1967).
Unit history of 3rd Panzer Division.

Geschichte des Großen Vaterländischen Krieges der Sowjetunion (Deutscher Militärverlag, East Berlin, 1965).
A translation of Soviet works on the history of war.

Geschichte des Zweiten Weltkrieges (Deutscher Militärverlag, East Berlin, 1975–1985).
A translation of Soviet works on the history of war.

Getman, A.L., *Tanki idut na Berlin* (Voenizdat, Moscow, 1982).
Unit history of 6th Tank Corps (later 11th Guards Tank Corps).

Glantz, David, *From the Don to the Dnepr, Soviet Offensive Operations December 1942–August 1943* (Frank Cass, London, 1991).
One chapter deals with the offensive against Belgorod and Kharkov in August 1943.

Graser, Gerhard, *Zwischen Kattegat und Kaukasus, Weg und Kämpfe der 198.Infanterie-Division 1939–1945* (Selbstverlag, Tübingen, 1961).
Unit history of 198th Infantry Division.

Green, W.C. and W.R. Reeves, (eds), *The Soviet Military Encyclopedia, Abridged English Language Edition*, Vols A–F (Westview Press, Boulder, CO, 1993).
A translated and abridged version of the Soviet Military Encyclopedia.

Green, William, *War Planes of Second World War, Fighters*, Vol. III (MacDonald, London, 1968).
Technical dictionary of fighter aircraft.

Griehl, Manfred and Joachim Dressel, *Flugzeuge gegen Panzer, Deustche Panzerjäger und Schlachtflugzeuge* (Podzun-Pallas, Friedberg, 1990).
A short history about German methods of tank-hunting with aircraft during World War II.

Groehler, Olaf, *Geschichte des Luftkriegs 1910–1970* (Militärverlag der DDR, Berlin, 1975).
A general history of air warfare from 1910 to 1970.

—, *Geschichte des Luftkriegs 1910–1980* (Militärverlag der DDR, Berlin, 1981).
A general history of air warfare from 1910 to 1980.

Grylev, A.N., *Dnepr, Karpaty, Krym* (Nauka, Moscow, 1970).
The campaigns to liberate western Ukraine winter/spring 1944.

Guderian, Heinz, *Panzer Leader* (Futura, London, 1982).

Inspector General of the German Armoured Forces.

—, *Panzerleader* (Natraj, New Dehli, 1985).

Inspector General of the German Armoured Forces.

Gunston, Bill, *Allied Fighters of World War II* (Salamander, London, 1981).

Technical dictionary of fighter aircraft.

Gurkin, V.V. and A.E. Ivashchenko, *5-ya Gvardeiskaya Kalinkovichskaya* (Voenizdat, Moscow, 1979).

Unit history of 5th Guards Rocket Artillery Division.

Hahn, Fritz, *Waffen und Geheimwaffen des deutschen Heeres 1933–45*, Band 1–2 (Bernard & Graefe, Koblenz, 1986 and 1987).

Deals with all weapon systems used by the German Army.

Hallion, Richard P., *Strike from the Sky. The History of Battlefield Air Attack 1911–1945* (Airlife, Shrewsbury, 1989).

A history of tactical air support up to 1945.

Harris, J.P. and F.N. Toase (eds), *Armoured Warfare* (Batsford, London, 1990).

Essays concerning the development of armoured forces.

Haupt, Werner, *Das Buch der Infanterie* (Podzun-Pallas, Friedberg, 1982).

A general history of the German infantry during World War II.

—, *Die Schlachten der Heeresgruppe Mitte 1941–1944* (Podzun-Pallas, Friedberg, 1983).

The soldier's viewpoint in Armygroup Centre from 1941 to 1944.

Healy, Mark, *Kursk 1943 (Campaign Series No. 16)* (Osprey, London, 1992).

A short history of Operation Zitadelle.

Hinze, Rolf, *Die 19.Panzer-Division 1939–1945 (im Bild)* (Podzun-Pallas, Friedberg, undated).

Photo-history of 19th Panzer Division.

Hogg, Ian, *German Artillery of World War Two* (Book Club Edition, London, 1975).

Technical directory of all guns in the Hitler war machine.

Istoriya Vtoroi mirovoi voiny 1939–1945, Vols 4–8 (Voenizdat, Moscow, 1976).

A general history of the war.

Jentz, Thomas L., *Panther Tank* (Schiffer Military History, Atgen, 1995).

Deals with all aspects of the Panther Tank.

—, (ed.), *Panzertruppen 1943–45* (Schiffer Military History, Atgen, 1996).

Combat experience and organization of Panzer regiments, battalions and companies.

Jukes, Geoffrey, *Kursk – The Clash of Armour* (Macdonald & Co., London, and Ballantine, New York, 1969).
A battle history.

Jung, Herman, *Die Ardennen-Offensiv* (Musterschmitt, Göttingen, 1971).
A German account of the Ardennes offensive 1944.

Kardashov, B., *5 Iyulya 1943* (Molodaja Gvardija, Moscow, 1983).
A short history of Kursk.

Katukov, M.E., *Na Ostrie Glavnogo Udara* (Voenizdat, Moscow, 1974).
Commander of 1st Tank Army.

Kehrig, M., *Stalingrad* (Deutsche Verlagsanstalt, Stuttgart, 1974).
A thorough analysis of the battle for Stalingrad.

Kleine, Egon and Volkmar Kühn, *Tiger, Die Geschichte einer legendären Waffe 1942–1945* (Motorbuch, Stuttgart, 1981).
Unit histories for all Tiger units.

Klink, Ernst, *Das Gesetz des Handels, Die Operation 'Zitadelle' 1943* (Deutsche Verlags-Anstalt, Stuttgart, 1966).
The history of Operation Zitadelle. (The best available account about the German forces.)

Knobelsdorff, Otto von, *19. Panzer-Division* (Verlag Hans-Henning Podzun, Bad Nauheim, 1958).
Unit history of 19th Panzer Division.

Kolomiets, M. and M. Svirin, *Kurskaya Duga* (EksPrint NV, Moscow, 1998).
A short history of the battle.

Koltunov, G.A. and B.G. Solovev, *Kurskaya Bitva* (Voenizdat, Moscow, 1970).
This book is the best Soviet account of the battle.

Konev, I.S., *Zapiski Komanduyushcheyo Frontom 1943–1944* (Nauka, Moscow, 1972).
Commander of the Steppe Front.

Kozhevnikov, M.N., *The Command and Staff of the Soviet Army Air Force in the Great Patriotic War 1941–1945* (Moscow, 1977) (translated Washington, DC).
General history of the Soviet air force during the war.

Kozlov, M.A. (ed.), *V plameni srazhenii* (Voenizdat, Moscow, 1973).
Unit history of 13th Army.

Krivosheyev, G.F., *Grif Sekretnosti Sniat* (Voenizdat, Moscow, 1993).
Soviet military losses in all wars fought by the Soviets.

Krupchenko, I.E. (ed.), *Sovetskie Tankovye Voiska 1941–45* (Voenizdat, Moscow, 1973).
General history about Soviet tank forces during the war.

Kurowski, Franz, *Der Panzerkrieg* (Moewig, München, 1980).
General history of the German Panzer forces.

Lehmann, Rudolf, *The Leibstandarte* Vol. III (J.J. Fedorowicz, Winnipeg, 1990).
Unit history of the 1st SS-Panzergrenadier Division.

Losik, O. (ret.), *Stroitelstvo i boevoe primenenie Sovetskik Tankovych Voisk v gody Velikoi Otechestvennoj Voiny* (Voenizdat, Moscow, 1979).
General history of the Soviet tank forces during the war.

MacDonald, C.B., *The Battle of the Bulge* (Weidenfeld & Nicholson, London, 1984).
A battle history of the Ardennes offensive 1944.

Madej, Victor, *The Russo-German War, July 1943–May 1945* (Valor, Allentown, PA, 1986).
Eastern front, based on German material.

Manstein, Erich von, *Soldat im 20.Jahrhundert* (Bernard & Graefe, Bonn, 1997).
A book which deals with von Manstein's whole active life not just World War II.

—, *Verlorene Siege* (Athenäum-Verlag, Bonn, 1958).
Memoirs of the Commander of Army Group South.

Manteuffel, Hasso von, *7.Panzer-Division 1935–1945* (Podzun-Pallas, Friedberg, undated).
Photo-history of 7th Panzer Division.

Mellenthin, F.W. von, *German Generals of World War II* (University of Oklahoma Press, Norman, OK, 1977).
Short portraits of German commanders, von Manstein and Model among them.

—, *Panzerbattles* (Futura, London, 1979, first print 1955).
The memoirs of the officer who was chief of staff of XXXXVIII Panzer Corps during Zitadelle.

Merker, Ludwig (ed.), *Das Buch der 78.Sturmdivision* (Selbstverlag, Tübingen/Neckar, undated).
Unit history of the 78th Assault Division.

Montgomery, B.L., *Normandy to the Baltic* (Hutchinson, London, 1946).
Deals with the western front, 1944–45.

Morozova.V.P. (ed.), *Kurskaya Bitva* (Tsentralno-Chernozemnoe, Voronezh, 1973).
A collection of essays dealing with different aspects of Kursk.

Moskalenko, K.S., *Ha Yugo Zapadnom Napravlenii 1943–45* (Nauka, Moscow, 1973).
Memoirs of the Commander 40th Army.

Moskalenko, K.S. (ed.), *Bitva na Kurskoi duge* (Nauka, Moscow, 1975).
A collection of essays dealing with different aspects of Kursk.

Müller-Hildebrand, B., *Das Heer*, Volume III (Mittler & Sohn, Frankfurt am Main, 1969).
The development and organization of German ground forces from 1941 to 1945.

Murray, Williamson, *The Luftwaffe 1933–45, Strategy for Defeat* (Brassey's, Washington/London, 1996).
A history of the Luftwaffe's battle losses.

Nehring, Walther, *Die Geschichte der deutschen Panzerwaffe 1916 bis 1945* (Weltbild, Augsburg, 1995).
General history of the German Panzer forces by Panzergeneral Nehring.

Overy, Richard, *Russia's War* (Penguin Books, New York, 1998).
A general history of the war on the eastern front.

Paul, Wolfgang, *Brennpunkte. Die Geschichte der 6.Panzerdivision (1.leichte) 1937–1945* (Biblio, Osnabrück, 1993).
Unit history of the 6th Panzer Division.

—, *Geschichte der 18.Panzer Division 1940–1943 (mit Geschichte der 18.Artillerie Division 1943–1944)* (Selbstverlag, Freiburg, 1975).
Unit history of the 18th Panzer Division.

—, *Panzer-General Walther K.Nehring* (Motorbuch, Stuttgart, 1986).
A biography of General Walther Nehring (Commander XXIV Panzer Corps).

Pawlas, Karl R., *Datenblätter für Heeres-Waffen, Fahrzeuge und Gerät* (Publizistisches Archiv für Militär- und Waffenwesen, Nürnberg, 1976).
Technical information about German equipment.

Perrett, Bryan, *A History of Blitzkrieg* (Robert Hale, London, 1983).
Concerning armoured warfare, mostly World War II.

—, *Knights of the Black Cross. Hitler's Panzerwaffe and its Leaders* (Robert Hale, London, 1986).
A general history of the German Panzer forces.

Plocher, Hermann, *The German Air Force versus Russia 1943* (US Air Force Historical Studies, No. 155, Arno Press, New York, 1967).
A post-war evaulation made by Luftwaffe personnel for the US Air Force.

Price, Alfred, *Focke Wulf Fw 190 in Combat* (Sutton, Stroud, 1998).
A history of the use of the Fw 190 in combat.

—, *Luftwaffe Handbook 1939–1945* (second edition) (Ian Allan, Shepperton, 1986).

An introductory handbook concerning the Luftwaffe.

Radzievskii, A.I, *Tankovii Udar* (Voenizdat, Moscow, 1977).
General history about the use of Soviet tank armies in operations.

Rebentisch, Ernst (ed.), *Zum Kaukasus und zu den Tauern, die Geschichte der 23.Panzer-Division 1939–1945* (Selbstverlag, Esslingen a.N., 1963).
Unit history for 23rd Panzer Division.

Restayn, Jean, *Tiger I on the Eastern Front* (Histoire et Collections, Paris, 1999).
Photo-history of Tiger units on the eastern front.

Rokossovsky, K., *A Soldier's Duty* (Progress, Moscow, 1970).
Commander of the Central Front.

Rotmistrov, P.A., *Stal' naya gvardiya* (Voenizdat, Moscow, 1984).
Commander of the 5th Guards Tank Army.

Rubbel, Alfred (ed.), *Erinnerungen an die Tigerabteilung 503 1942–1945* (Selbstverlag, Bassum, 1990).
Unit history of the 503rd Heavy Tank Battalion (Tiger).

Ruppental, *US Army in World War II, Logistical Support of the Armies*, Vol. I (Office of the Chief of Military History, Dept of the Army, Washington, DC, 1953).

Rysskii Archiv: Velikaya Otechestvennaya 4(4), Kurskaya Bitva, Dokumenti i Materiali 27 Marta–23 Avgusta 1943 goda (Terra, Moscow, 1997).
Selected archival documents dealing with the battle.

Samchuk, I.A., P.G. Skachko, I.N. Babikov and I.L. Gnedoi, *Ot Volgi do Elby u Pragi, Kratkii Ocherk oboevom puti 5-i Gvardeiskoy Armii* (Voenizdat, Moscow, 1970).
Unit history of the 5th Guards Army.

Samchuk, I.A., *Gvardeiskaya Poltavskaya* (Voenizdat, Moscow, 1965).
Unit history of the 97th Guards Rifle Division.

Samchuk, I.A. and P.G. Skachko, *Atakuyot Desantniki* (Voenizdat, Moscow, 1975).
Unit history for the 9th Guards Airborne Rifle Division.

Saucken, Dietrich von, *4.Panzer-Division, Der Russlandfeldzug von Mai 1943 bis Mai 1945* (Selbstverlag, Coburg, 1968).
Unit history of the 4th Panzer Division.

Schaub, Oskar, *Aus der Geschichte Panzer-Grenadier-Regiment 12 (S.R.12)* (Selbstverlag, Bergisch Gladbach, 1957).
Unit history of the 12th Panzergrenadier Regiment (4th Pz Div).

Schäufler, Hans, *So lebten und starben sie, Das Buch von Panzer-Regiment 35* (Kameradschaft ehem.Pz Regt 35, Bamberg, undated).
Short essays about the 35th Panzer Regiment during the war.

Schramm, P.E., *Kriegstagebuch des oberkammandos der Wehrmacht*

(Wehrmachtführungsstab), Vol. III (Bernarde Graefe, Frankfurt am Main, 1962).

The war diary of the OKW operations section.

Schrodek, G.W., *Ihr Glaube galt dem Vaterland, Geschichte des Panzer-Regiments 15* (Schild, Munich, 1976).

Unit history of the 15th Panzer Regiment (11th Pz Div).

Schwabedissen, W., *The Russian Air Force in the Eyes of German Commanders* (Arno Press, New York, 1960).

The German view of the Red Air Force during the war.

Scutts, Jerry, *JG 54, Jagdgeschwader 54 'Grünherz'* (Airlife, Shrewsbury, 1992).

Unit history of the Jagdgeschwader 54.

Senger und Etterlin, F.M. von, *Die Kampfpanzer von 1916–1966* (J.F. Lehmanns, München, 1966).

Deals with tanks from 1916 to 1966.

—, *Die Panzergrenadiere* (J.F. Lehmanns, München, 1961).

General history of the organization and equipment of the Panzer-grenadiers.

16-ya Vozdushnaya (Voenno-istoricheskii ocherk oboevom puty 16-i Vozdushnoy Armii 1942–1945) (Voenizdat, Moscow, 1973).

Unit history of the 16th Air Army.

Sharp, Charles C., *Soviet Order of Battle in World War II*, Vol. II, *School of Battle* (George F. Nafziger, West Chester, OH, 1995).

Soviet Mechanized Corps and Guards Armoured units 1942 to 1945.

—, *Soviet Order of Battle in World War II*, Vol. III, *Red Storm* (George F. Nafziger, West Chester, OH, 1995).

Soviet Tank Corps and Tank Brigades 1942 to 1945.

—, *The Soviet Order of Battle in World War II*, Vol. VI, *Red Thunder* (George F. Nafziger, West Chester, OH, 1995).

The organization of Soviet artillery.

—, *Soviet Order of Battle World War II*, Vol. X, *'Red Swarm'* (George F. Nafziger, West Chester, OH, 1996).

Deals with Soviet Rifle Divisions formed 1942 to 1945.

Shores, Christopher, *Duel for the Sky: Ten Crucial Air Battles of World War II* (Doubleday, New York, 1985).

Contains a chapter about the air battles around Kursk, July 1943.

Shtemenko, C.M., *Generalnyi Shtab v Gody Voiny* (Voenizdat, Moscow, 1975).

Viewpoint of an officer belonging to the Soviet General staff.

Shukman, Harold (ed.), *Stalin's Generals* (Weidenfeld & Nicolson, London, 1993).

Short portraits of Soviet commanders, among them Rudenko, Rokossovsky and Vatutin.

Skomorokhov, N.M. (ret.), *17-ya Vozdushnaya Armiya v Boyakh ot Stalingrada do Veny* (Voenizdat, Moscow, 1977).
Unit history of the 17th Air Army.

Smol' nyi, M.K., *7000 Kilometrov v Boyakh i Pokhodakh* (Voenizdat, Moscow, 1982).
Unit history of the 161st Rifle Division.

Solowjow, B., *Wendepunkt des Zweiten Weltkrieges, Die Schlacht bei Kursk* (Pahl-Rufenstein, Köln, 1984).
A general history of the summer of 1943.

Sovetskie Voenno-Vozdushnye Sily v Velikoy Otechestvennoy Voine 1941–1945 (Voenizdat, Moscow, 1968).
General history of the Soviet air force during the war.

Spaeter, Helmuth, *Die Geschichte der Panzerkorps Großdeutschland, Band 2* (Selbstverlag, Bielefeld, 1958).
Unit history of Panzergrenadier Division Großdeutschland.

Sperker, Karl Heinrich, *Generaloberst Erhard Raus, ein Truppenführer im Ostfeldzug* (Biblio, Osnabrück, 1988).
A biography of General Raus (Commander Corps Raus).

Stacey, C.P., *The Victory Campaign, the operations in NW Europe 1944–1945* (The Queens Printer and Controller of Stationery, Ottawa, 1960).
The western front, 1944–45.

Stachura, P., D. Bernád and D. Haladej, *Henschel Hs 129 (second edition)* (MBI, Praha, 1996).
A short history of the Hs 129.

Stadler, Sylvester, *Die Offensive gegen Kursk 1943. II.SS-Panzerkorps als Stosskeil im Grosskampf* (Munin Verlag, Osnabrück, 1980).
Unit history for II SS-Panzer Corps during Operation Zitadelle.

Stapfer, H-H., *Il-2 Stormovik in action* (Squadron/Signal Publications, Carrollton, 1995).
A short history about the Il-2 and its variants.

Stoves, Rolf, *Die Gepanzerten und Motorisierten Deutschen Grossverbände 1935–1945* (Podzun-Pallas, Friedberg, 1986).
Many short unit histories, covers all divisions and brigades in the German Panzer forces.

Strauss, Franz Josef, *Geschichte der 2. (Wiener) Panzer-Division* (Kurt Vowinckel Verlag, Neckargemünd, 1977).
Unit history of the 2nd Panzer Division.

Sydnor, Charles W., *Soldiers of Destruction: The SS Death's Head Division 1933–1945* (Princeton University Press, Princeton, NJ, 1977).

Unit history of the 3rd SS-Panzergrenadier Division.

Svirin, M., *Tyazheloe Shturmovoe Orudie Ferdinand* (Armada, Moscow, 1999).

A photo-history of the Ferdinand assault gun (Elefant).

Tessin, Georg, *Verbände und Truppen der Deutschen Wehrmacht und Waffen-SS* (Mittler & Sohn, Frankfurt am Main (Vols 1–5), Biblio Verlag, Osnabrück (Vols 6–14), 1966–1975).

Lists all German units during World War II, includes a short history.

Timokhovich, I.V., *Sovetskaya aviatsiya v bitve pod Kurskom* (Voenizdat, Moscow, 1959).

History of the Soviet air force around Kursk during the spring and summer of 1943.

—, *Operativnoe iskusstvo Sovetskikh VVS v Velikoy Otechestvennoy Voine* (Voenizdat, Moscow, 1976).

General history showing how the Soviet air force conducted its operations.

Ulrich, Karl, *Wie ein Fels im Meer, Kriegsgeschichte der 3.SS Panzerdivision 'Totenkopf'* (Munin, Osnabrück, 1987).

Unit history of the 3rd SS-Panzergrenadier Division.

Vasilev, S.I. and A.P. Dikan, *Gvardeitsy Pyatnadtsatoy* (Voenizdat, Moscow, 1960).

Unit history of the 15th Guards Rifle Division.

Vasilevskii, A.M., *Delo Vsei Zhizni* (Politizdat, Moscow, 1976).

A Stavka representative's viewpoint.

Venkov, B.S. and P.P. Dudinov, *Gvardeiskaya Doblest* (Voenizdat, Moscow, 1979).

Unit history of the 70th Guards Rifle Division.

Voennoe Iskusstvo, Vtoraya Mirovaya Voina, Vol. 2 (Nauka, Moscow, 1966).

Analyses different parts of the war.

Vopersal, Wolfgang, *Soldaten, Kämpfer, Kameraden*, Band 3 (Selbstverlag, Osnabrück, 1987).

Unit history of the 3rd SS-Panzergrenadier Division.

Vyrodov, I.Ya (ret.), *V Srazheniyakh za Pobedy* (Nauka, Moscow, 1974).

Unit history of the 38th Army.

Vysotskii, F.I., M.E. Makukhin, F.M. Sarychev and M.K. Shaposhnikov, *Gvardeiskaya Tankovaya* (Voenizdat, Moscow, 1969).

Unit history of the 2nd Tank Army (later Guards).

Weidinger, Otto, *Division Das Reich*, Band IV, 1943 (Munin, Osnabrück, 1986).

Unit history of the 2nd SS-Panzergrenadier Division.

Wood, Tony and Bill Gunston, *Hitler's Luftwaffe* (Leisure Books,

Turnhout, 1984).
Technical encyclopedia for German aircraft.
Zaloga, Steven J. and James Grandsen, *Soviet Tanks and Combat Vehicles of World War II* (Arms & Armour, London, 1984).
A history of the development of Soviet tank forces and armoured vehicles.
Zaloga, S., J. Kinnear, A. Aksenov, and A. Koschchavtsev, *Stalin's Heavy Tanks 1941–1945, The KV and IS Heavy Tanks* (Concord Publications, Hongkong, 1997).
A photo-history of heavy tanks in the Red Army.
Zhadov, A.S., *Chetyre Goda Voiny* (Voenizdat, Moscow, 1978).
Commander of the 5th Guards Army.
Zhukov, G.K, *The Memoirs of Marshal Zhukov* (Natraj, New Dehli, 1985).
A Stavka representative's memoirs.
—, *Vospominaniya i Razmyshleniya* (Vols I–III) (Novosti, Moscow, 1986).
A Stavka representative's memoirs.
Ziemke, Earl F., *The German Northern Theater of Operations 1940–1945* (Dept. of the Army, Pamphlet No. 20-271, Washington, DC, 1959).
A general history concerning German operations in the Arctic.
—, *Moscow to Stalingrad* (Military Heritage Press, New York, 1988).
The eastern front from Typhoon to Stalingrad.
Zvartsev, A.M. (ret.), 3-ya *Gvardeiskaya Tankovaya* (Voenizdat, Moscow, 1982).
Unit history of the 3rd Guards Tank Army.

PERIODICALS

Air International
Vol. 54, No. 6 (June 1998), Dr Alfred Price: *Tanks for the memories*, pp. 339–43.

Aktuellt och Historiskt
1968, K.J. Mikola, Finlands Försvarsmakt 50 år.

The International TNDM Newsletter
Vol. 1 No. 6 (June 1997). R.C. Anderson Jr, *Artillery Effectiveness versus Armor*, pp. 26–30.
Istoricheskii Archiv

No. 5 1993, *Obespechit Prevoskhodstvo Sovetskikh Tankov, Donkladnye zapinksi I. V. Stalin 1942–1944*, pp. 105–15.

Journal of Soviet/Slavic Military Studies
Vol. 6, No. 4 (December 1993) Edwin Bacon, *Soviet Military Losses in World War II*, pp. 613–33.
Vol. 6, No. 4 (December 1993) Documents, *The Defense Battle for the Kursk Bridgehead, 5–15 July 1943*, pp. 656–700.
Vol. 7, No. 1 (March 1994) Documents, *Tank Forces in Defense of the Kursk Bridgehead* and *Operational Maskirovka According to Voronezh Front Experience, July–August 1943*, pp. 82–137.
Vol. 7, No. 3 (September 1994) B.V. Sokolov, *The Role of Lend–Lease in Soviet Military Efforts, 1941–1945*, pp. 567–86.
Vol. 9, No. 4 (December 1996) N. Zetterling, *Loss Rates on the Eastern Front during World War II*, pp. 895–906.
Vol. 11, No. 1 (March 1998) N. Zetterling and A. Frankson, *Analyzing World War II Eastern Front Battles*, pp. 176–203.

Voenno-Istoricheskii Zhurnal
No. 8 1967 G. Zhukov: *Ha Kurskoi duge*, pp. 69–83.
No. 9 1967 G. Zhukov: *Ha Kurskoi duge*, pp. 82–97.
No. 6 1968 Dokumenty i Materialy: *Kurskaya Bitva v Tsifrakh (period Oborony)*, pp. 58–68.
No. 7 1968 Dokumenty i Materialy: *Kurskaya Bitva v Tsifrakh (period Kontrnastupleniya)*, pp. 77–91.
No. 4 1969 V. Fedorenko: *Primenenie Tankovykh Armii dlya Resheniya Oboronitelnykh zadach*, pp. 30–40.
No. 1 1970 P. Rotmistrov: *Bronetankovye u Mekhanizirovannye Voiska v bitve pod Kurskom*, pp. 12–22.
No. 7 1971 G. Khoroshilov: *Voopuzhenie Sovetskoi Artillerii v Gody Velikoj Otetjestvennoj Vojny*, pp. 81–7.
No. 9 1972 A. Vinskij: *Primenenie Inzhenernikh Zagrazhdenii v Oborone po Opytu Velikoy Otechestvennoy Voyni*, pp. 72–7.
No. 10 1972 I. Ananev: *Sozdanie Tankovykh Armii i Sovershenstvovanie ikh Organizatsionnoy Struktury*, pp. 38–47.
No. 7 1973 A. Babadzhanyan: *1-ya Tankovaya Armiya v Oboronitelnom Srazhenii*, pp. 41–50.
No. 8 1973 A. Babadzhanyan: *1-ya Tankovaya Armiya v Belgorodsko-Kharkovskoy Operatsii*, pp. 23–31.
No. 8 1973 G. Biryukov and A. Tokmakov: *Artilleriya v oborone 13-i Armii*, pp. 41–8.

No. 10 1973 V. Lupshev and N. Silin: *He otstupili ni na shag*, pp. 53–7.

No. 7 1974 A. Sidorenko: *Oborona 23-go Gvardeiskogo Strelkovogo Korpusa*, pp. 38–45.

No. 9 1974 R. Kiudmaa: *Artilleriyskoe Obespechenie Vvoda v Proryv 1-i i 5-i Gvardeiskoi Tankovykh Armii*, pp. 43–8.

No. 11 1974 G. Biryukov and S. Totrov: *Nekotorye Voprosy Primeneniya Artillerii vo Frontovykh Operatsiyakh*, pp. 11–17.

No. 7 1979 I. Zagryadskii: *Boevye Deystviya 27 Oiptabr na Oboyanskom Napravlenii (5–10 iyulya 1943)*, pp. 38–41.

No. 2 1980 N. Azyasskii, *O Vklade Partisan v razgrom gruppi armii 'Tsentr'*, pp. 29–35.

No. 5 1983 Dokumenti i Materiali: *Sovetskaya Aviatsiya v Bitve pod Kurskom*, pp. 40–4.

No. 6 1983 A. Bazhenov: *Razvitie Taktiki Oboronitelnogo Boya po Orytu Kurskoi Bitvy*, pp. 34–44.

No. 6 1983 A. Efimov: *Primenenie Aviatsii v Kurskoi Bitve – Vazhnyi Etap v Razvitii Operativnogo Iskusstva Sovetskikh VVS*, pp. 45–54.

No. 6 1983 A. Smirnov: *Kharakternye Cherty Operativnogo Iskusstva Voisk PVO Strany v Kurskoi Bitve*, pp. 55–62.

No. 7 1983 E. Kolibernov: *Osobennosti Organizatsii Inzhenernogo Obespecheniya v Kurskoi Bitve*, pp. 26–34.

No. 8 1983 A. Yakushevskii: *Kritika burzhuaznykh falsifikatsii Kurskoy bitvy*, pp. 29–37.

No. 4 1984 B. Piratov: *Organizatsiya i Provedenie Artilleriyskoy Kontrpodgotovki v Oboronitelhykh Operatsiyakh Velikoy Otechestvennoy Voiny*, pp. 74–80.

No. 9 1984 O. Losik: *Opyt Organizatsii i Vedeniya Krupnykh Tankovykh Srazhenii v Gody Velikoy Otechestvennoy Voiny*, pp. 12–21.

No. 8 1988 A.S. Gusev: *Razvitie Taktiki Oboronitelhogo boya v pervom i vtorom periodakh Velikoy Otechestvennoy Voiny*, pp. 10–18.

No. 4 1991 G.F. Krivosheyev, *Voina Broni i Motorov*, pp. 36–41.

No. 8 1993 N.G. Andronikov: *Gitlerovskii 'Fakel' Byl Pogashen na Ognennoi Dyge*, pp. 2–6.

Wehrwissenschaftliche Rundschau
Jahrgang 15 (1965), G. Heinrici and W. Hauck: *Zitadelle*, pp. 463–86, 529–44, 583–604.

Index

Africa, 2, 143n41
Aleksandrovka, 97, 194
anti-tank guns, German
  organization, 41–3
  Pak 36/37, 41–3, 55n65; losses, 125
  Pak 36 (r), 42, 192
  Pak 38, 41–3, 55n65, 192; losses, 124–5
  Pak 40, 19, 26, 41–3, 72n49, 192; losses, 124–5
  Pak 41, 42
  Pak 97/38, 42–3
anti-tank guns, Soviet
  AT-defence, 33, 35–6, 132–3, 141n3
  45 mm AT-gun, 34–5, 49, 193, 212
  57 mm AT-gun, 49, 212
  76.2 mm AT/Field-gun, 34–5, 49, 59, 132–3, 193
  85 mm AA/AT-gun, 42, 49, 52
  AT-Reserves, 33–4, 36
Ardennes, 45, 55n74, 112, 136
assault guns, German
  Sturmgeschütz III, 26–31, 42, 46, 52n6, 64–6, 68, 71n24, 72n32, 72n49, 138, 143n51, n52, 146, 183, 185–9, 192, 195–6, 210, 218, 221; losses, 120–1, 217, 221–2
  Sturmhaubitze, 26–9, 31, 65, 69, 72n48, 195–6, 212; losses, 222
assault guns, Soviet, 33–6, 47–9, 52, 54n39, 56n86, 57n97, n102, 67, 72n40, 73n53, 105–6, 108, 143n48
  SU-76– 49, 52, 67–8, 72n40, n46, 210
  SU-85– 68, 72n47
  SU-122, 49, 52, 69, 72n40, n48, 210
  SU-152, 69, 72n40, 210
Avdeevka, 194

Balkans, 2, 5
Barbarossa, see Operation Barbarossa
Bastogne, 136

Befehlspanzer, see Panzer Befehlswagen
Belgium, 2
Belgorod, xiii, 9, 48, 98, 116, 119, 127, 140, 145, 148, 192
Bell P-39 Airacobra, 79, 81
Berezovka, 95, 97–8
Bergepanther, 63, 182
Berlin, 4
Bitiug, 90
Black Sea, 1
Blizhniaia Igumenka, 92
Bogodukhova, 16
Breith, Hermann, 17
British Army, 15th (Scottish) Division, losses, 114
Brummbär, 17, 27, 58, 67, 195–6, 210; losses, 120–1, 217, 222
Bykovka, 85

Canadian Army, 3rd (Cdn) Infantry Division, losses, 114
Caucasus, 1, 6
Cherkasskoye, 85
Churchill tank, 105–6, 108, 126
Chistyakov, Ivan Mikhailovich, 34
Clausewitz, Carl von, 135
Cobra, see Operation Cobra

Daimler-Benz, 62
Dalniaia Igumenka, 92
Dniepr, 149
Don, 2
Donbass, 119–20, 127
Donets, 6, 9, 20, 85, 88, 95–6, 103, 113
Douglas A-20, 79
Dubrova, 88

Elefant, see Ferdinand
Esebeck, Lieutenant-General von, 23n6, 90, 94

Fatezh, 94
Ferdinand, 12n18, n22, 19, 27, 58, 60, 66, 71n28, 72n32, 102–3, 178, 210; losses, 120–1, 143n52, 217, 222
fieldworks, 22, 33, 35
flak, 30–1, 192
Flammpanzer, 29–30, 46, 63, 185–9, 195, 218; losses, 122, 217, 222
Focke-Wulf FW 190, 77, 79, 80, 83n38
France, 2

Generalovka, 88
German Army
  Army Groups
    A, 6; losses, 116
    Centre, 5, 9–10, 22, 32, 37, 48, 76, 95, 115, 134, 139, 181, 219; losses 116, 120–1, 198, 220
    North, 5; losses, 116
    South, 6, 9–10, 17–18, 29, 31–2, 37, 43–4, 63, 76, 98, 112, 115, 132–4, 137, 143n46, 181, 218–21; losses, 116, 122, 220
  Armies
    2nd, 17–8, 37, 44, 65, 116; losses, 200
    4th, 23n2; losses, 117, 200
    6th, 138, 152n25; losses, 117, 200
    7th, 109
    8th, see Kempf
    9th, 10, 15–6, 18, 23n6, n11, n15, n20, 25, 27, 32, 34, 43–4, 59, 65–7, 84, 95–6, 116, 123, 139, 141n18, 178, 219; losses, 112–3, 117, 120, 199–207
    16th, losses, 117, 200
    17th, losses, 117, 200
    18th, losses, 117, 200
    20th Mountain, losses, 200
    1st Panzer, 138; losses, 117, 200
    2nd Panzer, 16, 23n2, 24n39, 95, 116; losses, 117, 124–5, 200–1
    3rd Panzer, losses, 117, 200
    4th Panzer, 17–18, 23n15, 29, 32, 44, 59, 63, 65–6, 84–5, 88, 90–1, 98, 116, 123, 125, 135, 139, 141n4, 152n25, 174, 191–2, 217–18, 224–5; losses, 112–15, 117, 199–201
    Kempf, 17–18, 29, 32, 44, 59, 65, 84–5, 88, 116, 123, 125, 134, 174, 217; losses, 112–14, 117, 199–201
  Corps
    VII, 44
    XI, see Raus
    XIII, 44
    XX, 25, 44, 52n1
    XXIII, 25, 32, 44, 65, 84, 87, 91
    XXXXII , 18, 37, 44, 54n50, 113;

      losses, 114
    LII, 17, 29, 32, 44, 94, 225; losses, 115
    III Panzer, 17, 29, 30, 32, 59, 65, 85, 88, 90–5, 97–8, 101–10, 134, 175; losses, 114
    XXIV Panzer, 29, 31–2, 137–9, 143n41
    XXXXI Panzer, 25–6, 32, 44, 65, 84, 88
    XXXXVI Panzer, 25, 28, 32, 44, 52n1, 65, 84
    XXXXVII Panzer, 25, 27–8, 32, 44, 65, 84, 87–90, 94–5
    XXXXVIII Panzer, 17, 29, 32, 43–4, 63, 65–6, 85, 87, 90, 92, 94, 96, 98, 175, 178, 225; losses, 115
    Raus, 17, 29, 30, 32, 44, 65, 85, 88, 96, 103, 133; losses, 114
  Infantry Divisions
    6th, 22, 27, 38–9, 42–4, 84, 88; losses, 202–6
    7th, 22, 28, 42, 44, 84; losses, 202–6
    14th, losses, 206
    26th, 44, 142n35; losses, 206
    31st, 28, 38–9, 42–4, 84, 90, 94; losses, 202–6
    39th, 42, 44, 192; losses, 114
    45th, losses, 202–6
    57th, 225; losses, 115
    68th, 44
    72nd, 44; losses, 202–6
    75th, 44
    78th Assault, 25–6, 84, 87; losses, 202–6
    82nd, 44
    86th, 26, 44, 84; losses, 202–6
    88th, 44
    95th, losses, 206
    102nd, 28, 43–4; losses, 202–6
    106th, 30, 42, 44, 113, 192; losses, 114
    110th, losses, 206
    129th, losses, 206
    134th, losses, 206
    137th, losses, 202–6
    161st, 44, 192; losses, 114
    167th, 17, 29–30, 38, 42–4, 87, 192, 225; losses, 114–15
    168th, 30, 113, 192; losses, 114
    183rd, losses, 206
    198th, 31, 42, 44, 88, 92, 192; losses, 114
    211th, losses, 206
    216th, 25, 42, 44, 84; losses, 202–6
    223rd, 192
    251st, losses, 202–6
    253rd, losses, 206
    255th, 42, 44; losses, 115
    258th, 28, 42, 44, 84
    282nd, 44, 192; losses, 114
    292nd, 26, 84, 91, 94; losses, 202–6

293rd, 192; losses, 206
296th, losses, 206
299th, losses, 206
320th, 30, 44, 113, 192; losses, 114
321st, losses, 206
327th, 44
332nd, 29, 44, 97, 225; losses, 115
339th, losses, 206
340th, 44
355th, 192
383rd, 25, 44; losses, 202–6
393rd, losses, 206
707th, losses, 206
Jäger Divisions
  5th, 182
  28th, 182
Motorized Division
  36th, 94–5; losses, 206
Mountain Division
  3rd, 182
Panzer Divisions
  1st, 147
  2nd, 27, 46, 87–8, 90, 94, 141n18,
    142n35, 181; losses, 121, 202–6
  3rd, 29, 38, 40, 46, 88, 90–2, 94–5,
    97–8, 182, 185, 192, 218, 225; losses,
    115, 122
  4th, 22, 25, 28, 46, 88, 90, 94; losses,
    121, 202–6
  5th, 23n3, 94, 120, 181, 219; losses, 121,
    206, 222n9
  6th, 30–1, 46, 85, 91–2, 95–7, 100n40,
    102, 182, 188, 192, 218; losses, 114,
    122, 193–4
  7th, 30–1, 46, 91–2, 96–7, 102, 133,
    182, 189, 192, 218; losses, 114, 122,
    141n32, 193–4
  8th, 23n3, 94, 120, 181, 219; losses, 121,
    206, 222n9
  9th, 27, 45–6, 56n77, 87, 141n18, 181;
    losses, 121, 202–6
  11th, 29, 45–6, 53n15, 87, 91, 96–8,
    128n17, 181, 185, 218, 225; losses,
    115, 122, 141n32
  12th, 25, 28, 46, 94–5; losses, 121,
    202–6
  14th, 147
  16th, 147
  17th, 31, 137–9
  18th, 22, 26, 46, 88, 96, 141n18,
    143n41; losses, 121, 202–6
  19th, 23n15, 30–1, 46, 92, 95, 102, 182,
    189, 218; losses, 114, 122
  20th, 27, 38–40, 46, 84, 90, 94, 96;
    losses, 121, 202–6
  23rd, 31, 138–9
  24th, 147

25th, 147
116th, 45
Lehr, 45, 142n35
Panzergrenadier Divisions
  10th, 22, 25, 28, 29, 44, 94; losses,
    202–6
  20th, losses, 206
  Großdeutschland, 9, 17, 44, 46, 55n73,
    63, 87, 90–1, 94–5, 128n17, 139,
    181–3, 186, 218–20, 225; losses, 115,
    122, 125
Brigades
  10th Panzer, 63; losses, 122–3
  Group Manteuffel; losses, 202–5
Regiments
  25th Panzer (7.PD), 70n8
  39th Panzer, 63, 177, 182
  51st Rocket Artillery, 26
  87th Grenadier, 26; losses, 202–5
  656th Tank Destroyer, 26–7, 66–7;
    losses, 121
  Großdeutschland Panzer, 59, 85
Assault Gun Battalions
  177th, 26, 65, 221; losses, 121
  185th, 26, 65, 221; losses, 121
  189th, 26, 65, 221; losses, 121
  202nd, 65, 221
  228th, 30, 65, 102–3, 190, 192, 221;
    losses, 122
  244th, 26, 65, 221; losses, 121
  245th, 27, 65, 221; losses, 121
  904th, 27, 65, 221; losses, 121
  905th, 31, 65, 102, 190, 192, 221; losses,
    122
  909th, 28, 65, 221; losses, 121
  911th, 29, 65, 218, 221; losses, 121
  Großdeutschland, 66
Assault Tank Battalion
  216th, 26, 67; losses, 121
Heavy Tank Battalions
  503rd, 30, 59, 70n8, 95, 102, 182, 190,
    192; losses, 122–3, 134
  505th, 27, 59, 182; losses, 121
Heavy Tank Destroyer Battalions
  560th, 192
  653rd, 26, 66
  654th, 26, 66
Jäger Battalions
  8th, 26
  9th, 28
  10th, 28
  11th, 28
  13th, 26
Panther Battalions
  51st, 29, 63, 182
  52nd, 29, 63, 182
Panzer Battalion

211th, 12n9, 13n25
Companies
   312th Pz (Fkl), 27
   313th Pz (Fkl), 26
   314th Pz (Fkl), 26
   811th Pz Eng, 26
   813th Pz Eng, 26
   814th Pz Eng, 52n4
Batteries
   393rd Assault Gun, 31, 65, 102, 190,
     192; losses, 122
Goliats, 26, 52n3, n6
Gorki, 75, 82n6
Greznoe, 90–1
Guderian, Heinz, 8, 10, 62, 143n41, 148,
  178

Hausser, Paul, 101, 109
Heinkel He 111, 77, 79, 97
Henschel, 66
Henschel Hs 129, 79–80
Hetzer, 42
Hitler, Adolf, 5–6, 9–10, 32, 58, 75, 137
Hoth, Hermann, 17, 112
Hummel, SP Artillery , 27–31, 46, 192
Hungarian Army
  2nd Army, 2
Hungary, 4

Iakovlevo, 85, 94
Ilyushin Il-2, 79–81
Ilyushin Il-4, 79
IS-2, heavy tank, 60, 62
Italian Army
  8th Army, 2
Italy, 2, 5, 218
Izyum, 9

Jagdpanzer IV, 55n74
Jeschonnek, Hans, 10, 75
Junkers Ju 87, 79–80, 83n38
Junkers Ju 88, 79

Katukov, Mikhail Efimov, 37, 126
Katyusha, see rocket artillery
Kazache, 95
Kharkov, xiii, 6, 9, 48, 63, 115–16, 119–20, 124,
  127, 138, 140, 145, 148
Kiselovo, 95
Klaivenovo, 194
Kluge, Günther von, 10, 95
Konev, Ivan Stepanovich, 20, 23n24
Krasnaia Dubrova, 90
Krasnoye Anamya, 97
Krasnoye Snamya, 194
Krivosheyev, G.F., 117–18, 127, 148
Krivtsovo, 194

Kromy, 10
Krutoi Log, 88
Kuban, 6, 74
KV tank, 58, 64–5, 69, 178, 210

Lavochkin La-5, 79
Lehmann, Rudolf, 207
Leningrad, 1, 5, 152n33
long-range aviation, see Red Air Force units
Luchki, 87, 91
Luftwaffe: losses, 123–4
  Luftflotte
    1st, 76
    4th, 18, 76
    5th, 12n10, 76
    6th, 18, 76; losses, 123
  Air Corps
    VIII, 18, 76–7; losses, 123
  Air Division
    1st, 18, 76–7
  Geschwader
    51st Fighter, 77
    55th Bomber, 75, 77
Lukhanino, 88, 90–2

MacDonald, Charles B., 136
Malenkie Maiacki, 90
Malo Iablonovo, 97, 194
Maloarkhangelsk, 84
MAN, 62
Manstein, Erich von, 2, 9–10, 31, 116, 125,
  137–9, 148, 221
Marder, SP AT, 26, 42, 46, 67, 72n49; losses,
  124–5
Maybach, 61
Mediterranean, 6
Melekhovo, 91
Melovoe, 85
Merefa, 138
Messerschmitt Bf 109, 79
Mihailovka, 85
Mines, 22, 33, 35–6, 71n28, 85
Mius, xiii, 120, 139, 220
Model, Walther, 10, 28, 32, 90, 95, 137
Moskalenko, Kirill Semenovich, 72n32
Moscow, 4
Munich, 4
Myassoyedovo, 194

Nashorn, 192
Nebelwerfer, see rocket artillery
Nechaevka, 91
Nehring, Walther, 138, 143n41
Netherlands, 2
Normandy, 45, 109, 112–13, 137; losses, 128n4
Northern Donets, 20, 85, 88, 95–6, 103, 113
Norway, 2

Novenkoya, 98
Novo Cherkasskoye, 87

Oboyan, 90, 92, 94, 97–8, 138–9, 174
Ochki, 84
OKH Reserves, 11n1, 19
OKW, 197
Olkhovatka(north), 84, 87, 90, 94–5
Olkhovatka(south), 95
Olkhovka, 87
Operations: Barbarossa, 1, 20; Cobra, 137;
    Epsom, 115; Freischütz, 24n37;
    Nachbarhilfe, 24n37; Roland, 98;
    Zigeunerbaronen, 24n37
Orel, xiii, 1, 4, 8, 9, 10, 16, 47–8, 75, 96,
    115–16, 119–22, 125, 127, 138, 140, 145,
    148, 151n7, 219, 221–2
Orlovka, 92
Ozerki, 84

Pak, see anti-tank guns
Panther tank, 9–10, 15, 45, 58, 60–4, 68, 70n10,
    71n14, n18, 102, 103, 122–3, 125, 133, 134,
    142n31, 146, 182–3, 195, 210; battle
    analysis 177–80; losses, 122, 217, 222;
    production cost, 61, 70n12
Panzer I, 30, 31, 46
Panzer II, 27, 29–31, 46, 138, 185–9, 195, 218;
    losses, 194, 217, 222
Panzer III, 15, 27–31, 46, 52n6, 53n26, 61,
    63–4, 138, 185–9, 195, 210, 218–19; losses,
    121–2, 194, 217, 222
Panzer IV, 15, 27–31, 46, 58–9, 61–5, 68,
    71n14, 72n49, 124, 135, 138, 146, 181, 183,
    185–9, 210, 218–9; chassis, 67; losses,
    121–2, 194, 217, 222; production cost, 61,
    70n12
Panzer V, see Panther
Panzer VI, see Tiger
Panzer 38 (t), 195; losses, 217, 222
Panzer Befehlswagen, 56n77, 185–9, 195, 218;
    losses, 194, 217
Panzerfaust, 41, 55n63
Panzerschreck, 41, 55n63
partisans, 22, 24n36
Pavlograd, 9
Pershing, US tank, 62
Petlyakov Pe-2, 79
Pokrovka, 87, 94
Poltava, 119
Ponyri, 84, 87, 91
Porsche, 66
Pravorot, 108
Prokhorovka, 90, 95–7, 101–10, 139
Protasovo, 87
Psel, 92–5, 98, 103, 106
Pukhov, N.P., 33

Razumnoe, 88
Red Air Force units
    Air Defence (PVO), 76, 78
    Long-Range Bomber Command, 20, 76, 78,
        82n11
    Air Armies
        1st, 75, 82n13
        2nd, 75–6, 78, 81, 83n34
        5th, 75, 82n13
        15th, 75, 82n13
        16th, 75–6, 78–9, 81, 82n10
        17th, 20, 75–6, 79, 83n34
Red Army units
    Districts
        Baltic, 11n1
        Kiev, 11n1
        Leningrad, 11n1
        Moscow, 143n53
        Odessa, 11n1
        Steppe, 10, 13n50, 23n24, 139
        Western, 11n1
    Fronts
        Bryansk, 16, 75, 141n15, 151n7
        Central, 11, 16, 18, 20–1, 32–4, 50,
            53n31, 67, 69, 73n53, 75, 84, 87,
            120, 134, 149; losses, 118–19, 127,
            133
        Don, 149, 152n25
        Southwestern, 19–20, 54n50, 75, 88,
            149, 152n25
        Stalingrad, 149, 152n25
        Steppe, 10, 13n50, 13n52, 20, 23n24,
            73n53, 75, 92, 127, 129n24, 131n64,
            149; losses, 118–19
        Voronezh, 10–1, 18–21, 34, 36, 50, 67,
            69, 73n53, 75, 85, 88, 90–1, 96, 98,
            120, 131n64, 132, 134, 138, 141n4,
            149, 174; losses, 118–19, 127–8,
            131n65, 133, 141n9
        Western, 75, 141n15, 151n7
    Armies
        13th, 32–3, 53n31, 87–8
        27th, 92, 129n24
        38th, 90, 92, 132, 139, 141n4
        40th, 85, 90, 132, 139, 141n4
        47th, 129n24, 143n39
        52nd, 129n24
        53rd, 92, 129n24, 143n39
        69th, 34, 36–7, 92, 101, 107–8, 118,
            141n5
        70th, 34, 54n39, 87–8
        4th Guards, 129n24
        5th Guards, 92, 103, 105, 107–8, 118,
            138, 143n39
        6th Guards, 34–5, 37, 85, 92, 94, 107,
            132, 139, 141n4, 174
        7th Guards, 34–5, 85, 88, 90, 92, 96,

118, 132, 141n4, 174
3rd Guards Tank, 47–9, 56n86
5th Guards Tank, 47–9, 51, 70n10, 88,
  94, 96, 101–10, 118, 138, 143n39;
  losses, 126–7
1st Tank, 34, 36–7, 47–9, 51, 56n84, 85,
  90–1, 94, 98, 139, 141n5, 174–5;
  losses, 126, 133
2nd Tank, 34, 47–9, 130n58; losses, 126,
  133
4th Tank, 47–9
Artillery Corps
  4th Breakthrough, 33
Cavalry Corps
  3rd Guards, 129n24
  4th Guards, 129n24
  5th Guards, 129n24
Mechanized Corps
  1st, 56n83, 129n24
  2nd, 48, 56n83
  3rd, 36–7, 48, 51, 56n83, 88, 91–2, 94
  4th, 56n83
  5th, 56n83
  6th, 56n83
  3rd Guards, 129n24
  5th Guards, 48, 51–2, 101–2, 106–7, 175
  6th Guards, 48
Rifle Corps
  17th Guards, 33, 87, 90
  18th Guards, 33, 91
  22nd Guards, 34
  23rd Guards, 34, 35
  24th Guards, 35
  25th Guards, 35
  32nd Guards, 96
  33rd Guards, 96
  35th Guards, 34, 36–7, 85, 141n5
Tank Corps
  2nd, 48, 50–1, 88, 90, 105–6, 110n20,
    138, 143n39, 175
  3rd, 34, 48, 50–1, 87; losses, 126
  6th, 36–7, 48, 50–1, 90–1, 94
  9th, 34, 50–1, 91
  10th, 50–1, 88, 90–2, 94, 138, 143n39,
    175
  11th, 48
  12th, 48
  15th, 48
  16th, 34, 48, 50–1, 87; losses, 126
  18th, 48–51, 96, 102, 106–7, 175
  19th, 34, 50, 87
  29th, 48–51, 96, 102, 106–7, 175
  30th, 48
  31st, 36–7, 48, 50, 94, 175
  2nd Guards, 34, 36, 48–51, 85, 90–2.
    105–7, 109, 110n20, 133, 174–5
  3rd Guards, 129n24

4th Guards, 129n24
5th Guards, 34, 36, 50–1, 85, 87, 90–2,
  94, 174–5
Airborne Rifle Divisions
  2nd Guards, 33
  3rd Guards, 33
  4th Guards, 33
  9th Guards, 95
Artillery Division
  1st Guards, 34
Rifle Divisions
  8th, 33, 84
  15th, 33, 84
  16th, 84
  74th, 33, 84, 87
  81st, 33, 84, 87
  100th, 85
  107th, 92
  111th, 90
  132nd, 84
  140th, 88
  148th, 33, 84, 87
  161st, 90
  175th, 87
  183rd, 91–2
  204th, 92, 94
  213th, 35, 88
  270th, 90
  280th, 84
  305th, 92, 95
  307th, 33, 87–8, 91
  309th, 90, 94
  375th, 34–5, 85, 92
  6th Guards, 33, 87
  13th Guards, 96
  15th Guards, 36
  36th Guards, 36
  42nd Guards, 96
  51st Guards, 35, 85
  52nd Guards, 34–5, 85, 88, 105
  66th Guards, 96
  67th Guards, 34, 85, 88
  70th Guards, 33, 87
  71st Guards, 34, 85, 90
  72nd Guards, 36, 88
  73rd Guards, 36, 88
  75th Guards, 33, 87
  78th Guards, 36, 88
  81st Guards, 36, 88, 92
  89th Guards, 35, 92, 95
  90th Guards, 88, 90
  92nd Guards, 92
  93rd Guards, 92
  94th Guards, 92
  95th Guards, 96, 105
Rocket Artillery Division
  5th Guards, 54n35

Anti-Tank Brigades
1st, 34
10th, 106
13th, 34
14th, 36
29th, 141n4
31st, 36
32nd, 141n4
Destroyer Brigade
4th, 34
Mechanized Brigades
11th (5.GMC), 101, 107
12th (5.GMC), 101, 107
Tank Brigades
26th (2.GTC), 101, 107
51st (3.TC), 91
86th, 175
96th, 35, 107, 174
107th (16.TC), 87
129th, 33, 87
180th, 175
192nd, 175
201st, 174
11th Guards, 34; losses, 126
27th Guards, 174
Anti-Tank Regiments
4th, 141n4
12th, 141n4
130th, 34
222nd, 141n4
563rd, 34
869th, 141n4
1076th, 36
1244th, 141n4
1689th, 36
SU Regiments
1422nd, 87
1438th, 174
1440th, 174
1447th, 107
1529th, 107, 174
1549th, 106–7, 175
Tank Regiments
43rd, 90
58th, 90
59th, 175
60th, 175
148th, 36, 174
167th, 36, 174
230th, 35, 174
262nd, 36, 174
27th Guards Heavy, 91, 174
53rd Guards, 106–7, 175
rocket artillery: German (Nebelwerfer), 26–31,
44, 195; losses, 125, 202–5; Soviet
(Katyusha), 33, 35–6, 49, 52, 54n35, 87
Rodin, Aleksei Grigorevich, 126

Rokossovsky, Konstantin Konstantinovich, 18
Rostov, 9
Rotminstrov, Pavel Aleekseevich, 70n10, 101–3,
105–6
Rumania, 4
Rumanian Army, 3rd Army, 152n25
Rzhavets, 96, 194
Rzhev, 9

Samodurovka, 88, 90
Saratov, 75, 82n6
Sd Kfz 232, losses, 194
Sd Kfz 250, see SPW
Sd Kfz 251, see SPW
Sd Kfz 301, 27, 52n6
Seim, 92
Sevriukovo, 90
Sevsk, 16
Sheina, 194
Shumilov, M.S., 35
Smolensk, 119, 120, 127
Sokho-Solotino, 91–2
Sokolov, B.V., 117–18
Solntsevo, 92
Speer, Albert, 10
SPW, 26, 28, 45–6, 124–5
Stalin, Iosef, 6, 10
Stalingrad, 1, 4; counteroffensive, 149
Stalino, 6, 138
Stary Gorod, 85, 92
Stavka, 10, 88, 92
Stavka Reserve, 2, 5, 11n4, 20, 139–40, 145,
148, 151n7, 151n19
Strelnikov, 194
Sturmgeschütz, see assault guns
Sturmhaubitze, see assault guns
Sturm IG (assault infantry gun), 31, 53n26,
138
Sturmovik, see Ilyushin Il-2
Sturmpanzer, see Brummbär
SU-76, SU-85, SU-122, SU-152, see assault
guns
Syrtsev, 85, 90–2

T-34, 30–1, 37, 42, 44, 46, 50–1, 58–65, 68–9,
70n7, n10, 100n40, 105–8, 126, 138, 140,
210
T-34/85, 62, 68, 72n47
T-70, 37, 50–1, 67, 106–8, 108, 126, 210
tank losses, 8, 48, 81, 102, 108–9, 111–12,
120–3, 125–7, 129n31, 130n60, 132–5,
142n27, 145–8, 193–4, 216–23
tank shipments, 147, 181–4, 219
Teploe, 94
Teterevino, 87, 90, 92
Tiger I (heavy tank), 15, 27, 29–30, 46, 49,
55n73, 58–64, 66, 68, 70n4, n7, n8, 71n18,

102–3, 133–4, 146, 182–3, 185–9, 195, 210, 218–19; losses, 121–3, 217, 222; production cost, 61, 70n12
Tiger II (heavy tank), 58
Trosna, 94

Ukraine, 1, 2, 6
US Army
  Corps
    VIII, losses, 114
  Divisions
    4th Inf., losses, 114, 128n13
    9th Inf., losses, 128n13
    30th Inf., losses, 114
    83rd Inf., losses, 114, 128n13
    90th Inf., losses, 114
  Regiments
    110th Inf (28.ID), 136

Vatutin, Nikolai Fedorovich, 18, 141n19
Verkhopenoye, 91, 96
Voronezh, 2, 20
Vypolsovka, 194

Waffen-SS units
  Corps
    II SS-Panzer, 9, 17, 29–30, 32, 55n72, 63, 66, 85, 87, 91, 98, 101–10, 175, 225; losses, 115, 125, 141n21, 142n22, 207
  Divisions
    1st SS, 17, 30, 44, 46, 55n71, 56n77, 92, 94–6, 98, 103, 105, 107, 110n17, 139, 147, 181–2, 187, 218–9, 225; losses, 115, 122, 207

2nd SS, 17, 30, 38, 44, 46, 55n71, 63, 87, 91–2, 97, 103, 105, 107, 110n17, 139, 182, 187, 192, 218, 220, 225; losses, 115, 122, 207
3rd SS, 17, 30, 44, 46, 55n71, 87, 92, 94–6, 98, 103, 105, 107, 110n17, 139, 188, 192, 218, 220, 225; losses, 115, 122, 207
5th SS, 31, 55n71, 55n72, 137, 138, 192
8th SS (Cav), 192
9th SS, 55n71
10th SS, 55n71
12th SS, 55n71
  Regiments
    1st SS Panzer, 59
    2nd SS Panzer, 59
    3rd SS Panzer, 59
  Battalions
    2nd SS Panzer, 182–3, 219
    1st SS Stug, 66
    2nd SS Stug, 66
    3rd SS Stug, 66
Weidinger, Otto, 207
Werfer, see rocket artillery
Wespe, SP Artillery, 27–31, 46, 192

Yakolev Yak-1, 79
Yakolev Yak-7, 79
Yakolev Yak-9, 79
Yaroslavl, 75, 82n6

Zeitzler, Kurt, 10
Zhadov, Aleksei, 103
Zhukov, Georgy Konstantinovich, 10, 130n55